Sacre

MW01222599

Sacred Spaces

The Geography of Pilgrimages

edited by

Robert H. Stoddard

and Alan Morinis

GEOSCIENCE AND MAN, vol. 34
Geoscience Publications • Department of Geography and Anthropology
Louisiana State University • Baton Rouge, LA 70893-6010

DEDICATION

Dedicated to David Sopher,
to his memory, his teaching,
and his contribution to our work and lives.

The Geoscience and Man series of symposia, monographs, and collections of papers in geography, anthropology and geology is published and distributed by Geoscience Publications, Department of Geography and Anthropology, Louisiana State University.

Series Editor: Miles E. Richardson

Geoscience Publications Committee: Chair, Miles E. Richardson, professor of anthropology; ex officio, William V. Davidson, chair of the Department of Geography and Anthropology; M. Jill Brody, associate professor of anthropology; Carville Earle, professor of geography; Jay Edwards, professor of anthropology; Steven D. Hoelscher, assistant professor of geography; Mary Lee Eggart, research associate, art director; and Esther Shaffer, managing editor.

Library of Congress Cataloging-in-Publication Data

Sacred places, sacred spaces : the geography of pilgrimages / Robert H. Stoddard and Alan Morinis, editors.
      p. cm. — (Geoscience and man ; vol. 34)
    Includes bibliographical references.
    ISBN 0-938909-66-5
    1. Pilgrims and pilgrimages — Comparative studies. 2. Religion and geography. I. Stoddard, Robert H. II. Morinis, E. Alan. III. Series: Geoscience and man ; v. 34.
BL619.P5S24 1997
291.3'51--DC21   96-47392

Cover: Sacred footprints, marking sites where a diety has walked the land of mortals, are analogous to pilgrimage places, where humans gain access to the divine. The footprints shown here are those of Visnu at the Kesava temple at Belur, India. Photography by Sally Stoddard. Cover design by Mary Lee Eggart.

Contents

Prologue

Miles Richardson

During the course of its more than 20 year history, the Geoscience and Man series has published outstanding volumes on the whole range of subjects encompassed within the twin pursuits of the study of the earth and of humanity. In light of this history, Geoscience and Man is especially proud to offer to the scholarly public this fine work on pilgrimage. The subject of pilgrimage is particularly appropriate for the series. Pilgrimage brings together earth and humankind in a manner so distinctive as to make it stand out among the other endeavors we humans launch upon. Perhaps only with pilgrimages do spirituality and earthiness combine in such intriguing fashions. On the one hand, there is the pilgrim's quest for an extramundane revelation. Pilgrims travel to locations where, as described in their founding narratives, the ordinary life we experience at home and at work is replaced by the extraordinary. Consequently, the ways by which we expect things to occur become transformed. Miracles occur. On the other hand, at the location, the sacred, in the varied forms that cultures constitute it, achieves a physical presence. The location becomes a place, and as such, it shares in the sensory attributes of other places, only more so. For one thing, since the sacred has a physical presence, copies can be made, and if copies can be made, they can be sold and a profit turned. And the piety of the pilgrim is often matched by the money sense of the merchant.

The interplay between spirituality and earthiness, between piety and commerce, between the sacred and the profane appears wherever we turn. To me, the interplay makes pilgrimage overwhelmingly visual. True, the other senses inform the pilgrim's quest, and one of the goals of many pilgrims may be touching the sacred. In addition, verbal communication — prayers, songs, narratives of miracles, recitation of sacred text — constitutes key aspects of the process. Seeing, however, and especially seeing the sacred, seems the base upon which the pilgrimage phenomenon rests. Founding narratives commonly relate the appearance of the sacred in

Sacred Places, Sacred Spaces: The Geography of Pilgrimages, edited by Robert H. Stoddard and Alan Morinis, 1997. Geoscience and Man, vol. 34, pp. v-vii Dept. of Geography and Anthropology, Louisiana State University, Baton Rouge, LA 70893-6010.

physical form before the eyes of the original discoverer. The appearance may not be in the form of a material icon, but it may a vision, yet the vision is an objective one, that is, something that purports to be external to the eyes of the viewer. The shrine itself, to which the pilgrimage moves and at which it culminates, is frequently an architectural marvel, a visual feast, suitable for the site (and sight) of miracles.

In the American South, a region long famous for its intense religiosity, the original Bible Belt no less, pilgrimages, in the core meaning of the term, are all but absent. To be sure, scattered throughout the states of the old Confederacy are locations where the Christian Virgin is said to have presented herself. Some of these, such as the Virgin of Tickfaw, here in Louisiana, appear tied to resident Catholicism; others such as the Virgin of Conyers, Georgia, are less directly connected to "indigenous" Catholics. Significantly, in both cases, the Virgin appeared in visions and not as an physical image. For in the South, among the dominant evangelical groups, such as the Southern Baptists, the sacred resides in the Sacred Scriptures, within the interior subjectivities of worshipers, and wherever members congregate in God's name. Since the sacred never becomes visual in an external, objective sense, place is never holy, nor is Christ an icon to be knelt before in veneration.

Because of the absence of the physical presence of the sacred, pilgrimage in the American South becomes a metaphor. It may be applied to one's life, as in a gospel hymn cast in the traditional mode, titled "I Am a Pilgrim." The singer proclaims "I am a pilgrim and a stranger, traveling through this wearisome land," and goes to on to say "I've got a home in that yonder City...and it's not made by hands." Life is a pilgrimage, with the shrine awaiting the pilgrim in Glory. As a metaphor, pilgrimage may even be applied to specific locations to which people travel. Each spring, the city of Natchez, Mississippi, organizes the Natchez Pilgrimage. The focus of such an endeavor is the Old South. The antebellum mansions in the older city are thrown open, and the public enters the great halls to the greeting of ladies dressed in period costume. The pilgrimage-like quality takes a particular air as the travel here is not only through space to Natchez but also, at least in the wishes of the pilgrimage committee, through time, to the glory that used to be.

Away from the South, its Bible, its mansions, and its glories, pilgrimage also comes to stand for our own quest for understanding of how life unfolds. As the eye moves from page to page in this volume, we find much to aid in the search. In the earlier chapters, we encounter considerations of pilgrimage as such and geography's own contribution to its study. Then going from section to section, we meet many of the world's major religious faiths and the unique, yet common manner in which shrines arise and people travel to them. Ending our journey, we come to the final chapter, a true masterpiece by one of America's most erudite geographers.

In sum, in the same manner that pilgrimage conjoins the distinctive attributes of spirituality and earthiness, *Sacred Places, Sacred Spaces* brings together the general and the particular, the abstract and the concrete. In so doing, the work provides its own luster to a subject filled with luminosity and the resulting illumination is sure to light the paths of all who journey toward the truth.

INTRODUCTION

The Geographic Contribution to Studies of Pilgrimage

The religions of humankind, from the great traditions of Islam, Christianity, Buddhism, and Hinduism, to sectarian cults and tribal religions, have all singled out spatial referents as places that embody or enshrine the religious ideals of the culture. These sacred referents and the complex web of logistics, demographics, economics, and related activities that associate with the visitation patterns to such sacred places are the subject of this book.

Sacred places and sacred journeys of pilgrimage exist in important forms throughout the world. This universality is illustrated in this book by settings in Europe (Nolan and Nolan), Arabia (Rowley), Malaysia (Din and Hadi), the United States (Prorok, Rinschede), Japan (Shimazaki), and India (Caplan, Karan, McCormick, Singh, and Sopher). The greater number of discussions about South Asian pilgrimage arises mainly from the religious variety in this region, as reflected by papers concerning Jain (McCormick), Sikh (Karan), and Hindu (Caplan, Singh, and Sopher) traditions.

Even though these papers represent a variety of cultural settings and religious traditions, they focus on the basic contributions that the geographic perspective makes to the field of pilgrimage studies. Because of its integrative nature, geography provides an important framework for studying the complex phenomenon of pilgrimages. Scholars who seek to understand spatial relationships — the focus of geography — necessarily incorporate phenomena that may also involve anthropological, sociological, economic, religious, and environmental topics.

In addition to their integrative characteristics, geographic studies often focus on the perception of places — a perspective that is especially important in pilgrimage behavior. Pilgrimages occur because people believe specific places are holy, and, thus, undertake religious journeys so they can worship at those places. What makes a particular place sacred in the eyes of believers? This is a fundamental question for pilgrimage scholars in gen-

Sacred Places, Sacred Spaces: The Geography of Pilgrimages, edited by Robert H. Stoddard and Alan Morinis, 1997. Geoscience and Man, vol. 34, pp. ix-xi. Dept. of Geography and Anthropology, Louisiana State University, Baton Rouge, LA 70893-6010.

eral, and especially for geographers interested in explaining the movement of pilgrims. An answer is not easy to discern, but McCormick, Nolan and Nolan, and Prorok all discuss aspects of this question in this volume.

Also related to the topic of place perception is the attachment individuals have to a specific place. Love of home and reluctance to travel elsewhere are feelings that vary tremendously among people and, therefore, must be incorporated into any geographic model that is designed to explain spatial behavior. In pilgrimage studies, this attachment to place takes on additional meaning because, for some pilgrims, it adds to the sacrifice of the religious journey. Pilgrimage, therefore, pertains to attraction of places: the secure place of home and the distant place of the divine.

Pilgrimages invariably require spatial movements and, thus, involve the geographic concern with distance and its effect on behavior. The effects of distance are especially pertinent when contrasting pilgrimages with travel for economic goals. In contrast to the distance decay functions that apply to most human movement, where interaction between close places tends to be much greater than that between widely separated places, travel to pilgrimage sites may be expressed by contrasting spatial relationships. On the one hand, travel by pilgrims often does reveal the same effects of distance as movement for other purposes because, for many pilgrims, traveling is undertaken merely to get to a sacred place and long distances deter many potential travelers (as noted by Din and Hadi, for example,).

On the other hand, when movement itself is regarded as a form of worship or sacrifice, the role of distance may differ from the usual distance decay function. Distance is no longer regarded as a hinderance to travel, but instead, it becomes an opportunity because movement is something valued. The importance of movement per se is especially obvious in religious processions and circumambulations, where the goal is certainly not to arrive at a distant place. The importance of the act of traveling is less clear in journeys that involve a long circuit to several pilgrimage sites, such as the one around Shikoku Island (Shimazaki). The trip can be regarded as only a necessity required to get from each holy site to the next in the series, or the movement may be interpreted as part of the total act of worship. Clearly, for some pilgrims, the act of traveling to a holy place has religious significance, with greater merit resulting from more sacrificial forms of movement (a result discussed by Din and Hadi and by Shimazaki).

In addition to studying the effects of total distance on movement, geographers often examine routes of movement. Understanding routes may depend on network analysis where paths that minimize distance between origins and destinations are compared to the volume of traffic on specific routes. When applied to the movement of pilgrims, however, an optimal route cannot be defined just by time-distance or cost-distance because the ideal approach may be defined by a path of sanctity. Certainly pilgrims moving along a prescribed sacred way lined with shrines seldom follow a pilgrimage route that is the most direct line between origin and destination.

Geographic contributions to pilgrimage studies also include the examination of nodal regions (catchment areas or pilgrimage fields) generated by pilgrims (Caplan and Karan). Questions of relative sizes, hierarchical relationships, overlapping zones, and changes in each of these aspects of nodal regions are some of the topics that contribute to a better understanding of pilgrimages.

One of the fascinating modifications to the normal nodal region is one having a mobile node, which occurs when pilgrims are attracted to a "place" that wanders. Situations where the pilgrims' destination varies spatially may occur when the sacred position is that occupied by a wandering saint (McCormick) or an image of veneration that is carried from place to place (Nolan and Nolan).

These themes, as well as others addressed in this book, present a perspective that is geographic and, thus, contribute an essential component to the body of literature produced by several disciplines. Scholars seeking to understand the complex phenomenon of pilgrimage can achieve success best by combining the observations and insights obtained from a variety of academic fields.

Geographic research on pilgrimages may range from a focus on activities at a particular place, involving a specific religious tradition, to one concerned with more general characteristics of journeys to sacred places. The studies contained in this book incorporate aspects of both the general and the specific, which makes it difficult to organize the chapters in a sequence that is entirely consistent. Nevertheless, the topics in this volume commence with those addressing pilgrimages in general (Section I) and then focus on those in Christianity (Section II), Islam (Section III), Hinduism (Section IV), and Jainism, Sikhism, and Buddhism (all in Section V). The volume closes with a treatise on the quest of place by Wagner (Section VI).

We owe special thanks to two colleagues who contributed significantly to this publication: to Fred Clothy of the University of Pittsburgh, who kindly hosted the conference out of which this volume grew, and to Carolyn Prorok, who volunteered invaluable assistance with editing.

Robert H. Stoddard
Lincoln, Nebraska

Alan Morinis
Vancouver, British Columbia

Section I:
THE ROLE OF PILGRIMAGES

Geography and Pilgrimage: A Review

Surinder M. Bhardwaj
Kent State University

Abstract

Geographic studies of pilgrimages and holy places have covered substantial ground in the last three decades. Through their focus on the spatial dimension of pilgrimage, geographers have demonstrated a more adequate comprehension of this complex and dynamic religious circulation. The concepts "circulation" and "hierarchy" helped to relate pilgrim fields associated with varying levels of sacred places. In recent years, geographers have classified pilgrimages and holy places, examined their distribution, analyzed their temporal dimension, developed new themes, and pointed out several research directions. Replicable classification criteria for pilgrim places have been articulated, making comparative studies of pilgrimage possible in the future. Methodological changes in the broader field of geography itself are inevitably reflected in pilgrimage studies. Earlier couched in descriptive framework, subsequent pilgrimage research in the last three decades became increasingly empirical, analytical, and interpretative. Pilgrimage studies have begun increasingly to utilize endogenous cultural motifs, symbols, and perceptions. Humanistic studies, emphasizing experiential aspects of the place and process of pilgrimage have begun to appear.

Pilgrimages in South Asia, Western Europe, and the Americas have received considerable attention, but other world regions, especially sub-Saharan Africa, Southeast Asia, and Central Asia remain to be examined. Likewise, religious circulation in faiths other than Roman Catholicism, Hinduism, and Islam still needs scholarly investigation. Multi-religion pilgrimages, pilgrim tourism, and comparative studies of pilgrimages and of holy places are among the new areas of research. Furthermore, research on the triple conjunction of religion, pilgrimage centers, and health has only begun to surface. Increasingly, some geographers argue that the concept "pilgrimage" should not be restricted to religious motivation but broadened to incorporate sentimental journeys impelled by a variety of secular beliefs, including nationalistic symbols and cultural heroes. Such a shift opens even more possibilities for future pilgrimage studies.

Key words: pilgrimage studies, religious circulation, sacred/holy places, pilgrim tourism

Sacred Places, Sacred Spaces: The Geography of Pilgrimages, edited by Robert H. Stoddard and Alan Morinis, 1997. Geoscience and Man, vol. 34, pp. 1-23. Dept. of Geography and Anthropology, Louisiana State University, Baton Rouge, LA 70893-6010.

Introduction

Religion is not subject to being appropriated by a single academic discipline, however imperial the intellectual ambitions of that discipline may be (Graubard 1982, v). This fact was evident from the participation of scholars representing various disciplines in the International Conference, "Pilgrimage: The Human Quest," held at the University of Pittsburgh in 1981. Subsequent research has amply borne out the multidisciplinary character of pilgrimage as a religious phenomenon (Coleman and Elsner 1995). Nevertheless, each discipline has a view that adds further understanding about various phenomena, including religion (Erndl 1993). Perspectives that geography has brought to bear upon this topic have focused on the inherently spatial dimensions of pilgrimage.

The minimum elements of pilgrimage include the religiously motivated individual, the intended sacred goal or place, and the act of making the spatial effort to bring about their conjunction. Whatever the religion, or the terminology employed for religious journeys, one fact is common to all types of pilgrimage — the physical traversing of some distance from home to the holy place and back.

Pilgrimage is a complex religious phenomenon for which the English language concept "pilgrimage" is only a general referent. In the Islamic tradition, for example, hajj (pilgrimage to Mecca) refers in reality to "observance of specified acts at specified places in or near Mecca in Arabia, at a specified time" (Al Naqar 1972, xv). The performance of hajj, although a religious obligation, is tempered by the directive that "the pilgrim be able to afford the rite; we are not to make hajj if it brings hardship to those dependent upon us" (Kamal 1964, 9). Religious visits by Muslims to a place other than Mecca is not hajj (Martin 1987, 345) and is usually termed *ziarat*.

Victor and Edith Turner (1978, 232) have characterized Catholic pilgrimages to Jerusalem and Rome as originally voluntary undertakings, which became prescriptive, and extensions of ecclesiastical control later on. In the Christian tradition, pilgrimage is not a requirement in the same sense as in Islam, rather the "journey of the ideal pilgrim could be presented at the beginning of the Fourteenth Century as an elaborate allegory of the life of Christ from the Nativity to Resurrection" (Sumption 1975, 93). Despite its non-obligatory character in contemporary Christianity, pilgrimage is widespread and extraordinarily rich in content and symbolism, particularly where the population is dominantly Catholic (Nolan 1973; Turner and Turner 1978; Nolan and Nolan 1989).

In Hinduism, pilgrimage is a matter of personal preference. In Sanskrit, *tīrthayātra*, literally "tour of the sacred fords," connotes a journey for taking a holy dip in rivers or pools at the various sacred places. Visitation of the Hindus to a goddess shrine is, strictly speaking, just *yātra* (devotional visit). Thus, use of the English phrase "pilgrimage" in the Hindu context can obscure the considerable difference in journeys undertaken primarily for ritual bathing and those for the holy sight (*darśana*) of a specific deity in his or her temple. Moreover, in the Hindu tradition, a living holy person is often described as a *tīrtha* (Bharati 1970, 89; McCormick, this volume) and the visit to such a personage is tīrthayātra.

There is clearly a spatial dimension to pilgrimage, whether the focus is on religious circulation or the description of a holy place, its unique location relative to the physical or cultural characteristics of an area, its nodality in the religious circulation manifold, its relationship to other holy places, or its symbolic position in a religious system. Because of this concern with these spatial aspects, geographers have explored several facets of pilgrimage and sacred centers, many of which are reviewed here. For the purpose of this review, studies are grouped into categories suggested by the emphasis of the authors themselves.

Geographic Studies of Descriptive and Travel Genre

Until relatively recently, many libraries grouped geography and travel literature together, mostly due to the importance which classical geography itself attached to exploration and discovery in widening geographic horizons (James and Martin 1981). Within this idiographic and travel genre of geographic literature, occasional descriptions of the pilgrimage places or allusions to pilgrims occur. Carl Ritter, in his *Comparative Geography of Palestine and the Sinaitic Peninsula* ([1866] 1986, 32-39), traces the evolution of Christian pilgrimage to the Holy Land.

Some gazetteer-like works of nineteenth century geography mention holy places as a part of their description of places in general. For example, Symonds, in his *Geography and History of India* (1845, 95), notes: "Kanoje, Muttra, and Bindrabund ... still greatly venerated as places of pilgrimage."

The temple towns, being distinctive as a class, attracted the attention of some geographers (Naganatha Rao 1937; Thirunaranan 1957; Dube 1968). Naganatha Rao describes Conjeeveram (modern Kanchipuram) in southern India as a major Hindu sacred place with many Hindu temples. Dube focuses upon Varanasi, believed by many to be the holiest city of the Hindus. He considers pilgrimage as a form of tourism, and identifies two religious circuits which many pilgrims still follow to complete their Varanasi pilgrimage.

Only an occasional early pilgrimage study attempts geographic generalizations. Eldon Rutter (1928, 1929) made some clearly "geographic" observations relating the number of Mecca pilgrims to the "locational advantage" of their source regions. He noted that the "Malays, who inhabit a country 5,000 miles from Arabia, normally send the largest number of pilgrims to Mecca, because their islands lie on the great steamship routes between Europe and the Far East" (Rutter 1929, 271). Similarly, the effect of relative distance seems to have been illustrated in comparing the participation of Malays and Javanese with the Egyptians. Rutter pointed out that the former, though forty million in population, sent about 30,000 pilgrims whereas the thirteen million Egyptians sent 15,000 pilgrims (Rutter 1929, 271). His explanation for this greater-than-expected participation of the Egyptians was that the pilgrimage from Egypt could be accomplished in a much shorter time.

The smaller number of pilgrims from India is accounted for by the "extreme poverty of large numbers of them" (Rutter 1929, 272). Rutter tried to explain why Iranians formed a very small part of the pilgrim congregation in spite of the fact that Iran is far closer to Mecca than Indonesia. The explanation was sought in the dominant Shi'a population of Iran. In its scope, Rutter's study (1928) falls in the tradition of British geography of the time, which gave considerable academic prominence to exploration and travel. But, we should not dismiss it as a "mere" description because geographic concepts such as relative location, intervening opportunity, and the relevance of the social, religious, and political factors are clearly suggested, although these concepts and their interpretations are not fully developed.

The Concept of Circulation and Pilgrimage

The concept of circulation has had a major impact on the geography of pilgrimages, and its usefulness has not run out. Deffontaines (1948) was perhaps the first geographer to explicitly recognize pilgrimage as a circulation phenomenon in his *Geographie et Religions*. Although it was not primarily a theoretical study, it illuminates the many facets of pilgrimage, especially its spatial manifestations and numerous implications (Deffontaines 1948, 295-338). Were Deffontaines's work available in the English language, the study of pilgrimages might have "taken off" earlier in geography. Many of Deffontaines's subsection headings are still worthy as titles for further empirical work: religious and geographic localization of pilgrimages, periodicity of pilgrimages, and pilgrimages in relation to health, food, lodging, and commerce.

Of greatest contemporary interest for us, however, is the fact that the phenomenon of pilgrimage is addressed by Deffontaines under the rubric of the major French geography concept "circulation." Religious pilgrimage is but one of the forms of circulation under his broader concept *Religion et Circulation*. Deffontaines's study is clearly within what Lukermann (1965) characterized as probabilistic underpinnings of the French school of human geography. Circulation, in the Vidalian tradition of human geography, is considered to be a "double-edged sword." It is seen both as "a destructive force transforming traditional regional equilibria and stable *genres de vie*, and also as a creative process promoting the diffusion of ideas

... and the radiation of sociocultural influences from nodal centres" (Butt-imer 1971, 190) Maximilien Sorre has observed that circulation carries elements that renew *genres de vie* (Sorre 1962, 408).

Deffontaines, writing in the conceptual context of the French school of geography, saw pilgrimage as a process that had a centripetal function in the society. Many famous sacred centers such as Mecca and Jerusalem can and do seem to perform this role, at least symbolically, through pilgrim circulation. New Hindu temples in the United States and Canada are performing a significant centripetal function for the expatriate Hindus. Sri Venkateswara temple at Pittsburgh in the United States is one such example (Bhardwaj and Rao 1988, 159-188). This temple is beginning to serve as a symbol of the renewal of religious feelings and even religious security for many domiciled Hindus.

Pilgrimage in the stricter spatial behavioral sense is a type of "circulation" clearly differentiated from the migratory processes. According to Gould and Prothero (1975, 42), "if there is a specific desire on the part of the individual or group of individuals who are moving to return to their place of origin, and when before leaving in the first place his intention is clear, then the movement may be considered as circulation rather than migration." At the same time, in the functionalist sense, pilgrimage belongs to the circulation of the Vidalian tradition, for it seems to fulfill a role of renewal, of bonding, and of helping to maintain a religious system by repetitively emphasizing some of its systemic properties.

Pilgrimage as a circulation phenomenon has been elegantly analyzed by David Sopher (1968) in his "Pilgrimage Circulation in Gujarat." The reinforcing of regional as well as all-India identity through pilgrimage circulation has also been suggested (Sopher 1968; Bhardwaj 1973), although the degree to which such effects occur is open to debate. Pilgrim circulation was shown by Sopher to be related to certain social characteristics and categories rather than religious affiliation alone. Especially interesting was his interpretation of Jain pilgrimage activity based in part on a map of the distribution anomalies throughout India of *tapasvis* related to the Palitana pilgrimage (Sopher 1968, 420). Such a map poses further questions for the exploration of cultural determinants of pilgrimage.

An important and difficult question raised by Sopher (1968, 405) concerns the degree to which opportunity or commitment influence pilgrim activity. In his judgment, caste groups whose budgets are based more on cash income — generally non-agricultural castes — manifest more pilgrimage commitment. Although others have reached a similar conclusion (Bhardwaj 1971; 1973; Karan, this volume), the matter is far from resolved because none of these studies used any cognitive scale to measure the degree of a pilgrim's commitment. To verify the cash income hypothesis we need to relate agricultural commercialization to increased pilgrim participation of the farming castes. Since agricultural prosperity in the Green Revolution regions has greatly increased the cash economy, we should expect these areas to generate a much larger number of pilgrims compared to earlier times or compared to agriculturally less prosperous areas. Personal observation by the author indicates an intensified pilgrim activity from among the increasing urbanized *jatis* (caste groups).

Relationships of pilgrim circulation to politico-cultural regions and to the identification of regions of similar cultural behavior certainly need exploration (Sopher 1968, 1980). Spencer (1969, 52-56) has noted the implications of a sort of symbiotic relationship between temples and imperial influence in South India. Such important themes have been studied in much greater depth by historians than by historical geographers (Stein 1960).

The theme of religious circulation with some modifications continues to attract the attention of geographers working on pilgrimages of Europe (Nolan 1980; 1983; Nolan and Nolan 1989), North America (Nolan 1973; Gurgel 1976), Asia (Caplan 1980; Tanaka Shimazaki 1981a, 1981b), and the Middle East (Birks 1978; Shair and Karan 1979). However, many Anglophone language geographers do not use the concept of circulation with all the implications of the French geographers.

Combining the empirical and the participant observation techniques, Birks (1975; 1978) has studied the phenomenon of Muslim pilgrimage across the sub-Saharan savanna to Mecca, both as an example of general population mobility, and as a religiously motivated behavior. In this excellent geographic study of hajj, Birks sets this pilgrimage in the context of its milieu, as the participants move through it, and as the milieu itself changes eastward to Mecca. Pilgrimage is conceived by Birks not as a self-contained institution or an insulated flow of people, but as "people on the move" constantly interacting with other people, institution, cultures, and circumstances. Birks writes:

> To travel with the pilgrims is to experience a paradoxical world with the ascetic, aesthetic and religious intermingled with the secular, pragmatic and immoral. Some of the most pious behavior and exacting religious practices exist alongside appalling squalor, degradation and immorality: such are the compromises of the pilgrim road. (Birks 1978, xi)

Birks's conclusions clearly point out the very complex nature of pilgrimage, incorporating but not limited to religious motivation. More recently, Gold developed this theme in her work, *Fruitful Journeys: The Ways of Rajasthani Pilgrims* (1988). One of the geographically significant conclusions is that among some groups, overland pilgrimage is popular because of the pilgrims' belief that "more profound spiritual benefit may derive if hardships are endured en route — resulting in his greater esteem being accorded the pilgrim on his return home" (Birks 1978, 134). Pilgrimage behavior thus introduces somewhat different meaning into the law of minimum aggregate effort.

The Distribution of Sacred Places

In the geography of pilgrimage, one of the vexing issues has been the search for some order or generalization about the location and distribution of sacred places. The available generalizations seem to be rather narrow. Fickeler (1947) noted several associations between certain landscape features and sanctity: mountain tops, water bodies, groves, and the like. He found no earlier systematic geographic inquiry related to this subject.

The difficulty of arriving at associative generalizations arises partly from the fact that the same elements of the physical landscape may be sources of attraction for pilgrims in one culture, and to be avoided or shunned by the other (Fickeler 1947; Tuan 1978). Also, some pilgrimage centers are situated in large cities whereas some of the holiest places may have only ephemeral, though large, periodic congregations (Deffontaines 1948).

It would seem logical that pilgrimage places in the universalizing religions (Islam, Christianity, Buddhism, and Sikhism) and in some segmental religions, would be associated with the activities and movements of each faith's founder. However, in Western Europe, Christian pilgrimage centers are focused on Mary, not the founder of the faith (Nolan 1980). Similarly, most of the Muslim holy places of the world are not associated with the life of the founder of the faith but rather with Muslim saints and events of their lives.

Furthermore, any attempt to associate the locations of pilgrimage places with founders' activities is of little value with respect to the "complex ethnic" religions, especially Hinduism. Stoddard (1966) addressed this fundamental question of the distribution of Hindu holy places in his pioneering work, "Hindu Holy Sites in India." Stoddard sought to derive the distribution of Hindu holy sites on the basis of specific assumptions. Then, by carrying out rigorous statistical tests, he compared three theoretical distributions with the actual one. He concluded that the spatial distribution of Hindu sacred places in India does not conform to the concept of minimizing aggregate travel distance, is not similar to the arrangement of larger urban centers, nor is it related to selected social characteristics of the contemporary Hindu population (Stoddard 1968). Students of pilgrimage at the time, including myself, did not fully realize the implications of those important findings. In retrospect, Stoddard's results served to identify fruitful paths to be followed and the directions to be avoided. Two decades after Stoddard's study, we are still seeking an answer to the central question he had originally posed about the location and distribution of Hindu holy sites. Study of the distribution of thirty-three major pilgrimage places in the world led Stoddard (1994, 34) to conclude that most are located "in areas of low latitude, moderate climate, and large rural populations having low incomes."

An alternative approach to account for the contemporary distribution of Hindu holy places has been that of historical geography, in which the present pattern is seen as developmental (Bhardwaj 1973). However, there are problems of establishing accurate chronology for several data sources considered authoritative by religious belief. Therefore, the method of historical geography also has not produced a satisfactory answer to the question about the distribution of the entire set of Hindu holy sites.

Since there are several religious traditions and sects within Hinduism, however, it would seem logical to account for the distribution of their sacred places in reference to the development, sacred topography, and symbology of the religious groups separately. Serious effort in this direction can be made on the basis of important historical work already accomplished in *A Historical Atlas of South Asia* (Schwartzberg 1978).

When considering the distribution of Christian pilgrimage places in Western Europe as a whole, it is significant to note that all Western European countries have active Roman Catholic pilgrimage centers (Nolan 1980). Nolan and Nolan (1989, 28-35; this volume), in their analysis of regional variations in shrine distribution in Western Europe, point up the extremely high density of shrines in the predominantly Roman Catholic areas of Germanic Europe. The smaller number of shrines in other parts of Europe, as well as in Catholic regions of the United States, suggests some important cultural factors underlying the difference in shrine distribution.

Distribution of Muslim shrines in many countries has been virtually ignored by geographers, de Planhol's work (1959) being the major exception. There is much room for study of non-hajj pilgrimages to the tombs of saints and holy men, which abound in many Muslim countries, even though Sunnis discourage shrine visitation because they regard the hajj as the only proper pilgrimage.

Classification of Holy Places/Pilgrimages

Until recently, a major void in pilgrimage literature had been a geographically relevant scheme for classification of pilgrimages. Stoddard (this volume) proposed the first explicitly geographic classification, which should make a profound impact on future studies of pilgrimage due to the sheer logic of its conception. He selected three important criteria for classifying pilgrimages: scale, frequency, and routes. Although examples of each of the 27 types he identified may not be readily found, we now have some clearly defined and replicable schema.

Classification of holy places by their association with deities, persons, saints, sacred objects, legends, environmental attributes, relative popularity, pilgrim field or catchment area, and other such criteria will continue to have their selective utility in historical-cultural studies of pilgrimage centers (Nolan 1980; Nolan and Nolan 1989). Attempts to quantify pilgrim fields have been made using relatively simple statistical measures (Sopher 1968; Gurgel 1976), but the broader significance of pilgrim fields in the classification of sacred places is yet to be realized.

Sopher (1967) suggested an "informal hierarchy" of pilgrim circulation in India from the district through pan-Indian levels. On the basis of empirical data, Bhardwaj (1973) divided Hindu sacred places into five levels — local, sub-regional, regional, supra-regional, and pan-Hindu. It appeared from the data that pilgrimage activity differently manifested itself at these levels. The sociological, as well as motivational, characteristics of the pilgrims participating at each level seemed to differ significantly. Unfortunately, replication of such a study has not been done. Since the Dravidian cultural region of India was not included in that study, it is not clear whether the concept of levels as a classificatory device is generally useful, although some scholars found it appealing (Turner and Turner 1978; Gold 1988).

To recognize "levels" of holy places in Hinduism is in no way tantamount to implying an ecclesiastical hierarchy which assumes the existence of a single religious system. Some theoreticians of the hierarchy concept, however, argue that almost all the very large systems will ultimately have hierarchic organization (Simon 1973, 9). It seems that pilgrimage places — at least Hindu pilgrimage sites — may be studied using the concept of discrete but interacting levels of hierarchy suggested by Pattee (1973) to reveal some useful spatio-social relationships, for example, associating specific or general motives of pilgrims with the level of places.

Another suggestion for categorizing pilgrimage places involves a simplified three-part classification, the nomenclature of which is widely recognized in Hinduism: *jala tīrtha, mandir tīrtha,* and *kṣetra* (Bhardwaj 1987, 353-354). The first category represents the original meaning of the word *tīrtha* as a crossing/ford, as well as other fluvial sites. The second, mandir tīrtha, is literally a temple, place, "abode" or house of a particular deity or a deified person. This minimal, two-fold categorization fairly clearly differentiates between places where self-purification by immersion rites and symbolic "crossing" are the primary motives of pilgrimage, contrasted with those places where the devotee seeks proximity to the deity. Supplications, vows, *darśan,* and other relational expectations tend to dominate at the mandir tīrtha. These two classes of sacred places seem to represent, respectively, the two transcendental and existential components of Hindu life.

The motivational characteristics of pilgrims may be, more likely, related to the category of the sacred place, i.e., jala tīrtha vs mandir tīrtha, rather than only to its level as determined by some geometric or statistical measure. As with transcendental and existential aspects of life itself, the two type of sacred sites may also complement each other at all spatial levels. The two categories of sacred places may spatially coexist, but are nevertheless non-competitive, complementary aspects of the sacred space. Further sub-categorization of mandir tīrthas can be done, recognizing the great importance of the *pithas* (seats) of a mother goddess and holy places of different sects.

The third, though perhaps somewhat less distinct category, kṣetra (literally "field"), may include sacred areas, forests, groves, mountains, and the like. A more appropriate nomenclature might be needed for this category, but ksetra is, indeed, a sacred area, not a point or a sacred spot. It is cognitively rather than precisely demarcated. It is an area where the many activities of a deity unfold such as play, battle, hunt, and retreat. A kṣetra, being a larger spatial unit (than, say, a temple), may frequently include many sacred spots but is not itself necessarily dependent upon their existence within its sacred space. Pilgrims in the kṣetras are not motivated primarily by ritual self-purification or a desire for supplication, but rather are there to "witness" the deity's activity — the sport, the dance, the drama — and to experience the feeling of joy or awe in a space permeated with holiness. Visits to a kṣetra may be essentially a pilgrimage for participation in the holy experience.

The three proposed broad categories, i.e., jala tīrtha, mandir tīrtha, and kṣetra, cannot be totally exhaustive but they seem to emphasize, respectively, the transcendental, the existential, and the recreational aspects of life (Bhardwaj 1987). This simple classification may also help us to develop a comparative study of the holy places of different religions — an area that has been sadly neglected so far. It should be possible, for example, to compare pilgrimage to Hindu mandir tīrthas with shrines of the Muslim saints as, in fact, Agehananda Bharati has observed (1963, 142-143).

Sopher suggested a category of pilgrimages focused on living holy persons (personal communication, May 8, 1981). He pointed out that the focus of pilgrimage is not always a fixed place, but could be a living mobile individual. "Pilgrimage" to such holy men as Sai Baba (Hindu), Muni Vidyananda (Jain), and Mahesh Yogi (Hindu) may be included in this category (also see McCormick, this volume). Convergence of the Ismaili Muslims to meet their religious leader, the Agha Khan, and the thronging of Roman Catholics to see the Pope when the latter visits different places are geographically of the same genre as the visitations by Hindus or Jains to their respective religious leaders as they move from place to place. This little-examined class of religious travel helps to bring out the locational dynamism of pilgrimage activity instead of its normally emphasized nodal fixity.

Preston (1990, 17-19) proposes an eight-fold classification of Roman Catholic pilgrim places in the American context by focusing on the distinctiveness of each class. His method is somewhat akin to geographers' method of defining unique regions, each internally homogeneous, but each identified on the basis of different criteria. Similarly, Rinschede (1990, 114-117), after identifying 126 pilgrimage places in the United States, classifies them into eight types. These two classification schemes, developed independently, nevertheless have some commonalities because of the very nature of the American society. For example, both Preston and Rinschede recognize a class characterized by ethnicity. However, seasonality and catchment area are prominent in Rinschede's typology.

We now have classifications of pilgrimage places based on a universal set of criteria, as well as those based on a specific one, and there are distinctive combinations of criteria. Usefulness of each typology will be determined ultimately by the extent to which it aids in a better understanding of the pilgrimage phenomenon.

Some Recent Themes

Islamic Pilgrimage Studies

The last three decades have witnessed an upsurge in the study of hajj by geographers, both Muslim and others (King 1972; Isaac 1973; Birks 1975; 1978; Dunbar 1977; Makky 1978; Rowley and El-Hamdan 1978; Badawi 1979; Shair and Karan 1979; Rowley, this volume; Din and Hadi, this volume). This trend was led by Russell King after a hiatus of well over 40 years. Isaac noted this trend early and pointed out the need to understand Islamic religious historiography in order to comprehend the development of Mecca as the holiest city of the Muslims. He also proposed that comparative recency of conversion might be positively related with the popularity of hajj in Africa south of the Sahara. He rightly argued, also, that the history of hajj reflects a complicated interaction of politics, economics, and religion.

Dunbar (1977) focused on the growing Islamic pilgrimage literature, especially dealing with hajj from West Africa. He suggested that the rapid growth in the number of Muslim pilgrims from Nigeria was "an index not so much of piety as of prosperity" (1977, 483). He credits past hajj as being an important element in generating cultural uniformity in sub-Saharan Africa. Sopher (1981), in part of his extensive review of literature on the geography of religions, also documented the expanding interest in Islamic pilgrimage.

There seem to be two main reasons for the considerable number of recent studies on hajj. First, the development of a modern university system in the Middle East in general, and Saudi Arabia in particular, has inevitably drawn scholarly attention to research areas of central concern to Islam. Thus, the first "Hajj Seminar" was held in 1976 at the King Abdul Aziz University (Badawi 1979). As Islam continues to experience intellectual, political, and religious revival, some of its fundamental institutions will undoubtedly command commensurate scholarly attention.

Second, pan-Islamic revival and increasing ability of potential pilgrims to undertake hajj has meant a great increase in the number of pilgrims (Rowley and El-Hamdan 1978; Din and Hadi, this volume), which in turn has necessitated studies oriented toward planning to cope with hajj traffic, housing, sanitation, and other related concerns in Mecca. Large number of Muslim workers drawn to oil-rich Saudi Arabia and other Gulf nations from different countries have helped intensify hajj by relatives of these employees (Long 1979). Leaving aside the issue of ritual and religion, Rowley and El-Hamdan (1978) have addressed the practical problem of an increasing number of hajj pilgrims arriving in the host region with its finite resources. Likewise, the study of pilgrim accommodation at Mecca has been completed under the auspices of the Hajj Research Centre (Makky 1978).

Rowley and El-Hamdan (1978), using a multiple regression model, predicted almost a million hajjis (pilgrims) coming by air in 1993, whereas the total number for all modes of transportation in 1971-73 was about half a million. Their analysis may appear to be quantitatively sophisticated; but when examined against the backdrop of historical data provided by King (1972) and Shair and Karan (1979), the prediction about numbers may not follow the projected trends. Historical data show that the figure of 300,000 Mecca pilgrims arriving in 1909 was not exceeded until sixty years later, having declined in the interim to as low as 9025 in 1941. Even in recent years, variations in pilgrim arrivals have been 50% higher or about 20% lower than the previous year. Also, the Rowley and El-Hamdan model is silent about the hajj potential of the Islamic population in the Soviet Union and China.

Shair and Karan (1979) found, also through the techniques of regression analysis, that per capita national income is the most important determinant of the volume of pilgrims. An interesting aspect of the Shair and Karan study is the regionalization of the Muslim world into areas of strong, weak, and least commitment to Islamic tradition.

In spite of the pivotal importance of hajj, the virtual neglect by geographers of the non-hajj or ziarat type pilgrimage is somewhat surprising (with Stoddard's 1993 study being a minor exception). Countries with large Muslim populations such as India, Pakistan, Bangladesh, Indonesia, and Iran have important centers of ziarat, which focus on the tombs of well-known martyrs, saints, and *imams* (de Planhol 1959). Ziarat to major holy places, such as Ajmer Sharif in India and Jerusalem, is clearly of international importance, even though it does not rival hajj to Mecca. Due to the neglect of ziarat research, there is very little geographic understanding of Islamic religious circulation in the diverse regional, cultural context of Muslim societies world wide. Lily Kong (1990, 367) recently made a similar observation about insufficient attention by geographers to the culturally varied manifestations of religion.

Here is an open field for cultural geographers. It should be valuable to test in the varied Islamic context the ideas of "levels" of religious circulation observed in Hinduism. Although Hinduism differs from Islam, both religions encompass a great diversity of cultures. In each case, pilgrimage is symbolic of religious identity transcending linguistic boundaries. Certain structural similarities between Irish Christian and Hindu pilgrimages have been suggested already by Nolan (1983).

The Spatial Symbolic Focus

In the recent past, during the so-called post-positivistic era of geography, a variety of modes have been employed to study pilgrimages and sacred sites. Increasing attention is now being given to religious concepts, schema, and symbolism (Stoddard 1980; Tanaka Shimazaki 1981a; 1981b), Weightman 1990), and pilgrimage research in geography is increasingly being anchored to endogeneous cultural and perceptual worlds rather than to a priori spatial theories. The experiential dimensions of pilgrimage are beginning to be revealed, and some common ground between disciplines is evident (Osterrieth 1985; Gold 1988).

Hiroshi Tanaka Shimazaki's work in a series of published and unpublished papers (Tanaka Shimazaki 1977; 1978; 1980; 1981a; 1981b; 1988; this volume) best represents this new genre in geographic research about pilgrimage. Although description of Japan's pilgrimages and enumerations of the sacred centers in Japan had been available earlier (Usaku 1960), Shimazaki (Tanaka Shimazaki 1977; 1981b) provides a dynamic perspective on the geography of pilgrimage. He carried out a meticulous examination of the early development of the sacred circuit in Shikoku, of the decline and emergence of the associated sacred sites, and of the evolution of the whole set of holy places into one spatial, symbolic system called the "Shikoku 88." The result is an admirable blend of the geographic and the religious symbolic dimension into a holistic study.

Similarly, Robert Stoddard (1980, 1981) explored geographic implications of the Hindu cosmological schemata. One of the relationships he observed in the Kathmandu Valley, Nepal, is that at the local scale, regularity is considered very important in the layout/design of sacred space, but at the scale of the entire Kathmandu Valley a geography of sacred sites is not necessarily perceived. Stoddard (1981) finds "visual evidence of the mandala as a pervasive model for the design of the built environment" at the scale of individual buildings and rural settlements, but less clearly at the scale of towns.

Singh (1987, 493-524; this volume) has sought to illustrate how the myriad of pilgrimage paths, routes, circuits, and deities associated with these sacred traces in the Varanasi area symbolize the eternal human quest for an ordered relationship with the cosmos. In the process, Singh unravels numerous strands, spatial and temporal, from which the intricate pattern of Varanasi pilgrimage is woven. Combining extensive textual evidence with empirical and participation techniques, he shows that pilgrimage to Varanasi is not just a religious journey to a sacred spot but is rather symbolic of the very microcosm of the Hindu view of life in its innumerable dimensions.

Geographers and others have independently noted a general circular movement of pilgrims at various scales. At a subcontinental scale, Sopher (1968) noted the practice of a roughly clockwise circuit pilgrimage in India. The clockwise *junrei* (pilgrimage) of Shikoku's 88 Buddhist pilgrim places has been discussed by both Usaku (1960) and Shimazaki (Tanaka Shimazaki 1977). Dube (1968) mapped the routes of two circuit type pilgrimages around the sacred city of Varanasi. Circumambulation of sacred ponds and lakes and of temples (*parikrama*) is only too well known in India among Buddhists, Hindus, and Sikhs. Amin (1978) shows in spectacular photographs the Islamic rite of circumambulating the Ka'aba. All these "roughly circular" pilgrim movements, from the very local to a subcontinental scale, suggest some common theme, the spatial symbolism of which awaits elucidation.

Historical Dimension of Pilgrimage Geography

During the last few decades, historical geography has experienced a vigorous revival; however, only a few geographers have turned their attention toward the historical geography of pilgrimages. One of the few is Nolan (1983), who made a significant contribution to pilgrimage studies on the basis of data related to 5,130 Roman Catholic shrines in Western Europe. Of special note is her analysis of the pilgrimage cult formation from the eleventh century to the present. More recently, Mary Lee and Sydney Nolan (1989), in a major work, analyzed shrine formation Western Europe for the last two millennia! They brought out the cyclical nature of shrine formation periods and its relationship to the cultural history of Europe. Nolan (1983) has further pointed out fundamental differences between Irish and other European pilgrimage that have developed historically, and she has cautioned against the temptation to build general theory of Christian pilgrimage on the evidence of only one of these two regions.

In his study of the diffusion of certain art styles, Goswamy (1968) established the enormous significance of pilgrim records kept by priests at several Hindu holy places. Anita Caplan's careful examination (1982; this volume) of priestly records at a pan-Hindu pilgrimage center also provides the basis for further in-depth historical geography research. On the basis of such records, it should be possible to extend historically our understanding of pilgrimage fields, their nature and development. Caution is necessary in the use of these records, however, because they may reflect a bias in favor of the higher castes and more well-to-do pilgrims. Nevertheless, geographers might be able to suggest the degree to which religious centers were (or, were not) symbols of local/regional or higher-order identity for a caste, a sect, a cult, or a whole range of people (Caplan 1982). This issue, raised by Sopher (1968) and others, is still essentially unresolved.

Various secondary sources, of course, provide the background for constructing historical geographies. For example, *A Historical Atlas of South Asia* (Schwartzberg 1978), with its detailed maps of religion and bibliographic resources, could be utilized for additional study of past pilgrimage patterns and their social and political correlates.

Historical geography of the Islamic pilgrimage centers in regions of recent Islamization such as sub-Saharan Africa should be particularly interesting because it could throw light on the processes of spatial networks. Similarly, the evolution of "pilgrimage" centers of several segmental religions — such as the Ba'hai faith, the Nirankaris, and the Hare Krishna — deserve to be studied (Prorok 1982; 1986). From the perspective of historical geography, answers could be obtained about how religions utilize and modify pre-existing religious networks and flows.

New Pilgrimages

Systematic study of the evolving process of "pilgrimage" among expatriate communities has attracted some attention during the last decade (Bhardwaj and Rao 1988; Prorok 1994; Bhardwaj and Rinschede 1990; Rinschede 1990). Several Hindu temples have been completed, or are in the active construction state, in United States, Canada, Malaysia, Trinidad, and Great Britain. Some of these temples will, in effect, represent the famous temples of India. A question geographers might ask is whether "pilgrimage" to the new temples will reaffirm the previous Indian regional-linguistic ties or whether the "expatriate deities" will have a broader appeal since these centers of worship perform a broad range of social and cultural functions. Utilizing structuration theory, Durr (1996) investigated the evolving temple-focused pilgrimage of expatriate Hinduism in the United States.

Sacred Center as an Intersection of Religion, Medicine, and Disease

Medical geography has made rapid strides in the last two decades (Rosenberg 1983; Paul 1985). However, despite the fact that many sacred centers, especially in the developing world, are points of intersection of religion, disease, and medicine, few geographers have shown interest in the study of this triple conjunction. Intensification of pilgrim circulation and "pilgrim tourism" at the sacred places provide a ready-made diffusion mechanism for communicable diseases, unless vigorous preventive health measures have been ensured, because sanitation at many sacred places still leaves much to be desired during the massive fairs and pilgrimages.

A few descriptive studies of disease pertain to pilgrimage. Diffusion of cholera from Mecca in the 19th century, and even through the early decades of this century, is well known (Deffontaines 1948; King 1972). Similarly, morbidity due to cholera at Hardvar and diffusion from there in the early decades of this century has been studied (Dutta 1973). Hausherr (1978) made several pertinent observations regarding health issues related to the Kataragama pilgrimage in Sri Lanka. Not only are pilgrims to this place exposed to the hazard of malaria, but also some people who have not even visited the site may get waterborne diseases due to the consumption of holy water brought to them from Kataragama by friends (Hausherr 1978). However, none of the geographic studies about health problems at, or associated with, holy places has gone beyond the exploratory stages.

Some sacred centers have become symbols of the revival of indigeneous medicine that has its roots in religious beliefs. As geographers examine the role of indigeneous medicine in the developing world (Gesler 1984), the significance of interrelationships between medicine and religion will become more evident and the need to explore them more urgent. By focusing research on major sacred centers (Dubey 1987; Singh 1987), geographers may be able to study how religious symbolism partially underlies the diffusion of indigeneous medicine in societies characterized by medical pluralism.

Pilgrim Tourism

Compound expressions such as pilgrim tourism, religious tourism, "Pilgertourismus," and "Religionstourismus" instead of simply "pilgrimage" or "tourism" indicate a close relationship between the two activities. These terms also connote differences between the activities: one perceived to be a purely religious and the other primarily a secular activity. These compound expressions also indicate the practical difficulty of trying to differentiate, for analytical purposes, the tourist from the pilgrim at a holy place. Difficulties are likely to multiply as visitors to sacred places increase in number. Such problems also assume importance as people define themselves as tourists or pilgrims, depending on whether they would like to be perceived as modern or traditional. In addition, pilgrims to one sacred place may, after fulfilling religious obligations, proceed to visit other places of tourist value. To overcome such classification problems, phrases that encompass both types are convenient. Of course the neutral term "visitor" can be applied in preference to tourist, pilgrim, or pilgrim tourist. But, that obscures the all-important motive that may have impelled the person to undertake the journey in the first place.

Rinschede (1985; 1988; 1990; 1994) and Rinschede and Sievers (1985) have developed and utilized a schema especially suited for detailed case studies of pilgrim tourism. They systematically examine, in detail, the demographic, socioeconomic, motivational, and spatial characteristics of pilgrim tourists. In addition, they focus on the numerous spatial characteristics of the sacred place itself by noting the morphology related to sacred functions and tourist activities (Jackson, Rinschede, and Knapp 1990). These studies, spearheaded by Rinschede, make it possible to compare different pilgrimage centers, although each one has its own distinctiveness. They constitute a distinctive genera that should be valuable in comparative "peregrinology."

A closely related, though regionally focused, type of pilgrim-tourism study is exemplified by the well researched work of Kaur (1985). Kaur's region of pilgrim tourism in the Himalayan area of western Uttar Pradesh (India). Considered a sacred region in Indian mythology, studded with numerous sacred centers, serving as a retreat for holy personages, and endowed with spectacular scenery, the Himalayas have become the major tourist attraction for a rapidly increasing Indian middle class. Here is an area of pilgrim tourism about which many more detailed studies are sure to follow.

Some Research Directions

Although geographers have addressed many aspects of pilgrimage during recent decades, several areas remain to be cultivated.

By now some aspects of the pilgrimage process of Hindus, Jains, Muslims, Buddhist, and Christians have been examined in detail. A systematic study of the pilgrimage concepts and process of Sikhism, however, has generally been neglected (with Karan's contribution to this volume being an exception). This is all the more surprising because Sikhism is in an active state of religious and political revival. Moreover, there is an intensification of Sikh pilgrimages, contrary to the deemphasis on this institution in Sikh religious scriptures. One of few geographic publications dealing with some aspect of Sikh pilgrimage has been the atlases showing routes traversed by Sikh gurus and the related shrines that grew up along these routes (Singh 1968).

Another under-examined topic concerns pilgrimages that attract people from more than one religion. Studies of pilgrimage in the context of specific religions have had the effect of overemphasizing the interreligious boundaries. At many sacred centers, however, pilgrims ignore religious boundaries and barriers to visit a deity, a saint, or the cult spot of a religion other than their own. Many pilgrims, in apparent contradiction to the tenets of their own religion, regularly transcend boundaries to achieve a particularly desired goal at the shrine of a different religion (Bhardwaj 1987; Nolan 1987). Pilgrim streams to several goddess shrines in Himachal Pradesh (India) are composed of a substantial number of Sikhs, although Sikhism discourages such pilgrimages.

This behavioral dimension, especially in the context of folk religion (Kong 1990, 367), is worth investigation because, at some threshold level, personal commitment must become intense enough for the pilgrim to cross boundaries set by his/her formal religion. Difficult personal, psychological, and pathological conditions could impel an individual to search for healing across the conventional religious bounds. It could be hypothesized that shrines characterized by religiously diverse pilgrim streams tend to "specialize" in healing or other intensely personal goals. Or, conversely, shrines that specialize in "healing" (in the broad sense) have a religious diversity among pilgrims regardless of the formal affiliation of the sacred place. Geographers concerned with place and health relationships are beginning to explore the significance of religion in health, which is leading them to focus on shrines where health and well-being are a major motive for pilgrimage (Bhadwaj 1987, Gesler 1996; Rinschede 1985). Lourdes (France), Fatima (Portugal), and Ajmer (India) are among numerous examples of such pilgrimage centers.

Geographers have so far not undertaken any serious study of comparative pilgrimages. Outside of geography's disciplinary bounds, Bharati (1981) and Turner and Turner (1978) have provided some theoretical basis for potential comparative studies. Even the *Encyclopedia of Religion* (Eliade 1987) takes little note of this topic. Perhaps time has now come to search for some cross-cultural comparisons of pilgrimage behavior. An overview of the geographic literature on pilgrimage still echoes Sopher's conclusion about geography of religion in general: its channels of research "might well be broadened and deepened" (1981, 519). Jackowski's work (1991) on the pilgrimages of contemporary world religions should be useful in the quest.

Within the disciplinary confines of geography, the concept of circulation has proved to be most productive, although even its potential has not been fully realized. No clear methodological consensus yet exists on the demarcation of pilgrim circulation regions, and the concept of levels of circulation has not been critically examined outside of the Hindu pilgrimage system. The study of past pilgrim circulation regions is in its inception, although the development of some primary data banks (e.g., Caplan 1982; Nolan and Nolan 1989) portend deeper inquiry.

There appears to be no clearly defined epistemological concern among pilgrimage geographers in spite of the fact that during the last two decades the profession itself has been hearing a deafening noise of diverse philosophical bells. Although not exclusively concerned with pilgrimage, Osterreith's "Space, place and movement" (1985), employing an existentialist mode, sets pilgrimage in the totality of movement experienced in life. Geographers should find her dissertation a rich resource for pilgrimage studies. More recently, Weightman (1990) defined a framework for the study of geography of religion using the humanistic approach. By and large, however, writings by pilgrimage geographers are characterized by eclecticism and pragmatism. Perhaps this is inevitable in light of the interdisciplinary nature of pilgrimage research. And yet, truly collaborative interdisciplinary studies of pilgrimage are rare.

A promising area of further research seems to be opening up with re-examination of the concept "pilgrimage" in light of a wider definition of religion. If freed from the confines of formal religions, "pilgrimage" can connote a spatial behavior motivated by pan-human sentiment (Bhardwaj 1990). When the source or the object of this sentiment is associated with a belief in the supernatural, this ensuing spatial behavior is a conventional religious pilgrimage. On the other hand, there is a whole series of journeys that are impelled not by the supernatural faiths but by what Zelinsky (1990, 253) terms "civil religions," which are characterized as "nationalistic pilgrimages." War memorials, tombs and graves of national martyrs, memorials to social reformers, and numerous sites of similar origin attract many visitors who may be described as pilgrims because of the sentiment motivating their visit.

Davidson, Hecht, and Whitney (1990) have examined the phenomenon of "pilgrimage" focused on the Rock and Roll hero, Elvis Presley. This is not a nationalistic but rather a truly secular pilgrimage. Secular pilgrimages may be focused on folk heroes of various types, including sports heroes. It can be argued that the sports halls of fame in the United States, which enshrine sports heroes, are, in fact, America's major shrines (Kelsey 1993; Kelsey and Bhardwaj 1990).

The role of environment in pilgrimage is another topic that has not been adequately investigated. A dialogue between the geographers of religion and the *Religionswissenschaftler* (historians of religion) was proposed by Buttner (1974), who argues that the geography of religion is in the "synthesis" stage of the long dialectic process between religion and the environment (both biophysical and sociocultural). At this stage the concern with one-sided "influences" should give way to the study of "reciprocal relationships" between religion and the total environment. The 1988 interdisciplinary symposium, "Religion und Umwelt," organized by G. Rinschede and his colleagues at the Katholische Universitat, Eichstatt, Germany, addressed several of these issues.

It is abundantly clear that many questions about the spatial aspects of pilgrimage remain to be answered. Some of the most cherished geographic concepts — circulation, diffusion, and spatial hierarchy — have been only marginally employed in the understanding of the "integrative" role of pilgrimages. Nevertheless, geographers have demonstrated that pilgrimage, a complex and dynamic phenomenon, cannot be adequately comprehended without the inclusion of the spatial perspective. Geographers, along with scholars in many other disciplines, will continue to be a part of the perpetual human quest.

References

Al Naqar, U. 1972. *Pilgrimage tradition in West Africa*. Khartoum: Khartoum University Press.

Amin, M. 1978. *Pilgrimage to Mecca*. London: Macdonald and Jane's.

Badawi, M. A. Z. 1979. Introduction. In *Hajj studies*, v. 1, eds. Z. Sardar and M. A. Z. Badawi, 15-26. London: Croom Helm.

Bharati, A. 1963. Pilgrimage in the Indian tradition. *History of Religions* 3:135-67.

——. 1970. Pilgrimage sites and Indian civilization. In *Chapters in Indian civilization*, v. 1, ed. J. W. Elder, 85-126. Dubuque, Iowa: Kendall/Hunt.

——. 1981. Theoretical approaches to the anthropology of pilgrimage. Paper at Conference on Pilgrimage: The Human Quest, University of Pittsburgh.

Bhardwaj, S. M. 1971. Some spatial and social aspects of the Mother Goddess cult in North India. Paper at the Third Punjab Studies Conference, University of Pennsylvania, Philadelphia.

——. 1973. *Hindu places of pilgrimage in India: A study in cultural geography*. Berkeley: University of California Press.

——. 1987. Single religion shrines, multireligion pilgrimages. *National Geographical Journal of India* 33:457-68.

——. 1990. Sentimental journeys: Thoughts on the nature of pilgrimage. Paper at the Association of American Geographers, Toronto.

Bhardwaj, S. M., and M. Rao. 1988. Emerging Hindu pilgrimage in the United States: A case study. *Geographia Religionum* 4:159-88.

Bhardwaj, S. M., and G. Rinschede. 1990. Pilgrimage in America: An anachronism or a beginning. *Geographia Religionum* 5:9-14.

Birks, J. S. 1975. Overland pilgrimage in the savanna lands of Africa. In *People on the move: Studies on internal migration*, eds. L. A. Kosinski and R. M. Prothero, 297-307. London: Methuen.

——. 1978. *Across the savannas to Mecca: The overland pilgrimage route from West Africa*. Totowa, NJ: Frank Cass and Company.

Buttimer, A. 1971. *Society and milieu in the French geographic tradition*. Chicago: Rand McNally.

Buttner, M. 1974. Religion and geography: Impulses for a new dialogue between religion-swissenschaftler and geographers. *Numen* 21:163-96.

Caplan, A. L. H. 1980. Geography of a Hindu pilgrimage: Prayag's Magh mela. Paper at Association of American Geographers.

——. 1982. Pilgrims and priests as links between a sacred center and the Hindu culture region: Prayag's Magh Mela pilgrimâge (Allahabad, India). Ph.D. diss., University of Michigan.

Coleman, S., and J. Elsner. 1995. *Pilgrimage: Past and present in the world religions.* Cambridge: Harvard University Press.

Davidson, J., A. Hecht, and H. Whitney. 1990. The pilgrimage to Graceland. *Geographia Religionum* 9:229-52.

Deffontaines, P. 1948. *Geographie et religions.* Paris: Gallimard.

de Planhol, X. 1959. *The world of Islam.* Ithaca: Cornell University Press.

Dube, K. K. 1968. Tourism and pilgrimage in Varanasi. *The National Geographical Journal of India* 14:176-85.

Dubey, D. P. 1987. Kumbha mela: Origin and historicity of India's greatest pilgrimage fair. *National Geographical Journal of India* 33:469-92.

Dunbar, G. S. 1977. West African pilgrimage to Mecca. *Geographical Review* 67:483-84.

Durr, J. 1996. Social spaces and sacred places: Structuration theory and Hindu pilgrimage. M.A. thesis, Kent State University.

Dutta, M. K. 1973. The diffusion and ecology of cholera in India. *Geographical Review of India* 35:248-62.

Eliade, M., ed. 1987. *The Encyclopedia of religion.* New York: McMillan and Free Press.

Erndl, K. M. 1993. *Victory to the mother: The Hindu goddess of northwest India in myth, ritual, and symbol.* New York: Oxford University Press.

Fickeler, P. 1947. Grundfragen der religionsgeographie. *Erdkunde* 1:121-44.

Gesler, W. 1984. *Health care in developing countries.* Washington, DC: Association of American Geographers.

———. 1996. Lourdes: Healing in a place of pilgrimage. *Health and Place* 2:95-105.

Gold, A. G. 1988. *Fruitful journeys: The ways of Rajasthani pilgrims.* Oxford: Oxford University Press.

Goswamy, B. N. 1968. *Pahari painting: The family as the basis of style.* Bombay: Marg.

Gould, W. T., and R. M. Prothero. 1975. Space and time in African population mobility. In *People on the move,* eds. L. A. Kosinski and R. M. Prothero, 39-49. London: Methuen.

Graubard, S. R. 1982. Preface to the issue, "Religion." *Daedalus* 111:v-vi.

Gurgel, K. K. 1976. Travel patterns of Canadian visitors to the Mormon culture hearth. *Canadian Geographer* 20:405-17.

Hausherr, K. 1978. Kataragama: Das heiligtum im Dschungel Sudost - Ceylons - aus geographischer sicht. In *Buddhism in Ceylon and studies on religious syncretism in Buddhist countries, symposien zur buddhismusforschung,* I, H. Bechert, ed., 234-80. Gottingen: Vandenhoeck und Ruprecht.

Isaac, E. 1973. The pilgrimage to Mecca. *Geographical Review* 63:405-09.

Jackowski, A. 1991. *Zarys geografii pielgrzymek.* Krakow: Uniwersytetu Jagiellonskiego.

Jackson, R. H., G. Rinschede, and J. Knapp. 1990. Pilgrimage in the Mormon church. *Geographia Religionum* 5:27-62.

James, P. E., and G. J. Martin. 1981. *All possible worlds:A history of geographical ideas.* New York: John Wiley & Sons.

Kamal, A. 1964. *The sacred journey: Being pilgrimage to Makkah.* London: George Allen and Unwin.

Kaur, J. 1985. *Himalayan pilgrimages and the new tourism.* New Delhi: Himalaya Books.

Kelsey, M. 1993. The cultural geography of sports halls of fame. Ph.D. diss., Kent State University.

Kelsey, M., and S. M. Bhardwaj. 1990. Sports shrines and secular pilgrimage. Paper at the Association of American Geographers, Toronto.

King, R. 1972. The pilgrimage to Mecca: Some geographical and historical aspects. *Erdkunde* 26:61-73.

Kong, L. 1990. Geography and religion: Trends and prospects. *Progress in Human Geography* 14:355-71.

Long, D. E. 1979. *The Hajj today: A survey of the contemporary Makkah pilgrimage.* Albany, NY: State University of New York Press.

Lukermann, F. 1965. The 'Calcul des Probabilites' and the Ecole Francaise de geographie. *Canadian Geographer* 9:128-37.

Makky, G. A. W. 1978. *Mecca, the pilgrimage city: A study of pilgrim accommodation.* London: Croom Helm.

Martin, R. C. 1987. Muslim pilgrimage. In *The Encyclopedia of religion,* ed. M. Eliade, 11:338-46. New York: McMillan and Free Press.

Naganatha Rao, V. E. 1937. Conjeeveram: A temple town. *Indian Geographical Journal* 12:205-28.

Nolan, M. L. 1973. The Mexican pilgrimage tradition. *Pioneer America* 5:13-27.

———. 1980. Spatial and temporal aspects of contemporary Western European pilgrimage: A preliminary report. Department of Geography, Oregon State University, Corvallis.

———. 1983. Irish pilgrimage: The different tradition. *Annals of the Association of American Geographers* 73:421-38.

———. 1987. Christian pilgrimage shrines in Western Europe and India: A preliminary comparison. *National Geographical Journal of India* 33:370-78.

Nolan, M. L., and S. Nolan. 1989. *Christian pilgrimage in modern Western Europe.* Chapel Hill, NC: University of North Carolina Press.

Osterreith, A. 1985. Space, place and movement. Ph.D. diss., University of Washington.

Pattee, H. H. 1973. Unsolved problems and potential applications of hierarchy theory. In *Hierarchy theory: The challenge of complex systems,* ed. H. H. Pattee, 131-56. New York: George Braziler.

Preston, J. 1990. The rediscovery of America: Pilgrimage as a spatial-symbolic system. Paper at 24th International Geographical Congress, Tokyo.

Prorok, C. V. 1982. New Vrindaban and the devotees of Hare Krishna: A geographic assessment. M.A. thesis, University of Pittsburgh.

———. 1986. The Hare Krishna's transformation of space in West Virginia. *Journal of Cultural Geography* 7:129-40.

———. 1994. Hindu temples in the Western world: A study in social space and ethnic identity. *Geographia Religionum* 8:95-108.

Rinschede, G. 1985. Das pilgerzentrum Lourdes. *Geographia Religionum* 1:195-256.

———. 1988. The pilgrimage center of Fatima, Portugal. *Geographia Religionum* 4:65-98.

———. 1990. Catholic pilgrimage places in the United States. *Geographia Religionum* 5:63-135.

———. 1994. Catholic pilgrimage centers in Quebec, Canada. *Geographia Religionum* 8:169-92.

Rinschede, G., and A. Sievers. 1985. Sozialgeographische untersuchungen zum pilgerphanomen. *Geographia Religionum* 1:183-94.

Ritter, C. (1866) 1986. *The comparative geography of Palestine and the Sinaitic Peninsula.* 2 v. Trans. by W. L. Gage. New York: Greenwood Press.

Rosenberg, M. W. 1983. Accessibility to health care: A North American perspective. *Progress in Human Geography* 7:78-87.

Rowley, G., and S. A. S. El-Hamdan. 1978. The pilgrimage to Mecca: An explanatory and predictive model. *Environment and Planning,* A 10:1053-71.

Rutter, E. 1928. *The holy cities of Arabia.* London: G. P. Putnam's Sons.

———. 1929. The Muslim pilgrimage. *Geographical Journal* 74:271-73.

Schwartzberg, J. E., ed. 1978. *A historical atlas of South Asia.* Chicago: The University of Chicago Press.

Shimazaki, see Tanaka.

Shair, I. M., and P. P. Karan. 1979. Geography of the Islamic pilgrimage. *GeoJournal* 3:599-608.

Simon, H. A. 1973. The organization of complex systems. In *Hierarchy theory: The challenge of complex systems,* ed. H. H. Pattee, 3-27. New York: George Braziller.

Singh, F., ed. 1968. *Travels of Guru Gobind Singh.* Patiala: Punjab University.

Singh, R. P. B. 1987. The pilgrimage mandala of Varanasi (Kasi): A study in sacred geography. *National Geographical Journal of India* 33:493-526.

Sopher, D. E. 1967. *Geography of religions.* Englewood Cliffs, NJ:Prentice-Hall.

——. 1968. Pilgrim circulation in Gujarat. *Geographical Review* 58:392-425.

——. 1980. The geographic patterning of culture in India. In *An exploration of India: Geographical perspectives on society and culture,* ed. D. E. Sopher, 289-326. Ithaca, NY: Cornell University Press.

——. 1981. Geography and religions. *Progress in Geography* 5:510-24.

Sorre, M. 1962. The concept of genre de vie. In *Readings in cultural geography,* eds. P. L. Wagner and M. W. Mikesell, 399-415. Chicago: University of Chicago Press.

Spencer, G. W. 1969. Religious networks and royal influence in Eleventh Century South India. *Journal of the Economic and Social History of the Orient* 12:42-56.

Stein, B. 1960. The economic function of a medieval South Indian temple. *Journal of Asian Studies* 19:163-76.

Stoddard, R. H. 1966. Hindu holy sites in India. Ph.D. diss. University of Iowa, Iowa City.

——. 1968. An analysis of the distribution of major Hindu holy sites. *National Geographical Journal of India* 14:148-55.

——. 1980. Perceptions about the geography of religious sites in the Kathmandu Valley. *Contributions to Nepalese Studies* 7:97-118.

——. 1981. The mandala as a geographic phenomenon. Paper at the Association of American Geographers, Los Angeles.

——. 1993. Regional Muslim pilgrimages: Marabouts in the Maghreb. Paper at the Association of American Geographers, Atlanta.

——. 1994. Major pilgrimage places of the world. *Geographia Religionum* 8:17-36.

Sumption, J. 1975. *Pilgrimages: An image of mediaeval religion.* London: Faber and Faber.

Symonds, A. R. 1845. *Geography and history of India.* Madras: American Mission Press.

Tanaka Shimazaki, H. 1977. Geographic expression of Buddhist pilgrim places on Shikoku Island, Japan. *Canadian Geographer* 21:116-24.

——. 1978. Sacredness in a changing Buddhist pilgrimage in Japan. Paper at the Tenth International Congress of Anthropological and Ethnological Sciences, New Delhi.

——. 1980. The evolution of a pilgrimage as a spatial-symbolic system. Paper at the 24th International Geographical Congress, Tokoyo.

——. 1981a. Japanese multiple pilgrim places as physical, behavioural, spatial, and symbolic complexes. Paper at Conference on Pilgrimage: The Human Quest, University of Pittsburgh.

——. 1981b. The evolution of a pilgrimage as a spatial-symbolic system. *Canadian Geographer* 24:240-51.

——. 1988. On the geographic study of pilgrimage places. *Geographica Religionum* 4:21-40.

Thirunaranan, B., and N. A. Padmanabhan. 1957. Tiruttani: Study of a temple town. *Indian Geographical Journal* 32:33-56.

Tuan, Y-F. 1978. Sacred space: Exploration of an idea. In *Dimensions of human geography,* ed. K. W. Butzer, 84-99. Chicago: University of Chicago, Department of Geography.

Turner, V., and E. Turner. 1978. *Image and pilgrimage in Christian culture: Anthropological perspectives.* New York: Columbia University Press.

Usaku, S. 1960. Les pelerinages au Japon. In *Source Orientales, les pelerinages,* eds. A. Esnoul et al., 343-66. Paris: Editions du Seuil.

Weightman, B. A. 1990. Religious symbols in landscape and life worlds: A humanistic perspective. Paper at the Association of American Geographers, Toronto.

Zelinsky, W. 1990. Nationalistic pilgrimages in the United States. *Geographia Religionum* 5:253-67.

Pilgrimage, Travel and Existential Quest

Anne Osterrieth
Federal Office for Scientific, Technical and Cultural Affairs, Belgium

Abstract

Humanistic geography, with its concern for "place," has neglected the importance of travel. In contrast to the view that "journey is misery," this chapter stresses the value of rootedness and the benefits of self-realization that are gained from interaction with the environment. People may seek travel, particularly pilgrimage, to achieve a form of inner transformation and to fulfill a quest — a cognitive and behavioral process involving a redefinition of one's identity and place in the world. Accomplishment of a quest involves both geographical adventure and the pilgrim's spiritual goal.

Questers who embark on pilgrimages discard their initial identities partly by breaking away from their home places. These quests always entail risks, such as outright danger, or milder sources of tribulations such as discomfort, inconveniences, hostility, and similar occurrences faced in an alien environment (i.e., "wilderness"). Thus, the questers, rather than behaving in a risk-avoidance manner, willfully set off into the wilderness to size themselves up. But without risk there is no test of competence that confirms one's own worth. Thus, pilgrimage is intrinsically rewarding because the journey offers occasions for the pilgrim to gain a sense of achievement and confidence that he/she is worthy to appear before the Almighty.

These attributes of pilgrimage, which are evident in the writings of medieval pilgrims, can be divided into four stages: departure, journey, encounter, and feast and return. Each stage contributed to a transformation that involved an enlarged consciousness of self and of the world.

Key words: pilgrimage, quest, rootedness, self-realization, humanistic geography.

Introduction

This research stems originally from the necessity of building a formal organization of knowledge in humanistic geography.[1] In so doing, it attempts to correct the current overemphasis on human attachment to places and the value of rootedness. It also seeks to elaborate the idea that interaction with the environment may serve the purpose of self-realization.

Sacred Places, Sacred Spaces: The Geography of Pilgrimages, edited by Robert H. Stoddard and Alan Morinis, 1997. Geoscience and Man, vol. 34, pp. 25-39. Dept. of Geography and Anthropology, Louisiana State University, Baton Rouge, LA 70893-6010.

One of the first formulations of geographical experience from an existential viewpoint was Tuan's essay on the relationship between space and place (1974), expanded in other writings (1975; 1976; 1977). The term "place" acquired a central status in humanistic geography because its definition requires both spatial and environmental elements, and human appraisal of them (Buttimer 1976; 1980; Entrikin 1976; Relph 1976; Seamon 1981; Pocock 1981). Concern with the experience of space and place gave birth to a series of other concepts now part of the lexicon of the humanistic geographer — at homeness, rootedness and rootlessness, insideness and outsideness, dwelling and exile — all terms which reflect the degree to which one belongs to and associates or dissociates oneself with place (Pocock 1981; Seamon 1981).

Conspicuously missing from this perspective is the positive value of travel.[2] No vocabulary describes the types or stages of journeys. The bias in favor of rootedness promotes the view that "outsideness" (not belonging) is a negative state of affairs (Seamon 1981) and that "journey is misery" (Tuan 1971). This research aims to correct such a view by exploring some of the values of travel through the analysis of a particular form of travel, which is pilgrimage.

This paper proposes a theoretical model of the quest, one that incorporates a geographical framework based on the anthropological theory on rites of passages and the psychological theory on intrinsic rewards. The quest is defined as a cognitive and behavioral process involving a redefinition of the individual's identity and place in the world. Medieval narratives of pilgrimages to Compostela, Spain, and Jerusalem, which provide the data for this work, give ample evidence of the nature of the quest process. The relations between the geographical adventure and the pilgrim's spiritual goal are essential to the accomplishment of the quest.[3]

Such findings suggest two types of conclusions. Firstly, people sometimes travel and submit themselves to certain environments in order to achieve a form of inner transformation. Secondly, places can be identified where people seek particular experiences, such as the experience of wilderness and danger or the experience of transformative release from the limitations of daily life.

The Model of the Quest
Setting up the Quest

The quest, as existential pursuit, is defined by two parameters: an object and a subject (Hiernaux 1977). The object, which motivates the quest, is symbolized here (fig. 1) by O+. The subject perceives his relationship to the object as one of relative deficiency with regards to a potential accomplishment. The subject in a state of deficiency (negative self-evaluation) is

$$\begin{cases} 0+ = \text{forgiveness (intercession, indulgences. . .)} \\ S\text{-} = \text{a sinner} \text{ ->} \quad S+ = \text{redeemed} \end{cases}$$

REDEEMING PILGRIMAGE

$$\begin{cases} 0+ = \text{miracle (thaumaturgic object)} \\ S\text{-} = \text{the sick} \text{ ->} \quad S+ = \text{the cured} \end{cases}$$

THERAPEUTIC PILGRIMAGE

$$\begin{cases} 0+ = \text{revelation (vision, presence. . .)} \\ S\text{-} = \text{alone} \text{ ->} \quad S+ = \text{oneness with God} \end{cases}$$

MYSTICAL PILGRIMAGE

Fig. 1. The quest patterns in Medieval pilgrimages. The object is symbolized by O+. The subject in a state of deficiency is S-; the subject transformed into the accomplished self is S+.

S-. The quest for the object is the process by which the subject is transformed into S+, or accomplished self.

In the Catholic religion, the object of the quest is God's grace. Initially the subject's state is that of a sinner, but with God's grace the subject is redeemed ("redeeming pilgrimage" in fig. 1). Medieval texts show the prevalence of such beliefs among pilgrims. An early 15th century narrative by Nompar de Caumont[4] best expresses these feelings:

> To seek forgiveness and remission from our sins...asking that, given my humility, He have pity on my wretched soul...I have undertaken with the help of God...the holy crossing overseas to Jerusalem to visit the holy sepulchre of Jesus Christ. (Noble 1975, 22).[5]

In the great pilgrimages, other types of emotional mobilization could be found, such as the quest for the cure of the body ("therapeutic pilgrimage" in fig. 1) or the quest for revelation ("mystical pilgrimage" in fig. 1); but the quest for salvation motivated most pilgrims. Indeed, in medieval times, a terror of Hell and an overwhelming sense of sin were quite common. Thus the dramatic prospects of Hell and damnation made it imperative to set normative criteria for action. The one who wanted salvation would seek God's forgiveness through penance and prayer, for example in the form of a pilgrimage.

From this initial presentation, two conclusions can be drawn. First, pilgrimage stems from an individual decision and aims at personal transformation, which relies on the subject's own actions. Pilgrimage thus qualifies as an individual quest. Second, dramatization and norm setting are the ways by which the individual structures his emotional energies into a quest pattern (Hiernaux 1977).

The Process of Quest

Basically, the quest is a matter of acquisition of competence as well as a performance (fig. 2). Competence and performance are the central stages of the quest. According to semiologists (Greimas 1970; 1983; Everaert-Desmedt 1981), competence means acquiring both the power and knowledge necessary to complete one's task,[6] while performance is the activity required to reach the object of the quest. In the quest, the subject undergoes trials and tribulations in order to acquire competence and achieve success.

The quest, although an individual pursuit, is usually framed in a social context. The quester is sent on a mission — this is the contract stage. Upon achievement of the quest, he receives consecration and is feasted — this is the sanction stage. Contract and sanction are ways to express on the cognitive plane the quester'sinitial state of relative deficiency with regard to his later accomplishment. The quester's identity changes through the quest; each trial brings the subject further along in his transformation.[7]

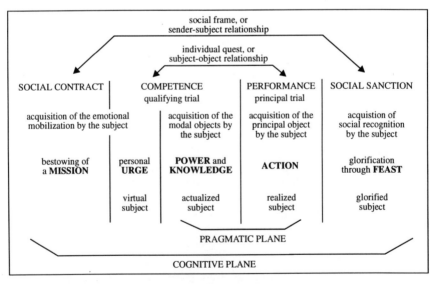

Fig. 2. The stages of a quest. *Source*: **Everaert-Desmedt 1981.**

During contract and sanction stages, the relationship of the subject is directed towards relevant others, such as his community or the Church, and his actions have high communicative content. This is why contract and sanction are considered the stages which set the cognitive plane of the quest. In contrast, competence and performance are the pragmatic stages of the quest: the quester is almost entirely involved in actively pursuing his goal. The relationship of the subject is directed toward the object of his quest.

The Spatio-Symbolic Course of the Quest

But the evolution of the quester between his initial situation and his final one can also be read as stages of passage (Gennep 1908; Turner 1978) (fig. 3). In the first stage, that of separation, the quester relinquishes statuses and roles that make up his identity, and prepares himself for his endeavor. During the second stage, the subject lives in a marginal state (or state of liminality) between two identities or social positions. This particular state may attract a temporary status which expresses some degree of disengagement of the subject from local community rules, routines, and responsibilities, and which afford him a certain freedom of action. During this second stage, the subject evolves at the margins of society and undergoes initiation. In initiation, one receives fundamental knowledge, and this knowledge is a source of both power and responsibility. One also undergoes trials by which one shows that one is apt and worthy to hold the new status that will be bestowed. These trials also symbolically represent the death and rebirth process.

During the final stage — that of aggregation (incorporation or reintegration) — the new identity or status is established, for the quest has been accomplished: the quester has reached the object of his quest. Given the high degree of emotional mobilization, this meeting with the object of the quest is interpreted as aggregation to the sacred. Yet, as the quester has achieved his ends, he may now celebrate his feat with others and return to ordinary life. Aggregation to the sacred is doubled by aggregation to the profane, which is usually expressed through a feast. The feast serves as outlet to the emotional energies which were invested in the quest.

On the cognitive plane, the quester discards his initial identity or status to move towards another situation. Symbolically (fig. 3), S_1 is the initial identity of the subject; nS_1 the rejection, or negation, of this identity; and S_2 the identity wished for. To this cognitive movement often correspond a geographical and social movement because the discarding of one's self is made easier by breaking away from the people and place with which one was involved (Leach 1976; Turner and Turner 1978). Movement on the social plane is accomplished through trials and initiation, which, in anthro-

Levels of displacement	Stage I	Stage II	Stage III
Social movement	separation	liminality or marginality	aggregation
Cognitive movement	$S_1 \longrightarrow nS_1$		$\longrightarrow S_2$
Geographical movement	to leave	to journey	to settle or to return

Fig. 3. Levels of displacement in the quest. Subject is shown as S with S_1 the initial identity; nS_1 the negation of this identity; and S_2 the identity wished for.

pological terms, embody death and rebirth. Both a journey and a liminal place may serve as a geographical frame for the endeavor.

The quest always entails a certain degree of risk. For without risk, there would be no trial, and thus no test of competence, and thus no value to the endeavor. The risks to be faced may not be outright dangerous, but, instead, milder sources of tribulations such as inconveniences, discomfort, hostility, or difficulties of all kinds. These are frequent occurrences in alien environments. Such an environment thus qualifies as "wilderness." The quester then willfully sets off into the wilderness to size himself up, a surprising finding in view of the current research in environmental behavior, which mainly stresses risk-avoidance behavior.[8]

Danger plays a triple role in the quest. First, the greater the hazard, the more dramatic the pursuit and the more valuable the object of the quest. Danger plays an essential role in the emotional mobilization of the quester. Second, the recurrence of risks helps to maintain the necessary tension and focus on what is relevant for one's quest. Danger sustains involvement in the quest. Third, the difficulties to be surmounted provide the necessary trials which serve as a competency test to the quester. Danger meters one's worth. Seen in this light, wilderness, which is the geographic embodiment of danger, is a necessary component of the quest.

But, in a quest, there are also sacred places. These are marginal places, where initiation occurs. One sacred place stands out as holding the object which initially motivated the quest. At this sacred place, the subject finally reaches his object of desire and comes to the understanding of this achievement: he is transformed. Thus the quest in itself ends at the sacred place, although the quester may further his travel, for example to return home.

The models describing the quest process and its spatio-symbolic course can be blended together. Separation takes place at the contract stage of the quest. Liminality corresponds to the competence stage and is enacted by a journey in the wilderness. Aggregation to the sacred happens at the sacred place and corresponds to the achievement of the quest (performance). The feast (sanction stage), which follows the performance and celebrates the end of the quest, expresses the reintegration of the individual to his community, thus making it possible for him to resume normal life.

The Intrinsic Rewards of the Quest

The issue of trial and wilderness deserves particular attention. People choose to confront difficult or precarious situations, apparently to obtain some prized object or reward. Yet a closer scrutiny shows that the situation in itself can be a source of satisfaction. Indeed, the fact of being on a quest holds its own intrinsic reinforcements, independently of the final prized object which initially motivated the pursuit.

Psychologists distinguish between three types of intrinsic rewards: they result from the desire for novelty and optimal stimulation, from the wish for personal causation, and from the desire for ego-transcendence. Stimulation of one's physical and/or mental faculties will be optimal when the situation to be faced requires a level of skill performance equal to the level of competence which the individual possesses (White 1959; Csikszentmihalyi 1975). Linked to that first factor, the desire for personal causation corresponds to the pleasure of being at the origin of decisions and of potentially controlling the issue of a challenge (deCharms 1968), while the desire for ego-transcendence qualifies the need to relate and identify with the outside world, and in so doing, to stretch the limits of the self to new domains of knowledge and competence (Caillois 1958; Csikszentmihalyi 1975).

In the quest, the discovery of foreign places and the meeting with the unexpected are sources of stimulation. The personal decision to go on a quest and the achievement of the quest by one's own doing satisfy the need for personal causation. Through this great adventure, the subject discovers new parts of the world, learns how to handle certain situations, and gains confirmation of his own worth. The enlarged awareness of self and the world resulting from this experience is a source of transcendence.

The Pilgrim's Experience
Departure

Accounts from Medieval pilgrimages confirm this theoretical argument. Pilgrimage can be divided into four stages: departure, journey, encounter, and feast and return (fig. 4). Departure was socially enacted by a religious ceremony where the priest blessed the pilgrims, and where the assembly prayed for the welfare of those undertaking the long and perilous journey. This ceremony qualifies both as social contract and as rite of separation.

For the pilgrim, departure implied a clean break. The unconscious aim was the divestment of social persona and the destructuring of habitual life patterns, which in religious terms were defined as those perpetuating sin (Turner and Turner 1978). The journey, which involved anonymity, relative poverty, and constant mobility, continued this process of detachment.

Stage I	Stage II	Stage III	Stage IV
preparation for departure	journey	encounter	feast and return
home	wilderness	sacred place	festive place
$S_1\ldots\ldots nS_1\ldots\ldots\ldots\ldots\ldots\ldots\ldots\ldots\ldots\ldots\ldots\ldots\ldots\ldots\ldots\ldots\ldots\ldots\ldots S'_2\ldots\ldots\ldots\ldots\ldots S''_2$			
separation	limen	aggregation to the sacred	aggregation to the profane
virtual subject	actualized subject	realized subject	glorified subject
contract (competence)	competence (performance)	performance	sanction

Fig. 4. A summary of the pilgrim's quest. Subject is shown as S as in figure 3; the accomplished identity has both a sacred, S'_2, and a profane, S''_2, aspect.

Once in *terra incognita*, the pilgrim could no longer count on roles and statuses which normally mediated his social interactions; neither could he rely on his earthly possessions to supply his comfort and lifestyle. Going *per agros* (literally "across fields," which refers to the tradition of religious wandering) left a man naked to the immediacy of experience. In other terms, the dissolution of structure entailed by the journey helped "unshield" the psyche and leave it open for new imprints.

Journey

During the journey, money, a passport, and possibly a guidebook gave the pilgrim the material competence to accomplish his travel. Money and a passport were necessary to undertake the trip. The passport authenticated the pilgrim's sacred status; it entitled him to food and shelter in hospices along the way and was supposed to exempt him from road tolls. The passport was thus a powerful means to achieve one's trip.

The guidebook was also useful. It provided the literate pilgrim with some practical knowledge about the journey, such as the stages to be covered, the food to be bought, and the places with drinkable water. It also informed him of the places of worship, of the indulgences to be received, and of the hagiographic tales which revivified his faith. The guidebook thus served both a material and a spiritual function.

On the spiritual level, competence was acquired through prayer and penance. Most pilgrims considered it necessary to perform one's devotions at as many shrines as possible along the way. In the late Middle Ages, such practice turned into a hoarding of sacred graces, which culminated with an emphasis on collecting indulgences, these metered remissions of God's punishment for one's sins (Dupront 1973).

Penance — especially walking barefoot — was seen as a means of increasing the penitential value of one's task (Jusserand 1891; Sigal 1974). Thus the journey was technically the means by which to acquire competence for the final performance, that is, the encounter with God at the pilgrimage site (fig. 4). Yet the feat of crossing hundreds of miles of foreign territory was lived as a performance in itself.

Indeed, in the Middle Ages, long distance travel was perilous and exacting (Barret and Gurgand 1978; Sumption 1975). Each day, food and shelter had to be secured, and one had to find one's way through foreign country. With each sunrise came the endless task of walking. These necessities put to the test the pilgrim's ingenuity and determination. In addition, the traveler suffered hunger, thirst, and other discomforts; yet more serious hardships were expected on the long haul. Most feared were the risks of getting lost in desolate areas, of falling prey to bandits and wild beasts, of being drowned crossing rivers or seas, of falling into the hands of Turkish pirates, and of becoming ill. Hear the complaint of a French pilgrim at sea:

> It wouldn't do to be fussy
> About food for it happens
> Many times and quite often
> That stinking food must be eaten.
>
> Badly covered and sunbaked,
> Eating dishes nearly rotten,
> And wines with sorts of foul taste,
> Them many, they drink often.
> (Nicole Louve, in Bonnardot and Longnon 1878, 111-112).

On the way to Compostela, the geographical areas considered most hazardous were the Landes near Bordeaux, the Massif Central, and the Pyrenees. In the pilgrimage to the Holy Land, it was the Alps, the Mediterranean Sea, and the deserts of Palestine and Egypt. This pilgrimage was particularly deadly: dysentery and sunstroke easily took away the men weakened by their travel.

Danger of course increased the value of the pilgrimage task. It also gave the measure of the pilgrim's determination and faith. And because the pilgrim believed that God had saved his life in moments of danger, he thus understood that God could also save his soul. Danger was thus part of both trial and initiation.

But the pilgrim's journey was not all devotion and mortification. The traveler also enjoyed tourism. Most pilgrims marveled at great works of art like fortifications and at the prosperity of certain cities. The Lord of Anglure and Canon Casola praised the riches of cathedrals (Bonnardot and Longnon 1878); Newett 1907). Thomas Brygg and Sir Richard Guylforde showed a fascination for the topography of sacred places and for their legends (Hoade 1952; Ellis 1851). Friar Fabri expressed his astonishment at seeing camels, elephants, and bananas (Prescott 1954; 1957). He also loved to learn about foreign ores and to gape at new landscapes. It is clear that these pilgrims, in discovering new parts of the world, took great pleasure in satisfying their curiosity.

The pilgrim also drew pride from his capacity to undertake the long journey. Becoming a seasoned traveler, he enjoyed the feeling of competence stemming from his skill at solving the material aspects of his task. Moreover, the travel experience gave him a new perspective on himself, his faith, and the world. Friar Felix Fabri, for example, reflected on his journey:

> Who, I ask you, would ever have dreamed that F.F.F. would be the friend of heathens ... agree with Tartars, be civil to Arabs and Egyptians, show respect to Mahomet, and walk humbly with the barbarian? ... the (Mediterranean) sea brings all together. (Prescott 1957, 266).

In pilgrimage, journey was intrinsically rewarding.

In summary, the journey offered occasions for trials and for learning, which provided the pilgrim with a sense of achievement. In addition, the profane experience acted as positive reinforcement to the religious endeavor.

But the success of the quest was uncertain until the final encounter with God. And thus, the longer the expectation, the stronger the desire to reach one's goal. In such conditions, the final meeting with the sacred would unleash the emotional tension accumulated along the way and would provide a psychological climax interpreted by the pilgrim as spiritual rebirth (Turner and Turner 1978).

Encounter; Feast and Return

Most pilgrims chose to arrive at the pilgrimage site during festival season. At that period, since many pilgrims congregated at the holy grounds, the scene was in tumult. All those who had toiled on the roads for weeks and months arrived with their expectations pitched to a peak. A fever could be felt in the crowd. They hurried to the sacred grounds in order to accomplish the final rituals. They participated with great emotion in religious ceremonies. Swept up in the general fervor, the pilgrim experienced rebirth and felt redeemed. Here is a 15th century account of such emotion in Rome:

> It would be well beyond my powers to describe the feelings of devotion and piety which overcame the crowds then, or to tell you what public displays of repentance and humility were to be seen ... They hoped to wash away their guilt with tears, to purge the stains of sin with groans of pain. And from such weeping and anguish, such general lamentation, there emerged consolation, rejoicing, happiness, and even jubilation at having experienced a spiritual renewal. A sudden change of mood from sorrow to joy overcame the crowd. (Ariosto, in Sumption 1975, 250).

The pilgrim had thus achieved his quest. Success left him elated. He shared this euphoria with other pilgrims by singing, drinking, and letting loose (Labande 1966; Barret and Gurgand 1978). Both the tension accumulated in the daily walking performance and the final joy of the pilgrim made the outlet of the feast necessary. And this feast would be repeated upon his arrival home, where family and friends would congratulate him.

Thus, at a pilgrimage site, the pilgrim finalizes the process of spiritual transformation (fig. 4). This last leg of the quest is characterized both by performance and glorification. The quest ends with the establishment of a new identity: the spiritual rebirth. Aggregation with the sacred is followed and mixed with aggregation to the profane, expressed in an explosion of feasting. At festival season, fairgrounds provided the locale for the merry-going.

In contrast, the return home was uneventful. Most medieval narratives do not even mention the return journey. The pilgrim took the shortest route; he no longer sought to visit places of worship. His main concern was to end his travel as soon as he could. The sacred in the landscape no longer mattered; the sacred was with him.

A Summary of the Pilgrim's Quest

It is now possible to summarize the pilgrim's quest. By making the decision to go on pilgrimage, the individual had taken in hand his own destiny and modified the course of his life. Through the ordeals of the journey and the graces accumulated along the way, he had acquired the competence to meet his God. And from this achievement, his sense of self came out renewed and reinforced. This transformation was all the more irreversible because it had been tied to an enlarged consciousness of self and of the world stemming from the mundane experience. The pilgrim felt fulfilled.

Conclusion

These results have several implications for geographical research. First, the pilgrimage example shows that mobility may be used as divestment of social persona, in order to build a new identity and new course to one's life.[9] Second, it seems that people willingly seek out difficulties and danger because they draw satisfaction from the challenge as well as increased self-esteem. This implies that travel as "time out" may be a mode of reassessing one's environmental competence and of regaining a sense of control over one's destiny. Finally, wilderness, sacred places, and festive places have been identified as playing specific psychological functions in human endeavor.

Notes

1. This paper is drawn from the author's doctoral dissertation, completed at the University of Washington in March 1985, under the title "Space, Place and Movement: The Quest for Self in the World."

2. For exceptions to this tendency, see Samuels (1978), Sopher (1979), Morissoneau (1979), and Salter (1981).

3. This paper emphasizes the individual experience of pilgrimages and its geographical context. The relation between the individual pilgrim and medieval society has been treated elsewhere (Osterrieth 1989).

4. All translations are the author's.

5. Bibliographical references of the early pilgrimage narratives are the following:

Anonymous. Histoire anonyme de la première croisade. 1095. (Bréhier 1924).
Anonymous. Le voyage de la saincte cyté de Hiérusalem. 1480. (Schefer 1882).
Aymery Picaud. Liber Sancti Jacobi. 1139. (Vielliard 1950).

Bertrandon de la Broquière. Le voyage d'outremer. 1432. (Schefer 1892).
Canon Pietro Casola. Pilgrimage to Jerusalem. 1494. (Newett 1907).
Friar Simon Fitzimmons. Itinerary. 1322-1324. (Hoade 1952).
Friar Felix Fabri. Evagatorium. 1484. (Prescott 1954; 1957).
Jean de Joinville. The life of Saint Louis. 1248-1254. (Shaw 1963).
(Lord) Ogier d'Anglure. Le saint voyage de Jhérusalem. 1395-1396. (Bonnardot and Longnon 1878).
Nicole Louve. Bailaide ... fuis suis mer en revenan don Saint sepulchre. 1428. (Bannardot and Longnon 1878).
Nompar de Caumont. Le voyatge d'oultremer en Jhérusalem. 1418 (Noble 1975).
Sir Richard Guylforde. Pylgrymage to the Holy Land. 1506. (Ellis 1851)
Thomas Brygg. The itinerary in the Holy Land. 1392. (Hoade 1952).

6. In semiologists' terms, urge, power, and knowledge are *modal* objects, modal because they influence the performance of the quest (Everaert-Desmedt 1981, 45). They are not to be confused with the object of the quest, which is also called the *principal* object.

7. In Everaert-Desmedt's typology (fig. 2), acquisition of the emotional mobilization creates a virtual subject, virtual because the subject, not having yet accomplished anything, cannot claim status except in terms of future events. Acquisition of the principal object means accomplishing the transformation of self, hence the realized subject. Social recognition of the feat produces a glorified subject.

8. Indeed many geographical studies stress risk-avoidance behavior and tend to overlook the positive value of "danger." One reason is that urban ills have pointed towards the need for security ("defensible space," etc.), for rest from sensory overload, and from crowding stress (see Porteous 1977). Each of these ills stems from situations where environmental stimuli are overwhelming; in consequence the individual can no longer control the situation for a positive outcome. The concept of environmental competence should, however, also be explored in the context of risk-taking behavior. Individuals may take calculated risks in order to increase their environmental competence. Mountaineering would be a good example of such behavior (Csikszentmihalyi 1975).

9. Such findings have potential applications in migration research as well as in the study of specific forms of travel (foreign assignments, tourism, etc.) More globally, they ascertain the positive value of travel in existential terms.

References

Barret, P., and J-N. Gurgand. 1978. *Priez pour nous à Compostelle*. Paris: Hachette.
Bonnardot, F., and A. Longnon. 1878. *Le saint voyage de Jhérusalem du seigneur d'Anglure (Ogier VIII)*. Paris: Didot.
Bréhier, L. 1924. *Histoire anonyme de la première croisade*. Paris: Champion.
Buttimer, A. 1976. Grasping the dynamism of the lifeworld. *Annals of the Association of American Geographers* 66: 277-92.
———. 1980. Home, reach, and the sense of place. In *The human experience of space and place*, eds. A. Buttimer and D. Seamon, 166-87. London: Croom Helm.
Caillois, R. 1958. *Les jeux et les hommes*. Paris: Gallimard.
deCharms, R. 1968. *Personal causation*. New York: Academic Press.
Csikszentmihalyi, M. 1975. *Beyond boredom and anxiety*. San Francisco: Jossey-Bass.
Dupront, A. 1973. Pèlerinage et lieux sacrés. In *Mélanges offerts à Fernand Braudel*, II: 189-206. Toulouse: Privat.
Ellis, H., ed. 1851. *The pylgrymage of Sir Richard Guylforde to the Holy Land, A.D. 1506*. London: Camden Society.

Entrikin, N. 1976. Contemporary Humanism in Geography. *Annals of the Association of American Geographers* 66: 615-32.

Everaert-Desmedt, N. 1981. *Sémiotique du récit*. Louvain-la-Neuve: Cabay.

Gennep, A. van 1908. *Les Rites de passage*. Paris: Nourry.

Greimas, A. 1970. *Du sens*. Paris: Seuil.

———. 1983. *Du sens II*. Paris: Seuil.

Hiernaux, J. P. 1977. L'institution culturelle. Thèse de doctorat, Institut de Sociologie, Université Catholique de Louvain, Louvain-la-Neuve.

Hoade, E. o.f.m. 1952. *Western pilgrims*. Jerusalem: Franciscan Printing Press.

Jusserand, J. J. 1891. *English wayfaring life in the Middle Ages (XIV Cent.)*. Trans. L. T. Smith. London: Fisher Unwin.

Labande, E. 1966. 'Ad limina': Le pèlerin médiéval au terme de sa démarche. In *Mélanges offerts à René Crozet*, v. 1. Poitiers: P. Gallais et Y. J. Riou.

Leach, E. 1976. *Culture and communication: The logic by which symbols are connected*. Cambridge: Cambridge University Press.

Morissonneau, C. 1979. Mobilité et identité quebécoise. *Cahiers de Géographie du Québec* 23: 29-38.

Newett, M., ed. and trans. 1907. *Canon Pietro Casola's Pilgrimage to Jerusalem in the Year 1494*. Manchester: Manchester University Press.

Noble, P. S. 1975. *Le voyage d'oultremer en Jhérusalem de Nompar, seigneur de Caumont*. Oxford: Basil Blackwell.

Osterrieth, A. 1989. Pilgrimage: Society and individual quest. *Social Compass* 36: 145-57.

Pocock, D. 1981. *Humanistic geography and literature*. London: Croom Helm.

Porteous, J. D. 1977. *Environment and behavior*. Reading, MA: Addison-Wesley.

Prescott, H. 1954. *Jerusalem journey. Pilgrimage to the Holy Land in the 15th C*. London: Eyre and Spottiswoode.

———. 1957. *Once to Sinai: The further pilgrimage of Friar Felix Fabri*. London: Eyre and Spottiswoode.

Relph, E. 1976. *Place and placelessness*. London: Pion.

Salter, C. 1981. Perspectives on exploration. Is travel a terminal disease? *Landscape* 25: 40-41.

Samuels, M. 1978. Existentialism and human geography. In *Humanistic geography: Problems and prospects*, eds. D. Ley and M. Samuels, 22-40. Chicago: Maaroufa Press.

Seamon, D. 1981. Newcomers, existential outsiders and insiders: Their portrayal in two books by Doris Lessing. In *Humanistic geography and literature*, ed. D. Pocock, 85-100. London: Croom Helm.

Schefer, Ch. 1882. *Le voyage de la saincte cyté de Hiérusalem*. Paris: Ernest Leroux.

———. 1892. *Le voyage d'outremer de la Broquière*. Recueil de voyages et de documents pour servir à l'histoire de la géographie depuis le XIIIe siècle jusqu'à la fin du XVIe siècle. Vol. XII. Paris.

Shaw, M. R. B., ed. and trans. 1963. *Joinville and Villehardouin: Chronicles of the crusades*. Harmondsworth: Penguin.

Sigal, P. A. 1974. *Les marcheurs de Dieu: Pèlerinages et pèlerins au Moyen-Age*. Paris: Armand Colin.

Sopher, D. E. 1979. The landscape of home: Myth, experience, social meaning. In *The interpretation of ordinary landscapes*, ed. D. W. Meinig, 129-49. Oxford: Oxford University Press.

Sumption, J. 1975. *Pilgrimages: An image of Mediaeval religion*. London: Faber and Faber.

Tuan, Y-F. 1971. Geography, phenomenology, and the study of human nature. *Canadian Geographer* 15: 181-92.

———. 1974. Space and place: Humanistic perspective. *Progress in Human Geography* 6: 213-52.

———. 1975. Place: An experiential perspective. *Geographical Review* 65: 151-65.

———. 1976. Humanistic geography. *Annals of the Association of American Geographers* 66: 266-76.

———. 1977. *Space and place: The perspective of experience*. Minneapolis: University of Minnesota Press.

Turner, V., and E. Turner. 1978. *Image and pilgrimage in Christian culture*. New York: Columbia University Press.

Vielliard, J. 1950. *Le guide du pèlerin de Saint-Jacques de Compostelle*, 2ème éd. Mâcon: Protat.

White, R. W. 1959. Exerpts from motivation reconsidered: The concept of competence. In *Environmental psychology*, eds. H. M. Proshansky, W. H. Ittelson, and L. G. Rivlins, 125-34. New York: Holt, Rinehart and Winston.

Defining and Classifying Pilgrimages

Robert H. Stoddard
University of Nebraska

Abstract

To make comparisons among the many forms of religious journeys, scholars need both an acceptable definition of the phenomenon called pilgrimages and a workable classification scheme that reveals significant differences. Following a discussion about the elements that should be incorporated into a definition of pilgrimages, a formal statement is presented. This provides a basis for separating those traveling activities that should be studied as pilgrimages from all other forms of human movement.

Further differentiation among pilgrimages can be achieved by categorizing them into a few distinct classes. Several criteria that logically could be utilized for dividing pilgrimages into various types are examined, but the final classification scheme depends on three factors. Each criterion is subdivided three ways, which produces a set of twenty-seven potential types of pilgrimages.

Key words: pilgrimage, pilgrimage defined, pilgrimage classified.

•Shortly before taking an examination, a college student travels by bus from Colombo to worship at the Kataragama shrine.

•During the Hajj period, Muslims from numerous countries assemble at Mecca to participate in prescribed rituals.

•Hundreds of Americans drive to Atlanta to attend a rally conducted by a famous evangelist.

Do these three events have any common characteristics? If so, can the term pilgrimage be applied meaningfully to all three events? Even if all three can be subsumed conceptually under the definitional category of "pilgrimage," are there significant differences that could be indicated logically by subdividing the entire pilgrimage set? The purpose of this paper is to provide a basis for answering these questions by presenting a definition of pilgrimages and a scheme for classifying them.

Sacred Places, Sacred Spaces: The Geography of Pilgrimages, edited by Robert H. Stoddard and Alan Morinis, 1997. Geoscience and Man, vol. 34, pp. 41-60. Dept. of Geography and Anthropology, Louisiana State University, Baton Rouge, LA 70893-6010.

41

The Role of Definitions and Classifications

A standardized definition and accompanying classification scheme can benefit pilgrimage studies in two major ways. They can promote clarity in communication and they can provide the means for establishing relationships among phenomena.

Definitions are essential for linguistic communication because the very basis of language involves the grouping of individual elements into semantic categories. Classification can also aid communication because greater linguistic precision can be achieved by dividing broad definitions into smaller groups. For example, travelers have been defined as "pilgrims," "tourists," or "religious wanderers" (Cohen 1981; Smith 1981; Graham 1981). Likewise, the group defined as "pilgrims" can be divided into subgroups, such as "Buddhist" pilgrims, "Christian" pilgrims, or "Sikh" pilgrims.

Another benefit resulting from a classification scheme is its potential role in establishing relationships among phenomena. To detect geographic relationships between pilgrimages and other human and environmental features, it is necessary to observe and measure variations. Although a few characteristics of pilgrimages, such as distance traveled and number of pilgrims, can be measured quantitatively, most aspects of pilgrimages can not be differentiated by applying numbers. Qualitative differentiation requires classification.

Only by discovering associations among variations in pilgrimages and other related phenomena can generalizations be accomplished. In other words, classification is a prerequisite for moving pilgrimage studies from being only a collection of descriptive accounts about unique events to a body of knowledge that facilitates making comparisons, finding relationships, and producing principles of geographic behavior.

Defining the Pilgrimage Phenomenon
Some Definitions of Pilgrimages

It is not surprising that a human activity as complex and varied as a pilgrimage has no universally accepted definition. Lack of unanimity not only complicates separating pilgrimages from non-pilgrimages but also implies differing criteria for classification. These difficulties become apparent by examining some definitions that have been published elsewhere.

Consider the following three definitions:

Definition #1: A journey to a sacred place as an act of religious devotion (Sykes 1982, 776).

Definition #2: Pilgrimage involves three factors: a holy place; attraction of individuals or crowds to this place; a specific aim, i.e., to obtain some spiritual or material benefit (Brandon 1970, 501).

Definition #3: The term pilgrimage is used in at least three senses. (1) There is first the "interior pilgrimage," the "journey of the soul" in a lifetime of growth from spiritual infancy to maturity. (2) There is, second, the literal pilgrimage to some sacred place as a paradigm of the intent of religion itself. This literal journey may be called "extroverted mysticism" (Turner 1973). (3) Finally, every trek to one's local sanctuary is a pilgrimage in miniature insofar as it acts out on a small scale some transition or growth and experience of the sacred and new community which pilgrimage in general affords (Crim 1981, 569).

Although these definitions possess common elements, there are differences that should be examined. Also, of great importance to the emphasis in this paper is the fact that they cannot be operationalized without further clarification. Even though adequately conveying conceptual meaning, they lack the precision needed to measure the differences between a pilgrimage and other kinds of journeys. Before examining the individual elements of these definitions, however, it should be noted that the first sense of the third definition — the "journey of the soul" — will be excluded here because such is not the phenomenon of physical travel that is manifested geographically.

Distance of Movement

One of the most basic elements in a definition of pilgrimage is movement. Most of the conceptual ambiguity of this element has been removed here by excluding the mystical or spiritual thoughts of a person who does not actually travel. For geographic purposes, at least, pilgrimages must involve the physical movement of persons from one place to another.

The primary definitional problem, however, concerns the minimum distance required for movement to be termed a pilgrimage. The issue is exposed in the third definition cited above, which suggests in the third sense that a stroll to a local sanctuary is also a kind of pilgrimage. Indeed, some pilgrimage scholars do regard every shrine as a center of pilgrimage (Bharati 1970). Does this mean that all movements to sacred places, irrespective of how short they are, are properly called pilgrimages? If so, this is an easy solution to the scale problem because we do not need to worry about the distance element. All travel which satisfies the other criteria for being a pilgrimage (see below) meets the movement requirement.

The third definition, however, does not really remove all uncertainty about the question of minimum distance because, since this "third sense" is presented as a distinct category, it evidently must differ from the preceding sense of the term. How is such a difference recognized? Is it based only on length of travel? If so, what distance separates the "miniature pilgrimages" from regular ones?

These questions about distance partly reflect the dilemma of scale inherent in all geographic study. Generalizations about spatial behavior are always influenced by scale — both the size of the total area in which the phenomena are observed and the size of the minimum unit for measuring variations. As an illustration, consider the following two situations. One is a map of the Anuradhapura area of Sri Lanka. It includes Sri Mahabodhi, Ruvanveli Dagaba, and the six other sacred spots within an area of approximately 15 square kilometers. The detail is such that the mapped paths of pilgrimage movements show the circumambulations around the *dagaba*s (stupas) and the approach to the Bodhi-Tree.[1] The second map, at a different scale, covers all of Sri Lanka. A single symbol represents Anuradhapura, and pilgrimage paths converge on the city along highways and rail routes. It is very apparent that many relationships, such as that between distanced traveled and number of pilgrims, will be quite different in these two situations.

The contrast between these two situations typifies the basic definitional issue of minimum distance. Virtually everyone would affirm that traveling from Colombo to Anuradhapura for the purpose of worship constitutes a pilgrimage. In contrast, most scholars would not regard the movement from Sri Mahabodhi to Ruvanveli Dagaba as a separate pilgrimage event.

In fact, common usage in the English language does not include such movements as weekly trips to a neighborhood church or daily strolls to a nearby shrine. Certainly the popular conceptualization of pilgrimage regards the movement as being longer than local travel. Furthermore, most pilgrimage scholars, including the Turners, have insisted that going on a pilgrimage involves movement away from the "local" environment (Turner and Turner 1978).

The exclusion of local movements from the definition of pilgrimage introduces questions about exceptional cases, such as persons who live near famous pilgrimage sites. For example, according to Neame (1968), most inhabitants of Lourdes attend the parish church and have little to do with the famous Marian shrine. When a resident of Lourdes does visit the shrine, however, the question arises about whether such a short trip should be regarded as a true pilgrimage. For consistency, that movement cannot be called a pilgrimage because the term applies only to "farther than local" journeys.

Excluding local journeys from the definition of pilgrimage is consistent with the general meanings of "procession" and "circumambulation." These terms usually imply a journey longer than just ritualistic movements inside a very confined space, but yet they still pertain to local movements. Conceptually, however, long processions and circumambulations seem to merge into short pilgrimages. Under some circumstances, a lengthy "procession," consisting of a group moving along a prescribed route for religious purposes, might be considered a short "pilgrimage." For example, should the movements from Mecca to Mina and Arafat and back to Mecca be called processions or short pilgrimages?

Similarly, even though "circumambulation" refers to movement around a sacred object or area, there is no definitional limit on the length of the circular journey. When the circumference of the route is several kilometers long, such as the 80-kilometer Pancha Kroshi Parikrama around the sacred area of Varanasi (Singh, this volume), movement certainly approximates the distance conventionally associated with that of a pilgrimage. Is it only the absence of a central focus that makes the famous circular movement around Shikoku a pilgrimage rather than a gigantic circumambulation? Or, does its greater distance of 1,385 kilometers shift it from one definitional category to the other?

The goals of definitional standardization can be achieved best by not expressing the "minimum distance" of a pilgrimage in quantitative terms. This is already demonstrated by the discussion about long circumambulations. The term "local" cannot be quantified meaningfully for all circumstances because of the variability in sizes of communities (or culture regions), the availability of transportation networks, and modes of travel. Therefore, rather than stating that the minimum distance must exceed, for example, 30 kilometers, here the term "pilgrimage" is defined as movement that is "longer than local."

Motivation

A second element in the definition of pilgrimage concerns the motive for the movement. As seen in the definitions quoted above, the motive is usually religious. It is true that if a portion of the second definition, which includes the phrase "to obtain some ... material benefit," is taken literally, it does not exclude vendors and pickpockets. Nevertheless, there is general agreement that the motivation of the traveler must be religious for the event to qualify as a pilgrimage.

Such agreement soon dissipates, however, when a definition of the term "religious" is attempted. The term "religion" is as vague and lacking standardization as the phenomenon being defined here. However, to avoid deviating into another discussion about the boundaries of terms, the word "religious" will be accepted as a definitional primitive.

Even with an assumed working definition of "religious," the actual separation of motives is virtually impossible. Neither observers nor travelers themselves can differentiate motives that are primarily religious from a multitude of other reasons for making a journey to a place where pilgrims congregate. At a popular pilgrimage site where fairs, festivals, sporting events, and markets concurrently attract pilgrims, tourists, vacationers, excursion groups, traders, and hustlers, the true religious pilgrims cannot always be identified.

It is true that some scholars have attempted to determine the motives of persons at pilgrimage sites by asking them to declare their reasons in an interview or on a questionnaire (Jindel 1976; Vidyarthi, Jha and Saraswati 1979; Naidu 1985). Although some clues about motivations may be obtained by this technique, it is questionable whether data are entirely representative and valid.

Furthermore, even if the "true motives" of travelers to pilgrimage sites were known, some definitional problems remain. One is the fact that motives change. If a person decides to visit a pilgrimage place because of curiosity but experiences a religious conversion while at the site, has the journey become a personal pilgrimage?

Another definitional problem results from the fact that trips are taken for multiple reasons. If a person travels to a foreign area as a tourist but while in that vicinity also makes a religious journey to a sacred site, is that person a pilgrim? The issue is well illustrated by the uncertainty about whether the large number of participants in commercial tours to religious sites should be counted as pilgrims (Nolan and Nolan 1989).

The operational solution to this definitional problem generally has been to count all who come to a pilgrimage site as pilgrims. Even though all who have made the journey probably have not done so for primarily religious motives, an inclusive count is accepted because of the virtual impossibility of operationalizing the term "religious."

In some respects, counting all who travel to a "pilgrimage site" as religious pilgrims shifts the definitional burden to that of differentiating among various types of destinations. That is, if Mecca is accepted as a sacred site, then there is some justification for regarding travelers to Mecca as pilgrims. If, on the other hand, Canterbury is no longer revered as a sacred place, then to be consistent, visitors to that place should not be defined as religious pilgrims. In any case, the nature of the destination is an important element in the definition of pilgrimage.

The Destination

To be called pilgrimage, the movement normally must be to a destination that is regarded as sacred. Conceptually this condition is clear; but operationally it requires the ability to measure sanctity. Because there are no inherent characteristics at a site that reveal its holy attributes, it is difficult to objectively identify places that are sacred and thus attract pilgrims.

Even conceptually there is not a sharp delineation between "sacred" and "nonsacred" places. Researchers are confronted with the task of deciding whether a family gravesite, a tree containing the spirits of a tribal community, or an altar in an urban mission should be included or not. In some cases, a childhood home or a national shrine have been termed sacred. It is necessary, therefore, to rate places that may or may not be considered sacred for the purpose of identifying those that exceed a minimum level of sanctity.

Several methods have been employed in attempts to rate places according to sanctity (Stoddard 1966, 1994; Bhardwaj 1973; Preston 1981). One method bases sanctity on statements in holy texts (Salomon 1979). Places enumerated in the indigenous literature as being sacred are accepted as equivalent to places of pilgrimages. This is generally an unsatisfactory method for identifying contemporary sacred sites, however, because of tremendous changes (Bhattacharya 1953; Sopher 1987; Tanaka Shimazaki 1988). The locations of some places cited in ancient texts are unknown today, while other places (e.g., La Salette, Lourdes, Knock, Fatima, and Medugorje) have become popular pilgrimage destinations only recently.

Another method relies upon empirical data that pertain either to number of pilgrims or to distance traveled. When using count data, it is assumed that a large number of persons traveling to a specific site indicates a high level of sanctity. Equating total number of pilgrims to sanctity is somewhat inappropriate for definitional purposes here because it involves cyclical reasoning, namely, that "pilgrimages" are movements to places that are defined as "sacred" because those places are where pilgrims go.

Reliance on travel data associates sanctity of a place with the distance worshippers have journeyed; that is, longer average distances (or greater variances in distances) indicate higher-order pilgrimage places (Bhardwaj 1973). As a definitional element, however, this method does not contribute additional support because it duplicates the "distance of movement" component.

A third method of measuring the sanctity of places is by obtaining the opinions of a group. When the group consists of the general population, sanctity of places is operationally defined on the basis of the collective responses of a sampled group (Bhardwaj 1973; Stoddard 1980; Jackson and Henrie 1983). In many ways, this comes closest to measuring the concept of sacred places, but it is costly to acquire the data through the necessarily large survey.

Alternately, a survey of experts can produce an index of sanctity. Admittedly, this method lacks the objectivity desired in an operational definition because it essentially states that a place is sacred if the experts affirm that such is the case. Nevertheless, most places that are regarded as sacred by larger populations are those that have been observed, identified, and reported as such by pilgrimage scholars (Stoddard 1994).

Besides the difficulty of measuring the sanctity of places, another type of definitional issue occurs when the destination of worshippers is not a fixed site, but rather a person who wanders. In India, where pilgrims are frequently attracted to the temporary residences of highly revered traveling monks (Bhardwaj, this volume; Eck 1985; McCormick, this volume), this might complicate the specification of sacred places. In general, these circumstances present no major problem because they can be subsumed under the comprehensive definition of pilgrimages to sacred places. If the immediate space around a revered person is regarded as holy, irrespective of how short the duration, then mass attraction to this place should be considered as a pilgrimage event. Presenting greater definitional difficulty, though, are the religious journeys of "flexible pilgrimages" of the Spiritual Baptists of Trinidad (Glazier 1983).

Magnitude

A fourth definitional issue concerns the magnitude of movement to a sacred place. Here a very important distinction is made between the concept of pilgrimage and an operational definition of this phenomenon of mass movement. Conceptually, the definition of pilgrimage should include any religious journey, including that of a single individual, to a sacred place. Consistently, then, an individual pilgrimage unit would be the travels of one person. The goal here, however, is to operationally define an event that involves the flow of a large collection of pilgrims. The aspect that presents uncertainty is the size or magnitude of the collection constituting a pilgrimage event.

A single pilgrimage event is defined here as the movement of numerous worshippers traveling to a sacred destination, usually during a special occasion. Many pilgrimages occur at the time of a religious holiday and/ or a specially announced occasion and, therefore, the question about whether a pilgrimage occasion has occurred does not arise. But, theoretically, the issue of magnitude is pertinent if very few pilgrims actually came at the same time of an announced ceremony or, conversely, if a large number of pilgrims spontaneously converged at a holy site at a time unassociated with a religious holiday.

The definition of "numerous" can be operationalized by attaching the condition of "significance." That is, if at a particular time, the number of visitors to a sacred site is significantly greater than the norm, that qualifies as a "pilgrimage event." It is not essential that "significance" be given a formal statistical meaning; a qualitative definition of the term is also satisfactory. Basing the definition on significant deviations from the normal number of pilgrims traveling to a place, of course, means that no absolute value determines a pilgrimage event. At places visited by several hundred pilgrims daily, a special occasion is marked by thousands of pilgrims;

whereas at other places that rarely have visitors, a pilgrimage event could be indicated by a few hundred pilgrims.

An Operational Definition of a Pilgrimage Event

Converting the concept of pilgrimage into an operational definition that will apply equally well to all cultural settings is difficult. This is partly because of differences in linguistic usage. In India, for example, people who undertake a journey for the purpose of being in the presence of a famous traveling monk are usually called pilgrims. In contrast, Americans who travel to national religious rallies and conferences to listen to famous spiritual leaders are seldom referred to as pilgrims. Thus, even though many characteristics of these two situations are similar, popular terminology does not equate them.

Nevertheless, certain key elements do need to be recognized as basic to an operational definition of pilgrimage. Thus, the following definition is suggested for the meaning of pilgrimage: *an event consisting of longer than local journeys by numerous persons to a sacred place as an act of religious devotion.*

Criteria for Classification

Within the set of all events defined as pilgrimages are innumerable variations, which, for analytical purposes, should be further characterized by dividing them into classes. The utility of a classification scheme, of course, is highly dependent on the criteria used to differentiate individuals (or events) because the selected criteria affect the way variations among the total population are observed and the way relationships may be detected. Therefore, several potential criteria are examined here for their merits and limitations before selecting three that probably possess the greatest discriminatory power for a geographic classification.

Length of Journey

A fundamental element in the definition of pilgrimage concerns the distance of movement, which means that it is a critical variable in understanding this phenomenon. The incorporation of this variable into a classification scheme, therefore, is essential for geographic understanding.

Pilgrimage scholars from a variety of disciplines have found merit in differentiating pilgrimage places on the basis of travel distance. Often discussions concern variations in the size and characteristics of the inherent nodal regions because, in effect, they are delineated by lengths of journey. Although other terminology, such as "catchment area" and "pilgrimage field," is sometimes utilized (Turner 1973; Preston 1981; Messerschmidt and Sharma 1989), it still taps into the abundance of studies dealing with nodal regions.Because distance can be easily measured quantitatively, it is tempting to delineate classes of pilgrims on the basis of linear units. The disadvantages of a numerical differentiation of journey distances are essentially the same as those advanced against quantitatively defining the upper limit of "local." That is, the travel implications of, say, 20 kilometers, varies greatly with conditions. It varies with mode of travel, as illustrated by the greater friction, or deterrence, of distance resulting from walking over mountainous terrain than from riding in a car on a superhighway. It varies with size of communities, especially if a 20-kilometer journey does, or does not, take the pilgrims outside their home territory into a region of foreign inhabitants and unfamiliar environments.

An alternative way of classifying distanced traveled by pilgrims is by utilizing ordinal categories such as regional, national, and international. (Of course, a category of "local" could be included also, if such were not excluded from an operational definition.) This means of classifying distance traveled has been the strategy of several scholars of pilgrimages (table 1).

The main limitation of an ordinal scheme for differentiating the travel distance of pilgrims is its imprecision in measurements, especially as it concerns national units. Because countries vary tremendously in size, the distinction between "national" and "international" does not correlate well with distance. For example, an "international" trip from Spain to France may be shorter and easier than a "national" one the length of India. Also, the size of a country influences the concept of "regional." That is, a regional pilgrimage in Brazil may encompass a much larger area than a regional one in Sri Lanka.

Table 1. Classification of pilgrimages, by selected authors

Bhardwaj 1973	Jackowski 1987	Preston 1980	Turner 1973
Local	Local	Local	Intervillage
Subregional		District	
Regional	Regional	Regional	Regional
Supraregional	National		National
pan-Hindu	International	All-South Asia	International

In spite of these limitations, this three-fold division is feasible. It is partially justified by the fact that we do live in a world in which international boundaries have a tremendous effect on human movement and related activities. The division between "national" and "international" recognizes this condition. Furthermore, the concept of regions and regionalism is well established in geography, so the term "regional" carries much more meaning than the expression "a shorter distance than national."

If desired, the conversion of these distance categories to a classification of a pilgrimage, as an event attended by a large number of pilgrims, can be accomplished by quantitative guidelines. As an illustration, if more than 30 percent of the pilgrims to a particular site are categorized as international, the event they are attending could be considered an "international" pilgrimage. If fewer than 30 percent of the pilgrims are international but more than 50 percent are national, then the occasion might be classified as "national." According to this proposed scheme, all other pilgrimages would be classed as "regional" (fig. 1). Thus, an event in which the percentage of pilgrims identified as international, national, and regional are respectively 10, 20, and 70 is categorized as a regional pilgrimage. With the accumulation of more empirical data, these limiting percentages could be adjusted to better fit world variations in pilgrimage distances.[2]

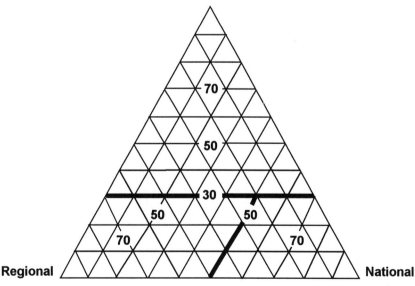

Fig. 1. Three types of pilgrimages — Regional, National, and International — are defined on the basis of the percentage of pilgrims who have traveled specified distances. The triangular graph illustrates how various percentages are combined to define each of the three pilgrimage types.

Pilgrimage Route

A second criterion that spatially distinguishes pilgrimages is the kind of route followed by pilgrims. One kind, which here is called "converging," is merely the collection of all direct-line paths taken by pilgrims going from their homes to a sacred site. In most respects, these resemble those converging on any other type of nodal center and are associated with least-effort connections, as expressed in time, ease, and cost of travel, and with perceptions and knowledge of route choices.

When a pilgrim makes a journey to more than one pilgrimage site, we would expect the entire connecting route to approximate a type of least-effort connectivity. Although it may not match the optimal pattern of the traveling-salesman type, the route is chosen by personal preferences of each pilgrim on the basis of time, costs, and similar factors.

Labeling this kind of pilgrimage travel as just another example of convergence to a nodal center, however, is not intended to deny the factor of sacrifice. For many pilgrims, greater merit can be obtained at the destination if the trip has been arduous. Unfortunately, the importance of this negative factor has not been studied in depth. It is known that the path of least effort is shunned by some pilgrims, but its cumulative effect on the selection of specific routes is unknown. In some cases, sacrifice is probably achieved through the mode of travel rather than by the route (Turner 1973; Stoddard 1988).

A second class of pilgrimage routes consists of paths prescribed by religious texts, teachings, and/or practice. A pilgrimage along a route that is prescribed essentially extends the religious domain far beyond a single holy site because the entire pilgrimage way is usually regarded as a sacred path. Often the total journey is an act of devotion, especially if it involves worshipping at numerous sites along the route. In fact, in some situations, there is no dominant holy spot, but rather, a series of places visited by pilgrims as they follow the pilgrimage route (Tanaka Shimazaki 1977; Hoshino 1981; Shimazaki, this volume).

Prescribed routes can be divided into two subcategories: circular and non-circular ("processional"). Circular routes do not necessarily form a shape that matches a circle, but they consist of a closed traverse. All pilgrims, irrespective of whether they commence and terminate at the same place or join the path at numerous entry points, complete the prescribed route. For example, when pilgrims in the Kathmandu Valley of Nepal make the 60-kilometer journey around to the four Ganesh shrines, they may join the circular route at the position closest to their home (Stoddard 1980). Consequently, a journey along a prescribed circular pilgrimage route has some of the characteristics of a large circumambulation, except that a sacred object or area may not necessarily be encircled.

A prescribed non-circular route invariably focuses on a pilgrimage site. The prescribed route functions as the sacred approach which prepares the pilgrim for the encounter at the holiest place. At the farthest distance, it may be that no route is prescribed so pilgrims join one of several branches only after they get closer to their destination. As they approach the goal, they are channeled into a single pathway, which may be lined with sacred way stations (Turner and Turner 1978; Miller 1981). When the pilgrimage site is located in a rather inaccessible place, the route restriction may be reinforced by physical constraints (Messerschmidt and Sharma 1989).

It is recognized that operationalizing the extent to which a pilgrimage route is prescribed involves the question of scale. When the scale is confined to the spatial movements within the immediate environs of the sacred area, ritualistic movement will often be partly or wholly prescribed (Shimazaki, this volume). Consistent with the rest of the classification scheme proposed here, such large-scale movements are disregarded.

In summary, it is recommended that pilgrimage routes be grouped into three classes: convergence, prescribed circular, and prescribed processional (non-circular).

Frequency of Pilgrimage

A third criterion that is helpful in observing variations in pilgrimages is their frequency of occurrence. Although this aspect is not as spatial as the other two criteria, time is certainly related to space in geographic analyses. This temporal component is not the view of time divided into historic periods; instead, it may refer either to the number of events that occur within a designated unit of time or the amount of time between pilgrimages. The latter is adopted here.

Frequency of pilgrimages occurs as a continuous variable, ranging from very rare events to almost continual religious journeys, which means the positions and number of class boundaries are not universally recognized as "natural." Because numerous religious celebrations occur annually, the classification proposed here is based on a year. If annual pilgrimages are separated from those taken less frequently and from others occurring more often, three classes result. To avoid having the middle class being restricted to exactly one year and to include annual cycles that do not match the Gregorian calendar, its boundaries are quantitatively expanded from merely 12 months to a period of 10 to 14 months. Here these three classes are termed "frequent" (for those occurring more often than every 10 months), "annual" (once every 10 to 14 months), and "rare" (more than 14 months between pilgrimages).[3]

Location of Pilgrimage Destination

Pilgrimages can be classified according to their locations by site or situation. The former pertains primarily to the characteristics at a particular location while the latter refers to the relative location of the place.

Site characteristics Site characteristics may be an integral part of a sacred place and, thus, serve as an appropriate classificatory criterion. Environmental characteristics that might be observed are high places, springs or wells, streams, coastal protuberances, caves, or a combination of several physical features (Nolan 1987; Sopher 1987).

Unfortunately for classification purposes, the environmental condition of many sites is not regarded as the reason for the site's sacredness. The Nolans, for example, found that more than half of the Christian pilgrimage sites they examined in western Europe were not meaningfully associated with a site feature (Nolan and Nolan, this volume). Sites where divine events were manifested and/or revered persons were born or martyred may be quite unrelated to the natural setting, yet be important destinations for pilgrims. Another limitation to classifying natural sites is created by pilgrimage goals that are mobile, that is, those associated with traveling monks. These factors do not exclude using site features as a criterion for classifying pilgrimage destinations, but they do reduce the potential for explanatory relationships.

Relative location Pilgrimage places can be classified also by the relative location, i.e., their geographic situation. The related phenomena may be the distributions of total or selected populations (Stoddard 1966; Sopher 1968; Bharati 1970; Bhardwaj 1973), transportation networks, or the origins of attending pilgrims. The latter has been expressed in terms of the core or periphery of the nodal region (Turner 1973; Sopher 1987; Tanaka Shimazaki 1988).

One argument against the inclusion of relative locations as a classificatory criterion is its potential for use as an explanatory variable. That is, the designation of a classification scheme always involves the question about the optimum number of criteria. Increasing the number of criteria concurrently does increase the precision of differentiating among individuals, but this achievement usually sacrifices opportunities for measuring relationships with variables that could otherwise be used as explanatory phenomena.

In this case, logic favors the exclusion of this variable — the relative location of the pilgrimage destination — from the classification scheme. It is more logical to have the option of correlating pilgrimage types with the geographic positions of their destinations than to incorporate this locational factor in the classification scheme.

Importance of Pilgrimage Places

Places may range from the holiest of holy places to sites that differ little from the surrounding profane space (Eliade 1959); therefore, another way pilgrimages might be categorized is by their degree of sanctity or, as emphasized by Preston (1981), their "spiritual magnetism." Any one of the methods used for measuring sanctity for definitional purposes (see above) can be utilized for classifying places.

Measuring the sanctity of a place by the number of pilgrims attracted to it is consistent with geographic studies of other phenomena drawn to a nodal center. The nature of religious motivations and behavior, however, complicates using this in, at least, three ways. One is that attendance is partly a function of the size of each religious group. For example, the Wailing Wall in Jerusalem may be regarded by Jews as very sacred, but the world population of Jews is comparatively small, especially in contrast to the Hindu population. Consequently, more Hindu pilgrims may attend a place perceived as having lesser sanctity than the number of Jewish pilgrims going to the Wailing Wall. Applying a measurement based on number of pilgrims would greatly limit cross-religious studies of pilgrimage.

A second complication results from uncertainty about the most appropriate time unit. To illustrate, compare (1) the 100 daily pilgrims to place X with (2) the 36,500 pilgrims that go to place Y at the time of annual festival with (3) the 438,000 that attend the one-in-12-years' holy occasion at place Z, which is virtually unattended at other times. On a 12-year basis, these three places are equally sacred; but when measured by a time unit of a year, places X and Y are more important than Z except for one year in twelve. If the sanctity of a site is measured by the magnitude of daily pilgrims, then place X is usually the most sacred.

A third reason for not equating number of pilgrims coming to a site with its sanctity is the feeling by some devotees that popularity diminishes its sacredness. A place that is very accessible and is patronized by numerous tourists, vendors, and others with marginal religious motives loses some of its spirituality (Stirrat 1979). Conversely, a place that requires much physical effort to reach may be perceived as especially sacred, partly because it is not crowded with casual visitors (Aziz 1982). It is difficult to assess the extent to which this factor is applicable to pilgrimage sites in general, but it may diminish the validity of using attendance data as a surrogate for the sanctity of a place.

Although the sanctity level of a pilgrimage site may be determined by methods other than its popularity, the alternative methods also have weaknesses that limit their effectiveness as way of grouping pilgrimages (as discussed in the definitional section). Therefore, the criterion of sanctity holds less promise for a classification scheme than those ultimately accepted here.

Motivation of Pilgrims

By definition, the primary motive for each traveler is religious, but this general category can be subdivided. Primary motives may be (1) to request a favor, (2) to offer thanks, (3) to fulfill a vow, (4) to express penitence, (5) to meet an obligation, and (6) to gain merit and salvation. Illustrations of the first type — requests for favors — include the birth of a son, the protection from a disease, an increase in material wealth, success in an examination, a worthy marriage, and a multitude of other human desires.

The second type of reason may be the offering of thanks for specific items (e.g., the safe birth of a child) or for general conditions. If the journey is made as a vow or promise of thanks for favors previously requested, such illustrates the third motivation class. A fourth possible motive is to endure sacrificial hardships as an act of worship or penitence. (In earlier centuries, this category might include those required to go on a pilgrimage as a form of punishment and supposedly to repent of their sins; see Davies and Davies 1982).

A fifth reason results from religious obligations to participate in one or more pilgrimages (such as the Hajj). A similar motive — the sixth listed here — is to acquire merit toward an ultimate salvation (in its broadest sense).

Just as the objectives for most travelers are mixed, making it difficult to assess the importance of religion in general, the various religious motives themselves overlap. To objectively group pilgrims from a wide variety of religious traditions and cultural settings according to their primary inner motivations for worship seems virtually impossible. This is not to deny the value of in-depth studies into motivating factors (Gross 1971; Pruess 1974); but the general application of this criterion is not promising.

Characteristics of Pilgrims and Other Factors

Pilgrimages differ in terms of the attributes of the participants such as their age, life stage, gender, family status, occupation, income, and religious affiliation. Information about each of these variables is fairly easy to obtain visually or by interviewing pilgrims. Furthermore, they are factors that contribute to differences among pilgrimage events.

A major disadvantage in using these variables results from their potential as explanatory associations. As discussed above (see "Relative Location"), the utility of a classification scheme is improved by keeping the discriminating criteria to a minimum and then by detecting relationships with other phenomena. Powerful generalizations about pilgrimages will be most successful when a classification scheme having a parsimonious number of criteria is employed to detect relationships with other phenomena. Therefore, characteristics of the pilgrims themselves should be avoided in designing a classificatory tool for differentiating pilgrimage events.

The criteria discussed here do not exhaust the potential list of classifying factors. For example, pilgrimages can be differentiated according to their historical period (Turner and Turner 1978; Nolan and Nolan 1989; and this volume). Nevertheless, the criteria enumerated here do include the primary components essential for spatial analyses.

A Classification Scheme

One of the purposes of this paper is to suggest a classification of pilgrimages according to their geographic characteristics. The goal is to select criteria that can be used effectively to describe differences and to measure variation that can be utilized in detecting relationships. Although greater precision in differentiating pilgrimage events can be achieved with many criteria, effective utilization by scholars will probably result from only a few criteria. Therefore, the scheme recommended here is based on three variables.

Classification of pilgrimages is based on (1) length of journey, (2) frequency of pilgrimage event, and (3) the pilgrimage route. These are given highest priority because of their conceptual importance (e.g., both length of journey and event frequency are closely related to the definition of pilgrimage) and because they can be effectively measured.

Of lesser utility for a classification scheme are the other criteria discussed here: (4) location of pilgrimage destination, (5) importance of pilgrimage place, (6) motivation of pilgrims, and (7) characteristics of pilgrims. Although these tend to have less direct bearing on pilgrimage movements than the first three criteria, one or more could be incorporated into an alternative classification scheme if greater specificity is desired.

According to the scheme suggested here, each of the three criteria are divided into three categories. The length of journey is divided into regional, national, and international; the frequency of pilgrimage events is typed as frequent, annual, and rare; and, the pilgrimage route is categorized as convergence, prescribed circular, and prescribed processional. Consequently, a total of 27 potential pilgrimage classes result (fig. 2).

One of the merits of this scheme is its capability for conveying immediately certain characteristics of a particular pilgrimage. For example, the Hajj (Din and Hadi, this volume; Rowley, this volume) represents an international, annual, converging pilgrimage.

A second advantage of this classification scheme is its utility in cross-cultural comparisons. The prescribed circular pilgrimage around Varanasi (Singh, this volume) can be analyzed for similarities and contrasts with the prescribed circular pilgrimage on Shikoku (Shimazaki, this volume).

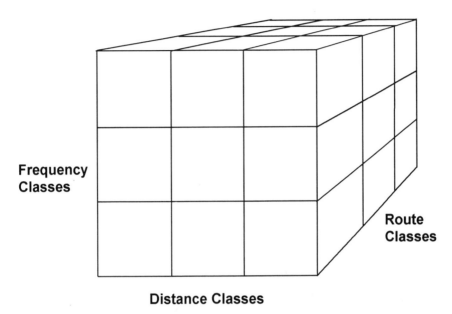

**Frequency
Classes**

**Route
Classes**

Distance Classes

Fig. 2. The classification scheme proposed here is based on three criteria: distance (length of journey), frequency (frequency of pilgrimage event), and route (pilgrimage path). Because each criterion is divided into three classes, a total of 27 pilgrimage types are defined.

A third benefit of this classification scheme is its potential for detecting spatial regularities and relationships with other variables associated with pilgrimages. Only with the ability to measure variations with a classification scheme will geographers some day be able to state, for example, that pilgrimages of type X normally display patterns of movement deviating from traditional gravity models. The classification scheme presented here contains the ingredients of a valuable aid for discovering numerous geographic characteristics of pilgrimage behavior.

Endnotes

1. *Bodhi*, from Sanskrit, means "wisdom," which for Buddhists refers to perfect wisdom or enlightenment. In one sense, the Bodhi-Tree (or Bo-Tree), or the "tree of enlightenment," is the pipal tree under which Gautama sat in meditation until enlightenment came to him and he became the Buddha. However, a shoot from the original tree in northern India was taken to Sri Lanka in the third century B.C. and planted in the city of Anuradhapura; and this offspring tree — said to be now the oldest historical tree in the world — is also called the Bodhi-Tree.

2. The percentages selected here for illustrative purposes are not based on accumulated data concerning travel distances for the major pilgrimages of the world, which should be the case to make the operational delineation of class boundaries truly meaningful.

3. It is appropriate to note the relationship between the extreme limit of the frequent (oftener-than-annual) class, the magnitude of the an event, and the distances traveled. If the operational definition of a pilgrimage event had not been restricted to a magnitude of "numerous" pilgrims (as proposed above), then the classification scheme would need to include the religious journeys of only a few individuals. However, it would have been almost impossible to identify discrete pilgrimages that occur at places (such as at Varanasi) visited by a small number of pilgrims almost continuously throughout the year.

Similarly, extreme values of this frequency variable would have been much different if the distance criterion in the definition proposed here had not excluded local movements. That is, if moving only a few meters or kilometers had been regarded as a pilgrimage, then all the daily journeys to a local place of worship would have produced a group of pilgrimages with very high frequencies. That is, the exclusion of local movements from the definition of pilgrimage events simultaneously excluded most of the very frequent trips to neighborhood shrines.

References

Aziz, B. N. 1982. A pilgrimage to Amarnath: The Hindu's search for immortality. *Kailash, Journal of Himalayan Studies* 9:121-38.

Bharati, A. 1970. Pilgrimage sites and Indian civilization. In *Chapters in Indian civilization*, v. 1, ed. J. W. Elder, 85-126. Dubuque, Iowa: Kendall/Hunt.

Bhardwaj, S. M. 1973. *Hindu places of pilgrimage in India: A study in cultural geography*. Berkeley: University of California Press.

Bhattacharyya, S. 1953. Religious practices of the Hindus. In *The religion of the Hindus*, ed. K. Morgan, 154-205. New York: The Ronald Press.

Brandon, S. G. F., gen. ed. 1970. *A dictionary of comparative religion*. London: Weidenfeld and Nicolson.

Cohen, E. 1981. Pilgrimage and tourism — convergence and divergence. Paper at Conference on Pilgrimage: The Human Quest, University of Pittsburgh.

Crim, K., gen. ed. 1981. *Abingdon dictionary of living religions*. Nashville: Abingdon.

Davies, H, and M-H. Davies. 1982. *Holy days and holidays: The medieval pilgrimage to Compostela*. Lewisburg: Bucknell University Press.

Eck, D. 1985. *Darśan: Seeing the divine image in India*, 2nd ed. Chambersburg, Penn.: Anima Books.

Eliade. M. 1959. *The sacred and the profane: The nature of religion*. Trans. by W. R. Trask. New York: Harcourt, Brace & Co.

Glazier, S. D. 1983. Caribbean pilgrimages: A typology. *Journal for the Scientific Study of Religion* 22:316-25.

Graham, W. A. 1981. The paradigm of the quest. Paper at Conference on Pilgrimage: The Human Quest, University of Pittsburgh.

Gross, D. R. 1971. Ritual and conformity: A religious pilgrimage to northeastern Brazil. *Ethnology* 10:129-48.

Hoshino, E. 1981. On the Shikoku pilgrimage in Japan. Paper at Conference on Pilgrimage: The Human Quest, University of Pittsburgh.

Jackowski, A. 1987. Geography of pilgrimage in Poland. *The National Geographic Journal of India* 33:422-29.

Jackson, R. H., and R. Henrie. 1983. Perception of sacred space. *Journal of Cultural Geography* 3:94-107.

Jindel, R. 1976. *Culture of a sacred town: A sociological study of Nathdwara*. Bombay: Popular Prakshan.

Messerschmidt, D. A., and J. Sharma. 1989. The Hindu pilgrimage to Muktinath, Nepal. Part 1: Natural and supernatural attributes to the sacred field. Part 2. Vaishanava devotees and status reaffirmation. *Mountain Research and Development* 9:89-104.

Miller, D. 1981. Hindu monasteries as a point along the pilgrim's path: The Sivananda ashram at Rishikesh. Paper at Conference on Pilgrimage: The Human Quest, University of Pittsburgh.

Naidu, T. S. 1985. Pilgrims and pilgrimage: A case study of Tirumala-Tirupati Devasthanams. In *Dimensions of Pilgrimage: An anthropological appraisal*, ed., M. Jha, 17-25. New Delhi: Inter-India Publications.

Neame, A. 1968. *The happening at Lourdes: The sociology of the grotto.* London: Hadder and Stoughton.

Nolan, M. L. 1987. Christian shrines in Western Europe and India: A preliminary comparison. *The National Geographical Journal of India* 33:370-78.

Nolan, M. L., and S. Nolan. 1989. *Christian pilgrimage in modern Western Europe.* Chapel Hill, NC: University of North Carolina Press.

Preston, J. J. 1981. Sacred centers and symbolic networks in South Asia. *Mankind Quarterly* 20:259-93.

——. 1980. Sacred places: Schemes of classification. Paper at Conference on Pilgrimage: The Human Quest, University of Pittsburgh.

Pruess, J. B. 1974. Veneration and merit-seeking at sacred places: Buddhist pilgrimage in contemporary Thailand. Ph.D. diss., University of Washington.

Salomon, R. 1979. Tirtha-pratyamnath: Ranking of Hindu pilgrimage sites in Classical Sanskrit texts. *Zeitschrift der Deutschen Morganlandishen Gesellschaft* 129: 102-27.

Smith, V. 1981. Quest in quest. Paper at Conference on Pilgrimage: The Human Quest, University of Pittsburgh.

Sopher, D. E. 1968. Pilgrim circulation in Gujarat. *Geographical Review* 58:392-425.

——. 1987. The message of place in Hindu pilgrimage. *National Geographical Journal of India* 33: 353-69.

Stirrat, R. L. 1979. A Catholic shrine in its social context. *Sri Lanka Journal of Social Science* 2:77-108.

Stoddard, R. H. 1966. Hindu holy sites in India. Ph.D. diss. University of Iowa, Iowa City.

——. 1980. Perceptions about the geography of religious sites in the Kathmandu Valley. *Contributions to Nepalese Studies* 7:97-118.

——. 1988. Characteristics of Buddhist pilgrimages in Sri Lanka. In *Pilgrimage in World Religions*, eds. S. M. Bhardwaj and G. Rinschede, 99-116. Berlin: Dietrich Reimer Verlag.

——. 1994. Major pilgrimage places in the world. In *Pilgrimages in the old and new world*, eds. S. M. Bhardwaj and G. Rinschede, 17-37. Berlin: Dietrich Reimer Verlag.

Sykes, J. B. 1982. *The concise Oxford dictionary of current English*, 7th ed. Oxford: Clarendon Press.

Tanaka Shimazaki, H. 1977. Geographic expression of Buddhist pilgrim places on Shikoku Island, Japan. *Canadian Geographer* 21:116-24.

——. 1988. On the geographic study of pilgrimage places. In *Pilgrimage in world religions*, eds. S. M. Bhardwaj and G. Rinschede, 21-40. Berlin: Dietrich Reiner Verlag.

Turner, V. 1973. The center out there: Pilgrim's goal. *History of Religions* 12:191-230.

Turner, V., and E. Turner. 1978. *Image and pilgrimage in Christian culture: Anthropological perspectives.* New York: Columbia University Press.

Vidyarthi, L. P., M. Jha, and B. N. Saraswati. 1979. *The sacred complex of Kashi.* Delhi: Concept Publishing Co.

Section II:
PILGRIMAGES IN THE CHRISTIAN TRADITION

Regional Variations in Europe's Roman Catholic Pilgrimage Traditions

Mary Lee Nolan, Oregon State University, and
Sidney Nolan, Academic Video and Research Associates

Abstract

Pilgrimage traditions are compared among eight major regions of Europe extending from Ireland and the United Kingdom across the continent to former Eastern Bloc states in which Roman Catholics are, at least, significant minorities. Variations in levels of shrine importance, periods of shrine formation, subjects and objects of veneration, sacred site features, and types of shrine origin stories are examined. Data on 6,380 shrines are analyzed, including 230 cases from Central European countries, thus updating the Nolans' 1989 publication, *Christian Pilgrimage in Modern Western Europe*.
Key words: religion, pilgrimage, Christian, Roman Catholic

The Roman Catholic pilgrimage tradition originated in the European heartland of Western Christendom. Although influenced by Eastern Mediterranean ideas, this is an essentially indigenous tradition with roots in the region's various pagan belief systems. It has evolved within the context of Europe's shifting political, socio-economic, folkloric, and intellectual orientations over the past 2,000 years, and pilgrimage remains an important, dynamic element of European culture. Today, at least 6,380 Roman Catholic shrines in Europe draw approximately 70 to 100 million visitations per year.[1]

Continually interacting cultural forces have produced similarities of pilgrimage expression throughout Catholic Europe. However, regional variations in shrine characteristics and pilgrim behaviors have persisted through the centuries. This discussion presents a survey of aggregate variations in shrine and pilgrimage characteristics by comparing the shrines of eight European regions (fig. 1).[2] The addition of 230 shrines in those Central European countries with large Roman Catholic populations broadens

Sacred Places, Sacred Spaces: The Geography of Pilgrimages, edited by Robert H. Stoddard and Alan Morinis, 1997. Geoscience and Man, vol. 34, pp. 61-93. Dept. of Geography and Anthropology, Louisiana State University, Baton Rouge, LA 70893-6010.

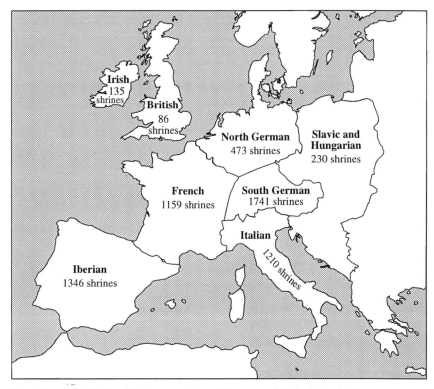

Fig. 1. Roman Catholic pilgrimage regions of Europe and their shrine totals.

the regional framework beyond that presented in our 1989 book, *Christian Pilgrimage in Modern Western Europe*.

The regions considered here are: (1) an Italian region, which combines Italy (fig. 2) with the Italian linguistic region of Switzerland; (2) a French region consisting of France, French Switzerland, and Walloon Belgium; (3) an Iberian region encompassing Spain, Portugal (fig. 3), and Andorra; (4) a South German region including Austria, Germanic Switzerland and the southern German regions of Baden-Württemburg and Bavaria (fig. 4); (5) a North German region consisting of the rest of Germany, Flemish Belgium, Luxembourg, the Netherlands and the Scandinavian countries; (6) a Slavic/Hungarian region made up (in 1991) of Poland, the Czech Republic, Slovakia, Hungary, Slovenia, Croatia, and Bosnia; (7) a British region of England (fig. 5), Scotland and Wales, and (8) an Irish region composed of the Republic of Ireland (fig. 6) and Northern Ireland. These regions conform to generalized cultural-linguistic areas and tend to reflect major historical-cultural variations in pilgrimage traditions.[3]

Fig. 2. Saint Peters at the Vatican, Rome, Italy.

Fig. 3. Part of a procession, coming and going, in honor of Sao Bento, Seixas, Portugal.

Fig. 4. The Blood Ride at Weingarten, Bavaria, southern Germany. This procession is held to honor a relic of Christ's Holy Blood venerated at the Weingarten monastery since the eleventh century.

Regional variations considered relate to (1) levels of shrine importance; (2) periods of shrine formation; (3) subjects and objects of pilgrim veneration; and (4) sacred site features. Discussion of these topics is followed by an examination of shrine location relative to settlements and by a brief summary of current pilgrimage practices and apparent trends.

Levels of Shrine Importance

Differences related to levels of shrine importance are among the most noticeable to the visitor. At great pilgrimage centers such as Rome, Lourdes, or Fátima, one typically finds pilgrims and tourists from all over the world. Crowds swell to the tens or hundreds of thousands on special pilgrimage days, and even during off-seasons there is some activity. The shrine complex is usually extensive and centered on a large pilgrimage church. Souvenir stands, parking lots, and facilities for housing and feeding visitors often augment the principal religious buildings. Shrines noted for cures, such as Lourdes, may have hospitals and other special facilities for the sick, infirm, and handicapped.

At the other end of the spectrum are the numerous small shrines visited by pilgrims from a few villages or urban neighborhoods. These shrines tend to be scenes of pilgrim activity only once or twice each year.

Fig. 5. The spot where Tyburn gallows stood, London, England. Many Catholic priests, some now canonized, were martyred on this site in the centuries following the Protestant Reformation.

Fig. 6. Lady's Island, Wexford, Ireland.

The casual visitor to a minor country chapel is likely to find solitude, and frequently a locked door. In Ireland, and occasionally elsewhere, a minor shrine site may be marked only by a holy well, a hilltop cross, or a weather-beaten statue standing vigil over a sacred stone.

Shrines of regional importance are of varied types. Some display many of the physical characteristics found at great shrines, whereas others are less obvious as pilgrimage centers. Regional shrines often serve multiple purposes. Some are parish churches while others are retreat centers, homes for the aged, or sites for youth encampments. Many are popular for weddings and baptisms, and those in the countryside may offer accommodations for a contemplative vacation.

Shrines at all levels of importance may be sites of active monasteries or convents and nearly 150 European shrines are located in cathedrals. It is important to note, however, that Europeans consider few of their parish churches, cathedrals, and monastic establishments to be centers of pilgrimage.

Measurement of shrine importance can theoretically be based on three criteria: (1) the size of the geographical area from which the shrine draws all or most of its religiously oriented visitors; (2) the number of annual visitations, and (3) the fame of the shrine as suggested by the frequency with which it is mentioned in various sources of published information (Stoddard 1994). Adequate data on the first two criteria are not always available. The third might be of value within a given culture region, but it is of marginal analytic utility in a general European context because most descriptive compendia deal only with specific regions or countries and are published in the regional or national language. Even when a survey extends across regional boundaries, the choice of shrines described is often biased toward the region in which the work is published. These factors have the effect of imposing region-specific pilgrimage characteristics on the general European scene.

The task of ranking shrines, which was extensively discussed by churchmen and other participants at the First Vatican Conference on Pilgrimage held in Rome in the Spring of 1992, is further complicated by the fact that some shrines draw small numbers of devotees from all over the world, whereas others are visited by hundreds of thousands of pilgrims each year from limited regions. In addition, some sites, while attracting only a few pilgrims from a small area, are major tourist destinations. As a result, these places are well represented in literature on shrines because of the place's art, architecture, historical associations, or colorful holy day celebrations. For example, Conques, France, registers more than 100,000 tourist visits a year to its Romanesque church, but the Medieval pilgrimage cultus focused on Saint Foy is now virtually extinct. The famous church does qualify as a place of district pilgrimage, however, because it contains an image of the Virgin Mary that is especially venerated by people from the town and its immediate vicinity.

Due to these complex ranking criteria, European shrines are best allocated to two highly generalized categories, major and minor.[4] Major shrines are defined as those which claim to draw at least 10,000 religiously motivated visitors per year from areas at least as large as a typical European province, or one of the larger diocese such as all of Brittany or all of Andalucía. Of the 6,380 shrines identified, 830, or 13 percent, fell into the major category. The Italian, French, and Iberian regions have the largest numbers of major shrines, and the Italian region has the largest proportion of its shrines classified as major ones (fig. 7). This suggests that the lack of emphasis on Germanic pilgrimage in most English-language literature may partly reflect the scarcity of major pilgrimage centers in these regions. A lack of major shrines is especially notable in southern Germanic lands where there are many places of pilgrimage, but only a few that are known or visited beyond their immediate districts. The densely populated, and largely Protestant, Northern Germanic region has relatively few shrines, but many of these are in the major category because they draw many visitors from nearby countries. However, these shrines are not generally well

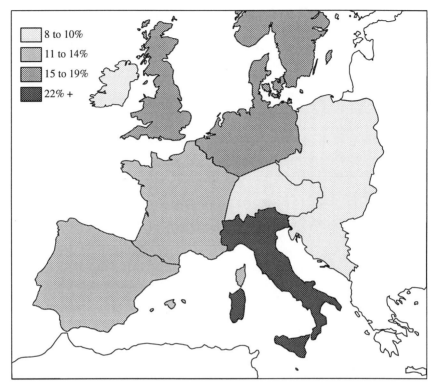

Fig. 7. Regional variations in percentage of shrines that are major pilgrimage centers.

known outside the Germanic culture region because pilgrims primarily come from areas where Germanic languages are spoken and from overseas German communities and missions.

The 5,320 shrines ranked as minor pilgrimage places make up 87 percent of the inventory. Some of these were classified as minor due to a lack of information, so there is a possibility that some of these sites may actually be of substantial importance. Most of the shrines categorized as minor, however, are sub-regional and district shrines that attract a modest number of pilgrims, usually for one or two special events each year. The minor category also includes 153 shrines that appear to be dormant or in a stage of advanced decline as pilgrimage centers.

As should be expected, minor shrines outnumber major shrines in all regions, but are proportionately the most numerous in the South German, Eastern, and Irish regions. The South German area contained the largest number of shrines classified as declining, but is also characterized by substantial numbers of recently developed and revitalized shrines. Thus, the fairly high number of declining shrines may reflect a highly dynamic tradition of district pilgrimages rather than any real decline in enthusiasm for pilgrimage per se. The highest proportion of declining shrines was found in Ireland, an area where traditional ideas about proper pilgrimage are currently undergoing major reinterpretations.

There seem to be few important distinctions between the broad categories of major and minor shrines in terms of most of the other variables considered. Major and minor pilgrimage centers stem from the same periods of cult formation, honor much the same set of holy persons with the same kinds of relics and images, and are about as likely to have some kind of sacred site feature associations. Certain types of stories about shrine origins, however, are more common at minor pilgrimage centers. Votive shrines, created as a thank offering for salvation from some impending catastrophe, are rarely important beyond a limited area. In contrast, shrines founded at the site of a claimed appearance of the Virgin Mary, or some other holy person, are more likely than most to be places of major drawing power.

As a rule, attributes of European shrine traditions vary to a considerably greater degree between regions and among shrines established during different time periods than they do among shrines of greater or lesser importance. Above the level of purely local pilgrimages, major and minor pilgrimage centers appear to be part of the same system, reflecting much the same set of spatial and temporal variations in orientations toward sacred places.[5]

Periods of Shrine Formation

Anthropologists Victor and Edith Turner (1978, 19) suggested that "the epoch of genesis is of crucial significance in determining the lines along which a specific pilgrimage has developed...." In keeping with this intuitively plausible generalization, the Turners developed a temporal model of Christian pilgrimage traditions based on three assumptions that were long common in English language literature on Roman Catholic pilgrimages. First, they assumed that new shrine formation and expressions of pilgrimage declined radically throughout Europe in the aftermath of the sixteenth century Protestant and Catholic Reformations. Secondly, they argued that during the Post-Reformation period when pilgrimage was presumably in decline throughout Europe, "...the Medieval mode of Catholic pilgrimage was given a new lease on life in the overseas empires of Spain, Portugal, and France" (Turner and Turner 1978, 201). As examples of their "fourth stage" in a typology of Marian shrines, these authors turned to the Americas where they found "...colonial shrines, which replaced, as it were, the shrines destroyed by the Reformation in Europe" (1978, 162-63). Finally, according the Turners, the new shrines of early-to mid-nineteenth century Europe sprang up dramatically after a three-century lull in cult-formative activity in that part of the world and were characterized by a radically new type of "post-Industrial" Marian apparition (1978, 38, 49, 203, 236).

The Turners' model, based on a now-outmoded common knowledge, was widely accepted and has influenced current interpretations of Christian pilgrimage evolution in both Europe and Latin America. Although we agree with the Turners about the importance of the period of pilgrimage genesis as a critical factor in the interpretation of current shrine traditions, our data refutes their interpretations of limited post-Reformation pilgrimage activity in Europe. Our temporal model of Christian shrine evolution, based on information about the formation periods of 4,237 active shrines, indicates the importance of post-Medieval changes in cult-formative events dating from the fifteenth and early sixteenth centuries. In addition, it reveals the Catholic Reformation period as extremely important for new shrine formations in many parts of Europe as well as on the mission frontiers, as is acknowledged in some recent publications (Barber 1991).

Dating the Shrines

Christian pilgrimage developed within the context of an essentially literate tradition. A majority of current shrines publicize an exact date, or a general time period of pilgrimage formation. Although some of these dates may be questionable, the numbers are sufficient for defining broad periods of time and establishing regional generalizations. The addition of the founding dates of the Roman Catholic shrines of Central Europe affected little change in the overall temporal pattern except to place an even stronger emphasis on shrine formation between 1540 and the late eighteenth century.[6]

Logical boundaries for time periods were based on the founding dates of more than 4,000 shrines. When plotted by decade, the data reveal a cyclical pattern of decline and florescence in cult formative activity. Low points in the cycle served as indicators for identifying the boundaries of shrine-formative periods.

Because founding dates of many Medieval and earlier shrines are imprecise, periods before 1529 were divided at the nearest turn of the century. This procedure generated six periods of Western European pilgrimage: (1) the Early Christian period: First Century to 699, (2) the Early Medieval period (fig. 8): 700 to 1099, (3) the High Medieval period: 1100 to 1399, (4) the Late Medieval/Renaissance period: 1400 to 1529, (5) the Post-Reformation period: 1530 to 1779, and (6) the Modern period: 1780 to present. These cult formative periods correspond with periods of major

Fig. 8. The Exterstein, an Early Medieval carving in the Teutoberger Wald, Germany. This former Christian pilgrimage center was sacred in pre-Christian times.

social change in Europe and probably provide a reasonably good surrogate indicator of general pilgrimage activity (fig. 9; table 1).

Pilgrimage participation probably drops off during low cycles of cult formation and picks up again at older shrines during times of marked new cult formation. It seems likely that new cycles of pilgrimage florescence begin with a series of adaptive transformations that improve the fit between pilgrimage and a changed intellectual, socio-economic, and technological order. These adaptations often begin at newly established shrines, but are then selectively grafted onto expressions of pilgrimage at older shrines that experience renewed vitality.

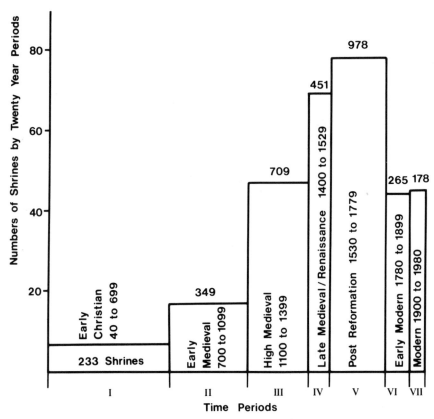

Fig. 9. Periods of cult formation in Western Europe.

Regional Variations in Periods of Shrine Formation

The Early Christian period, which began in the first century and ended with the turn of the eighth century, accounts for only six percent of today's shrines. Seventy-three percent of these are currently dedicated to saints. Most of the rest probably began as saint's shrines, but became Marian pilgrimage centers during the Middle Ages or later.

This early period is strongly represented by the shrines of Ireland where numerous holy places dedicated to the early Celtic saints have survived, often at sites marked by holy wells, sacred stones, and monastic ruins (Nolan 1983).[7] Many early shrines in Britain were similar in type to those of Ireland, but most did not survive the Reformation.

Table 1. Regional variation in numbers of shrines during pilgrimage formative periods

Region	Early Chrisitan		Early Medieval		High Medieval		Late Medieval		Post-Reformation		Modern		Total Number
	No.	%	No.	%	No.	%	No.	%	No.	%	No.	%	
Italian	61	6	68	7	187	20	207	22	289	30	141	15	953
French	63	8	143	18	211	26	100	12	167	21	117	15	801
S. German	16	1	80	6	214	17	196	15	633	49	156	12	1295
N. German	6	2	30	11	67	25	39	15	74	28	51	19	267
Iberian	12	2	82	15	209	38	77	14	140	26	29	5	549
British	4	5	2	3	1	1	2	3	5	6	66	83	80
Irish	86	83	2	2	4	4	2	2	0	0	10	10	104
Slavic/ Hungarian	1	1	4	2	26	14	19	19	116	62	12	12	188
Europe Total	249	6	411	10	919	22	642	15	1424	34	592	14	4237

Note: % shows percent of Region's total.

On the continent, this period is fairly well represented in the French and Italian regions, but is of little importance in the German regions, most of which were not Christianized before the eighth century. Early Christian shrines in Iberia generally were extinguished or forced into a long period of dormancy by the early eighth-century Muslim conquest of the peninsula.

The Early Medieval period (700-1099) accounts for 10 percent of today's shrines. About a third of these are dedicated to saints. As with earlier shrines, many pilgrimage places from the period, which are now devoted to Mary, probably began as saints' shrines. Early Medieval shrines are proportionately most numerous in the French, Iberian and North Germany regions.

The High Medieval Period (1100 to 1399) is usually thought of as a golden age of European pilgrimage. This was the time of the most pilgrim traffic to such famous shrines as the tomb of Saint James in Santiago de Compostela, Spain, the murder site and tomb of Saint Thomas Becket in Canterbury, and the reliquary of the Three Kings in Köln. In addition, the first official Holy Year Pilgrimage to Rome was celebrated in 1300. This period accounts for the formation of 22 percent of the shrines considered. Although several of the most famous High Medieval shrines honor saints, about three-quarters of those dated to the period are primarily dedicated to the Virgin Mary. Most of these appear to have originated as Marian shrines as an upsurge of devotion to the Virgin spread through Europe.

Extant shrines of High Medieval origin are most numerous in the French region, although Iberia leads in the proportion of shrines from this period. Many Spanish and Portuguese shrines sprang up in the wake of the Christian reconquest of the peninsula from the Muslims. Here the "Shepherd's Cycle" story of miraculously found images reached its peak in both time and space. Few of the once numerous Early and High Medieval shrines of Great Britain survived the Reformation, although several modern shrines in England, Wales and Scotland are located at the sites of Medieval pilgrimage places. The low proportion of Medieval shrines in Ireland suggests that Protestant British repression was more successful in uprooting that Catholic island's Medieval shrines than in eliminating the earlier cults of the Celtic saints.

The Late Medieval/Renaissance period, from 1400 through 1529, has sometimes been dismissed as a declining phase of Medieval pilgrimage expressions. This is not the case, however, with surviving cults. Fifteen percent of today's shrines were established during this 130-year span, which is considerably more per annum than during the 300-year High Medieval period. The Renaissance also marks a time of major changes in patterns of shrine formation, including the first documented Marian apparitions that meet the Turners' (1978) criteria for fully modern or "post-industrial" apparitions.[8]

Formation of pilgrimages with survival value tapered off in France and the German regions during the second decade of the sixteenth century, but remained high through the 1520s in Spain and on the Italian peninsula. The Italian region, with the highest proportion of shrines dating from this period, may have been the region of origin for most of the influential innovations in the manifestation of Renaissance pilgrimage. In addition to "modern-type" Marian apparitions, a more personalized relationship between humanity and divinity is indicated by the emergence of painted ex-voto offerings graphically giving thanks for divine intervention in times of individual stress (Cousin 1981). Votive shrines established by relatively ordinary individuals, as opposed to communities or kings, became increasingly evident among the shrines of Renaissance Italy.

The Post-Reformation years (1530 to 1779) account for 32 percent of the dated shrines. Cult-formative activity was high throughout Catholic Europe. It was especially prevalent in the South German region, where nearly half of today's pilgrimage places date from the period, and the Slavic/Hungarian region where 62 percent of identified shrines are from that era.

The shrine-formative events of the Catholic Reformation are clearly important for interpreting the development of modern European pilgrimage. The period is also critical for understanding the implantation of Christian pilgrimage in the Americas. Despite the fact that the carriers of Christian pilgrimage traditions across the Atlantic were Catholic Reformation missionaries, not Medieval men, the notion of a transplantation of Medieval European pilgrimage to Latin America persists in the literature. More attention should be paid to the influence of Renaissance and Catholic Reformation re-interpretations of European pilgrimage on the missionaries' actions than to lingering Medieval notions. Also neglected is the influence of missionaries of South German origin who journeyed to the Americas under the auspices of Spanish monarchs of the Austrian Hapsburg family (Nolan and Nolan 1991).

The Modern period of 1780 to the present accounts for 14 percent of active shrines. Because it takes a number of years for a new pilgrimage to become firmly established and publicly acknowledged, the relatively small number of new shrines identified for recent decades does not necessarily indicate any decrease in cult-formative activity. Revitalization of shrines in the Slavic/Hungarian region is currently in process, so additional studies in that region should be undertaken within the next few years.

As the Turners and other scholars have emphasized, some of the most famous shrines of the past 200 years are found at sites where apparitions of the Virgin Mary are believed to have occurred. However, shrines stemming from apparition events make up only nine percent of the pilgrimages established since 1780. Such famous Marian apparitional shrines as Lourdes, Knock, and Fátima are clearly important, but cannot be considered fully representative of modern trends in shrine formation. During the twentieth century, there has been a greater tendency toward the development of pilgrimage around people with a reputation for holiness than has been apparent since the Middle Ages. Places associated with such persons as Pope John XXIII, the stigmatized Italian Capuchin Padre Pio, the German Jesuit Father Rudolph Meyer, and several other people whose lives exemplify an attempt to live by Christian principles in a twentieth century world, each draw more than a million visitors per year from many nations. These shrines are as much a part of modern pilgrimage as are the great Marian apparitional shrines. They convey a different symbolism from that emphasized in the Turners' analysis of Modern pilgrimage; not apocalyptic or anti-modern, but instead a message of hope and an example of personal courage in difficult times.

As in other periods, there are interesting regional variations. Britain has a high percentage of Modern shrines. Some, as at Walsingham and Canterbury, are revivals of Medieval and earlier shrines. Others were formed as entirely new cults after Britain developed more permissive attitudes toward religious freedom in the nineteenth century. In contrast, Iberia has a very low percentage of Modern shrines. This primarily reflects a Spanish resistance to new shrine establishments that persisted throughout the nineteenth and early twentieth centuries. However, several important shrines in Portugal, including Fátima, are of recent origin.

Subjects and Objects of Pilgrim Veneration

Most European pilgrimage centers focus on devotions related to specific historical persons including the Virgin Mary, Christ, or one of the saints, including folk saints, exemplary holy persons, and officially canonized saints. Some shrines have a dual focus, but most pilgrims consider one subject of devotion to be more important than the other.

The Virgin Mary is the predominant personage of pilgrim veneration for Europe as a whole. Sixty-five percent of all active shrines have Mary as their primary devotional subject (table 2). There is, however, considerable regional variation in the degree of focus on Mary. She is most important in the Slavic, Italian, and French regions. The exceptionally high proportion of 81 percent of Marian shrines in the Slavic/Hungarian region probably reflects the ability of her pilgrimage places to survive periods of religious repression. It is also possible that most of the shrines in that region for which no subject could be identified are devoted to saints.

In Iberia, the Virgin Mary is venerated at more than two-thirds of the shrines, although her pilgrimage centers are proportionately less common in northern Portugal and the northwest Spanish province of Galicia where

Table 2. Regional variation in subjects of primary devotion

Region	Christf		Mary		Saints		Unknown or None		Total
	No.	%	No.	%	No.	%	No.	%	No.
Italian	40	3	933	77	235	19	2	1	1210
French	23	2	933	71	270	23	42	4	1159
S. German	207	12	997	57	522	30	15	1	1741
N. German	52	11	258	55	154	33	9	2	473
Iberian	129	10	922	68	278	21	17	1	1346
British	1	1	34	40	49	57	2	2	86
Irish	1	1	16	12	106	79	12	9	135
Slavic/ Hungarian	5	2	187	81	3	6	25	11	230
Europe Total	458	7	4171	65	1627	26	124	2	6380

Note: % shows percent of Region's total.

numerous district and sub-regional shrines are dedicated to saints. Somewhat more than half of the Germanic shrines are devoted to the Virgin. In Britain, she is less often found as a primary subject than are the saints. Marian shrines are relatively rare in Ireland, but include one of that island's most important pilgrimage centers, the nineteenth-century apparitional site at Knock.

Saints, who are the primary devotional subjects at 26 percent of Europe's shrines, make up the next most important category of pilgrims' veneration (fig. 10). Most saints are represented by only one or two important shrines, but 20 saints have 10 or more shrines of greater than local significance. The most commonly found are shrines dedicated to Saint Anne, the traditional name for the mother of Mary, and to Saint Anthony of Padua, a follower of Saint Francis of Assisi. The shrines of these two saints are numerous and widespread, and most are attracting increasing numbers of pilgrims. Italian shrines associated with Francis of Assisi have recently grown in popularity as a result of this saint's associations with ecology. In 1980, the Vatican officially designated Francis as the Patron of Ecologists. Other saints' shrines, including the German livestock patrons Leonard, Wendel, and Ulrich, have diminished in significance during the past century, but are still well represented among district-level shrines in their regions.

By far the highest proportion of saints' shrines are found in Ireland where 79 percent of the identified shrines are dedicated to holy persons, many of them the traditional saints of ancient Celtic lore. More than half of the British shrines are also dedicated to saints, ranging in type from near mythic folk saints to martyrs of the English persecution of Catholics dur-

Fig. 10. Musicians at the Shrine of Saint Hubert, patron of hunters. Saint Hubert, Belgium.

ing the Reformation. The lowest proportion of saints' shrines was found in the Slavic/Hungarian region, but this may reflect the relatively limited amount of information obtained for that region. The highest numbers of saints' shrines are found in the Southern Germanic region with a particular concentration in Switzerland and western Austria. Saints' shrines are also common in the Netherlands, Portugal (fig. 11), and northwestern Spain.

For Europe in general, pilgrimage centers focused on Christ are surprisingly few, making up only seven percent of the shrines. Christ is most often found as a subject of pilgrim veneration in Germanic regions where the oldest and most persistent expressions of this cultus are found. Except for southernmost Portugal and the provinces bordering France, Iberia is also an important region for Christ-oriented pilgrimages. In all regions, a majority of Christ-oriented pilgrimages date from the Catholic Reformation period. This is important, but rarely considered, in studies of the numerous Christ-centered shrines of Latin America, most of which were established during the peak period of popularity for this type of cultus in Europe (Kendall 1991; Straub 1991; Sallnow 1991).

The holy person to whom Catholic pilgrims pay respect usually is symbolized at the shrine by one or more small, potentially moveable ob-

Fig. 11. Bus load of pilgrims en route to the shrine of Sao Torcato, Portugal.

jects (table 3). Most often, these are small images in either two- or three-dimensional form. In addition, there are the bodily remains of saints and other relics, such as pieces of cloth associated with a holy person or splinters believed to come from Christ's Cross.

Shrines without moveable cult objects are most common in Ireland, and, to a lesser extent, Britain. In these regions, large numbers of venerated relics and images were destroyed during the sixteen and seventeenth centuries. Thus, particularly in Ireland, a Celtic predisposition toward focus on sacred site features was reinforced by a Protestant attack on more easily eliminated symbols of devotion.

Regional preferences for certain types of relics and images are apparent. Bodily remains of saints are most frequently found in the North German, British, and Italian regions, and are least common in the Iberian, South German and Slavic/Hungarian traditions. Northern Germanic lands have the highest proportion of other types of relics, largely due to a greater than ordinary concentration of fragments of the "True Cross,"

Table 3. Regional variation in objects of primary veneration

Region	Bodily Remains		Other Relics		Images		None		Total Number
	No.	%	No.	%	No.	%	No.	%	
Italian	75	7	15	2	904	87	45	4	1039
French	95	14	17	2	550	79	33	5	695
S. German	96	7	41	3	1228	87	53	4	1418
N. German	48	18	24	9	177	69	13	4	262
Iberian	27	3	12	1	744	93	18	2	801
British	27	33	0	0	26	32	29	35	82
Irish	5	5	1	1	6	6	91	88	103
Slavic/								?	150
Hungarian	2	1	0	0	148	99	?	?	150
Europe Total	375	8	110	3	3783	83	282	6	4550

Note: % shows percent of Region's total.

along with remnants of Eucharistic miracles in which the host or wine of the Mass was believed to have turned into actual flesh or blood.

The Italian and Germanic traditions are more inclined to use two-dimensional imagery, and this tendency intensifies toward the east in the Slavic/Hungarian region (table 4). It seems likely that the Eastern Orthodox avoidance of venerating three-dimensional images has had some impact in the most easterly parts of Catholic Europe. Curiously, there are very few two-dimensional cult objects in the French and Iberian regions. The scarcity is so great as to suggest a cultural bias against the attribution of miraculous qualities to paintings and frescos in these parts of Europe, a possibility supported by several Spanish shrine stories that refer to an original two-dimensional cult object being replaced by a statue that was presumably deemed more suitable as a devotional object.

The phenomenon of miraculous black or dark-skinned paintings and statues is, at present, most pronounced in France where nearly 12 percent of the images have dark skin tones. Dark Madonnas are nearly as common among the images of the Northern Germanic and Slavic/Hungarian regions. The famous Spanish *morenas*, or dark images of Mary, are dramatic in their elaborate vestments, but are less prevalent than in the other two regions. The Italian, South German, and British regions have relatively few dark images.

Dark images, which range in hue from medium brown to jet black, are usually portrayals of Mary, but there are at least two highly venerated dark Christ images, one at Lucca in Italy and the other in the Netherlands.

Table 4. Regional variation in types of images

Region	Total Number of Images	Two-Dimensional		Black or Dark	
		No.	%	No.	%
Italian	798	390	49	21	3
French	514	13	3	64	12
S. German	1171	372	32	33	3
N. German	149	24	17	16	11
Iberian	464	17	4	35	8
British	28	2	7	2	7
Irish	5	2	40	0	0
Slavic/ Hungarian	148	106	72	17	11
Europe Total	3277	926	28	188	6

Note: % shows percent of Region's total

A few statues of European and Eastern Mediterranean saints are also noted for their darkness.

Sacred Site Features

In spite of the strong emphasis on potentially movable objects, many European shrines also display ties to specific natural settings, as indicated by the presence, or former presence, of sacred features at their sites (table 5). Among the classified shrines, one-third have some kind of association with one or more sacred natural features. The majority of these have only one sacred site feature, although at about one-fifth of the shrines with site features, two or more different aspects of the environment have sacred significance. Examples include sacred grottos located on mountain heights and sacred stones by curative wells overhung by holy trees.

Shrines that focus on natural features are by far the most common in Ireland, a region where most surviving shrines are old, and where relics and images are much less common as cult objects than is the case elsewhere in Europe. On the continent, sacred site features are most frequently found at Italian, French and South German shrines. Proportions are somewhat below the European average in the Iberian, British and Slavic/ Hungarian regions, and substantially below average in the North Germany area.

Although sanctification of natural features has continued to occur as new shrines have been founded through the centuries, pilgrimage centers

Table 5. Regional variation in types of natural features

Region	Total Number of Shrines	Shrines with Site Features		High Place		Water		Trees		Stones		Grotto	
		No.	%	No.	%	No.	%	No.	%	No.	%	No.	%
Italian	1210	427	35	242	57	99	23	87	20	38	9	72	17
French	1159	379	33	174	46	137	39	80	21	26	7	37	10
S. German	1741	625	36	268	43	223	36	162	26	53	8	29	5
N. German	473	85	18	43	51	26	31	27	32	3	4	2	2
Iberian	1346	361	26	202	56	91	25	57	16	23	6	49	14
British	86	24	28	7	29	20	83	5	21	2	8	2	8
Irish	135	121	90	16	13	104	86	14	11	60	50	4	3
Slavic/ Hungarian	230	62	27	16	26	37	60	26	42	7	11	3	5
Europe Total	6380	2084	33	968	46	737	35	458	22	212	10	198	10

Notes: Several sites have more than one feature so the percent of a Region's total may sum to more than 100; % shows percent of Region's total.

dating from the first 1,200 years of the Christian era are more likely to have site feature associations than those from later periods. The vast majority of the shrines that have three or more sacred site features were holy places in pre-Christian times. This suggests that sanctification of natural features at shrine sites, although now thoroughly Christianized, represents the continuation of ancient European traditions of nature veneration (Nolan 1986).

The natural landscape feature most commonly associated with pilgrimage shrines is a hill, mountain, or other height. Of the shrines having a sacred site feature, 46 percent are located on high places. There is, however, no single criterion for defining a sacred high place. Some shrines are located on hills or mountains specifically referred to as "holy mountains." Only a few are found on the summit of the highest prominence in the area. Other shrines are on mountain spurs, foothills, or abrupt rock outcrops in areas with much higher surrounding mountains. Many more are on slopes above valley towns, often about one-third the way to the summit. Some shrines, described in the literature as located on high places, are actually nestled in high mountain valleys or situated on relatively flat plateau surfaces above valley settlements. These might more accurately be described as high elevation shrines than high place shrines.

High place shrines are especially common in Italy and Iberia, and are most numerous in a Mediterranean coastal belt extending from the eastern shores of Spain through Southern France and down the western margins of the Italian peninsula. High place shrines are least prevalent in the British, Irish, and Slavic/Hungarian traditions, although all of these regions have some important holy mountains.

Holy waters are the next most common type of sacral site feature and are found at 35 percent of shrines that have such associations (fig. 12). Sacred water appears to have been a more common site feature in the past. Several shrine stories, especially in Germanic lands, refer to a holy well or spring that has either dried up or is no longer a focus of pilgrim activity.

Sacred water in the European tradition is usually found in a spring or well, although there are a few exceptions. The famous Lough Derg in County Donegal is one of several holy lakes in Ireland, and there are a few sacred lakes in northern Italy. In northern Spain and in Ireland, there are a few places where ocean waters or tidal pools are believed to have special qualities. Some places along the Mediterranean coasts of France and Italy continue rituals that involve carrying a miraculous image into the sea at a certain point.

Water which collects in stone hollows is thought to have especially curative properties at a number of shrines, particular in Ireland and Austria. In contrast to India, major rivers in Europe are not generally considered sacred, even at their sources. For example, there are no pilgrimage

Fig. 12. Collecting water at a curative spring at Pannamaria in Slovakia, site of a vision of
the Virgin Mary in the 1950s.

shrines at the sources of the Rhine, Rhone, or Danube rivers. A few small
streams, especially in Austria, are thought to have sacred qualities at specific spots along their banks. One such place is said to be the spot where
Mary knelt to wash the Christ Child during a somewhat round-about
flight from the Holy Land to Egypt.

Emphasis on sacred water is most prevalent in Ireland where 86 percent of the site-feature shrines have a holy well or other water feature. Water sources are nearly as common at site-oriented shrines in Great Britain,
and are also found at a substantially above average proportion of site feature shrines in the Slavic/Hungarian region. The least emphasis on water
as a sacred feature is found in the drier Italian and Iberian regions, suggesting that Christian veneration of water sources is not directly related to
a relative scarcity of water resources.

Indications of tree and/or grove cultus are found at 22 percent of Europe's site feature shrines. Occasionally, as at La Sainte Baume in southern
France, a sacred grove has endured since pre-Christian times. In Italy, several forests have been maintained for centuries as a result of an association
with Medieval saints, particularly Francis of Assisi. The majority of tree

cults, however, are related to an apparition or discovery of an image of the Virgin Mary in a tree that is no longer in existence. Frequently, such holy trees are destroyed by pilgrims who strip the bark, pluck the leaves, and whittle-away the wood to carry home as talismans. In some cases, enough wood is preserved to carve a cult image.

The Slavic/Hungarian and Germanic regions have the highest emphasis on groves, trees, and legends associated with trees. This may partly reflect ancient Teutonic and Slavic rituals involving trees and forests. Certainly it is noteworthy that when a miracle involving the Virgin Mary or her image occurs in a tree named by species, the tree is most often an oak. Cultic tree connections are least prevalent in Ireland, but where they are found, there is usually a living tree, most often a thorn tree. Rags torn from clothing are still hung on such trees, as well as on barbed wire that fences some sacred sites. These thank offerings provide a means of transferring problems from something associated with the pilgrims' person to the tree or fence.

About 10 percent of the shrines with site features have rocks or stones with cultic associations. Some focus on curious natural rock formations. Others are characterized by rituals involving dolmens, menhirs, old grinding holes in rock outcrops, and occasionally the stone ruins of Roman temples or ancient churches. Although shrine churches in and of themselves do not seem to be thought of as cult objects in Europe, the ruins of churches may acquire such qualities over time so that a form of stone cultus seems to be associated with the ruins of a few long-abandoned early Christian structures. In Ireland, some of the hidden Mass rocks of penal times have recently become focal points for district pilgrimages. Stone cultus is particularly prevalent in the Irish tradition, and it is least evident in the North German region. Austria and the Brittany region of France have higher than usual proportions of shrines with sacred stones than is typical for the South German and French regions in general.

Another 10 percent of Europe's site-feature shrines are associated with natural caves or grottos. Artificial grottos, usually imitations of the famous Lourdes apparition site, are very common, but were not included in our count. The largest proportions of natural grottos are found at shrines in the Italian and Iberian regions. The North German and Irish traditions have the smallest proportions. Typically, sacred caves are shallow and have relatively easy access.

The manner in which landscape features acquire a special sanctity is often recounted in shrine formation stories. These origin stories, which can be categorized into seven basic types, also usually included a rationale for shrine locations (table 6).

Table 6. Regional variation in types of origin stories

Region	Significant Site		Ex-voto		Found Object		Acq'd Object		Miracle		Apparition		Devotional		Total Number
	No.	%	No.	%	No.	%	No.	%	No.	%	No.	%	No.	%	
Italian	125	14	126	14	136	15	112	13	156	18	181	21	42	5	878
French	105	19	126	23	113	21	55	10	64	12	52	10	30	6	545
S. German	112	12	254	28	111	12	159	18	188	21	33	4	51	6	908
N. German	44	23	24	13	30	16	47	25	13	7	7	7	24	13	189
Iberian	57	12	69	15	168	36	67	14	34	7	66	14	11	2	472
British	53	67	0	0	5	6	13	16	1	1	5*	6	2	3	79
Irish	46	84	1	2	0	0	1	2	3	5	3	5	1	2	55
Slavic/Hungarian	12	7	27	15	32	18	36	20	44	24	26	14	5	3	182
Europe Total	554	17	627	19	595	18	490	15	503	15	373	11	166	5	3308

Note: % shows percent of Region's total.
* The five British apparitions pre-date the Reformation, but the tradition has remained so strong that they have been classed as apparitional shrines in the nineteenth- and twentieth-century re-establishments.

Shrine Locations

There is extensive speculation in both the geographical and anthropological literature about the relative location of holy places, but the identification of general models and rules has proved elusive (Sopher, this volume; Turner 1973; Tanaka Shimazaki 1988; Eade and Sallnow 1991; Scott and Simpson-Housley 1991). It is evident that some shrines are extremely central in their locations by any definition of centrality. Others may be considered peripheral in a variety of ways, depending on how the term is defined, and still others are clearly remote from the mainstreams of human activity, although in the case of rural shrines, not necessarily that far away from the homes of their primary devotees. In our exploration of this problem, we asked a two-part question. Where are shrines actually located relative to communities of different sizes, and what are the differences between shrines that are clearly central and those that are obviously remote by some measurable set of criteria?

After intensive mapping and field work, we found that a substantial majority of European pilgrimage centers are located in proximity to communities. Most are referenced by communities, which is, of course, about the only way they can be found. The reference community is considered the shrine town, whether or not the shrine is actually located in the town. Of the 3,454 shrines for which we have detailed location information, about 40 percent are located within the built-up area of their towns. Another 13 percent are on the edge of town or within one kilometer of the edge, and 39 percent lie between one and ten kilometers from their towns. Only about eight percent are located more than ten kilometers by road or path from a settlement, and some of these are monastic establishments with a sizable resident population.

Shrine towns vary greatly in sze. In predominantly Catholic countries, large cities, such as Paris, Madrid, Rome, and Vienna, typically have numerous shrine churches with distinctly different pilgrimage traditions. Most predominantly Catholic cities with populations of 100,000 or more, have at least one shrine. As a rule, the smaller the community, the less likely it is to be a shrine town. This relationship, however, results partly from the constraints of this study because purely local shrines, which are often associated with small settlements, were excluded.

About 18 percent of the shrines are associated with cities that had 25,000 or more inhabitants in the early 1980s. This figure includes the multiple shrines of very large urban centers. Another 18 percent of the shrines are found in or near towns with 5,000 to 24,999 inhabitants, and 23 percent are associated with communities of 1,000 to 4,999 residents. About one-third are located in or near villages with fewer than 1,000 inhabitants.

If all shrines associated with communities of fewer than 5,000 are combined with all those found on or beyond the edge of larger towns and

cities, the proportion of pilgrimage centers that can be considered peripheral to large population centers stands at about 80 percent. There is an apparent relationship between the size of a shrine community and the
likelihood that the shrine will be located within the built-up area of the
town. Of those shrines associated with cities of 25,000 or more, 79 percent
are either in town or no more than a kilometer from its outer edge. In contrast, only 58 percent of the shrines associated with settlements of 1,000 to
24,999 are in or near the town. Fewer than half of the shrines associated
with villages of less than 1,000 are in the village or with a kilometer of its
edge. Several explanations for this pattern are possible. One of the most
obvious is that Europe's larger communities have grown out to encompass
some of the shrines originally built in the countryside beyond them. Except for the fact that shrines in the countryside are more likely to have sacred environmental features than those in towns, differences between
pilgrimage centers located in communities and those located more than a
kilometer beyond them were not apparent in our data.

As already observed, most shrines are neither highly central nor extremely remote. It is only by comparing the extreme ends of the spectrum
from central to remote shrine locations that obvious differences emerge. In
order to make this comparison, we defined central shrines as those lying
within the built-up area of a city of 25,000 or more people. Remote shrines
were defined as those located more than fifty kilometers from a city with
a population of 25,000 or more, and not associated with a town of more
than 1,000 people. In addition, remote shrines had to be located well off
main highway routes as these were indicated by a fairly standardized series of Esso road maps that were available for most of Western Europe in
the late 1970s and early 1980s.

Our initial data run had a disproportionately large number of Irish
cases among the remote shrines. Because Irish shrine patterns are different
in most respects to those found in continental Europe, we excluded the
Irish cases from our comparison of central and remote shrines.

Although much has been written about the mystique of shrine peripherality, we found that central shrines in Europe are more than twice as
likely to be of major importance than are remote shrines. Even when Irish
cases are excluded, remote shrines are more likely than urban shrines to
depend primarily on the mystique of site feature veneration as opposed to
a primary focus on relics or images. Shrines with three or more sacred site
features are three times more likely to be remote than urban.

Certain powerful types of cult objects such as relics of Christ's Passion, saints' tombs, and dark images are much more likely to be venerated
at central shrines. There is also a decided difference in frequencies of certain cult formative stories. Central shrines are much more likely to be the
sites of significant events in the lives of saints, or places sanctified because

images or relics were acquired, than are remote shrines. Weeping or bleeding images also tend to be associated with central shrines. In contrast, remote shrines are more likely to have come into being because of apparitions or the mysterious finding of relics or images. Legends about images repeatedly returning to the place they were found, and other stories suggesting divine intervention in the choice of the shrine location, are three times as likely to be told at remote shrines. Shrines in out-of-the-way places are also more likely to be located at sites that were sacred in pre-Christian times.

The differences between central and remote shrines suggest that shrine location in continental Europe reflects a number of different and sometimes conflicting ideals. In some cases the pull of a sacred site embellished with one or more stationary environmental features justifies a shrine's remote location. When cults focus on moveable images and relics, the choice of shrine placement must be made by resolving the conflict between two ideals of holy object location. On the one hand, such objects should be venerated in a central place so that their power can bring the greatest good to the largest number of people. In addition, Europeans have long been aware that possession of a very miraculous object can increase a city's importance and that holy shrines generate substantial income. On the other hand, there is an equally strong idea that a holy object should be kept in a place that is somewhat difficult to reach and removed from the contamination of everyday urban life. The fact that about three-quarters of all shrines are neither central nor very remote suggests that location debates often have been resolved through compromise.

Some pilgrimage traditions include regularized movement of the cult object that can be interpreted as solutions to the problem of where such object should be placed for veneration. In mountain districts of France, Spain and Italy, some miraculous images are transhumant — residing in town during the winter and making a processional trek to their country chapels in summer. In Andalucía, miraculous images of Mary are ordinarily kept in country chapels. Once or twice a year, people from all the surrounding communities gather at the chapel to celebrate a *romeria* in honor of the Virgin. Then, at a different time of year, the image is taken in procession to the town that considers this particular manifestation of the Virgin its patroness. During a period of one to four weeks, the image is honored in the town's most important church. Then the patroness is carried back to her country shrine.

In a few places, including the Lipari Islands off the coast of Sicily, the image rather than the devotees makes the pilgrim journey by being carried to several communities in a set annual pattern. Such images, however, usually have home shrines that may be visited by the faithful when the need arises during other times of year.

Summary and Conclusions

Pilgrimage throughout Europe, although rooted in the same basic system of beliefs and behaviors, shows a considerable amount of regional variation. In terms of several variables, regional differences tend to be greater than differences between major and minor pilgrimage places.

Variations between regions on the continent are less striking than are those which set Ireland apart from mainstream European traditions, but even within continental Europe there are still marked differences in historical periods during which the largest number of shrines were established, in tendencies to grant sanctity to certain kinds of environmental features, in the frequencies with which certain holy persons are honored with shrines, and in the kinds of objects that represent these persons. There are also regional differences in the frequencies of certain kinds of shrine origin stories and in commonly recurring shrine legends.

The Slavic/Hungarian region, not dealt with in any previous publication, is interesting in the degree to which it conforms to overall continental patterns. The very strong concentration of shrine formations in the Post-Reformation period, and particularly the eighteenth century, reflects aspects of the region's history that are quite different from events in lands farther to the west. The peak of Polish shrine formations in the seventeenth century corresponds to a period when Poland was a viable, although war-wracked state. Here, cult formations seem to have declined precipitously in the eighteenth century, an era when the country was weakening and ultimately subjected to partition between powerful, predominantly non-Catholic neighboring states. However, a florescence of pilgrimage followed liberation of Hungary from Ottoman Turkish control in 1699. As a result, 36 percent of active Slavic/Hungarian region shrines date from the eighteenth century, a period of low cult formative activity elsewhere in Europe, and only 12 percent were founded after 1780. Interestingly, what may become one of the most important Marian apparition cults of the 20th century began in 1981 at Medjugorje in Bosnia, then part of Yugoslavia.

The emphasis on Marian shrines and on images as cult objects in the Slavic/Hungarian region may partly reflect limited amounts of data from the region, although it seems likely that Marian cultus was better able to resist suppression during the period of Communist control than were some other forms of religious expression. This region also amplifies the South German emphasis on two-dimensional images as well as on shrine origin stories involving spontaneous miracles. This should be expected, given the historic influence of Imperial Austria on much of the Slavic/Hungarian region.

In spite of the regional variations in European pilgrimage, there is a commonality in the adaptations of pilgrimage to a modern world. Current trends include provision of more facilities at shrine centers for diverse religiously-oriented activities, a decrease in the number of colorful processions and other public displays, a growing emphasis on pilgrimage for the sick, and an effort to create a better fit with modern work-leisure patterns by shifting traditional fixed-date pilgrimages to weekends. Some shrine administrators must deal with the problem of accommodating large numbers of secularly-oriented tourists. Strategies include scheduling pilgrimage events at times when touristic visitation is low, curtailing advertisement of special pilgrimage events, reducing folkloric display of a kind likely to attract tourists, and/or developing interpretive displays and programs to inform the casual visitor about the religious significance of the shrine.

It seems evident that pilgrimage is undergoing major changes in late twentieth century Europe, but is in no danger of dying out. Vatican officials, aware of increasing visitation at shrines during a period when attendance at Mass is declining, convened the first church conference ever held on the subject of pilgrimage in April 1992.

Meanwhile, new shrines are developing in various parts of Europe. Several of these places are of special importance to pilgrims from urban industrial areas who visit the sites to share, and thus confirm, their beliefs that traditional miracles still happen. Pilgrims from the industrial centers of Liverpool, Ludwigshafen am Rhein, and Milan encountered at places such as Collevalenza and San Damiano in Italy and San Sebastían de Grabandal, Spain, seemed to be seeking the miraculous as a confirmation of traditional faith in a changing world. This is in contrast to the attitude of the country Irish who tend to say that miracles happen only when you believe.

The men and women who care for established shrines and attend the needs of their visitors often suggest that the paramount miracle of late twentieth-century pilgrimage relates to gaining peace of mind and an increased ability to cope with circumstances. As one priest put it, "It is a miracle that so many people come here, and that their lives are better because they came."

Acknowledgments

This study was made possible by grants from the National Endowment for the Humanities, the Oregon State University College of Liberal Arts Research Program, the Oregon State University Research Council, and the OSU Foundation. Partial support for field work was provided by Educational Video Network, Huntsville, Texas.

Notes

1. Visitation estimates were derived from data provided by shrine administrators, and from field observations in Europe between 1976 and 1991. The estimates are conservative because these attempt to describe only religiously motivated visits, thus discounting the large numbers of tourists at many well-known shrines. The figures do not provide any indication of the number of individuals who visit European shrines because the same person may visit a given shrine more than once per year, and many may visit several different shrines.

2. Our inventory of shrines is based on a wide variety of sources including general and regional compendia and correspondence with European bishops and shrine administrators. For a more complete discussion of data sources on Western European shrines see Nolan and Nolan (1989). Basic data on Central European shrines was collected by correspondence with bishops and shrine personnel between 1985 and 1988. Field work in the region includes visits to Yugoslavia in 1976 and 1978, to Czechoslovakia and Hungary in 1987, and to the East German area in 1990 as the reunification process was taking place.

3. Shrines of the Trentino-Adige subregion are included in the Italian region although as a group they are more South German than Italian in character. Likewise, the shrines of Alsace, an area of strong Germanic influence, are included in the French region reflecting current national boundaries.

4. For a finer breakdown of importance categories see Nolan and Nolan (1989).

5. We did not attempt to inventory places described as local in visitation, that is, those drawing devotees only from a single rural community or urban neighborhood. Some of the shrines originally included in the inventory proved to be highly localized when more information was obtained. When the characteristics of these 414 places were analyzed separately they proved as a group to be substantially different from the norm in several respects. Christian (1981), in a study of popular religion in sixteenth century Castile, found similar differences between local shrines and those that draw pilgrims from more extensive areas. It seems likely that there are structural differences between the characteristics of sacred places with only a local following and those of importance to several communities. More comprehensive data on localized European devotions would be useful for comparison with Bhardwaj's (1973) data that indicate differences between major and localized pilgrimage systems in Hindu India.

6. For a detailed discussion of problems related to dating pilgrimages see Nolan and Nolan (1989).

7. Because Irish shrines are different from those on the continent in many ways, caution should be used in employing early Irish shrines as examples of Early Christian shrines in general. The Turners' (1978, 104) use of Saint Patrick's Purgatory in Ireland as the primary example for their category of Archaic pilgrimage illustrates this point. This pilgrimage, unique even for Ireland in its penitential nature, may always have been atypical of European shrines in any age.

8. In the Medieval Shepherd's Cycle type of apparition, Mary appears with her babe in arms. If she says anything, she gives simple instructions on where her image may be found and/or asks that a shrine church be built at the apparition site. The finding of an image usually follows the apparition and confirms the validity of the visionary's experience. The "modern" type of Marian apparition, according to criteria suggested by the Turners, involves an apparition of Mary alone. She delivers a fairly lengthy message to the visionary, often including statements of an apocalyptic nature. No image is found at the site or nearby, although a graphic representation of the apparitional event is usually created to serve as a visual focus for veneration at the new apparitional shrine.

References

Barber, R. 1991. *Pilgrimages*. Woodbridge, U.K.: Boydell Press.

Bhardwaj, S. M.. 1973. *Hindu places of pilgrimage in India: A study in cultural geography*. Berkeley: University of California Press.

Christian, W. A. 1981. *Local religion in sixteenth century Spain*. Princeton: Princeton University Press.

Cousin, B. 1981. *Ex-voto de Provence: Images de la religion populaire et de la vie d'autrefois*. Paris: Desclee de Brouwer.

Eade, J., and M. J. Sallnow, eds. 1991. *Contesting the sacred: The anthropology of Christian pilgrimage*. London and New York: Routledge.

Kendall, C. 1991. The politics of pilgrimage: The Black Christ of Esquipulas. In *Pilgrimage in Latin America*, eds. N. R. Crumrine, and A. Morinis, 139-56. New York: Greenwood Press.

Nolan, M. L. 1983. Irish pilgrimage: A different tradition. *Annals of the Association of American Geographers* 73(3): 421-38.

——. 1986. Pilgrimage traditions and the nature mystique in Western European culture. *Journal of Cultural Geography* 7(1): 5-20.

Nolan, M. L., and S. D. Nolan. 1989. *Christian pilgrimage in modern Western Europe*. Chapel Hill: University of North Carolina Press.

——. 1991. The European roots of Latin American pilgrimage. In *Pilgrimage in Latin America*, eds. N. R. Crumrine and A. Morinis, 19-49. New York: Greenwood Press.

Sallnow, M. J. 1991. Dual cosmology and ethnic division in an Andean pilgrimage cult. In *Pilgrimage in Latin America*, eds. N. R. Crumrine and A. Morinis, 281-306. New York: Greenwood Press.

Scott, J., and P. Simpson-Housley, eds. 1991. *Sacred places and profane spaces: Essays in the geographics of Judaism, Christianity, and Islam*. New York: Greenwood Press.

Stoddard, R. H. 1994. Major pilgrimage places of the world. *Geographia Religionoum* 8: 21-40.

Straub, E. S. 1991. Through the fields of Amatitlán. In *Pilgrimage in Latin America*, eds. N. R. Crumrine, and A. Morinis, 157-71. New York: Greenwood Press.

Tanaka Shimazaki, H. 1988. On the geographic study of pilgrimage places. *Geographia Religionoum* 4: 21-40.

Turner, V. 1973. The center out there: Pilgrim's goal. *History of Religions* 21(3): 191-230.

Turner, V., and Turner, E. 1978. *Image and pilgrimage in Christian culture: Anthropological perspectives*. New York: Columbia University Press.

Pilgrimage Studies at Different Levels

Gisbert Rinschede
Universität Regensburg

Abstract

Geographical aspects of the pilgrimage phenomenon can be studied at different levels which often imply varying types of investigation. The four levels of geographical studies examined here are: (1) pilgrimage phenomena at single places (or what are sometimes called "micro case studies"); (2) pilgrimage phenomena within countries and cultural regions (that is, "meso studies"); (3) pilgrimage phenomena in a general and worldwide perspective (or "macro studies"); and (4) pilgrimage phenomena examined for interdisciplinary integration (here termed "mixed studies"). Each of these levels has its own characteristics and emphases, and demands specific methods of investigation and presentation. This paper treats some aspects of these differences. The intention is to make explicit and systematic the categories that geographers use to compare pilgrimages.

Key words: geographic scales, pilgrimage, U. S. Catholic pilgrimages, pilgrimage studies, data collection

Pilgrimage Phenomena at Single Places

One type of geographical study focuses on the pilgrimage phenomenon as it occurs at a single place. Such investigations normally commence by collecting several kinds of data that are useful in attempting to understand the geographic aspects of pilgrimages.

An important item is the identification of the religious event that, as expressed by Eliade (1959), "manifests itself in the profane" (fig. 1). Although the origins often lie outside today's sacred history, the driving force behind the steady flow of pilgrims is often associated with belief in miraculous healings, supernatural apparitions, and similar events. These beliefs are linked to a particular place with its own sacred geography and "spiritual magnetism" (Preston 1990). Geographic understanding, there-

Sacred Places, Sacred Spaces: The Geography of Pilgrimages, edited by Robert H. Stoddard and Alan Morinis, 1997. Geoscience and Man, vol. 34, pp. 95-115. Dept. of Geography and Anthropology, Louisiana State University, Baton Rouge, LA 70893-6010.

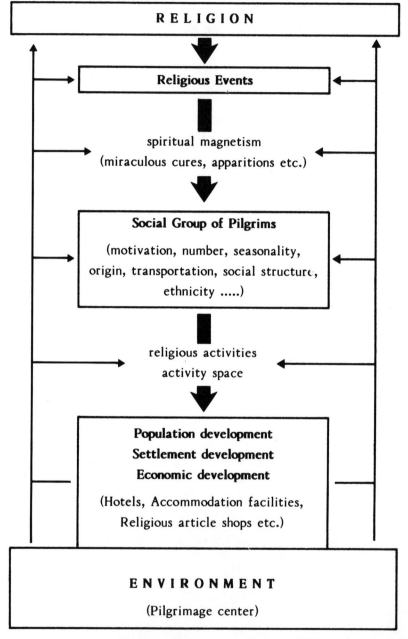

Fig. 1. Model of religion/environment-relationship at pilgrimage places. *Source:* Author's investigation.

fore, requires a careful examination of the site and all its religious attributes.

The relative location (or geographic situation), however, is also important because the magnetism of a site may reflect the ease of access. Links to airports and major highways and proximity to large agglomerations of population tend to attract a larger number of pilgrims than religious sites located at inaccessible places, although there is, by no means, a perfect correlation. Thus, in the United States, major pilgrimage places such as San Juan, Texas, Belleville, Illinois, and Orlando, Florida, are located with easy access to interstate highways. Proximity to large tourist attractions is proven to be particularly advantageous. Thus, the positive development of the "Our Lady of the Snows" shrine in Belleville can be understood by considering the city of St. Louis, situated on the opposite bank of the river, which attracts large tourist streams every year. The location of the "Our Lady of Fátima Shrine" in Youngstown, New York, just a few miles north of Niagara Falls, has undoubtedly attracted additional pilgrims and contributed to the rapid rise of the shrine. This seems to have been taken into account in establishing the pilgrimage place, "Mary Queen of the Universe," in Orlando, Florida, just a few miles away from Disney World and Epcot Center (Rinschede 1990a).

The next step, after noting the site and situation of a particular pilgrimage place, should be an analysis of the religious motivation of pilgrims. To do this, the connection between the "spiritual magnetism" of the pilgrimage place and the motivations of the pilgrims has to be examined. A distinction should be made between the "true pilgrims" with primarily religious motives, such as fulfilling a vow or praying for a healing, and at least two other kinds of visitors. These include "pilgrim tourists," who have a high proportion of free time, and "ordinary tourists," who visit the site out of curiosity or cultural interest. Classifying pilgrims on the basis of their motivation, however, can be extremely difficult (Nolan and Nolan 1989). This is partly because pilgrimage journeys today are increasingly tied to other forms of tourism. They are multifunctional journeys, even when the religious factor seems to dominate. This complicating factor is especially evident in industrialized countries where the relationship to other touristic forms is much closer than in developing countries in which mass tourism is still in its beginnings.

Also to be considered is the number of pilgrims, even though acquiring such data may be difficult in practice. Accurate information may be available only about organized and registered pilgrim groups, but local authorities may provide rough estimates for recent years. In general, the best statistics are found at major pilgrimage places, such as Lourdes (fig. 2). If data on the number of pilgrims by dates are obtained and tabulated, various temporal relationships can be established. Typical relationships

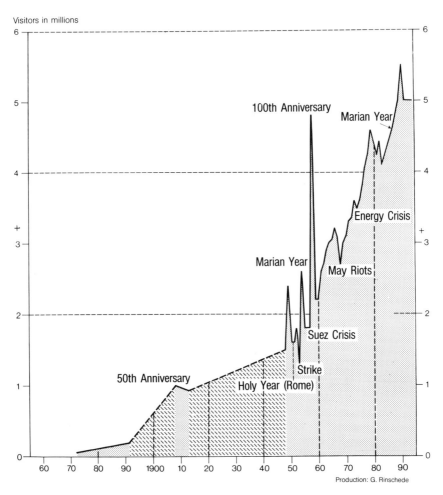

Visitors in millions

Fig. 2. Number of visitors to the pilgrimage place of Lourdes, France 1872 - 1994. Data are extrapolated for several dates prior to 1950. *Source:* **Rinschede 1986 (revision 1995).**

are built on a correlation between pilgrim flow and climatic factors, farming calendars, or seasonal religious events. In general, the pilgrim season in the northern latitudes is limited to the summer months of April/May - October because pilgrimage activities often take place in the open air (fig. 3). Religious ceremonies and commemoration days certainly play a large, if not a decisive, role in the motivation of the pilgrims. Thus, the days of the apparition in Fátima on the 13th of each month from May to October and in Guadalupe on the 12th of December represent the high points of the pilgrim streams (fig. 4).

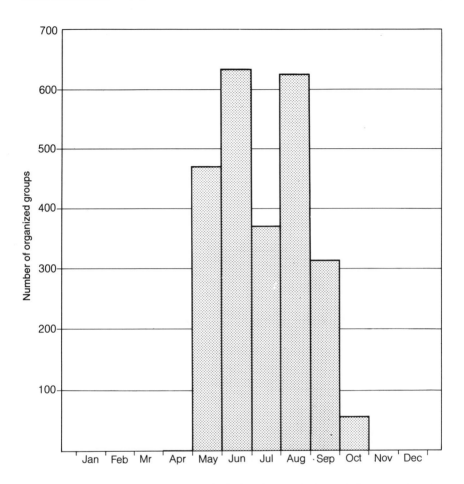

Fig. 3. Number of organized groups of pilgrims in Cap-de-la- Madeleine, Québec, by months in 1988. *Source:* Information of the Shrine Office 1989 (Rinschede 1992b, 1994).

Additional data that an investigator should attempt to obtain from the pilgrims concerns their previous journeys, their origins, their modes of travel, and their social and ethnic characteristics (Caplan, this volume). With data about previous journeys, one can gain insight into the degrees of involvement endured by individual pilgrims and the aggregate strength of pilgrimage as a ritual performance within a given population.

Information about pilgrims' homes and the origin of their journeys provides an opportunity for substantial derived knowledge such as patterns of participation (fig. 5). Data about regions of attraction can aid in describing the pilgrimage place by type of nodal region or "catchment area" and can suggest areal variations in support of the religious node. The pil-

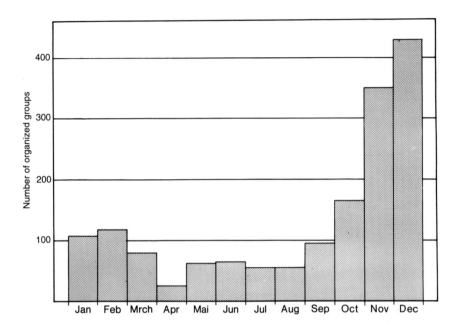

Fig. 4. Number of organized groups of pilgrims to "Nuestra Señora de Guadalupe," Mexico City, by months, 1986. *Source:* Author's investigation, April 1988 (Rinschede 1988, 1990b).

grimage places can be easily arranged in a classification system of local, regional, supra-regional, national, and international catchment areas. Rome, Lourdes, Fátima, Mecca, and Jerusalem are examples of pilgrimage places with international importance. The "National Shrine of the Immaculate Conception" in Washington, D.C., is of great importance nationally, with visiting pilgrims coming from all dioceses in the United States. This broad national support results partly from the fact that dioceses often engage a pilgrim representative who is responsible for organizing trips to Washington. Most other pilgrimage places in the United States are of regional or supra-regional importance. Their catchment areas extend only as far as neighboring states.

Data about the modes of transportation (e. g., by foot, rail, bus, car, truck, ship, and airplane) allows the researcher to discover changing patterns of pilgrimage behavior (Din and Hadi, this volume). For example, with the shift away from journeys made mainly by foot, many nodal regions ("catchment areas") have increased in size. Data about the routes of transportation may reveal certain routes that are particularly important.

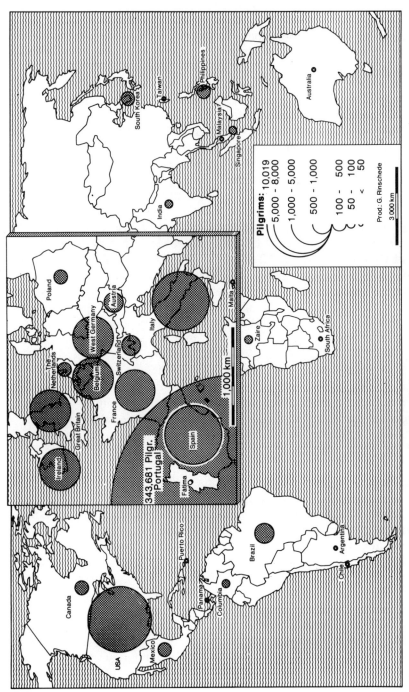

Fig. 5. Number and origin of pilgrims in organized groups to Fátima, Portugal, 1987. *Source:* Information from the "Serviço de Peregrinos - SEPE," Fátima (Rinschede 1988, 1990b).

Illustrative of important sacred ways are the routes of St. James to Santiago de Compostela and the Hedscha railroad from Damascus to Mecca.

In the United States, pilgrimage by foot did not develop as a tradition. Today it is customary only in Chimayo, New Mexico, probably the oldest Catholic pilgrimage place in the United States. Until about 1955, many pilgrims arrived at pilgrimage places like Auriesville, New York, Carey, Ohio, and Starkenburg, Missouri, on special trains, but these rail services have now been discontinued. Almost all pilgrims in the United States nowadays reach the holy places by road, travelling either by bus or car.

Collecting socio-ethnic data makes it possible to establish numerous relationships between pilgrim characteristics and the pilgrimage to a specific site. Some pilgrimage sites attract pilgrims who are distinguished by their sex, age, schooling, income, occupation, and/or ethnicity. Around 10 percent of all pilgrimage places in the United States are visited exclusively by one specific ethnic group. For example, the "Sanctuary of Christ of Chimayo," New Mexico, is visited by Indians and Mexican Americans, "Our Lady of Charity Shrine" in Miami by Cuban exiles, and the "National Shrine of our Lady of Czestochowa" in Doylestown, Pennsylvania, by Polish people. Nearly all other pilgrimage sites display a strong ethnic component in their pilgrim numbers, reflecting old immigrant groups from Western, Southern, and Eastern Europe, as well as the more recent immigrant groups from Latin America, and from Asia (fig. 6) (Rinschede 1990a). Pictures, statues, altars, and other objects at shrines often reflect the ethnicity of their visitors. For example, a statue of Saint Anthony of Padova, one of Saint Patrick, and one of the Infant of Prague respectively indicate patronage by Italian, Irish, and Czech pilgrims. A pilgrimage place may serve in part to affirm the identity of an entire national ethnic group, or of an ethnic minority, within an foreign majority, as was shown by Prorok (1988, 1994), who investigated different Hindu communities in the West.

The magnitude and nature of religious activities and the areal extent of the activity space affect the general development of the pilgrimage place. Another phase of a micro case study, therefore, should concern the development of population numbers, settlement patterns, and economic activities. In fact, the spatial impact of pilgrims assembling at a place is one of the most important aspects of the study of pilgrimage phenomena (Rowley, this volume). Although the effects on pilgrimage places in the open country may be easier to detect than effects on those in large metropolitan centers, all places are affected (although in many different ways) by the periodic influx of pilgrims. An effective way of observing impacts is through an historical examination of population, settlement, and the economy of a place. If possible, the situation at the time of the first religious events should be recorded along with those of other significant

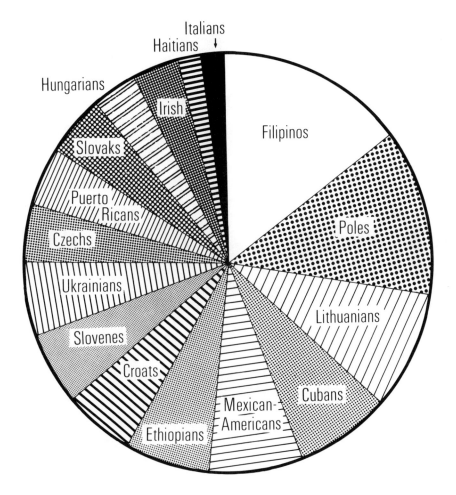

Fig. 6. Number of ethnic pilgrims (estimated) to the "National Shrine of the Immaculate Conception," Washington, D C 1987. *Source:* Information of the Shrine Office 1987 (Rinschede 1990a).

times. Data may be acquired from oral comments by local authorities, archival materials, maps, and aerial photographs.

Since they became pilgrimage sites, nearly all holy places have experienced a constant population growth. Some pilgrimage places like Fátima, Lourdes, and Loreto have sprung up in the open countryside under the influence of pilgrimage streams and have developed rapidly. The development of settlement patterns and economic structures of a place are closely tied to the rapid population growth. In the well-known cities of Lourdes, Fátima, and Loreto the development was strictly planned (fig. 7).

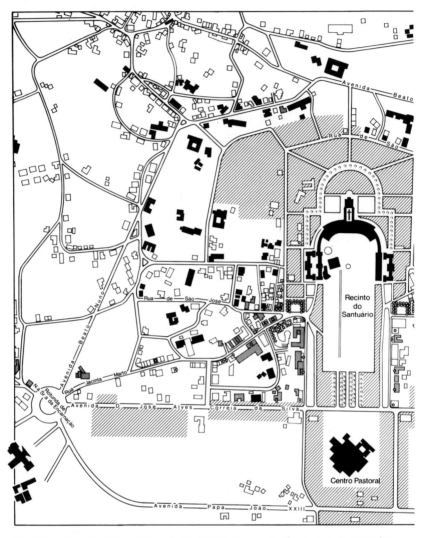

Fig. 7. Functions in Fátima (Cova da Iria), 1986. *Source:* Author's mapping 1985/86 .

The core of the city became the religious center surrounded by other religious sites such as monasteries and hospitals. The impact of pilgrims on
the economic structure is of particular significance and is reflected in the
hotels, restaurants, religious article shops, and numerous other businesses
that cater primarily to pilgrims. In essence, the functional organization of
a place can be derived by examining a map of land use. Seen as a whole,
the economy of an entire city and its surroundings (Fátima, Lourdes) and

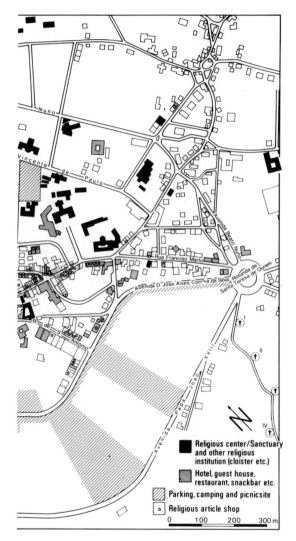

(Rinschede 1988, 1990).

sometimes of an entire country (Mecca, Saudi Arabia) can be influenced by the pilgrim streams.

In the United States, the influence of the pilgrimage place on the population and settlement structure of its surrounding area cannot be clearly established for any place. The influence on the economic structure is also limited, even when in some cases 100 or more staff members are employed. This is partly caused by the fact that pilgrimage places in the United States are relatively self-sufficient, with incomes from gift shops, book stores, motels, restaurants, snackbars, and similar support facilities. In contrast, the influence exerted by the surrounding area on the pilgrimage place is of much greater importance. Natural surroundings, attractive cities, and other touristic places of interests within reach have a positive effect on pilgrim numbers and on the development of the pilgrimage place. Recognition of these effects is evident by their being taken into account in the planning of new pilgrimage places. On the other hand, changes in the environmental setting may negate some of the originally expected advantages. For example, some pilgrimage places built in smart residential areas find themselves in a less attractive run-down environment within a few decades.

The land use pattern caused by pilgrims corresponds with the activity spaces of pilgrims (Singh, this volume). Variations in activity spaces will reveal differences in pilgrimage groups (e. g., organized tours versus private travelling parties) and areas of focus (such as a religious site and its supporting zone distinguished from the primarily secular region). Since the distance between the home location and the pilgrimage place can be considerable, frequently pilgrims visit other religious places on the same trip when possible. In the United States, pilgrim tours can be found more in the Eastern states, where there is the larger number of pilgrimage places. For example, pilgrims from New York City and Boston who undertake regular tours of Canadian pilgrimage centers in Québec also visit shrines in Youngstown, Fonda, and Auriesville, New York.

The relationship of human activities and the natural environment — the ecological theme of geography — is another type of investigation that merits attention. Studies often deal with some aspect of the interacting and reciprocal effects of the natural setting on pilgrims and their impact on the environment (Tanaka Shimazaki 1977, 1988).

Pilgrimage Phenomena within Countries and Cultural Regions

A different level and scale of study is achieved by considering an entire country or large cultural region rather than looking at just a single place. By dealing with several places, comparisons and generalizations about pilgrimage are possible. This is not to suggest that a different kind of information is examined; in fact, the most useful studies are the very ones that have comparable data that can be investigated under standardized conditions.

First, the distribution of pilgrimage places in a country or cultural region could be examined. For example, the concentration of Catholic pilgrimage places, which were established by early immigration groups to the United States, generally corresponds to the concentration of Catholics. However, recent immigrant groups from Asia and Latin America represent an important percentage of pilgrims today and are influencing existing pilgrimage places in different ways (fig. 8).

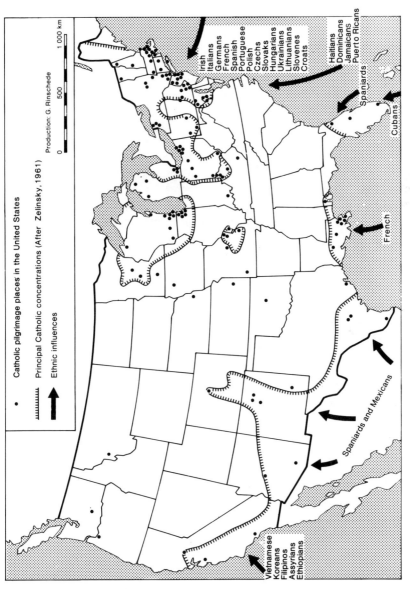

Fig. 8. Distribution of Catholic pilgrimage places in the United States and ethnic influences, 1989. *Source: Rinschede 1990a.*

Because comparisons and generalizations are often based on classification, the categorization of pilgrimages is common. For example, A. Sievers (1987) categorized pilgrimage places in Sri Lanka according to their major religious affiliation (Buddhism, Hinduism, Islam, and Christianity); and S. M. Bhardwaj (1973) classified sacred places in India on the basis of presiding deities. Nolan and Nolan (1989) classified pilgrimage places of Western Europe several ways, including shrines devoted to health-related cults. They noted, for instance, that shrines devoted to the health and well-being of livestock are predictably concentrated in the cattle-raising countries of Switzerland, Austria, and Ireland, and the regions of Bavaria, Northern Portugal, and Bretagne (Nolan 1988, 1994).

Numerous scholars have differentiated pilgrimage places according to the number of visitors during a specified period (fig. 9). Combining the number of pilgrims with a map showing the origins of pilgrims to particular places provides a basis for categorizing pilgrimages as local, regional, supraregional, national, or international (Stoddard, this volume).

Another way of characterizing pilgrimage is by using a set of criteria for which descriptive types are noted. One proposed set of criteria is the following:

Worship rites
Age and origin
Founders and administrators
Location
Size and facilities
Catchment areas and number of pilgrims
Ethnicity of pilgrims
Effect on settlement and economy

An illustration of descriptive types for this set of criteria is provided by listing the appropriate response for each criterion when examining the typical Catholic pilgrimage place in the United States (Rinschede 1990a):

Worship rites	Marian with an increasing ecumenical character
Age and origin	Established in the 20th century
Founders and administrators	A religious order
Location	Originally at the edge of a large city, situated in the Midwest
Size and facilities	Large and abundant
Catchment areas and number of pilgrims	Regional with 10,000 - 100,000 per summer season
Ethnicity of pilgrims	Strong ethnic affiliation
Effect on settlement and economy	Very little

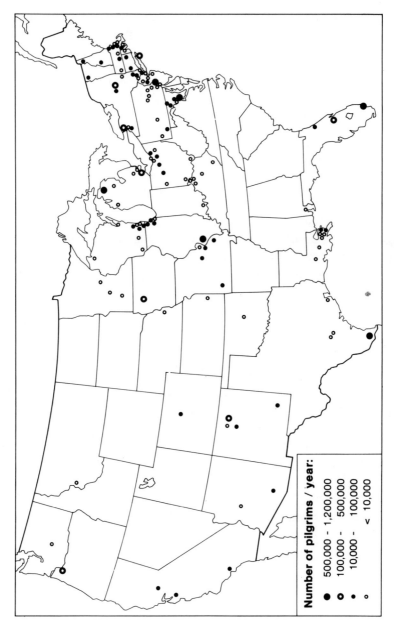

Fig. 9. Size of Catholic pilgrimage places in the US, 1989, by number of pilgrims per year in 1989. *Source:* Rinschede 1990a.

Thus by studying several pilgrimage places within a country or cultural region, a scholar can ascertain not only variations, which are indicated by classificatory differences, but also those aspects that places have in common. For example, Lourdes, Fátima, and Loreto all typify settlement and economic conditions that apply to many other pilgrimage centers in Europe (see fig. 7). Likewise, the common characteristics of Catholic pilgrimage sites in the United States can be generalized by a "model" of land use patterns (fig. 10). Such generalizations can then serve as a basis for comparisons between regions. For instance, a typical pilgrimage site in the United States is generally more isolated and has less impact on the surrounding countryside than in Europe.

Another benefit that can be gained by studying a set of regional places is the expanded ability to understand historical changes. The changes that most pilgrimage places undergo through time can be examined not only as a series of events in isolation but also as a set of interacting places that affect each other. Furthermore, these interacting units can be interpreted within the context of general changes in religious attitudes, economic conditions, social values, and political influences of the entire region (Karan, this volume).

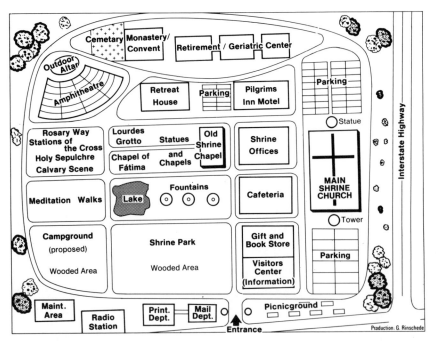

Fig. 10. Model of a Catholic pilgrimage place in the US. *Source:* Author's investigation 1986-1989 (Rinschede 1990a).

Pilgrimage Phenomena in a General and Worldwide Perspective

A third level of study concerns pilgrimage places in general. Rather than being restricted to particular cultural regions or religious affiliations, pilgrimages are examined as a universal phenomenon. Although pilgrimages have been analyzed from psychological, sociological, and religious perspectives by numerous scholars, not many geographers have attempted to generalize about pilgrimages across religious and international boundaries.

Basic to developing geographic principles about pilgrimages is the identification of a useful classification. One way of defining the major pilgrimage places in the world is according to numbers of visitors. However, because such data are presently lacking for many religious centers, this method of identification is difficult to implement. Another strategy for defining the major pilgrimages places is by a consensus (expressed in publications and through direct surveys) of pilgrimage scholars (Stoddard 1994).

After a set of places has been identified and mapped by location, generalizations about their geographic relationships can be developed (fig. 11). The map itself allows for the detection of distributional concentrations, especially those for certain religions. The spatial distribution of pilgrimage places can be related to other phenomena, such as latitudinal position, climatic setting, and distance to large agglomerations of population (Stoddard 1994). From such locational bases, areal associations between pilgrimage places can be examined for altitude, morphological location, and numerous other features.

Pilgrimage Phenomena Examined for Interdisciplinary Integration

A fourth level of study occurs when geographic investigations accompany those in other disciplines. The geographic perspective already integrates aspects of pilgrimages that are studied by other disciplines because geography is concerned with numerous phenomena that interrelate spatially and ecologically. Nevertheless, insights into the complex phenomenon of pilgrimage are enhanced when studies have been designed to integrate the approaches of multiple disciplines. In other words, a comprehensive understanding is best achieved through the cooperation of scholars from several disciplines.

Although a study designed for the purpose of integrating the results with that obtained by other scholars can be conceived as a fourth level, this does not mean that such an approach is restricted to just one geographic level. Multi-disciplinary studies can focus on pilgrimages as they occur at one place, within a region, or throughout the world. In this sense, this type of pilgrimage study overlaps the three levels discussed above. Its concep-

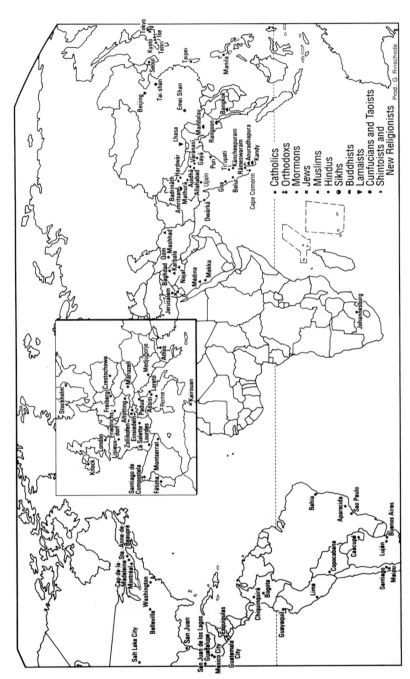

Fig. 11. Pilgrimage places/religious centers of national and international importance. *Source:* Rinschede 1990b.

tual classification as a fourth level, therefore, depends upon the degree to which the results are suitable for interdisciplinary integrations.

Theoretically, pilgrimages can be examined from any perspective involving human actions and beliefs. Nevertheless, the main disciplines dealing with pilgrimages, in addition to geography, have been history, psychology, sociology, economics, anthropology, and religious studies. There is a continued necessity for studies that are compatible across disciplinary lines (Preston 1990), and geographers have an important role in promoting this goal.

The need for this level of study was made apparent by multi-disciplinary conferences that have been held in recent years, such as at Pittsburgh in 1981, Eichstätt in 1988, and London in 1988. Since then quite a few volumes with contributions to the pilgrimage phenomenon from different perspectives and disciplines have been published (Eade and Sallnow 1991; Smith 1992; Bhardwaj and Rinschede 1988; Bhardwaj, Rinschede and Sievers 1994). The different articles resulted from independent research projects that were not coordinated in the beginning. Even better would be projects that are already coordinated at an early stage. So, in the late eighties P. Giuriati and the author started projects to study religio-sociological and geographical aspects in different Catholic shrines, such as Lourdes, Fátima, Loreto, Montreal, Guadalupe, Belleville, and Czestochowa (Giuriati 1992; Giuriati and Lanzi 1994; Rinschede 1992a, 1994).

Conclusion

The purpose here is not to suggest the superiority of a particular level of pilgrimage study. The skills and interests of scholars, opportunities for field work, and the changing body of accumulated information all affect scholars as they plan and undertake pilgrimage research. Irrespective of the kind of study, it is imperative that researchers as they commence their work consider the level of investigation and how it will best contribute to the growing body of knowledge about pilgrimages.

References

Bhardwaj, S. M. 1973. *Hindu places of pilgrimage in India: A study in cultural geography.* Berkeley: University of California Press.

Bhardwaj, S. M., and G. Rinschede, eds. 1988. *Pilgrimage in world religions,* Geographia Religionum, 4. Berlin: Dietrich Reimer Verlag.

Bhardwaj, S. M., G. Rinschede, and A. Sievers, eds. 1994. *Pilgrimage in the old and new world,* Geographia Religionum, 8. Berlin: Dietrich Reimer Verlag.

Eade, J., and M. Sallnow, eds. 1991. *Contesting the sacred: The anthropology of Christian pilgrimage.* London and New York: Routledge.

Eliade, M. 1959. *The sacred and the profane: The nature of religion,* trans. by W. R. Trask. New York: Harcourt, Brace & Co.

Giuriati, P., ed. 1992. *J. Pellegrini alla Santa Casa di Loreto. Indagine socio-religiosa*, Loreto: Congregazione Universale della Santa Casa.

Giuriati, P., P. M. G. Myers, and M. E. Donach. 1990. Pilgrims to Our Lady of the Snows in Belleville, Illinois, in the Marian Year: 1987-1988. In *Pilgrimage in the United States*, eds. G. Rinschede and S. M. Bhardwaj, 149-192. Geographia Religionum, 5. Berlin: Dietrich Reimer Verlag.

Nolan, M. L. 1988. Pilgrimage and perception of hazard in Western Europe. In *Pilgrimage in world religions*, eds. S. M. Bhardwaj and G. Rinschede, 41-64. Geographia Religionum, 4. Berlin: Dietrich Reimer Verlag.

———. 1994. Seasonal pattern of Christian pilgrimage. In *Pilgrimage in the old and new world*, eds. S. M. Bhardwaj, G. Rinschede, and A. Sievers, 17-36. Geographia Religionum, 8. Berlin: Dietrich Reimer Verlag.

Nolan, M. L., and S. Nolan. 1989. *Christian pilgrimage in modern Western Europe*. Chapel Hill, NC: University of North Carolina Press

Preston, J. 1990. The rediscovery of America: Pilgrimage in a promised land. In *Pilgrimage in the United States*, eds. G. Rinschede and S. M. Bhardwaj, 15-26. Geographia Religionum, 5. Berlin: Dietrich Reimer Verlag.

Prorok, C. V. 1988. Hindu temples in Trinidad: A cultural geography of religious structures and ethnic identity. Ph. D. diss., Louisiana State University.

———. 1994. Hindu temples in the Western World. A study in social space and ethnic identity. In *Pilgrimage in the old and new world*, eds. S. M. Bhardwaj, G. Rinschede, and A. Sievers, 95-108. Geographia Religionum, 8. Berlin: Dietrich Reimer Verlag.

Rinschede, G. 1986. The pilgrimage town of Lourdes. *Journal of Cultural Geography* 7:21-34.

———. 1988. The pilgrimage center of Fátima, Portugal. In *Pilgrimage in world religions*, eds. S. M. Bhardwaj and G. Rinschede, 65-98. Geographia Religionum, 4. Berlin: Dietrich Reimer Verlag.

———. 1990a. Catholic pilgrimage places in the United States. In *Pilgrimage in the United States*, eds. G. Rinschede and S. M. Bhardwaj, 63-135. Geographia Religionum, 5. Berlin: Dietrich Reimer Verlag.

———. 1990b. Religionstourismus. *Geographische Rundschau* 42:14-20.

———. 1992a. Forms of religious tourism. *Annals of Tourism Research* 19:51-67.

———. 1992b. Catholic pilgrimage centers in Québec, Canada. In *Geographical snapshots of North America*, ed. D. G. Janelle, 292-95. New York, London: The Guilford Press.

———. 1994. Catholic pilgrimage centers in Québec, Canada. In *Pilgrimage in the old and new world*, eds. S. M. Bhardwaj, G. Rinschede, and A. Sievers, 169-92. Geographia Religionum, 8. Berlin: Dietrich Reimer Verlag.

Rinschede, G., and A. Sievers. 1987. The pilgrimage phenomenon in socio-geographical research. *National Geographical Journal of India*, 33:213-17.

Rinschede, G., and S. M. Bhardwaj, eds. 1990. *Pilgrimage in the United States*, Geographia Religionum, 5. Berlin: Dietrich Reimer Verlag.

Sievers, A. 1987. The significance of pilgrimage tourism in Sri Lanka. *National Geographical Journal of India* 33: 430-47.

Singh, L. and Singh, R. P. B., eds. 1987. *Trends in the geography of belief systems*. The National Geographical Society of India. Research Publication Series: 34, Varanasi: Banares Hindu University

Smith, V., ed. 1992. Pilgrimage and tourism: The quest in guest. *Annals of Tourism Research* 19 (1).

Stoddard, R. H. 1966. Hindu holy sites in India. Ph. D. diss., University of Iowa.

———. 1994. Major pilgrimage places of the world. In *Pilgrimage in the old and new world*, eds. S. M. Bhardwaj, G. Rinschede, and A. Sievers, 17-36. Geographia Religionum, 8. Berlin: Dietrich Reimer Verlag.

Tanaka Shimazaki, H. 1977. Geographic expression of Buddhist pilgrim places on Shikoku Island, Japan. *Canadian Geographer* 21:116-24.

——. 1988. On the geographic study of pilgrimage places. In *Pilgrimage in world religions*, eds. S. M. Bhardwaj and G. Rinschede, 21-40. Geographia Religionum, 4. Berlin: Dietrich Reimer Verlag.

Tyrakowski, K. 1994. Pilgrims to the Mexican highlands. In *Pilgrimage in the old and new world*, eds. S. M. Bhardwaj, G. Rinschede, and A. Sievers, 193-246. Geographia Religionum, 8. Berlin: Dietrich Reimer Verlag.

Becoming a Place of Pilgrimage:
An Eliadean Interpretation of the Miracle
at Ambridge, Pennsylvania

Carolyn V. Prorok
Slippery Rock University

Abstract

People attach sacred significance to specific places through their interpretation of extraordinary experience. Parishioners at Holy Trinity Croation Catholic Church in Ambridge, Pennsylvania, believe that a miracle occurred in their church; on Good Friday in 1989 a young man serving mass noticed that the crucifix suspended over the altar had closed its eyes. Thousands of pilgrims visited the church within weeks of the event. This paper presents an Eliadean interpretaion of the miraculous event and proposes an understanding of the formation of new places of pilgrimage as the transcendance of paradox, a fixed point in a community's shared faith and as a symbol of group experience.
Key words: miracle; Ambridge, PA; crucifix; Elidean analysis; pilgrimage; U.S. pilgrimage.

Introduction

Exceptional events, miracles, experiences which motivate one to wonder and marvel: these inspire the creation of sacred objects and places. Extraordinary experience binds people to objects and places, a process that is part and parcel of the progressive transformation of ordinary space into sacred place. Parishioners of Holy Trinity Croatian Catholic Church in Ambridge, Pennsylvania (a small community northwest of Pittsburgh), have had such an extraordinary experience, and thousands of others have traveled to Ambridge to share it.

Intrinsically of interest to geographers is the exploration and understanding of the nature of sacred places. How does a certain place take on sacred significance? How is that significance sustained? Why do people

Sacred Places, Sacred Spaces: The Geography of Pilgrimages, edited by Robert H. Stoddard and Alan Morinis, 1997. Geoscience and Man, vol. 34, pp. 117-139. Dept. of Geography and Anthropology, Louisiana State University, Baton Rouge, LA 70893-6010.   117

behave as if that place is extraordinary? Answering questions like these can be attempted by first elucidating events connected to the incipient sacredness of a specific place, and secondly by explaining the circumstances encompassing that place within a framework that at once helps us to hang the experiences of a few people at a certain time and place onto a universal peg, while at the same time maintaining the integrity of their individual encounters with the sacred.

Events surrounding the crucifix at Holy Trinity provide a unique opportunity for a geographer to observe, as it happens, the transformation of an ordinary church into a place of pilgrimage in the making. Mircea Eliade's (1959) seminal work on the nature of sacred places provides us with a "humanistic framework" for understanding people's experiences in Ambridge. The events at Ambridge illustrate the spiritual integrity of those involved in the transformation of the church and its crucifix, while at the same time exemplifying a human drama that has been repeated in many times and places for millenia.

Study Area

Ambridge is a small town approximately 20 miles north of Pittsburgh, down the Ohio River, with slightly fewer than 10,000 people. The settlement of Old Economy, established in 1824 by the Utopianist George Rapp, predates the town known as Ambridge. In 1904 the Borough of Ambridge was established (Toker 1986, 296-7) and by 1905 included the Old Economy settlement (Wagner 1924, 23). One of the largest steel plants in the Pittsburgh area, LTV's Aliquippa Works, was built across the river in 1907. It attracted large numbers of immigrant workers from a wide range of European ancestry (Couvares 1984, 89; Toker 1986, 297). Today, Ambridge's population reflects a varied immigrant background. Each ethnic group built its own church. For example, within a few blocks of each other can be found Holy Trinity Croation Catholic Church (the church under study fig .1), St. Stanislav Polish Catholic Church, and St. Peter and Paul's Ukranian Catholic Church.

Ambridge's population has been in decline since the 1970s, mainly due to outmigration (Andriot 1983, 681). At one time, the Aliquippa Works regularly employed 14,000 people and spun out sheet metal at the speed of seventy miles an hour. Today it is practically shut down and unemployment has been high for over a decade (Toker 1986, 298).

During these stressful times of unemployment and outmigration a miracle is believed to have occurred in Ambridge. The faithful do not doubt its authenticity. This faith, and the need to commune with that which is extraordinary, has drawn thousands to this small community.

Fig. 1. Holy Trinity Croatian Catholic Church, Ambridge, PA. Note restrictions on parking near the church. (Artwork by Mary Lee Eggart.)

The Miracle

The word miracle comes to English from Old French and ultimately Latin: *mirari*, to wonder at (OED). Nolan and Nolan (1989, 360) state that a miracle is a "...person, thing, or event that excites admiring awe."

Events surrounding the crucifix at Holy Trinity Croation Church on Melrose Street in Ambridge, Pennsylvania, are believed to be a miracle. Holy Trinity's crucifix is life-size and has been in the church for 58 years of the Church's 60 year history. It had hung on the wall behind the altar and was moved when the church was remodeled in 1965. A stained glass window depicting a crucifix was then placed in the wall behind the altar, so the life-size crucifix was placed in the baptistry. Later it was moved again to the church balcony and again to the side of the sacristy where people could light votive candles and touch the cross (Anonymous 1989). Sometime during one of these moves, the crucifix was damaged when a painter fell from a scaffold and bumped into it. The crucifix was cracked, but the painter was "miraculously" unhurt (Card 1989). For approximately 20 years the congregation shared a special intimacy with the life-sized crucifix in their church, as they were able to closely direct their gaze toward the image of Jesus.

When Father Vincent Cvitkovic became pastor of Holy Trinity in 1985, he decided to have the crucifix repaired. An artist, Dominic Leo, refurbished the crucifix, and it was eventually suspended 22 feet above the altar in January 1989 (Anonymous 1989) (fig. 2). At that time Father Vincent told the congregation, in the dedication of the hanging of the crucifix, that, "it was a very rare thing to see a crucifix with the eyes open" (Card 1989). Father Vincent went on to explain that the crucifix represented a still living Christ with eyes and mouth partially open (Twedt and Hasch 1989) (fig. 3).

It is difficult to determine just how rare it is in modern times to have a crucifix depicting a live Christ. Bainton (1974, 146-148) points out that early representations of the crucifix in the fifth and sixth centuries usually depicted a live Christ, and representations of a dead Christ on the cross were not typical until the eleventh and twelveth centuries. Regardless of the history and frequency of the crucifix displaying a live Christ, the priest and congregation of Holy Trinity viewed the cross in their church as unusual. Furthermore, the special qualities associated with this cult image may be related to its supension over the altar. Nolan and Nolan (1989, 181) indicate that the importance of an image is dramatized by its position high over an altar. Finally, the raising up of the crucifix, after it had rested at eye-level for so many years, could have had a vivifying effect on people's perception of it. Thus, the act of elevating the crucifix only a few months before

Fig. 2. Interior of Holy Trinity showing the crucifix 22 feet above the altar. (Artwork by Mary Lee Eggart.)

Good Friday operated at two levels; it created both a physical and spiritual milieu that was primed, if you will, for extraordinary interpretation.

No one actually saw the eyes of Christ's image close on that memorable day. It is significant, though, that the miracle occurred on Good Friday, the day commemorating Christ's death. During the evening Good Friday Mass on March 24, 1989, the young men serving the mass thought the eyes of the crucifix were different. According to Father Vincent, his nephew Jim Cvitkovic (19 years old) looked up at the crucifix and noticed that the eyes were closed. After serving Mass the four young men were found by the priest crying in a room to the side of the altar. They explained that the eyes were closed on the crucifix, whereupon Father Vincent got a ladder and looked for himself. Parishioners were filing out of the church at the time. Father Vincent noticed the artist, Dominic Leo, had not left yet, and so called to him. Mr. Leo looked at the crucifix and concurred that the eyes were indeed closed. In an interview for the television program "Unsolved Mysteries" (Cosgrove/Meurer 1989), Mr. Leo reported that the eyes ap-

Fig. 3. The crucifix at Holy Trinity, considered by the parishioners to be rare for having both eyes and mouth partially open, representing a still living Christ. (Artwork by Mary Lee Eggart.)

peared fleshy and teary and, he added, "...the left eye was closed and the right one was slightly open" (Cosgrove/Meurer 1989). Soon after Mr.Leo's observation of the crucifix, other parishioners knew of the miracle of Christ's image closing its eyes. Many returned to pray at the altar late into the evening.

While praying, a young man believed that he received a message from Jesus. He wrote the message on paper and gave it to Father Vincent. The message was:

> I have given this sign for all those who have faithfully come to me week after week offering up their sorrows, joys, many sufferings and crosses. It pleases me to see so many people converted through this prayer group. Truly, my presence is within this church. You must be prepared, for within the weeks and months to come, many will flock to see what I have done. Many will doubt. However, through your example and faith, they will be converted. Have patience. Welcome them with open arms just as the people of Medjugorje welcome those who flock to see my mother. Don't base your beliefs on these signs that happen, but in what you know to be true in your heart and in the Gospel. (Papale 1989a)

Father Vincent reported, "I looked at it dumbfounded; it would explain everything" (Papale 1989a).

The reference to Medjugorje in the message is relevant to the miracle experience for Holy Trinity parishioners and significant in terms of sustaining what I call the place's future "sacrality," i.e., an environment that generates sacred observances and rites. A place's sacrality involves the tangible, outward "thingness" of sacred action that in turn creates a milieu where future participants can create anew their spiritual sentiments while sharing in the collective project of making space sacred.

Medjugorje is the Croation town (in Bosnia and Herzegovina) where visions of, and messages from, the Virgin Mary, Queen of Peace, have been attracting millions of visitors from around the world since 1981. In 1988, the Pittsburgh Center of Peace, a prayer group dedicated to praying for the Medjugorje visionaries (and known also as the Queen of Peace prayer group or the Medjugorje prayer group), was established at Holy Trinity by one of the parishioners. It is one of only 16 chapters nationwide whose members accept the messages of Medjugorje (Ireton 1989).

The parishioners in the prayer group meet every Friday night for several hours. The Medjugorje group met the night of the miracle and they believe that the miracle is a sign that Christ is pleased with them (Card 1989). Notable is the fact that the Good Friday miracle did not occur during the morning mass for all parishioners, but at the prayer group's regular Friday evening mass. According to one parishioner, "I feel this church was chosen by the Almighty a long, long time ago. I've been to Medjugorje two times, and when I have come back from Medjugorje, to the prayer group, I feel like I am in a little Medjugorje. I can feel the same presence there" (Papale 1989a). Many of the 150 members of the group have made a pilgrimage to Medjugorje. For them, the miracle experience on Good Friday reconnects them to the miracle experiences of Medjugorje (Card 1989). The miracle not only occurred during a prayer group service with many pilgrims who had been to Medjugorje, but also four of the priests that have served Holy Trinity since its establishment were born in Medjugorje (Cosgrove/Meurer 1989). Moreover, Father Vincent Cvitokovic is a member of the order of Croatian Franciscans, whose international headquarters is in Croatia and whose members have traditionally served the Medjugorje parish (Card 1989).

Once the story of the crucifix spread through Ambridge, and then was picked up by the Pittsburgh media and eventually national media, thousands of people came to see the crucifix for themselves. The Pittsburgh Catholic Diocese, administered by Bishop Donald Wuerl, was compelled to investigate the miracle, one of only a few investigations done by the church in the U.S. in recent times (Milbank 1989). The investigation by the diocese took over three months. In the meantime, thousands visited Holy Trinity and reported their own spiritual experiences, which included seeing the eyes opening and closing in quick succession, bleeding on the face, paling of skin color, cures, fulfilling of prophecy, and a returning to the church of lost souls (Utterback 1989a, 1989b; Card 1989).

The national, prime-time program "Unsolved Mysteries" came to Ambridge to film the mystery of the crucifix on June 6th, 1989. Parishioners gathered to re-enact the Good Friday Mass for the cameras and, during the filming, they believed they saw the eyes open again. Witnesses explained that at approximately 3:30 a.m. early Wednesday morning, when the filming crew was wrapping up the night's work by filming individuals climbing a ladder to see the crucifix better, one parishioner exclaimed the eyes had opened about three-fourths of the way. Others said that they had been taking pictures throughout the evening and they noticed the eyes had reopened (Card 1989). And so, a process of reaffirming faith through extraordinary experiences continued to accrue to the crucifix at Holy Trinity.

Eventually the Diocese Commission published its report in early July. The report indicated that the eyes of the crucifix did not miraculously close (Fodiak 1989, 1). Commission members based their report on interviews with witnesses, before and after photographs, and video tapes of the crucifix from different angles. According to the report, some photos do "...show a difference in the eyes from one photo to the other. This, however, is clearly attributable to varied lighting combinations and the various angles from which the eyes are viewed" (Guo 1989).

By the time the report came out, Father Vincent had left the parish for a retreat in order to relieve stress related to the events since Good Friday (Papale 1989b). After the report was publicized, the pastor resigned his post as Holy Trinity's priest, much to the disappointment and chagrin of family members and parishioners (Card 1989; Haynes 1989). Despite the commission report, the parishioners and many of the pilgrims to Ambridge believe that something unusual is happening at Holy Trinity. Mr. Leo, the artist who refurbished the cross, indicates that, as a good Catholic, he will not challenge the commission's findings, but he will not accept them either. He states, "I know what I saw. I was there. They're telling me their decision is based on what they saw in pictures. What God made happen in that church was the real thing. Those photographs don't mean anything to me. I worked on that crucifix. I know what I saw" (Papale 1989b).

Modern Christ-Centered Pilgrimage

In their book, *Christian Pilgrimage in Modern Western Europe* (1989), Mary Lee and Sidney Nolan treat the Christian pilgrimage experience from a geographic perspective. Since most pilgrims to Holy Trinity are descendants of European immigrants, and because the Nolans' work is probably the most comprehensive of its kind to be published, the following section will be based on their findings and will describe those patterns of European Christian pilgrimage that are pertinent to this study.

Journeying to sacred places for the fulfillment of a vow, to ask for favors and give thanks, or merely to express one's personal devotion has been a common practice among Europe's Christians, especially Catholics, for centuries, despite the fact that undertaking a pilgrimage has never been a Christian duty (Nolan and Nolan 1989, 20, 38). For Christians, those places most intimately connected to the life of Jesus are holiest. In Europe, Christ-centered places account for approximately 12 percent of Western European shrine sites (Nolan and Nolan 1989, 20, 157). The Christ cultus spread to the New World, primarily through Spanish colonization efforts. Today, approximately 28 percent of Latino shrines surveyed by the Nolans (1989, 124) are Christ-centered.

Dating mainly from the Renaissance and Catholic Reformation periods, images of the suffering Christ, or a man in agony, appear to be the most common cult images at Christ-centered shrines in Western Europe (Nolan and Nolan 1989, 188). Moreover, German culture, having sustained contact with Byzantine Rite Christians, may have been influenced by the typical Byzantine portrayal of a suffering Christ with bowed head (Nolan and Nolan 1989, 363). Although data on this subject are lacking for the United States, and patterns cannot be ascertained, the Ambridge crucifix appears to fit the above description. The miracle of Ambridge, as a catalyst for shrine formation, has precedence in Europe. Veneration of

Christ images, especially that of Jesus suffering the crucifixion, were common in Germanic areas by the 12th century. Twenty-five percent of Christ-centered European shrines have miracles associated with them.

Belief in the many stories of bleeding, crying, moving or speaking images has been attributed to the early cultus surrounding pilgrimage shrines in Western Europe (Nolan and Nolan 1989, 171, 217, 221). The Nolans (1989, 218, 241) classify shrines established by themes of wondrous events that characterize ordinary objects (even those found in churches) or places with extraordinary holiness as 'spontaneous miracle shrines', a type of shrine formation most popular in Italy and Germanic regions. In fact, 86 percent of shrines formulated due to belief in an image moving, crying or bleeding are found in Italy and German speaking areas (Nolan and Nolan 1989, 245). Since Croatia is proximate to both of these regions, it is possible that Croatians share some of the same cultural attributes.

The Pilgrims to Holy Trinity

Because modern pilgrims may identify with figures who represent the potential for sanctity, especially during times of hardship or great stress, the large numbers of people visiting Ambridge is not unusual. By the end of March 1989, only a week after the miracle, visitors numbered in the thousands (Card 1989). By early April, attendance at the daily evening masses was about 600, and as many as 800 individuals attended the Friday night Medjugorje prayer group (Card 1989). As a result of all the activity, the priest extended the church's open hours to 15 a day, with repeated masses. By early May, so many people had descended on the small church that some local residents around the church indicated annoyance with the crowds (Card 1989).

When the author began surveying the pilgrims in June, the visitation rate had slowed. Most people were now visiting Holy Trinity on the weekends, with smaller numbers on weekdays (Card 1989). A questionnaire survey was administered from June 16th to July 13th, 1989. A notebook of survey forms and a pen were mounted on a lectern and established in the church's lobby. It was checked periodically and resupplied with new forms when necessary. The survey included questions concerning the origin and ethnicity of the pilgrims, their reasons for visiting Holy Trinity and methods of transportation to the church, and acquisition of information regarding miraculous events. This survey does not represent a random sample and can only provide a crude indication of the characteristics associated with modern American pilgrims.

Over 1600 people from twelve nations responded to the survey. Since this represents only a fraction of the total, the number of pilgrims visiting Holy Trinity in such a short period of time is phenomenal by modern United States standards. During the same period 294 pilgrims signed the registry of the National Shrine of Our Lady of Lebanon in North Jackson, Ohio, and during the entire summer of 1988, 1,275 pilgrims signed the registry of the National Shrine of Our Lady of Consolation in Carey, Ohio (Faiers and Prorok 1989). The greater attraction of Holy Trinity appears to be the recent miracle that has gained national recognition, while the other shrines are older and have had less media attention.

The vast majority of pilgrims to Holy Trinity were Americans (table 1). Less than two percent of the visitors were foreign, many of whom indicated that they were visiting relatives and friends in the area when they heard of the events at Ambridge.

The ditstribution of pilgrims from the United States is extensive in areal distance from the shrine in that 37 states and the District of Columbia are represented (table 2). Despite this wide distribution, few pilgrims travelled great distances to the shrine. Pennsylvania is the origin of most pilgrims (65 percent) and states contiguous to Pennsylvania account for nearly 20 percent more. The majority of pilgrims originate in a radial zone of approximately 100 miles from the shrine (fig. 4). This is reinforced by the responses of pilgrims, in that nearly 99 percent traveled to the shrine by car or chartered bus and returned home the same day.

Table 1. Origins of Holy Trinity pilgrim by country

Country of origin	Number of pilgrims	% of total
United States	1557	96.10
Canada	11	0.70
Spain	3	0.20
Czechoslovakia	2	0.10
Australia	1	0.06
Northern Ireland	1	0.06
Hungary	1	0.06
Philippines	1	0.06
Poland	1	0.06
Belgium	1	0.06
India	1	0.06
Germany (not specified)	1	0.06
Responses not usable*	39	2.40
Total	1620	99.98

Source: Survey by author, 1989
* Responses were illegible, given by individuals who were parishioners of Holy Trinity, or left unanswered.

Table 2. Origins of Holy Trinity pilgrim in the
United States

Place of origin	Number of pilgrims	% of total
Pennsylvania	1011	65.00
Ohio	189	12.10
Florida	46	3.00
New York	45	2.90
California	31	2.00
New Jersey	29	1.90
Virginia	28	1.80
Michigan	24	1.50
Maryland	21	1.40
Texas	18	1.20
Illinois	14	0.90
West Virginia	12	0.80
Massachusetts	10	0.60
North Carolina	8	0.50
Arizona	6	0.40
Louisiana	6	0.40
Wisconsin	6	0.40
Colorado	5	0.30
Connecticut	5	0.30
Georgia	5	0.30
South Carolina	5	0.30
Tennessee	5	0.30
Washington (State)	5	0.30
Indiana	4	0.30
Utah	2	0.10
Oklahoma	2	0.10
New Mexico	2	0.10
New Hampshire	2	0.10
Kentucky	2	0.10
Delaware	1	0.06
Minnesota	1	0.06
Washington, D.C.	1	0.06
Kansas	1	0.06
Mississippi	1	0.06
Missouri	1	0.06
Nebraska	1	0.06
Nevada	1	0.06
Wyoming	1	0.06
Total	1557	100.00

Source: Survey by author, 1989

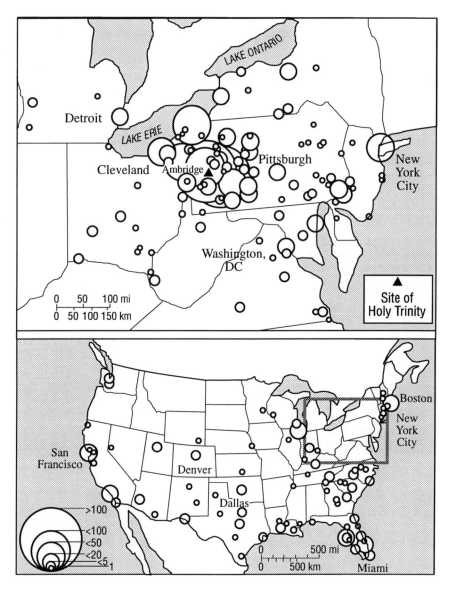

Fig. 4. Distribution of origins of pilgrims to Holy Trinity Coatian Catholic Church, Ambridge, PA.

Alhough national media coverage of the miracle was intense for a short period of time, and even though pilgrims came from as far away as California and Florida, pilgrimage to Ambridge is predominantly a regional phenomenon. Nolan and Nolan (1989, 24) indicate that the range of drawing power for a shrine in Europe may be influenced by the degree of outmigration from the area in which the shrine is located. Minor or modest shrines may have very large catchment basins because they draw emigrants and their descendants. These pilgrims usually combine a family visit with the shrine visit. This appears to be the case with many Holy Trinity pilgrims who come from afar. A large proportion (65 percent) of visitors originating 500 miles or further from Ambridge indicated that they were visiting family in the area. Even more long-distance pilgrims may have been visiting family, since nearly 85 percent of respondents from 500 miles or more from Ambridge indicated that they learned of the miracle event from family members. This pattern of visiting the family in no way detracts from the spiritual experience of visiting the shrine.

Holy Trinity's pilgrims represent many ethnic groups traditionally regarded as Catholic in the United States (table 3). More than one third of the pilgrims are of Slavic ethnicity (such as Poles and Slovaks), while nearly another third are represented by individuals of Italian and Germanic descent. The role of ethnicity in relation to the formation of American pilgrimage shrines only reflect the high numbers of a particular, traditionally Catholic group in the region of the shrine. In this case, Western Pennsylvania has a high proportion of Italians, Poles and other Slavs, Irish and German Irish, and German Catholics, especially in its urban areas (Toker 1986, 10, 12). This also accounts for the low proportion of French and Spanish-heritage Catholics visiting the shrine. Other ethnic groups represented by small numbers of pilgrims are groups that are traditionally non-Catholic.

If ethnicity plays any role at all in this shrine's formation as a pilgrimage site, then it supports and reinforces the proclivity of Catholics in general to visit a place noted for miraculous events. Certain traditions, however, may be passed on to the descendants of immigrants to America. It is interesting to note the Nolans' (1989, 245) indication that four-fifths of Western Europe's spontaneous miracle shrines that developed due to wondrous events surrounding an image are found in Italy and Germanic areas, while only one-seventh are found in France and Iberia, a region of Western Europe where apparitions and other shrine formation events are more common than the spontaneous miracle shrine (Nolan and Nolan 1989, 224-268).

It may be appropriate to speculate that if the events associated with Holy Trinity's crucifix are not considered typical of miraculous phenomena in France and Iberia, and if a supernatural sign is believed to have oc-

Table 3. Ethnicity of Holy Trinity pilgrims

Ethnicity	Number of pilgrims	% of total	Ethnicity	Number of pilgrims	% of total
Italian	328	17.6	Scotch	6	0.30
Irish	276	14.8	Portuguese	5	0.30
Polish	262	14.0	Lebanese	4	0.20
German	218	11.7	Ruthenian	4	0.20
Slovak	189	10.2	Dutch	4	0.20
Croatian	109	5.9	Asian Indian	3	0.20
American	67	3.6	Welsh	3	0.20
English	51	2.7	Syrian	3	0.20
Hungarian	45	2.4	Armenian	3	0.20
French	29	1.6	Chinese	2	0.10
Catholic	28	1.5	Bohemian	2	0.10
Slovenian	25	1.3	Belgian	2	0.10
Ukranian	24	1.3	Swiss	2	0.10
Slavic	18	1.0	American Indian	2	0.10
Russian	18	1.0	Indian (not		
Scotch-Irish	17	0.9	specified)	1	0.05
Lithuanian	15	0.8	Danish	1	0.05
Serbian	11	0.6	Jewish	1	0.05
Spanish	11	0.6	Presbyterian	1	0.05
Austrian	9	0.5	Russian Orthodox	1	0.05
Filipino	9	0.5	Greek Orthodox	1	0.05
Caucasian/White	9	0.5	Pennsylvania	1	0.05
Greek	8	0.4	Romanian	1	0.05
Byzantine Rite			Brazilian	1	0.05
Catholic	7	0.4	Turkic	1	0.05
African-American	7	0.4	Yugoslavian	1	0.05
Swedish	6	0.3	Korean	1	0.05
Hispanic		0.3	Laotian	1	0.05
Mexican/Columbian	6	0.3	Canadian	1	0.05
			Total*	1861	100.30

Source: Survey by author, 1989

*Some respondents did not indicate ethnicity, while others identified more than one, such as Italian and Irish; percentages are rounded up.

curred, then it is less likely that an individual would expect an image to close its eyes, or for a community of believers to accept that individual's experience as probable or true. Information is lacking on the regional patterns of shrine formation in Eastern Europe. Poland's and Croatia's proximity to Germany and Italy respectively, may be a link that would, in part, explain the spontaneous miracle of an image closing its eyes occurring in a Croation church and having such a high proportion of Polish devotees. This point is put forth for consideration because the author contends that preadaptation to the interpretation of a given human experience influences the integration of that experience for the individual and the community that identifies with it (Jordan 1989). That is, since spontaneous miracles associated with images are more commonly found in Italian and Germanic areas of Western Europe, then such an event is more likely to be believed by Italian and German Americans and less likely to be discounted by them. If the Ambridge area had been dominated by French and Iberian Catholics and not by Italian and Central European Catholics, then the response to information concerning the events of Good Friday may have been weaker. In fact, the miracle may have had a different character altogether.

Once the news of a miraculous event, such as that at Holy Trinity, goes beyond the experience of the individuals who first report it, the community of potential devotees has to determine the event's and the teller's believablity. One woman, calling Holy Trinity from New York City soon after the miracle, wanted to know if what had happened was a "real miracle" because she did not want to drive so far for nothing (Utterback 1989a). The question this woman raises is crucial to the formation of a pilgrimage shrine. If a person is going to travel to a place, in many cases a place to which they have never been to before, he or she usually has an important reason for doing so. Thus, authenticity of the shrine's sacrality presumes the potential success of the pilgrims' quest.

Holy Trinity pilgrims identified at least 14 general categories of reasons for visiting the church (table 4). Nearly 100 visitors stopped at Holy Trinity in passing, ostensibly out of curiosity. All shrines attract the curious, and in this case almost 7 percent of those surveyed visited the church for this reason. But most people had a more serious investment in the visitation of the shrine. Undoubtedly, hopes and desires are the focus of the pilgrimage experience for the faithful.

Approximately 60 percent of the respondents indicated a need to be close to the miracle, and, in that proximity to the miracle crucifix, derive inspiration and reaffirmation of their faith. Pilgrims expressed this need by such responses as: "I wanted to pray here," "I wanted to be close to a real miracle," "I believe in God and miracles," "I wanted to be in the prayer group," "I love Jesus," or "I wanted to praise God." Qualitatively, the above

Table 4. Pilgrim reasons for visting Holy Trinity

Reasons for visiting shrine	Number of pilgrims	% of total
To pray (mediate for inspiration or strength)	374	26.5
See the miracle (honor the miracle/be close to the miracle)	287	20.3
Ask for special favors	208	14.7
Belief in God (& in miracles)	150	10.6
To visit Mary & Jesus	117	8.3
Visit in passing (curiosity or only visiting family)	95	6.7
To get God's blessing (grace)	55	3.9
For mass/prayer group	27	1.9
Give thanks	26	1.8
I love Jesus	22	1.6
Praise God	20	1.4
Medjugorje	13	0.9
Called by God	8	0.6
Need hope	7	0.5
Other	4	0.3
Total*	1413	100.0

Source: Survey by author, 1989
* Some pilgrims did not respond to this question.

responses display a basic need to be close to an extraordinary thing or a place. The desire to be physically close to the supernatural, as it is understood by the devotees, is represented by the expression, "I wanted to visit Jesus," or "I wanted to visit Mary." Although less than 10 percent of the pilgrims made those statements, this type of response transcends the latter type in that it is straightforward about the physical presence of the supernatural, while the other statements only imply such a presence.

Finally, many pilgrims came to Holy Trinity because they believed that their requests might be answered. Asking specifically for God's grace was important, but requests for the cure of a loved one's illness and for a family member to find a job outnumbered the request for grace by nearly four to one. All of these responses are typical of pilgrims in many times and places, and the degree to which these pilgrims believe that their needs are met by the pilgrimage experience is the degree to which this formative shrine will sustain its new-found, extraordinary sacrality.

Eliadean Analysis

According to Eliade (1959, 11), that which is sacred, "...manifests itself, shows itself, as something wholly different from the profane." Hierophany literally means 'something sacred shows itself to us', and it is the term Eliade uses to indicate an experience of the sacred. For Christians, the most powerful of hierophanies is the incarnation of God in Jesus Christ (Eliade 1982, 408), while the most elementary of hierophanies would be the manifestation of the sacred in some ordinary object. For all practical purposes, the image of Christ on the crucifix is an ordinary object in Christian communities, and for that reason, the miracle at Ambridge would be considered an elementary hierophany.

The hierophanic nature of the event at Ambridge brings to bear a number of conditions that pertain to the formative sacrality and significance of the place and the pilgrims who visit it. These conditions include, but are not restricted to, the hierophany as paradox, as fixed point, and as a symbol of group experience.

Each and every hierophany is in and of itself a paradox because, as Eliade (1959, 11-12) indicates, even in the case of elementary hierophanies, any object becomes something else through the manifestation of the sacred, and yet it remains itself, since it continues to participate in its normal milieu. This paradox at once gives power and integrity to the believers and their faith, in that believers must be able to accept the paradox and then transcend it through faith for the hierophany to be possible in the first place. Thus, devotees who continue to visit Holy Trinity's crucifix have transcended the paradox implicit in the miracle, and, once transcended, the paradox of the miracle need not be questioned nor refuted. Therefore, the church's investigation only solves the mystery of what happened at Ambridge for non-believers and those who doubted the miracle from the beginning.

Furthermore, Eliade (1959, 21) points out that a hierophany, "...reveals an absolute fixed point ..." and, in doing so, possesses existential value for the faithful. The temporal and spatial fixed point orients believers and gives them direction, a direction that would have no meaning without an origin. For Christians, the absolute fixed point is the incarnation of God as Jesus Christ at a specific time and place. The world was literally 'created anew' by this magnificent hierophany (Campbell 1964, 334). This incarnation took on further significance at the death and resurrection of Christ, because it is through death and resurrection that a Christian becomes one with God. As time-distance decay occurs, from the fixed point, orientation of the believers may falter and, so, signs are needed to assist devotees in re-directing their faith. If a sign does not occur, it is provoked. Eliade (1959, 27) states that, "A *sign* is asked, to put an end to the tension and anxiety caused by relativity and disorientation...." A sign may be provoked and perceived in many ways, whether it be a physical event or merely a "feeling" that is acted upon by a devotee. What is crucial is the response of the community of believers when the sign manifests itself (Prorok 1986, 135). The Medjugorje prayer group needed such a sign, and the altar boys proved to be a valid and reliable vehicle for recognizing and reporting the hierophany. Moreover, the sign came from God through his incarnation in Christ. Thus, receiving the sign from God through a valid and believeable source, such as the young men who served mass, then orients the group during times of stress.

Finally, Eliade (1959, 211-212) explains that hierophanies are symbols through which humans find their way out of individual situations particular to themselves and open themselves to the general and universal. That is, "Symbols awaken individual experience and transmute it into a spiritual act, into a metaphysical comprehension of the world." Hierophanies are ultimate symbols, for by understanding the symbol, each and every believer succeeds in living in the universal (Eliade 1959, 212).

If the young man serving Mass had considered his experience with the crucifix peculiar, without context and unreasonable, then he probably would not have related his experience to the others, or if he did, it would have been in an offhand manner — a manner that would have discounted his belief in his own experience. But, the young man did not relate his extraordinary experience in an offhand manner for a number of reasons. First, the experience had the best context possible — a Good Friday Mass with the prayer group, a group intellectually and spiritually prepared to receive a sign. Secondly, the experience was eminently reasonable, given preadapted European, Christian notions of how the sacred manifests itself when an image of God is involved. Finally, the prayer group had most likely formed in response to the hard economic times faced by the Ambridge community, as well as a particularly strong connection to Medjugorje. It is probable that the group had been asking for a sign that they were doing the right thing: following a path that would lead them to solving their problems through God's intention. The hierophany was then reinforced by the "message" received by a prayer group member, clinching, if you will, the fixed point so necessary to the group's survival. Without the group's participation, the hierophany would not be a sign, but would only be a young man's personal experience. If that personal experience had been repudiated at the worst, or merely not supported at the least, then the young man's experience would have remained his personal fantasy, dream, or reverie. It was when his experience was recognized, accepted, and, moreover, exalted, that it became the group's experience and so was ontologically raised to the status of myth or miracle. It is precisely due to group acceptance that this place takes on its sacred significance, a significance that can only be sustained if individuals are continually able to integrate their personal world with that which the miracle symbolizes.

Conclusion

The miracle associated with the crucifix at Holy Trinity in Ambridge drew national attention to this small Pennsylvania town. The church and its image of Christ has taken on extraordinary sacredness since March of 1989, ostensibly from the believeability for the faithful of the experiences of the Medjugorje prayer group and the need to reaffirm one's faith. Eliade's concept of hierophany as a paradox to be transcended, as an event that fixes a point in the history of a devotee's faith, and as a group experience is well illustrated by the phenomena occurring in Ambridge. Thousands of people have visited the incipient pilgrimage shrine since that remarkable day in March in order to share the experience of the parishioners of Holy Trinity.

According to James Hannigan, a theologian at Duquesne University, the situation at Ambridge may be a part of a series of what are believed to be miraculous events, such as the apparitions in Lubbock, Texas, and Tickfaw, Louisiana, in 1989. Events like these have been reported in greater numbers in the United States since the phenomena of Medjugorje became well known in the early 1980s (Milbank 1989; Van Biema 1991). This wave of extraordinary events may only be a temporary phase in American Catholic life that weakens and then is forgotton within a relatively short time after the occurrence of the miracles, or they may be the beginning of a new era in shrine formation (Warner 1996).

If an incipient shrine like the one in Ambridge is to sustain its newfound sacrality, then people will have to continue having extraordinary experiences there, and they will have to share those experiences with friends and family. This sharing of experience motivates new pilgrims to visit Ambridge, and thereby sustains a cycle of new, potentially wondrous events and an ever-growing pilgrim population. The Nolans (1989, 247) explain that:

> One may conceptualize a kind of critical mass of sick persons. Once a certain level of visitation is reached, it is almost certain that cures will be credited to pilgrimages to the place. Cures will be said to stem from the journey in itself, from touching the cult object, or from drinking water from the shrine spring or well if there is one....As the stories are embellished and spread, there will be vows to make a pilgrimage to the shrine if one or one's loved ones get well. Among any large group of sick persons, some generally recover; thus, the shrine's ability to attract pilgrims grows.

This process is a difficult one in that a shrine has to attract a large number of pilgrims from the outset in order to increase the potential for sustaining extraordinary sacredness. Also, official sanction from the Church may create greater credibility for the shrine's sacrality, thereby increasing the potential number of pilgrims who will visit the cult object in the first place. Local and initial visitors to a potential shrine site often do need official Church sanction to continue believing in the efficacy of the shrine's sacredness, or a great number of visitors to a shrine site, and their consequent wondrous experiences, may preclude the need of Church sanction to sustain the shrine's sacrality. Nolan and Nolan (1989, 289) explain that the sparsity of modern pilgrimage shrines in Europe does not indicate a lack of contemporary sacred experiences that would lead to formation of a shrine, but instead represents the difficulty of receiving official church sanction and establishing continued pilgrimage to the modern shrine.

Lack of ecclesiastical toleration is related to the problem of modern pilgrimage shrine formation. Over 200 reports of apparitions have occurred in Western Europe since 1931, but only a few gained recognition by the Church. Many attracted a significant number of pilgrims and attention for a short time, but did not become an enduring place of pilgrimage (Nolan and Nolan 1989, 289). Establishment of a shrine is an attempt by lay people, assisted in part by local priests, to establish the appearance of the sacred, the ineffable, within their domain. The ecclesiastical hierarchy, using the reforms of Vatican II, whereby the word is privileged over icon, often rejects their attempt and reasserts it authority. Thus, the story of the shrine is not so much about why people would believe the eyes of an icon opened and shut, but about a conflict between the local parish and the hierarchy, and ultimately between icon and word. If the icon wins, a shrine is formed; if the word wins, it is only a "miracle" — a false understanding of the ineffable (Miles Richardson, personal correspondence 1995).

Will the miracle at Ambridge endure? If it does, it will be one of a few places of pilgrimage in the United States. This formative shrine certainly has the potential for enduring, despite the lack of ecclesiastical toleration. At the very least the miracle will endure in the minds and hearts of local devotees, and at best the possibility exists that the new shrine will become an enduring center of extraordinary sacredness in a modern desacralized world.

Acknowledgments

The author thanks Father Vincent Cvitkovic and the Holy Trinity pilgrims and parishioners for their assistance and participation in this study. Daphne Goh Tai Hoon and Melissa Sloan were particularly helpful for their assistance in data processing and display, and Mary Lee Eggart did the artwork.

A shorter version of this paper first appeared in *Scholars*, a publication of Pennsylvania's State System of Higher Education.

References

Andriot, J. 1983. *Population abstract of the United States*, vol. 1, McLean, Va: Andriot Associates.

Anonymous. 1981. History of the Holy Trinity Croatian Roman Catholic Church. Church paper. Ambridge, PA.

Bainton, R. H. 1974. *Behold the Christ*. NY: Harper & Row.

BBC — British Broadcasting Service. 1986. Madonna of Medjugorje. *Everyman Series*. London: BBC.

Campbell, J. 1964. *Occidental Mythology*. The Masks of God Series. NY: Penguin Books.

Card, T. P. 1989. Periodic reports. *Beaver County Times*. March to August. Beaver, Pa.

Cosgrove and Meurer Productions. 1989. Report on the miracle at Ambridge. "Unsolved Mysteries." September 9, 1989.

Couvares, F. G. 1984. *The remaking of Pittsburgh: Class and culture in an industrialized city, 1877-1919*, Albany: SUNY Press.

Eliade, M. 1959. *The sacred and the profane: The nature of religion*. W. R. Trask, trans. NY: Harcourt, Brace & Co.

——. 1982. *A history of religious ideas: From Gautama Buddha to the triumph of Christianity*. Chicago: University of Chicago Press.

Faiers, G. and C. V. Prorok. 1989. Pilgrimage to a "national" American Shrine: Our Lady of Consolation in Carey, Ohio." *Geographia Religionum* 5:137-147.

Fodiak, W. 1989. "Commission: No miracle in Ambridge." *Pittsburgh Catholic*, July 7, p. 1.

Gigler, R. 1989. "Pastor resigns at church of reported Good Friday miracle." *Pittsburgh Press*, August 14, sec. B1.

Guo, D. 1989. "Panel: Crucifix didn't blink." *Pittsburgh Post-Gazette*. July 6, pp. 1, 4.

Haynes, M. 1989. "'Miracle in Ambridge' church pastor resigns." *Pittsburgh Post-Gazette*. August 14, p. 1.

Ireton, G. 1989. "Mary seen: Couple among Medjugorje witnesses." *Pittsburgh Post-Gazette*. April 1, 1989, sec. B4.

Jordan, T. 1989. Preadaptation and European colonization in rural North America. *Annals of the Association of American Geographers* 79:489-500.

Milbank, D. 1989. "Miracles: They seem to come in waves." *Pittsburgh Post-Gazette*. July 6, 1989, p. 4.

Nolan, M. L. and S. Nolan. 1989. *Christian pilgrimage in modern Western Europe*. Chapel Hill: University of North Carolina Press.

Papale, R. A. 1989a. "Message links Yugoslavian town to local parish." *Beaver County Times*. March 28, sections A1, A8.

——. 1989b. "Diocese: No miracle," *Beaver County Times*, July 6, sections A1, A8.

Prorok, C. V. 1986. The Hare Krishna's transformation of space in West Virginia. *Journal of Cultural Geography* 7:129-40.

Toker, F. 1986. *Pittsburgh: An urban portrait*. University Park: Pennsylvania State University Press.

Twedt, S. and M. Hasch. 1989. 150 witness Good Friday "apparition" in Ambridge. *Pittsburgh Press*. March 27, sections A1, A4.

Utterback, D. 1989a. Hundreds flock to church to see "miracle." *Beaver County Times*. March 27, sections A1, A8.

——. 1989b. They come to witness a "miracle." *Beaver County Times*. March 28, sections A1, A8.

Van Biema, D. 1991. "Miracles, U.S.A." *Life* 9 (July 14): 38-39.

Wagner, E. M. 1924. *Economy of old and Ambridge of today*. Ambridge: Citizen Print.

Warner, Marina. 1996. Blood and Tears, *New Yorker* 8 (April): 63-69).

Section III:
PILGRIMAGES IN THE MUSLIM TRADITION

The Pilgrimage to Mecca and the Centrality of Islam

Gwyn Rowley
University of Sheffield

Abstract

Islam may be conceived as a plurality of individuals who, through shared expectations and experiences, take one another into account and are aware of a commonality. Much of this commonality is based on a system of information sharing, which is significantly enhanced by the Hajj.

Commonality is partly encouraged by the *hadith* or discussion circles, which are held between Hajj participants and sheiks (teachers). The process of dispersal and diffusion is further achieved when pilgrims return to their home communities. Likewise, a sense of belongingness is cultivated by *mutawifs* and their assistants, *wakeels*, who guide and serve pilgrims during their time in Mecca. By serving as travel agents for thousands of pilgrims prior to and during their performance of the Hajj, the mutawifs establish a link between pilgrims' homes and their common focus on the pilgrimage destination.

The annual number of pilgrims has been increasing in recent decades, not only from the increased world population of Muslims and the improved means of transportation, but also from the institutional support that reinforces and disseminates Islamic information. Activities centralized in Mecca, therefore, contribute to both a religious commonality and a concurrent desire within a growing population to perform the Hajj.
Key words: pilgrimage, Hajj, Mecca, religious commonality.

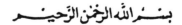

Sacred Places, Sacred Spaces: The Geography of Pilgrimages, edited by Robert H. Stoddard and Alan Morinis, 1997. Geoscience and Man, vol. 34, pp. 141-159. Dept. of Geography and Anthropology, Louisiana State University, Baton Rouge, LA 70893-6010.

وَأَذِّن فِى ٱلنَّاسِ بِٱلْحَجِّ يَأْتُوكَ رِجَالًا

وَعَلَىٰ كُلِّ ضَامِرٍ يَأْتِينَ مِن كُلِّ

فَجٍّ عَمِيقٍ "

صدق الله العظيم

And proclaim unto mankind the pilgrimage.
They will come unto thee on foot and every
lean camel; they will come from every deep ravine.

Holy Qur'an

Most Westerners view pilgrimages as cultural artifacts of a bygone day. For Islam, however, the pilgrimage to Mecca, the Hajj, is of a vital and precise importance (Burton 1893). Indeed, to comprehend its essentiality and purpose, the Hajj must be considered not simply as pilgrimage but as the fifth pillar of Islam that inexorably interrelates with the four other pillars or foundations of the faith. It must be viewed as part of the essential and overall unity of Islam in its spatial embrace.

Unlike other pilgrimages, the Hajj is in no way devoted to nor concerned with the glorification or sanctification of either a person nor any of the places and shrines being visited (Pfaffenberger 1983). Rather, the rituals represent a re-enactment of the Prophet Muhammed's obedience and submission to the injunctions and the will of God — the essence of Islam.

This paper will demonstrate the pivotal and centralizing nature of Islamic space, its dimensions, extents, and vitality, and will consider the importance of the Hajj in reinforcing the overall unity of Islam as a vibrant and interacting cultural realm. Some elements of the Hajj will be outlined, its tributary regions will be considered, and the recent and future growth of the Hajj will be evaluated.

The Religious Background for Islamic Pilgrimage

One contribution of the human geographer is the presentation of orderly descriptions and understandings of the human world. Geographically, pilgrimages, which are movements to places or points, can be considered as intricate spatial structures comprised of linkages and patterns that present complex interrelationships. The view here is that the overall integration of points, areas, and their linkages should be of particular concern because such a unified system can assist in our understandings of the human world.

In our present context, we must realize that, although the human geographer often views religion partly within an institutional framework that comprehends personal and shared beliefs concerning the supernatural, religion can also be considered as a complex of culture traits; a kind of group behavior, a reflection of different life styles, and a basis for both social integration and social conflict. For the geographer, one part of an academic problem is frequently to discover "composition and meaning of the geographic aggregate that we as yet recognize somewhat vaguely as the culture area" (Sauer 1962, 34).

Religion, according to Durkheim (1965, 7), is "a unified system of beliefs and practices relative to sacred things ... which unite into a single moral community, called a church, all those who adhere to them." A church in this sense is, in many ways, akin to a cultural region (Hicks 1976, 20).

An additional and fundamental factor in Durkheim's definition of religion (1965, 41) was his insistence that the beliefs be shared by an organized group:

> Religious beliefs are always common to a determined group, which makes a profession of adhering to them and of practicing the rites concerned with them.

Beliefs and rituals are thus forms of conduct that people share in groups within a framework of norms, roles, and other organizational components. Reflecting Barrington Moore's approach (1950), the moral order appropriate to any particular society has a necessary connection with the institutional forms within which thought and practice are expressed.

Furthermore, Durkheim stated (1965, 36):

> All known religious beliefs, whether simple or complex, present one common characteristic: they presuppose a classification of all things, real and ideal, of which men

think, into two distinct terms which are translated well enough by the words *profane* and *sacred.*

Durkheim viewed this distinction between the sacred and profane as absolute, as two quite distinct classes, with the sacred consisting of things "set apart, and forbidden" — that is, things and ideas considered as transcendent or ultimate. Once the sacred has been isolated, rites and rituals may be developed as rules of conduct that will bring man to confront the sacred.

Islam may thus be conceived as a plurality of individuals who, through shared expectations and experiences, are in contact with one another, who take one another into account, and who are aware of the significant commonality (Shils 1957). This is especially evident in the fundamental Islamic belief in the unity and oneness of God (*tawheed*). Throughout Islam such a commonality underlies developments on the macrocosmic political and social levels and serves further to differentiate Islam. Islam overall, as a vibrant community, is a fine example of this complexity.

Much of this commonality is based on a system of information sharing. Lévi-Strauss (1958) has emphasized that primitive religious systems are, like all symbolic systems, carriers of information in the technical Shannon-Weaver sense. Within Islam, this transfer of information and rededication to the pilgrimage plays a central regulative role, both to the person and to the community as a whole, by attuning human actions to a view of cosmic order and design.

Events of the Hajj
The Rites of the Hajj

According to Islamic law, every Muslim has to perform Hajj at least once in the course of one's lifetime, provided that health and other personal and family circumstances permit (Qur'an 3:96-7). The Hajj, literally "to visit the holy places," itself incorporates a number of quite specific rites and duties only to be performed by the *hajjis* (pilgrims) at quite precise times and locations in a specified order in the region in and about Mecca (the Haram). The related yet optional Al-Ziyarah, the visit to the tomb and mosque of the Prophet Muhammed in Medina, is undertaken either before or following the prime pilgrimage (Burton 1893; King 1972; Isaac 1973; Rowley and El-Hamdan 1977a).

Muslims, of course, may and do visit Mecca at other times outside the period of the designated pilgrimage (Din and Hadi, this volume). However, the Umrah (or the Lesser Pilgrimage) is not Hajj and pilgrims who undertake such a visit to Mecca and its holy places are not hajjis.

The Hajj itself commences on the eighth day of the twelfth month (Dhul-Hijjah 8) of the lunar year and ends on the thirteenth day (Dhul-Hijjah 13), a total of six days. The hajji performs the prescribed rites of prayers and physical movements to the various sites in the same order as the farewell pilgrimage performed by the Prophet Muhammed in A.D. 632.

The pilgrim enters into *ihram*, a state of physical and spiritual consecration to God, symbolized by donning the Ihram dress, comprised of two plain unsown white cloths and a pair of sandals. These are worn throughout the Hajj. Then the pilgrim commences a set of activities that requires considerable movement (fig. 1).

The main day of the Hajj occurs on Dhul-Hijjah 9. On this day it is preferable that the pilgrims arrive in Arafat (from Mina) before midday. After completing the midday prayer, the pilgrims return to their campsites and begin the "Standing in Arafat" (the Waqoof), which, in the words of the Holy Prophet, is the Hajj itself. In essence, the pilgrims gather on the Plains of Arafat and, while facing Mecca, meditate and pray until just before sunset. After sunset the pilgrims move to Musdalifah, collecting either 49 or 70 pebbles for use in the rites of the following day.

Early on Dhul-Hijjah 10 the pilgrims return to Mina to "Stone the Devils," symbolized by the casting of seven stones at one of three pillars, thereby signifying one's repudiation of all evil. Following the stoning, the pilgrim purchases a sheep or a part thereof for ritual slaughter in memory of Abraham's (Ibrahim's) willingness to sacrifice his son and to give thanks to God. On this particular day (Eid-al-adha), all Muslims throughout the world reaffirm Tawheed and its earthy manifestation in the community of Islam by conducting similar ritual slaughterings.

This ritual slaughter completes the major portion of the Hajj but other rituals remain to be accomplished: the journey to the Al-Haram mosque in Mecca, the circling (*tawaf*) of the Ka'bah (which is considered here to be the same as the sanctum sanctorum) seven times, the kissing of the Black Stone (Hajar al-Aswad) embedded in the Ka'bah, and "the running" (*sa'y*) in memory of Haggar's search for water for the infant Ishmael at Wedi Zamzam (Rowley and El-Hamdan 1977a).

Hajj-Islam Interaction

The overall unity of Islam and its powers of reinforcement through Hajj is demonstrated by the *hadith* or discussion circles. At the time of the pilgrimage, hadith are held by hajjis (participants in the Hajj) and sheiks (teachers) in and about Mecca. Such groups, ranging from formal seminars and conferences to informal discussion groups, are concerned with Islamic interpretations and views on problems of modern life as in family, education, and personal relationships. At its simplest level, the group

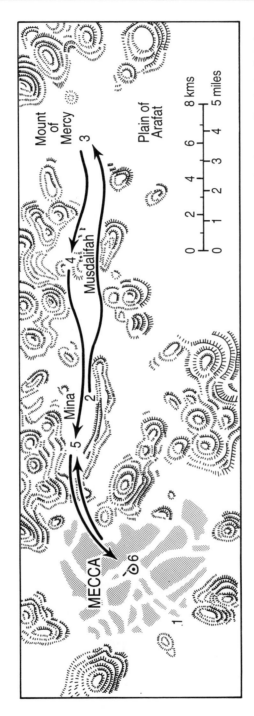

Fig. 1. Pilgrim site activities about Mecca: 1) enter Al Haram after donning the Ihram; 2) move to Mina; 3) "The Standing in Arafat"; 4) move to Musdalifah; 5) return to Mina, stone the devils, and perform the sacrifice; 6) make the Tawaf and kiss the Hajar al-Aswad.

consideration of ideas and values consists of a process of pooling whereby new learning takes place and from inchoate searchings clarifications emerge. Such views are derived from specific Islamic principles.

Whereas hadith-group composition is primarily dependent on nationality and language, facility in spoken Arabic by hajjis does result in considerable cross-fertilization, break-downs and recompositions of the primary discussion groups. Much interaction thus arises between groups and individuals. Of particular concern is the great deal of feedback that occurs throughout Islam. This process of information-dispersal from Mecca, as the center of diffusion and dissemination via the contact fields of returning hajjis, points to a research area of exciting and major dimensions. Such continuing processes of contagious diffusion through Islamic space furthers the base cultural continuity (Brown 1982).

Some Effects of the Hajj

The effect of the pilgrimage is clearly demonstrated in private sector employment, which accounts for more than 16 percent of the total employment within the five cities of Mecca (380,000), Medina (210,000), Jiddah (600,000), Taif (205,000), and Yanbu (36,000). Pilgrims provide a basis for hotel, transport, retailing, and financial services. Indeed, the last three decades have witnessed quite massive investments within the regional infrastructure to accommodate and serve the pilgrims. Improvements to local and international transport services include new super highways and greatly enlarged air and sea terminals at Jiddah (Rowley and El-Hamdan 1977b).

Another impact of the Hajj is the employment of persons who assist pilgrims, namely, the *mutawif*s. Prior to traveling, the intending pilgrim consults a copy of *The Pilgrims Guide* (Ministry of the Hajj and Waqifs 1984), which provides an outline of the practical problems that might arise and how to overcome them. It also gives information about arranging the pilgrimage, particularly in the introduction to the mutawif. The position of the mutawif is of prime importance in any understanding of how the average Muslim undertakes the pilgrimage. The mutawif's main function is to act as a travel agent and courier, to guide and serve the pilgrims during their visits to the holy places.[1]

Three thousand mutawifs are registered in Mecca. A third are essentially corporate business operators owning accommodations and receiving pilgrims in their own name, while the remainder are employed as assistants by the former group to assist and guide the pilgrims. A mutawif is contacted prior to the pilgrim's departure from home and complete arrangements are then made ahead of time by the mutawif and various assistants.

In addition to guiding pilgrims to the holy places and leading them in the performance of the rites and rituals, the mutawif service includes obtaining lodging in Mecca and Medina, and transport between the various sites. Typical accommodation in Mecca is in large dormitory blocks occupied by perhaps ten hajjis per room during the period of the Hajj. Such blocks are often empty for the remainder of the year.

The most successful mutawifs receive more than 20,000 pilgrims a year while others may cater to as few as a thousand. In 1986, the average charge for guidance was SR150 (US$45) per hajji while costs of accommodation, subsistence, and transportation within the Haram were extra. On the average, the hajji stays only two weeks in the Haram. In 1986, two-thirds of all pilgrims stayed for fewer than 30 days and only 6.2 percent remained for more than 70 days.

The mutawif profession tends to be hereditary. Formerly mutawifs catered to pilgrims from a certain country, with the mutawif speaking the country's language or languages. A survey taken in 1986 by El-Hamdan and Rowley (1986) indicates that over 43 percent of the mutawifs still cater to a single nationality.

Related to the mutawif is the *wakeel*, located in Jiddah, who operates as an agent or receptionist, usually for three or four mutawifs. The duties of the wakeel include meeting the pilgrims at the port of entry (sea, air, or road), attending to visas, health records, and perhaps accommodations in Jiddah, and arranging for their onward transportation to Mecca.

Overall, the organization and planning for the Hajj is the responsibility of the Ministry of the Hajj, a separate department of the Royal Government of Saudi Arabia. The constraints imposed on the space within the Mecca region and on time during Dhul-Hijjah 8-13 by the pilgrimage are now affecting specific planning procedures designed to facilitate and control pilgrim access to the Mecca region. At present, pilgrim quotas are in operation for most countries to offset problems of "excess numbers" which would create unacceptable levels of congestion at the various sites.[2]

Recent and Continuing Growth of the Hajj
Perspectives on Islam

Although a prime focus of this paper is on the continuity of the Hajj and the quite astounding recent growth in the numbers undertaking this pilgrimage, a background on the so-called Islamic resurgence requires some attention first. This is necessary to comprehend the continuity and ebullience of the Hajj, and of Islam itself (Watt 1961).

The Islamic community has been viewed in a variety of ways. What may be termed an ostensibly dominant and pervasive Imperialist worldview sees "superior" Western válues and "modernization" — indeed, "civilization" — as coming into contact with an essentially "peripheral" native or lower form of exotic culture. These "localisms" are then overcome or modified (Wallerstein 1983). Others view this "development" and supposed modernization as, in reality, a lumpen-Europeanization which destroys peripheral societies by overriding their culture and reduces "underdeveloped" areas to a type of dependency through domination from the "core." The goal of the economic core is to incorporate the periphery into the hegemonic capitalist world (Blaut 1987).

The economic primacy of the West has likewise been translated to the socio-cultural realm, stressing the superiority of Christendom and Western values. Confrontations with Islam, however, were always something quite different. Muslims recognized Islam itself as a core possessing specific values and as having an ascendancy and dynamism that overrode the viewpoints of the newcomers. That sense of centrality and equality — even superiority — is now becoming increasingly manifest within an Islamic resurgence.

Indeed, this Islamic resurgence and mounting disdain for Western values may be considered appropriately as a constancy of the base values and objectives of Islam. This contrasts with what may be considered a decline of Western systems with their increasing uncertainties and doubts about the primacy and resolution from within the West itself, the decline of religiosity, the break-up and erosion of traditional family structures, the disillusionment of youth, and the direct questioning of Western industrial-capitalist structures and work-ethic (Amin et al. 1982).

Numbers of Pilgrims

This mounting ebullience and vitality of Islam is associated closely with the growth of the Hajj itself. Since 1950 there has been an overall increase in the number of pilgrims undertaking the Hajj (fig. 2). In 1932, 90,662 foreign pilgrims entered Saudi Arabia, but the number rose to 100,471 in 1951 and a six-fold increase to 645,182 was achieved by 1973. The 1986 figure for foreign pilgrims was 1.64 million and, including those from Saudi Arabia, the total amount was more than 2.25 million. In the 1990s, the annual number of pilgrims has consistently exceeded three million.

During the later 1980s, the total number of hajjis increased to 2.8 million, of which over a half a million were from Saudi Arabia itself. Africa provided some 250,000 pilgrims per year, with almost a half of this total deriving from Nigeria. Arab countries, beside Saudi Arabia, contributed some one million pilgrims, with over 100,000 from both Egypt and Iraq, and some 75,000 from both Algeria and the Yemen. Syria, Libya, Morocco, and Jordan each contributed about 50,000 pilgrims per year. Over a million hajjis a year have come from further afield in Asia, notably Turkey (180,000), Pakistan (140,000), Indonesia (160,000), Iran (100,000), and India

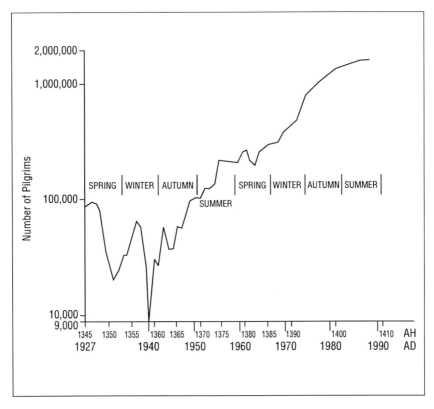

Fig. 2. The numbers of foreign pilgrims to the Hajj, 1927-1986. *Source*: Ministry of the Hajj, 1986.

(60,000). Of particular note is the recent increase in the number of hajjis from the countries of Central Asia, which were formerly republics of the Soviet Union.

The present overall rate of increase is likely to continue, and in 2-3 years to expand again quite markedly with the seasonal shift of the Hajj from summer to spring.[3] The expected increase is partly related to the increase of Muslims in the world. As of 1987, the overall population of Islam was conservatively estimated at 850 million (some 19-20 percent of the total human population). That figure is obtained by updating Weekes' early 1970s data (table 1) and making some allowance for external expansions (Weekes 1978; Institute of Muslim Affairs 1987). Islamic populations are increasing internally by some 3 percent or more per annum, while external conversions, especially from animistic sects in Africa and among Blacks in North America, point to even further growth. Updated data on world

Table 1. Muslim peoples of the world, 1977

Country	Total Population (1,000)	Muslim population (1,000)	% Muslim
Aden	1,250	1,225	98
Afghanistan	14,500	14,355	99
Albania	2,500	1,750	70
Algeria	17,800	17,266	97
Bahrain	300	273	91
Bangladesh	83,300	70,805	85
Benin	3,300	528	16
Bulgaria	8,800	924	10
Burma	31,800	1,272	4
Burundi	3,900	39	1
Cameroon	6,700	1,005	15
Central African Republic	1,900	95	5
Chad	4,200	2,100	50
China, PRC	850,000	17,850	2
Comoro Islands	314	251	80
Congo	1,400	14	1
Cyprus	600	108	18
Djibouti	114	107	94
Egypt	38,900	35,400	91
Ethiopia	29,400	11,760	40
France	53,400	534	1
Gabon	500	5	1
Gambia	600	540	90
Gaza	400	360	90
Ghana	10,400	1,976	19
Greece	9,100	182	2
Guinea	4,700	3,055	65
India	622,700	80,805	13
Indonesia	136,900	123,210	90
Iran	34,800	34,104	98
Iraq	11,800	11,210	95
Israel	3,600	288	8
Ivory Coast	7,000	1,750	25
Japan	114,200	1	-
Jordan	2,900	2,697	93
Kampuchea	8,000	96	1
Kenya	14,400	1,296	9
Kuwait	1,100	1,023	93
Lebanon	2,800	1,428	51
Liberia	1,700	255	15

(continued)

Table 1. (*continued*)

Country	Total Population (1,000)	Muslim population (1,000)	% Muslim
Libya	2,700	2,646	98
Madagascar	7,900	553	7
Malawi	5,300	795	15
Malaysia	12,600	5,544	44
Maldive Islands	100	100	100
Mali	5,900	3,540	60
Mauritania	1,400	1,344	96
Mauritius	900	153	17
Mongolia	1,500	143	10
Morocco	18,300	17,385	95
Mozambique	9,500	950	10
Niger	4,900	4,165	85
Nigeria	66,600	31,302	47
Oman	800	800	100
Pakistan	74,500	72,265	97
Philippines	44,300	2,348	5
Qatar	100	100	100
Romana	21,700	173	1
Rwanda	4,500	23	-
Saudi Arabia	7,600	7,220	95
Senegal	5,300	4,326	82
Sierra Leone	3,200	960	30
Singapore	2,300	345	15
Somalia	3,400	3,366	99
South Africa	26,100	313	1
Sri Lanka	14,100	1,128	8
Sudan	16,300	11,736	72
Surinam	400	80	20
Syria	7,800	6,786	87
Taiwan	16,600	20	-
Tanzania	16,000	3,840	24
Thailand	44,400	1,776	4
Togo	2,300	161	7
Trinidad and Tobago	1,100	66	6
Tunisia	6,000	5,520	92
Turkey	41,900	41,062	98
Uganda	12,400	744	6
United Arab Emirates	200	184	92
United States	216,700	807	-
U.S.S.R.	259,000	52,311	19
Upper Volta	6,400	1,408	22

(*continued*)

Table 1. *(concluded)*

Country	Total Population (1,000)	Muslim population (1,000)	% Muslim
Vietnam	47,300	52	-
Western Sahara	138	110	80
Yemen, Arab Republic	5,600	5,544	99
Yemen, Peoples Republic	1,800	2,620	90
Yugoslavia	21,800	4,142	19
Zaire	26,300	526	2
Zambia	5,200	52	1
Zimbabwe	6,800	3	-
Total		740,701	

Source: Weekes 1978

Muslim populations are to be released by the Institute of Muslim Affairs in late 1997. In the mid-1990s, however, the total Muslim population in the world is estimated at well over 1,000 million.

The continuing expansion of many Muslim economies, with more financial opportunities afforded to a wider range of people, also suggests that the potential number of pilgrims will continue to grow markedly over the next several years. Likewise, easier, faster (making possible shorter periods away from employment and home responsibilities), and relatively cheaper methods of transportation also point to an ever-increasing proportion of potential pilgrims. Indeed, for many, the pilgrimage can now be accommodated within the period of an annual vacation.

Travel Modes to the Hajj

Modes of travel to the Hajj partly reflect the world distribution of Muslims. The main concentration is in the northern hemisphere in Asia and Africa, extending in a broad belt from Senegal in the west to the southern Philippines and eastern Indonesia in the east (figs. 3 and 4).

From 1963, major changes have occurred in the methods of transport utilized by the pilgrims (fig. 5). Data on the origin and mode of arrival of pilgrims assembled by the Saudi authorities (Central Department of Statistics 1971-1986) reveal that air and land travel have increased dramatically in popularity at the expense of sea travel. Maritime travel accounted for 78 percent of foreign pilgrims arriving in Saudi Arabia in 1950 but only 19 percent in 1986. In 1950, 13 percent travelled by air but 52 percent did so in 1986. Likewise, in overland travel, the figures of 10 percent in 1950 rose to 29 percent in 1986. Furthermore, it is expected that both air and land

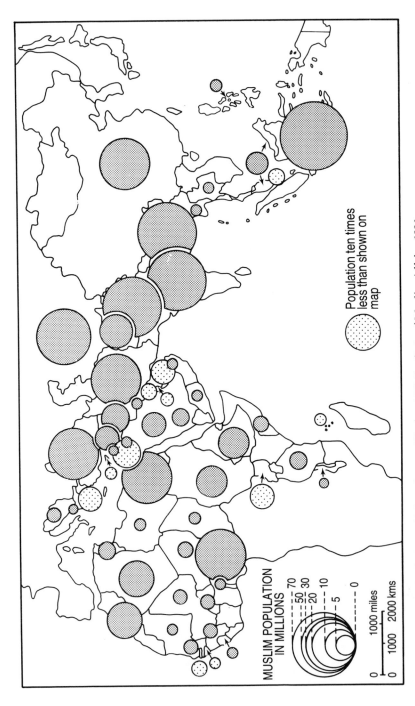

Fig. 3. The Muslim populations of Islam. *Sources:* Weekes 1978; Institute of Muslim Affairs, 1986.

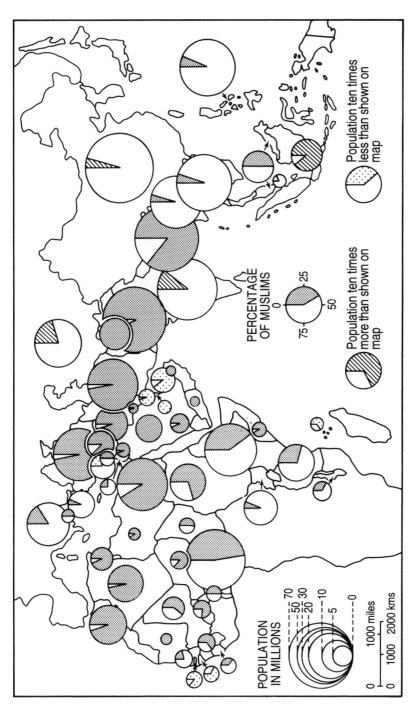

Fig. 4. Muslim components of total populations by country. *Sources:* Weekes 1978; Institute of Muslim Affairs, 1986.

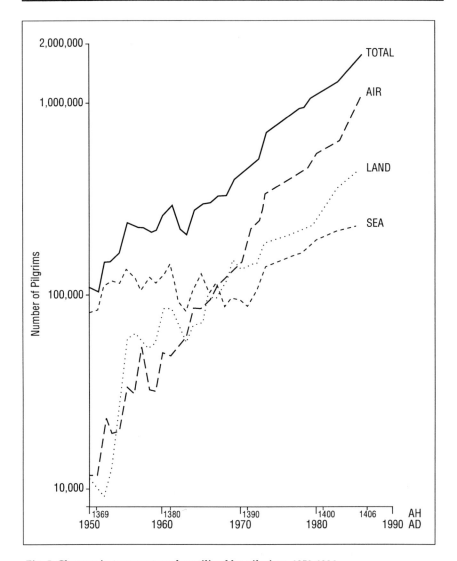

Fig. 5. Changes in transport modes utilized by pilgrims, 1950-1986.

routes will continue to make quite significant inroads into traditional sea transport.

In every country from which pilgrims travel, there are two or three methods of transport available, depending on their location relative to Saudi Arabia and maritime waters. During the period of study, countries from which more than 75 percent of the pilgrims travelled to the pilgrimage overland — by private automobile, truck, or bus — were adjacent to Saudi Arabia but also included the then Yugoslavia, Turkey, and Afghanistan (fig. 6). Pilgrims from Oman and particularly the eastern regions of south Yemen (the Hadramaut) have to contend with the difficult physical barrier of the Rub'al-Khali. From Oman they have a choice between air and sea; and from south Yemen pilgrims travel by air, sea, and land (Shair 1983).

Countries where pilgrims favor air travel include the north and west African countries and Iran. In 1986, the dominance of air travel to the Hajj from Iran resulted from the Iraqi-Iranian conflict. From Egypt, the percentage of hajjis travelling by land was less than 9 and by sea less than 1. Nigeria still had a sizeable but diminishing percentage of hajjis who traveled by sea (8.7), but the remainder flew. Travel by air was generally increasing in importance in Malaysia (see Din and Hadi, this volume), the Philippines, Thailand, and India; while overland transport accounted for 21.07% from Pakistan.

These data, however, refer to the mode of arrival in Saudi Arabia. Pilgrims from Chad and Niger, for example, travel overland to Port Sudan, then via ship to Jiddah. Their mode of travel to Saudi Arabia is then recorded as having been by sea.

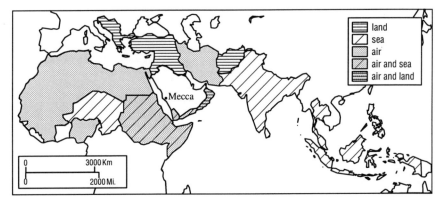

Fig. 6. Predominant modes of transport utilized by pilgrims (for countries with more than 2000 pilgrims annually).

Summary and Concluding Remarks

Human geographers have a role in the study of the Hajj because their viewpoints have a particular pertinence and relevance in developing understandings of structures. They seek to explore the cultural-communal frameworks and moral paradigms that underlie the external world and the agents in the process of "community maintenance and reinforcement" (Bernstein 1979, 224).

Indeed, the prospects for exciting research on the Hajj have received particular attention by the Social Sciences Research Council (SRRC) in the United States, with its program being orchestrated by the Joint Committee on the Comparative Study of Muslim Societies. Metcalf (1986, 6), in her then capacity as chair of that SRRC committee, emphasized "a pressing need" in the West "for more serious information" and its dissemination to a larger public on the deeper realities, dimensions, and base constancy of Islam and Muslim societies.

This brief essay has sought to demonstrate the overall unity of Islam that is perpetuated and, indeed, reinforced through the Hajj. The Muslim vision of the return of everything to its source in God (Allah) underlies the conception of God and fellowship in that quest. Thus, any study of Hajj that does not consider its functional, interactive perspective will fail to appreciate that constancy which is achieved through submission to the will of Allah, the quintessence of Islam.

Because the injunction to make the pilgrimage is strong and the desire of Muslims to visit Mecca is vital, the greater ease of transportation has resulted in increasing numbers of pilgrims. This increase in numbers, combined with participation by pilgrims in institutions which function to reinforce and disseminate Islamic information and values throughout the Muslim world, reinforces the overall unity of Islam as a vibrant and interacting cultural realm.

Notes

1. Many of the mutawif's services, therefore, resemble those provided by a Hindu paṇḍā (see Caplan, this volume).

2. Such quotas derive directly from the evaluations and recommendations of Rowley and El-Hamdan (1977b; 1978; and El-Hamdan and Rowley 1986).

3. The Muslim lunar year is 11 days shorter than the Gregorian year; hence, from the Western perspective, each year the Hajj occurs 11 days earlier than the previous year.

References

Amin, S., G. Arrighi, A. G. Frank, and I. Wallerstein.1982. *Dynamics of global crisis*. New York: Monthly Review Press.

Bernstein, R. J. 1979. *The restructuring of social and political theory*. London: Methuen.

Blaut, J. M. 1987. Diffusionism: A uniformitarian critique. *Annals of the Association of American Geographers* 77:30-47.

Brown, L. A. 1982. *Innovation diffusion*. London: Methuen.

Burton, R. F. 1893. *Personal narrative of a pilgrimage to al-Madinah and Meccah*, 2 v. London: Tylston and Edwards.

Central Department of Statistics. 1971-1986. *Statistical yearbooks 1391 AH - 1404 AH.* Riyadh: Ministry of Finance, Royal Government of Saudi Arabia.

Durkheim, E. 1965. *The elementary forms of religious life.* Trans. by J. W. Swain. New York: The Free Press.

Gibbs, H. A. R., and J. H. Kramer. 1961. *Shorter encyclopaedia of Islam.* Leiden: Brill.

El-Hamdan, S. A. S., and G. Rowley. 1986. *The Hajj, 1404, interim report on reception and direction criteria.* Riyadh: Ministry of the Hajj and Waqifs and Ministry of Municipal and Rural Affairs, Royal Government of Saudi Arabia.

Hicks, D. 1976. *Tetum ghosts and kin: Fieldwork in an Indonesian community.* Palo Alto: Mayfield.

Institute for Muslim Affairs. 1986. *Muslim populations of the World.* Riyadh: Institute for Muslim Affairs.

Isaac, E. 1973. The pilgrimage to Mecca. *Geographical Review* 63:405-09.

King, R. 1972. The pilgrimage to Mecca: Some geographical and historical aspects. *Erdkunde* 26:61-73.

Lévi-Strauss, C. 1958. *Structural anthropology.* New York: Basic Books.

Metcalf, T. 1986. New research priorities: Towards an orchestrated program on Muslim societies. Social Science Research Council, New York, NY. *SSRC Newsletter* Nov., 1986, p. 1.

Ministry of the Hajj and Waqifs. 1984. *The Pilgrims Guide: Essential information for pilgrims and general guide to the addresses of mutawifs in Mecca, Mina and Arafat.* Riyadh: Royal Government of Saudi Arabia.

———. 1986. *Pilgrim statistics 1404.* Riyadh: Royal Government of Saudi Arabia.

Moore, B. 1958. *Political power and social theory.* Cambridge, MA: Harvard University Press.

Pfaffenberger, B. 1983. Serious pilgrims and frivolous tourists: The chimera of tourism in the pilgrimage of Sri Lanka. *Annals of Tourism Research.* 10:57-74.

Rowley, G., and S. A. S. el-Hamdan. 1977a. Once a year in Mecca. *The Geographical Magazine* 49: 753-59.

———. 1977b *The Hajj — Pilgrims, sites, accommodations and related services: Assessments and projections.* Riyadh: Ministry of the Hajj and Waqifs and Ministry of Municipal and Rural Affairs, Royal Government of Saudi Arabia.

———. 1978. The pilgrimage to Mecca: An explanatory and predictive model. *Environment and Planning, A* 10: 1053-71.

Sauer, C. O. 1962. Cultural geography. In *Readings in cultural geography*, eds. P. L. Wagner and M. W. Mikesell, 30-34. Chicago: University of Chicago Press.

Shair, I. M. 1983. Geography pattern of Southwest Asian Hajjis: A regression model. *GeoJournal* 7: 291-98.

Shils, E. 1957. Primordial, personal, sacred and civil ties: Some particular observations on the relations of sociological research and theory. *British Journal of Sociology* 8: 130-45.

Wallerstein, I. 1983. *Historical capitalism.* London: Verso.

Watt, W. M. 1961. *Islam and the integration of society.* Evanston, IL: Northwestern University Press.

Weekes, R. V. 1978. *Muslim peoples: A world ethnographic survey.* Westport, CT: Greenwood Press.

Muslim Pilgrimage from Malaysia

Abdul Kadir Din and Abdul Samad Hadi
Universiti Kebangsaan Malaysia

Abstract

Since the early fifteenth century, Muslim pilgrims have traveled from Malaysia to the Holy Kaabah in Mecca to perform the Hajj and the Umrah, but the number who have made these religious journeys has varied over time. A study of these fluctuations suggests that they are related to changes in transportation technology, economic and political conditions, occurrences of the Grand Hajj, and organizational institutions in the source area. The effects of these factors can be shown by a generalized description consisting of five stages: prior to the eighteenth century, from the 1700s to the 1880s, the 1880s to 1969, 1969 to 1977, and post-1977.

The importance of pilgrimages in Malaysia is demonstrated by examining the expected number of pilgrims based on the two variables normally utilized in the standard gravity model: population and distance. In comparison with other Muslim countries, the number of Malaysian pilgrims is seven times larger than the general pattern of movement. This greater emphasis results from a strong commitment to the five pillars of Islam, encouragement provided by governmental institutions, ease of travel between Malaysia and Saudi Arabia, and a higher economic well-being in Malaysia than in several other Muslim countries.

Current trends indicate that the magnitude of pilgrim movements from Malaysia will continue to grow. The increasing ease of travel will undoubtedly make pilgrimages more feasible for a greater number of persons (although the very reduction in hardships and sacrifices associated with transportation technology may simultaneously diminish the religious merit in the eyes of some potential pilgrims). Secondly, pilgrimages may become more common as economic and political ties between Malaysia and Saudi Arabia become closer. Lastly, continued governmental support, as well as that provided by private tour organizers, is expected to assist an increasing number of Malaysian Muslims performing one or more pilgrimages to Mecca.

Key words: pilgrimage, Hajj, Malaysia, pilgrimage statistics.

*And proclaim unto mankind the Hajj. They
will come to thee on foot and on every lean
camel; they will come from every deep ravine,
that they may witness things that are of benefit*

Sacred Places, Sacred Spaces: The Geography of Pilgrimages, edited by Robert H. Stoddard and Alan Morinis, 1997. Geoscience and Man, vol. 34, pp. 161-182. Dept. of Geography and Anthropology, Louisiana State University, Baton Rouge, LA 70893-6010.

to them, and mention the name of Allah on
appointed days over the sacrificial animal He
hath bestowed on them. Then eat thereof and
feed therewith the poor unfortunate. Let them
make an end of their unkemptness and pay
their vows and go around the ancient House.
That [is the command]. And whoso magnifieth
the sacred things of Allah, it will be well for
him in the sight of his Lord.... Qur'an 22,
28-31 (as translated in Long 1979: xiii)

The above commandment was revealed to Prophet Abraham long before the Holy Kaabah (the sacred "House" of Allah) was reconstituted as
the center of the Muslim world (Long 1979). In spite of its changing for-
tunes through the centuries, the Holy Kaabah has become the focal point
of Muslim prayers and the Hajj. Muslim scholars are generally agreed that
the Hajj was prescribed as one of the pillars of Islam in A.H. 9 (A.D. 631).
Henceforth, each year Muslims from all over the world travel by land, sea,
and (nowadays) air to perform the Hajj (fig. 1).

The sheer volume and persistence of flows of pilgrims offers a wide
opportunity for academic analysis. Moreover, if the pilgrim flows are
viewed within the larger context of population movement, the Hajj forms
a special circulatory movement which is not only place specific but also
time specific. The circulation has many implications on the receiving area
as well as on the sending communities.

Conceptually, studies on Islamic pilgrimage have not progressed beyond empirical descriptions and, even at this stage, much more cross-cultural data are required before efforts can be made towards further
generalizations about this category of human movement. This paper aims
at providing an additional empirical description of the movement of Muslim pilgrims by examining those from Malaysia. Specifically, the paper
deals with the following questions:

    (1) What is the numerical importance of the pilgrimages from Malay-
       sia?
    (2) What are some factors related to variations in pilgrimage flows?
    (3) What are some historic relationships associated with pilgrimages?
    (4) What is the future of pilgrimages as indicated by trends?

Malaysians as Part of the Global Flows of Pilgrims

Performing the Hajj is the fifth and last pillar of Islam.[1] Essentially, every
adult male Muslim who is healthy and has the means to undertake the

Fig. 1. Organized prayer at the Holy Kaabah, Mecca. (Photograph provided by the Pilgrims Funds and Management Board, Malaysia, 1996.)

journey is required to perform the Hajj at least once in his lifetime. A primary motive for pilgrimage for Muslim males in Malaysia, therefore, is to fulfill the fifth pillar of Islam. Furthermore, in Malaysia a person who has performed the Hajj will be called a "Haji" and will acquire certain religious status. To the average person, especially in a village, the Haji may be looked up to as a person to officiate at religious functions and as a source for moral guidance.

The Hajj is place specific in that the pilgrims will have to make the journey to Mecca and to other prescribed areas in the vicinity of that holy city. It is also time specific since the pilgrims will have to perform the Hajj from the 8th to the 12th of Zul-Hijjah (the twelfth month of the Muslim lunar year).[2]

Apart from the Hajj, Muslims also travel to the Holy Kaabah to perform the Umrah, which is the lesser Hajj. Umrah is not *wajib* (obligatory), and it can be performed at any day and month of the year. It has its own prerequisites, rules, and rites. During the Hajj a pilgrim may also perform the Umrah, or he may perform it during off-peak periods when the number of pilgrims will be much smaller.

The Hajj and Umrah draw Muslims from the world over. Malaysia, as a predominantly Muslim country, is one of the contributing sources to the annual flow of pilgrims to Mecca. In fact, in 1982,[3] Malaysia ranked thirteenth as the national origin of pilgrims from outside Saudi Arabia (table 1). By looking at data for the preceding decade, it can be noted that the

Table 1. Pilgrims to Mecca: Top twenty sender countries, 1982.

Country	Number of Pilgrims	Rank Order of Size	Rank Order of Size, 1973
Egypt	98,408	1	5
Iran	89,503	2	4
Nigeria	81,128	3	3
Pakistan	72,844	4	1*
Yemen (YAR)	63,241	5	2
Indonesia	57,478	6	12
Turkey	43,788	7	8
Algeria	40,400	8	9
Syria	27,890	9	6
Sudan	26,983	10	7
India	26,229	11	13
Jordan	25,429	12	10
Malaysia	25,277	13	17
Iraq	23,179	14	11
Morocco	18,686	15	15
Libya	17,787	16	16
Bangladesh	12,258	17	-*
Tunisia	9,645	18	18
Oman	9,475	19	24
Kuwait	6,558	20	19

Sources: Long 1979, p. 130, and Ministry of the Interior (annual).

*"Bangladesh" included with Pakistan in 1973.

relative importance of Malaysia increased from its position of seventeenth in 1973.

The role of the country as a source region is also revealed by examining the percentage of pilgrims from outside Saudi Arabia who came from Malaysia annually for a couple of decades (table 2). By 1982, the percentage was close to 3.0 (fig. 2); and it became as high as 4.5 percent in 1990.

Greater insight into the numerical importance of Malaysian pilgrims can be obtained by comparing the observed flow with that expected based on a gravity model. It is not surprising, of course, that numerous pilgrims originate from Nigeria, Pakistan, and Indonesia because of the sizes of the Muslim populations in these countries. Likewise, the large number of pilgrims from Yemen can be explained in terms of the country's proximity to Mecca. Egypt and Iran are top source countries (table 1) because they have large Muslim populations as well as being located near the destination of the Hajj. In other words, the comparative magnitudes of pilgrim flows ap-

Table 2. Proportion of pilgrims to Mecca from Malaysia, 1973-95.

Year	Total* Pilgrims	Number of Malaysian Pilgrims	Percentage of Total Pilgrims from Malaysia
1973	647,898	12,983	2.0
1974	918,777	15,366	1.7
1975	886,052	15,735	1.7
1976	719,040**	3,506	0.5
1977	1,089,429	4,278	0.4
1978	821,236	7,498	0.9
1979	862,520	10,221	1.2
1980	812,982	14,346	1.8
1981	879,361	22,704	2.6
1982	853,555	25,277	3.0
1983	1,003,911	25,040	2.5
1984	919,671	24,749	2.7
1985	851,761	24,415	2.9
1986	856,718	24,640	2.9
1987	960,386	25,478	2.7
1988	762,755	30,357	4.0
1989	774,560	33,511	4.3
1990	827,236	37,464	4.5
1991	720,000***	27,456	3.8
1992	2,000,000	43,718	2.2
1993	2,033,353	37,620	1.9
1994	1,531,681****	24,344	1.6
1995	1,042,374	25,117	2.4

Source: LUTH, 1995.

*Excluding pilgrims from Saudi Arabia

** 1976 Hajj figures dropped owing to the introduction of a Saudi ruling which did not permit personal choice of Hajj guides. The new ruling was, however, rescinded in 1978.
*** 1991 Hajj figures dropped following outbreak of the Gulf War on 2 August 1990 which lasted for over five months.
**** 1994 Hajj figures dropped following the Saudi application of a quota system which limits the number of pilgrims from individual countries to 1% of the total population. Additional arrivals are nevertheless allowable at the direction of the Saudi authorities. The quota for Malaysia for 1995 was only 19,000, with a discretionary permission given to an additional 6,119 pilgrims.

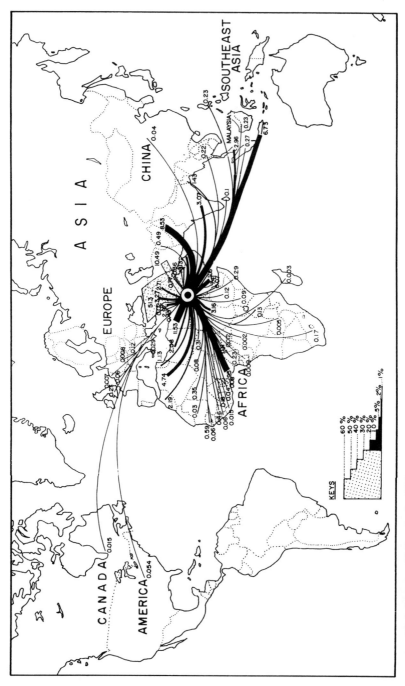

Fig. 2. Global foreign Hajj arrivals, 1982.

pear to result from a direct relationship with population and an inverse relationship with distance.

Factors Associated with Pilgrimage Flows
International Variations

The degree to which population and distance account for Malaysia's share of the pilgrimage flow can be examined by comparing the actual proportions with those predicted by the gravity model (table 3). Based on the Muslim population and the distance to Mecca, it is expected that 0.48 percent of all pilgrims from the twenty main countries would originate in Malaysia. The actual percentage in 1982 was 3.26. These results suggest that the Malaysian contingent is overrepresented by seven-fold. Outside of

Table 3. Expected and observed percentages of pilgrims to Mecca, 1982.

Country	Muslim Population*	Distance to Mecca**	P/d	Expected Percentage	Observed Percentage***
Egypt	39,600	1,280	30.938	14.44	12.68
Iran	38,316	1,952	19.629	9.16	11.53
Nigeria	38,681	4,016	9.632	4.50	10.45
Pakistan	90,210	3,536	25.512	11.91	9.38
Yemen (YAR)	5,500	832	6.611	3.09	8.14
Indonesia	135,900	8,016	19.954	7.92	7.41
Turkey	46,746	2,144	21.803	10.18	5.64
Algeria	20,100	3,872	5.191	2.42	5.20
Syria	8,536	1,368	6.240	2.91	3.59
Sudan	14,527	984	14.763	6.89	3.48
India	78,430	3,920	20.008	9.34	3.38
Jordan	3,276	1,280	2.559	1.19	3.28
Malaysia	7,285	7,040	1.035	0.48	3.26
Iraq	13,300	1,440	9.236	4.31	2.99
Morocco	22,077	4,704	4.693	2.19	2.41
Libya	3,104	2,880	1.078	0.50	2.29
Bangladesh	77,439	5,280	14.666	6.85	1.58
Tunisia	6,700	3,296	2.033	0.95	1.24
Oman	711	1,936	0.367	0.17	1.22
Kuwait	1,500	1,216	1.234	0.58	0.84

* Estimates of Muslim population (in thousands) for 1982 obtained from *The World Almanac and Book of Facts*, 1984.

**Shortest distance (in kilometers) between capital city and Mecca measured on Replogle World Nations Series globe (scale 1:41,849,600).

*** See data in table 1, countries listed in the same order.

Saudi Arabia and Oman, situated in the vicinity of Mecca, Malaysia is the most overrepresented sender country.

This overrepresentation may be attributed to three factors. First, there are indications which suggest that Malaysian Muslims have a strong commitment to Islam. This is manifested by the fact that Islam is declared constitutionally as the state religion and Islamic law operates besides common law. The national capital, Kuala Lumpur, is significantly the site for the International Islamic University, the venue for the annual Qur'an reading for the Islamic world, and the site for the headquarters of the Islamic Development Bank.

The second factor is related to the ease of travel since Kuala Lumpur is directly linked by air and sea to Mecca and travel facilities are augmented through government initiatives.

Finally, Malaysia, with a per capita GDP of over US$800 in 1982, is perhaps better endowed than most Muslim countries outside Southwest Asia. Thus, besides population and physical distance, the religious attitudes of the people, the time distance, and the economic well-being of pilgrims are unquestionably important in determining the desire and ability of Muslims to effect the Hajj.

Variations within Malaysia

The importance of population size can be analyzed also by looking at the numerical variations of pilgrimage source areas within Malaysia itself (table 4). Pilgrims originated from all the states in the country, with the largest numbers coming from Johore, Kelantan, Kedah, and Perak, the four states with the largest Muslim populations. As can be seen from a scatter diagram showing the proportion of pilgrims with the percentage of Muslims per state (fig. 3), these two phenomena tend to covary.

The Federal Territory, which has only four percent of the Muslim population but over fourteen percent of the pilgrims, is the major exception to this generalization about population size and proportion of pilgrims. This anomaly reflects the concentration of wealthy Muslims in Kuala Lumpur, where employment in the federal government is common. Although there are no available figures, it is known that most of the federal departments of the Muslim-dominated government are located in this core city.

In order to investigate the importance of income as a factor, the number of pilgrims per Muslim population was calculated for each state (table 5). The role of this variable is obvious from the fact that the number of pilgrims per 1000 Muslims ranges from only 1.9 in Selangor to 7.7 in the Federal Territory. Because of the relative wealth of the Federal Territory, it seems logical to examine whether this might be an explanatory variable in the sizes of pilgrimage flows in general.

Table 4. Muslim population and pilgrims, by Malaysian state, 1974-1978 and 1979-1982

State	Muslim Population, 1980	Percent of Total	Pilgrims 1974-78	Percent of Total	Pilgrims 1979-82	Percent of Total
Perlis	115,514	1.67	766	1.47	848	1.53
Kedah	784,215	11.33	6,271	12.06	4,973	8.95
Pulau Pinang	311,743	4.05	2,131	4.09	2,003	3.60
Perak	773,702	11.18	3,895	7..49	4,118	7.41
Selangor	650,718	9.40	9,510	18.30	7,377	13.27
N. Sembilan	267,564	3.72	1,900	3.66	1,912	3.44
Melaka	238,192	3.44	2,093	4.03	2,202	3.96
Johore	876,440	12.66	6,070	9.75	5,173	9.31
Pahang	496,383	7.17	1,809	3.48	2,355	4.24
Terengganu	493,511	7.13	3,086	5.94	4,271	7.69
Kelantan	795,649	11.50	6,729	12.94	7,896	14.21
Fed. Territory	312,474	4.51	4,991	9.60	7,263	13.06
Sabah	487,627	7.05	2,105	4.05	2,876	5.17
Sarawak	327,575	4.73	1,621	3.12	2,308	4.15
Total	6,921,307	100.00	51,977	100.00	55,575	100.00

Sources: Department of Statistics 1984; and LUTH 1974-1982.

On the basis of 1980 data, however, it appears that per capita GDP by states is not a factor (fig. 4). The Federal Territory does not stand out dramatically as a distinct source area. Interestingly, if any relationship does exist among the remaining states, it seems to display a tendency toward an inverse one, with high rates of pilgrims from the poorer states of Kelantan and Terengganu and low rates from states having a higher economic well-being like Selangor and Pulau Pinang. This tendency, however, is far from conclusive as it does not reveal intrastate income disparity.

If the pattern of income distribution of the country is examined (table 5), there is clearly an inverse relationship between GDP per capita and the proportion of Muslim population in each state. This reflects the inter-ethnic income inequality that has persisted since colonial times. In 1984, for example, the average income per capita among the indigenous groups, which were mostly Muslim Malays, was M$384, whereas the corresponding figure for the Chinese, almost all of whom were non-Muslims, was M$678 (Fifth Malaysia Plan 1986-1990, 1986: 116). Thus, the economic well-being of the rich states as indicated by the high per capita GDP is not an accurate reflection of the economic position of the Muslims.

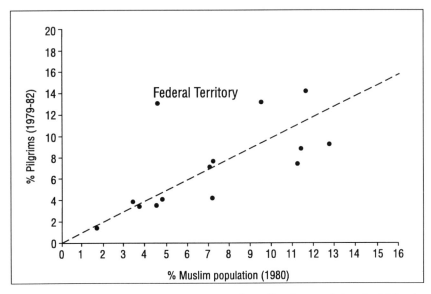

Fig. 3. Percentage of pilgrims by percentage of Muslims in population for Malaysian states.

Historical Perspective of Pilgrimage from Malaysia

Looking at pilgrimages through time can aid in understanding contemporary pilgrimage patterns. The earliest evidence of Islam in the Malay Peninsula dates back to the fourteenth century, in the form of an inscription on a stone slab. Islam subsequently gained influence when the first Malay chief of Malacca was converted to Islam in the early fifteenth century. Some mention of Malay pilgrimage is found in Malay folklore, court literature, and later in Malay annals written in the early nineteenth century.

Estimates of the number of pilgrims were, however, not available until the beginning of the twentieth century (Roff 1975). As in the case of the total number of pilgrims converging into Mecca, estimates of pilgrims leaving Malaya are raw and fragmentary (Long 1979). Prior to 1928, pilgrim passports were not compulsory. As a result, available figures have tended to undercount the actual number. Moreover, the figure recorded for 1927, for example, was inflated as it included pilgrims from Indonesia who had managed to obtain passports in Singapore and Penang. There were also those who went through India and consequently were not included in the enumeration of Malayan pilgrims (Roff 1975). As a result of these anomalies, available figures tend to vary among different sources.

Table 5. Wealth and pilgrims per Muslim population for Malaysian states, 1982.

State	GDP per Capita, 1980 (M$)	Moslem Percentage	Pilgrims per 1000 Moslems
Perlis	1101	79.8	4.4
Kedah	1101	72.9	4.3
Palau Pinang	2357	34.8	3.0
Perak	1583	44.7	2.3
Selangor	3176	45.7	1.9
N. Sembilan	1817	47.0	3.7
Melaka	1469	53.9	5.1
Johore	1726	55.8	2.7
Pahang	1486	65.0	2.0
Terengganu	1316	94.5	5.3
Kelantan	842	92.7	5.1
Fed. Territory	3176	34.3	7.7
Sabah	1847	51.3	2.0
Sarawak	1382	26.2	2.3

Sources: LUTH 1982; The Fourth Malaysia Plan 1981; and Department of Statistics 1984.

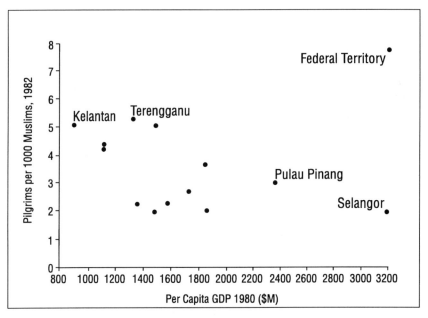

Fig. 4. Pilgrims per 1000 Muslims by per capita GDP for Malaysian states.

Roff's 1924-40 pilgrim statistics, for instance, are different from the figures available in reports by the Malayan Pilgrims Corporation (LUTH), which cover the period between 1900 and 1982 (LUTH 1982). Since there is no glaring contrast in the patterns derived from the two estimates and since the figures from LUTH are more comprehensive, those estimated statistics are used for this paper.

The past trend in Malay pilgrimage has been somewhat erratic with marked variations in the total number of pilgrims (table 6). Given the paucity of reliable information, it is difficult to describe the trend beyond a highly generalized impression. It appears (fig. 5) that the trend in Malay pilgrimage roughly follows the pattern discernible for the Muslim world as a whole. Two clear patterns may be identified from the figure: firstly, the trend for both the total and the Malaysian pilgrims increased over time, and secondly, numbers show marked variations from year to year.

Table 6. Malaysian pilgrims, 1900-1995.

Year	Pilgrims	Year	Pilgrims	Year	Pilgrims	Year	Pilgrims
						1972	10,395
1900	6,861	1924	13,024	1948	4,740	1973	12,983
1901	4,356	1925	-	1949	3,224	1974	15,366
1902	4,896	1926	550	1950	3,886	1975	15,735
1903	7,612	1927	1,940	1951	5,809	1976	3,506
1904	4,246	1928	9,875	1952	5,687	1977	4,278
1905	5,349	1929	4,646	1953	6,025	1978	7,498
1906	6,511	1930	4,353	1954	5,404	1979	10,416
1907	5,922	1931	1,334	1955	3,520	1980	15,259
1908	4,689	1932	329	1956	4,287	1981	22,835
1909	5,268	1933	320	1957	4,319	1982	25,277
1910	7,177	1934	514	1958	4,275	1983	25,040
1911	11,707	1935	712	1959	4,366	1984	24,749
1912	8,743	1936	1,046	1960	5,315	1985	24,415
1913	11,243	1937	2,882	1961	6,498	1986	24,640
1914	8,344	1938	5,115	1962	5,599	1987	25,478
1915	-	1939	2,059	1963	4,886	1988	30,357
1916	-	1940	45	1964	5,066	1989	33,511
1917	-	1941	-	1965	5,214	1990	37,464
1918	-	1942	-	1966	6,501	1991	27,456
1919	1,270	1943	-	1967	6,611	1992	43,718
1920	14,397	1944	-	1968	6,471	1993	37,620
1921	9,593	1945	-	1969	6,573	1994	24,344
1922	5,671	1946	138	1970	9,702	1995	25,117
1923	5,576	1947	1,636	1971	10,650		

Sources: LUTH 1975; 1981-82.

Both the total arrivals and the Malay component were determined principally by the availability of convenient transportation, the state of peace and security along the routes to and in Mecca, and the economic circumstances within the source areas. In general, the numbers declined during the political instability of the two world wars and the Hejaz War,[4] as well as during the period of world economic depression in the early 1930s (Din 1982). In contrast, the totals were high during times of favorable economic and political conditions. However, mention should also be made of the grand Hajj (Hajj Akhbar), the occasion when the visit to Mecca falls on a Friday. Muslims regard such instances as spiritually more rewarding since Friday prayers can also be performed at that time. For this reason, there was a peak in 1911, a year of Hajj Akhbar.

During the period before the Second World War, pilgrim passages were less institutionalized and there were few health and immigration controls imposed on the incoming pilgrims. Intending pilgrims often had to brave the seas in unsanitary sailing ships; and as many as 15 percent of the pilgrims were reported to have died on the way (Majid 1926). The famous Malay writer, Munshi Abdullah, whose account of the journey in the

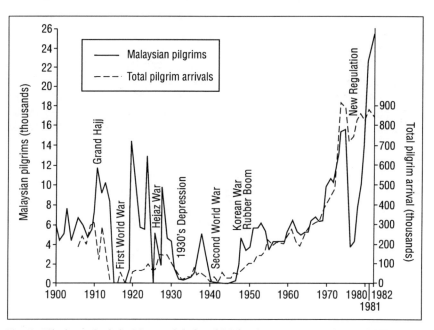

Fig. 5. Pilgrim arrivals in Mecca, global and Malaysian, 1900–1995. *Source:* LUTH 1995; and Ministry of Interior (annual).

late nineteenth century was published posthumously, died of cholera in Jeddah before visiting the holy city (Munshi Abdullah 1960).

Pilgrimage was suspended during the First World War period (1915-18). As a result, the year 1920 registered a record total of more than 14,000 pilgrims, some of whom appeared to have made up for the lost years. In the same way, the Wahabi victory in the Hejaz War resulted in more pilgrims, partly as a rebound from the absence of pilgrims during the fighting in 1925 and partly because one of ibn Saud's top post-war priorities was to rid the Hejaz region of threatening groups and to ensure the safe passage of pilgrims to Mecca. Thus, by 1928, the number of Malay pilgrims rose to nearly 10,000.

It was during this period that the Malay pilgrim component ranked as the largest ethnic group effecting the Hajj (Rutter 1929).

With the exception of 1938, the number of Malay pilgrims fell drastically between 1930 and 1946 as a result of the general world depression and the Second World War. The number of pilgrims swelled again during the 1950s when prosperity from the Korean War made possible many pilgrimages that had previously been deferred. It should be noted that, with improved health control and medical facilities, death rates among Malay pilgrims fell from 15 percent per year before the 1930s to under 2 percent after the 1960s. From then on, there was a steady increase both in the total number of Muslim pilgrims and in the Malay component, which reached a record of over 15,000 in 1975.

The high of 1975 was followed by an abrupt fall to 3,506 pilgrims in 1976 due to several factors. One was the delayed effects of the world oil crisis, which caused financial hardships in the ASEAN region. In that year, pilgrims traveling by air exceeded those using sea transportation (with the latter being completely phased out by 1977). By this date the cost of the trip had more than doubled that of the six preceding years. Also the prestige accorded to the title of Haji had decreased, as its attainment has become increasingly commonplace. Furthermore, the number of Malaysian pilgrims also declined due to the new regulations introduced by the Saudi authorities, which prescribed sheikh tour operators (*muassasah*) in Mecca rather than letting pilgrims choose their own Hajj guides.

After 1976, the number of pilgrims from Malaysia increased annually, up to a total of over 25,000 in 1982. During the next decade, the numbers remained approximately the same, although a record number of 43,718 Malaysians made the pilgrimage in 1992.

Traveling costs to Mecca had been fairly low before the 1970s when the predominant mode of transportation was by sea. The replacement of sea transport by air and the effects of inflation have resulted in a substantial increase in costs. A rough estimate based on the varying costs per passage (table 7), combined with the total number of pilgrims (table 6), would

Table 7. Cost of passage to Mecca for Malaysians.

Year	Cost per Pilgrim(M$)	Total Cost (in million M$)*
1926	600	3.3
1947	1500	2.5
1964	1500	7.6
1966	1700	11.1
1978	4000	30.0
1979	4500	46.0
1980	5000	72.0
1981	5000	113.5
1982	5000	126.4

Source: LUTH 1982.
* US $1 = M $2.25

suggest that the cumulative amount of money spent on pilgrimages since 1900 has exceeded M$1 billion. Even during earlier times, the total expenditures were large. An estimate by Lim (1977, 238) of pilgrim spendings totaling M$500 million between 1874 and 1941 appears to be somewhat overstated because extrapolation from 1926 data yields a sum approximately half that amount for the pre-1941 period. Nevertheless, even the lower estimate certainly does point to the magnitude of capital drain from the Malay community.

A simple retroactive calculation of the multiplier effects based on the above multiplicand spendings would certainly reveal a much higher loss of economic potential for the Malays. It is for this reason that the Hajj has been repeatedly singled out as the "extraordinary expenditure" which in the past has been one of the main religious obstacles to the economic development of the Malay peasantry (Swift 1964; Von der Mehden 1980).

The Evolution of Hajj Movement from Malaysia: A Generalized Description

The evolution of Hajj movements from Malaysia may be divided into five stages based on transport technology and organizational institutions (fig. 6). In essence, changes through time reflect the decreasing friction of distance. Along with the greater ease of movement have come organizational institutions that served the Hajj industry.

Era I: Prior to the 18th Century

During the pre-Colonial days but after the coming of Islam to Malacca in the early fifteenth century, the Malay community was known to have sent pilgrimage expeditions from the port of Malacca. These early pilgrims had to sail in small vessels, which depended entirely on the help of the seasonal monsoon and trade winds. The journeys, which were embarked un-

ROUTE	MODE	SCALE OF SOURCE AREAS	ORGANIZATIONAL INSTITUTIONS	TIME, DURATION OF JOURNEY
	small sailing vessels	localized riverline villages under chieftainships.	traditional non-formalized arrangements led by aristocrats.	Circa: pre 18th century, more than 6 months of sailing, dependent on trade winds.
	large sailing vessels	settlements under colonial govt. Straits Settlements. Federated and Unfederated Malay States.	under the charge of Colonial State Government. Travel arranged by the private sector.	Circa: pre World War I, sailing still dependent on trade winds.
	steamships	Colonial Malaya, subsequently Peninsular Malaysia.	under supervision of the Dept. of Haji Affairs, Ministry of External Affairs, later shifted to Pilgrims Control Board, Ministry of Home Savings Board established in 1969, under Ministry of National and Rural Dept.	Pre 1973, sailing in cargo steamships for 3 to 4 months.
	bimodal-steamships and planes	National-Federation of Malaysia.	Pilgrim Management and Fund Board (LUTH), Prime Minister's Dept. Travel arrangement by private sector.	1973-1977, sailing in converted cargo ships and medium size planes for less than 3 months.
	jumbo jets	National and Pan Islamic-Malaysia provides facilities for pilgrims from neighboring countries.	LUTH became the sole agents for intending pilgrims.	1977 onward, sailing phased out, journey by larger planes for less than 2 months.

Fig. 6. Evolution of Hajj movements, Malaysia.

der the patronage of Malay chiefs, would easily have taken more than six months to complete because they involved many stoppages along the coastal route.

Era II: 18th Century - 1880s

During this period, the duration of the journey was as long as the previous stage since, despite increased capacity of ships, sailing was still dependent on trade winds. Vagaries of bad weather, storms, attacks by pirates, and unsanitary conditions on board the ships, partly due to the absence of refrigeration, were some of the hazards faced by pilgrims during these periods.

The Colonial period saw several localized embarkations, which originated at the ports of the Straits Settlement at Penang, Malacca, and Singapore. Travel arrangements were organized mainly by state governments in collusion with Arab and Indian traders who provided passage in larger sailing ships.

Era III: 1880s - 1969

With the introduction of the steamships in 1827, the length of the journey to Mecca was reduced to between three and four months, which was about one-half the time taken during the earlier periods. Pilgrim departures became more organized and were subject to passport and foreign exchange controls. At this stage, a pilgrim officer was posted to the British consulate of Mecca to be in charge of welfare and surveillance activities.

Era IV: 1969 - 1977

To provide financial advice and savings facilities to intending pilgrims, another body (the Pilgrims Saving Fund Board) was set up in 1963. In 1969 this body was amalgamated with the Department of Hajj Affairs to form the Pilgrims Savings and Management Corporation (LUTH). The new corporation not only provided counseling, savings, and control facilities, but it also provided access to opportunities for investment in corporate economic ventures, thereby allowing intending pilgrims to invest in shares it acquired from public companies.

Intending pilgrims were able to prepare for the Hajj under the guidance of LUTH representatives stationed at sixty offices throughout the country. Careful interviews were held to ensure that only those who had the means to travel were allowed to embark on the journey. Qualified candidates were then required to attend a two-day course on the Hajj held in mosques and district centers. The course was intended to inform candidates on the ritual procedures and the religious significance of the Hajj, to brief them on health care facilities during the journey, and to create an awareness about the administration of the Hajj in Malaysia and in Mecca.

With the introduction of better supervision, and bimodal means of travel in faster steamships and air charter services, the time taken to bridge the seven thousand kilometers by sea to Mecca was further reduced to less than three months. Part of the delays that remained were the result of bottlenecks faced during transshipment in Saudi Arabia.

Bimodal facilities available during this period, while offering an option for either a cheaper or speedier mode of travel, posed problems of controlling health and immigration. By 1977, partly in an effort to take advantage of scale operations of charter flights, pilgrimages by sea were completely phased out.

Era V: Post-1977

Since the phasing out of sea passage in 1977, the Pilgrim Corporation has managed to ensure better services in terms of providing information, saving facilities, and health supervision. In 1982 a total of 304 LUTH personnel, including 178 medical staff, accompanied the Malaysian pilgrims. During the same year the Corporation also had taken a pan-Islamic role in providing passage facilities for a total of 175 intending pilgrims from neighboring countries. Furthermore, it had managed to reduce air fare to some extent and to secure better investment returns for pilgrims.

In line with the objective of involving Muslims more effectively in the economy, LUTH has invested its funds in industry, commerce, plantations, and real estate. About 75% of its funds are held in shares of public companies, 12% in subsidiary companies, either wholly or partly owned by LUTH, and 13% in land and buildings. The book value of these investments up to the end of 1981 was M$209 million while the market value was more than double that value. At that time, the profit gained from these investments was more than M$80 million. Thus, through its savings scheme LUTH has been able to channel Muslim capital into ventures that would not have been possible without collective efforts.

With greater efficiency in travel arrangements and more effective dissemination of Hajj instructions (which included the conduct of mock Hajj rituals at the district level, fig. 7), pilgrimage time has been further reduced to less than two months at the maximum. This reduction of time also owes in part to the efforts of the Saudi government in trying to solve the multitude of congestion problems occurring at the destination.

Summary of the Evolution of the Hajj Movement

This five-stage description serves to highlight the process of modernization of the Hajj passage. It is deliberately simplified; and there are obvious

Fig. 7. Circumambulatory practice around a model of the Holy Kaabah at the Pilgrim Complex, Kelana Jaya, Malaysia. (Photograph provided by the Pilgrim Funds and Management Board, Malaysia, 1996.)

overlaps in the periods. The choice of period breaks is largely based on significant changes in technological and institutional variables. The progressively speedier, efficient, and institutionalized passage, which catered to increasing size of service areas, provides one of the possible explanations for the relative increase in the size of the Malaysian contingent of pilgrims.

The trend towards institutionalized passage runs parallel to the worldwide trend in institutionalized mass tourism. Indeed, mention should be made also of Umrah (the off-peak pilgrimage), which is gaining popularity among Malaysians who are now able to book cheap charter flights offered by the state-owned Malaysian Airline System (MAS). In order to ensure the viability of cheap mass transportation, the government has recently introduced a ruling that all intending pilgrims must effect the Hajj solely through LUTH, and as a result has given a protective monopoly to the national carrier.

Expected Future Trends

To predict the future trends would require a thorough analysis of all conditions that have affected pilgrimages in the past. Many other factors were perhaps as important as, and undoubtedly worked in concert with, the technological and institutional variables. These include the increase in the standard of living in a relatively stable and peaceful economy, a resurgence of Islamic influence, political support, and a greater awareness of the outside world. Further analyses of these factors, however, would require a lengthy discourse (which is beyond the scope of this paper).

Barring unforeseen circumstances such as war, energy crisis, global depression, or restrictions by the Saudi authorities, several existing conditions provide a basis for anticipating future trends. Given the current Islamic resurgence in the country, the current policy that allows every government servant a forty-day fully paid leave for those embarking on the journey, the healthy national economic growth, fast and efficient jet transportation, the present trend of Hajj flows from Malaysia will continue into the future. At the same time, the total number performing the Umrah will increase. As a consequence, the Malaysian share in the total flow of pilgrims to Mecca is predicted to increase.

Looking at the trend in Hajj participation from another perspective, the special status accorded to pilgrims in the past may be devalued perceptually because the passage is now so easy to complete. Some may doubt its spiritual fulfillment, which originally was directed towards experiencing endurance of hardships and ascetic abstinence. If and when this feeling becomes prevalent, a reversion to sea passage may well be a more preferred alternative. That is, the concerns for speed and better journey conditions may be reversed by choice in the future. It seems quite probable that if the standard of living increases further there will be a sufficient demand to support economic operations by both air and sea. Also, with the current national policy favoring privatization, the next era may witness a reversion to bimodal transportation and the management of the Hajj industry by the private sector.

Within the context of international tourism, the convenience of Hajj in packaged tours, as already initiated by MAS, may encourage more travelling among Muslims. It is likely that the pilgrim profile will consist of a much younger group, members of which will live long enough to embark on more repeated visits. If the trend in Malaysia is a reflection of other parts of the Muslim world, one might say that the mystery surrounding the sacred journey and the distance gap between Arab lands and Asia will gradually be bridged. With more established Islamic ambience in Malaysia (such as the presence of the Islamic Development Bank, the International Islamic University, and the plans for future Islamic Hotels), more travellers from Malaysia can be expected to visit the Arab World and vice versa. This would re-link Malaysia to Southwest Asia — a situation comparable to the pre-Colonial times when there was a closer connection between the Muslim communities in Mecca and their regional counterparts in Atjeh, Patani, and Kota Bharu.

To date, a study on the economic impact of the Hajj on the Muslim community in Malaysia is yet to be undertaken. There is evidence, however, of change achieved by LUTH in transforming the Hajj practice, which was once regarded as a source of Malay poverty, into a profitable avenue of saving and investment.

As it is, LUTH is perhaps the only successful Malay corporation in the public sector that has sustained an impressive performance fully funded by Malays, and it promises to be a major frontier in Malay economic development. Because of this success, it seems that the present government-led management will continue into the distant future. Undoubtedly LUTH will not neglect its important role in ensuring better Hajj passage and education, for to do so would mean killing the goose that so far has been remarkable in producing the golden egg.

Conclusion

The empirical description of pilgrim flows from Malaysia suggests that Hajj from Malaysia has been part of the world movement of pilgrims since Islam came to the country in the fifteenth century. Taking distance and population into consideration, the Malays have been sending proportionally the biggest contingent to Mecca. Although this excess from the expected proportion must be related to the strength of Malay values and disposition to the Hajj, its persistence into the post-1970s must have been reinforced by government support through LUTH. Barring unforeseen circumstances such as war and terrorism, it is reasonable to expect the Malaysian contingent to increase in number as well as proportion in the foreseeable future as LUTH continues to improve its services.

Endnotes

1. The other four pillars are: a declaration that there is only one God and Mohammed is His messenger; performance of five daily prayers; fasting during the month of Ramadhan; and contribution of zakat (or tithe) to the community.

2. For a detailed guide on Hajj and its rites, see Kamal 1978.

3. For this research, most of the analysis of pilgrimage statistics is based on 1982 data.

4. The Hejaz War was a 16-month military confrontation between pro-British ibn Saud and pro-Turk Hussain 'Ali in the Hejaz, the western coast of the Arabian Peninsula. It ended in the defeat of the latter on December 25, 1925. The conclusion of the war marked the end of the Ottoman empire and the foundation of the present day Saudi Arabia. One of ibn Saud's top post-war priorities was to rid the Hejaz of its baser evils so as to ensure the safety of passage for pilgrims conducting the hajj from all over the world (Troeller 1976, 231-236).

References

Department of Statistics. 1984. *State housing report, 1980*. Kuala Lumpur, Malaysia.

Din, A. K. H. 1982. Economic implications of Moslem pilgrimages from Malaysia. *Contemporary Southeast Asia* 4:56-75.

Kamal, A. A. 1978. *Every man's guide to Hajj and Umrah*. Lahore, Pakistan: Islamic Publication Limited.

Lim, T. G. 1977. *Peasants and the agricultural economy in colonial Malaya, 1874-1941*. London: Oxford University Press.

Long, D. E. 1979. *The Hajj today: A survey of the contemporary Makkah pilgrimage*. Albany, NY: State University of New York Press.

LUTH (Lembaga Urusan dan Tabung Haji). 1975-1983. Perangkaan Haji, File LUTH/UH (05) 225/1, dan perangkaan bagi tahun 1975-1983. Kuala Lumpur: LUTH Headquarters.

Majid, H. A. 1926. A Malay's pilgrimage to Mecca. *Journal of the Malayan Branch of the Royal Asiatic Society* 4:270-87.

Malaysia 1981. Fourth Malaysia Plan 1981-1985. Kuala Lumpur: Government Printers.

Malaysia 1986. Fifth Malaysia Plan 1986-1990. Kuala Lumpur: Government Printers.

Ministry of the Interior. Annual. *Pilgrim statistics*. Riyadh: Royal Government of Saudi Arabia.

Munshi Abdullah, A. K. 1990. *Kisah Pelayaran Abdullah ke Kelantan dan ke Judah*. Kuala Lumpur: Oxford University Press.

Roff, W. R. 1975. The conduct of the Hajj from Malaya and the first Malay pilgrim officers. *SARI*, Institute of Malay Language, Literature and Culture, National University of Malaysia, Occasional Paper No. 1, 81-112.

Rutter, E. 1929. The Muslim pilgrimage. *Geographical Journal* 74:271-73.

Swift, M. G. 1964. Capital, saving and credit in a Malay peasant economy. In *Capital, savings and credit in peasant societies*, eds. R. Firth and B. S. Yamey, 133-57. London: George Allen and Unwin.

Troeller, G. 1976. *The birth of Saudi Arabia: Britain and the rise of Sa'ud*. London: Frank Cass.

Von der Mehden, F. 1980. Religion and development in Southeast Asia: A comparative study. *World Development* 8:545-53.

Section IV:
PILGRIMAGES IN THE HINDU TRADITION

The Goal of Indian Pilgrimage:
Geographical Considerations

David E. Sopher
Syracuse University
(see dedication page)

Abstract

Spatially peripheral locations of pilgrimages places are implied by Victor Turner's emphasis on liminal experiences, but such is not clearly evidenced in India. When the 12 or 45 most sacred Hindu pilgrimage places are classified as central, peripheral, or neither, fewer than half match the Turner proposition. Although there is some tendency toward central positions, they are not arranged according to centrality factors either.

A mixed message about the role of place also arises from Hindu pilgrimage. Pilgrims, with strong ties to their home places, seek distant destinations of sanctity, and the magnitude of Hindu pilgrimages attest to the strength of this message. Yet, ancient texts, philosophers, and folk tales all affirm that searching for particular places, even places of extreme sanctity, is unnecessary and that place is an illusion.

Key words: Hindu, pilgrimages, place, core-periphery.

To Victor Turner's proposition that pilgrimage provides a liminal experience, fostering a temporary dissolution of society's structure and engendering communitas,[1] there is attached a corollary that is of particular interest to geographers. In arguing that the social liminality of the experience involves and indeed seems to require a spatially peripheral location for the pilgrim's destination, Turner appears to have provided the kind of structural key to spatial pattern for which some geographers have been searching. But does the key really fit? Since Turner himself cites certain data from India in support of his argument (Turner 1973), I shall put that argument to a further test by scrutinizing the available body of material on Indian pilgrimage. The result of the investigation may also have some bearing on the social implications of the Indian institution of pilgrimage.

Sacred Places, Sacred Spaces: The Geography of Pilgrimages, edited by Robert H. Stoddard and Alan Morinis, 1997. Geoscience and Man, vol. 34, pp. 183-190. Dept. of Geography and Anthropology, Louisiana State University, Baton Rouge, LA 70893-6010.

A number of geographers have tried to explain the distribution of Hindu sacred places according to some general principles (Stoddard 1966; Sopher 1967; Bhardwaj 1973). Many important sacred places are associated in particular with streams, especially at confluences, with other bodies of water, or with hilltops. These are, however, only desiderata in the location of sacred places. They do not tell us which places associated with water and which particular hills will acquire special sanctity.

Because sacred centers provide the foundations of a civilization, Stoddard has wondered whether holy places are distributed in such a way as to tend to minimize the aggregate distance traveled to them by the population of that civilization (Stoddard 1966, 37). He has also recognized that the merit of pilgrimage in India, as elsewhere, increases when the goal is distant and the way there hard. Maintenance of this rule would make the distribution of major Hindu holy places far from optimal relative to the distribution of the Hindu population. Stoddard found that although the sacred places were not optimally distributed, their distribution was closer to an optimum than was the distribution of randomly selected sites and was therefore clearly different from a chiefly peripheral distribution.

In Turner's thesis there is some question about the geographic scale implied, but most of his comparisons across civilizations show his conception to involve a regional or national scale. Having stated that "peripherality of the holiest shrines is by no means confined to Christian pilgrimage systems," Turner (1973, 212) turns to India, although only Pandharpur and those truly peripheral locations in western Tibet — Mount Kailash and Manasarovar — are cited. This particular selection ignores the ancient tradition of sacred cities and is, as Stoddard's analysis suggests, incorrect even as a statement of general tendency. Since in Turner's theory "peripherality ... represents liminality and communitas, as against sociocultural structure" (Turner and Turner 1978, 214), should we not expect to find the opposition he poses between structure and anti-structure greatly reduced if not eliminated when centrality rather than peripherality marks the locus of the pilgrim's goal?

This seems to happen in certain kinds of Hindu pilgrimage. Bharati has emphasized the purposiveness of the Hindu pilgrim journey and the tightly structured performances in which the pilgrim takes part at the sacred center (Bharati 1963, 137). Pfaffenberger maintains that much the same is true among Hindu Tamils in Sri Lanka, even when the goal of the pilgrimage, Kataragama, happens to be way out there (Pfaffenberger 1979). On the other hand, Binford notes that fluidity and lack of structure mark the annual *mela* (religious fair) at the popular, non-puranic shrine of Ramdevra (Binford 1976, 140). The point at which communitas must yield to structure and division, as Turner says it always must, seems to depend then on the geographic location of the pilgrimage center, justifying attention to the topic.

I have taken the list of the forty-five "most sacred" Hindu places of pilgrimage compiled by Stoddard and have labeled these "central," "peripheral," or "neither to a marked extent." The scale I have used is frequently regional rather than pan-Indian. The point of doing so is neatly made by the case of Amarkantak. Marking the source of the sacred Narmada River, Amarkantak is located deep in the jungly interior of central India, and is thus clearly peripheral to settled, populous areas. Nevertheless, it happens to be closer to the center of gravity of the Indian population today than any of the other forty-four sacred sites, and would therefore be, by Stoddard's criteria, the most accessible sacred place in India! I have, however, intuitively marked it "peripheral." By my count, then, 24 percent of the sites are unquestionably central, 38 percent are peripheral, and the rest are neither or have a location that is in some sense problematic.

When the dozen most sacred places alone are considered, half of them are found to be central, only two — Rameswaram and Badrinath — are peripheral, and the remaining four are questionable. These results decisively invalidate Turner's generalization for India. All six very sacred places that have a central location are included among the holiest cities of ancient India, their sanctity being closely related to the sanctity of rivers. The primary sanctity of rivers in the Hindu scheme of religious topography itself suggests that it is a mistake to fasten on peripherality as a chief requisite in the location of sanctity in India. Rivers connote axiality. Their major confluences are nodal locations that epitomize centrality and, indeed, often become the sites of central cities, sacred or not.

Turning to the question whether communitas engendered by pilgrimage in the Indian context also generates a sense of geographically defined community, what is of interest is the degree to which Indian social structure is responsive to the potential of wider integration provided by the pilgrimage experience. That potential and its realization do not form an integral part of the Hindu theory of pilgrimage. In the Mahabharata, only solitary pilgrimage is considered. The purpose is individual salvation and the ritual prescriptions to be followed have always been addressed to the individual, not the collective. There is, then, at crucial moments a structuring away from communitas, precisely at those times when a human aggregate is on the point of becoming a "congregation." Pfaffenberger's Tamil informant, denying the influence of communitas as a motivation of pilgrimage, if not as an unsought concomitant of it (Pfaffenberger 1979, 257), expresses what is probably the understanding of pilgrims who follow the shastric or textually prescribed mode.

This is not to deny that the pilgrim assembly can at certain moments generate an enormous excitement, a collective self-realization symbolized by a simultaneous act of common worship, and that this can be anticipated as a part of the saving experience. I recall the tremendous surge of the crowd at the Puri *ratha jatra* (the pilgrimage procession of the deity in his chariot), the explosion of sound carrying the name of the god as the great car of Jagannath lurched creakingly forward to begin its triumphal procession across the town. Mira Binford speaks aptly of the common experience of people standing outside the temple, part of a great mass of people who worship Ramdev, as a kind of confirmation for them (Binford 1976, 141).

Binford points out, however, that the Ramdev Mela offers considerable opportunities for social mixing and sharing in contrast, as she says, to what is encountered in large pilgrimage centers like Kashi and Madurai. There, structure and division, in Turner's words, "keep breaking in," and they do so early and forcefully.

Nevertheless, the almost unanimous scholarly consensus is that the *tirtha yatra*[2] has been one of the great unifying forces in India since the first millennium before Christ. Among the more cautious statements to this effect is the suggestion by the Sanskritist J. Ensink that in a culturally diverse and politically divided subcontinent without any generally recognized hierarchy, "the sense of unity must have been strongly supported by travels to distant sanctuaries, by joining people from different regions in reverence for the god of one and the same temple" (Ensink 1974, 66).

We may have no reason not to agree with Ensink that the institution of pilgrimage must have had such an effect. Yet a concomitant message of the experience of pilgrimage in India must also be that the pilgrim is very much of the place from which he comes. Solidarity with the particular group or place from which one comes is often greatly reinforced by certain social features of pilgrimage in India, whereby a pre-existing community channels the current of communitas engendered by the pilgrimage experience. One example must suffice here: the custom in some villages of western Uttar Pradesh of the *jat ke git* ("pilgrimage songs") sung by both those who depart and those who stay at home (Chandola 1977). Generally, pilgrims from one village travel together to a subregional shrine of Devi and their departure from the village becomes a village-wide celebration. On such occasions, night-long *jagarans* (literally, "wakes") take place, during which a lamp is kept burning and long songs are sung which incorporate the names of all family members and close friends. Persons connected to anyone who has gone on the pilgrimage are named as if they, too, had gone. At other, broader scales of pilgrimage, too, it is solidarity of a small group that is usually increased, while communitas with the large pilgrim mass at the destination is perhaps experienced as a mood of common exaltation rather than through direct interaction with others.

Both Bhardwaj and I have noted in different ways how regional and caste structures retain their control of the pilgrims' activities when they travel to shrines of pan-Indian significance outside their home region. The institution of the *panda* (pilgrimage priest)[3] in its traditional form was intended to accommodate the distant pilgrim by providing him with food, lodging, and ritual instruction according to the custom of his own land (Caplan, this volume). The pilgrim would perform the necessary ritual acts, visit the appropriate sites within the sacred complex, experience awe or bliss or the healing power of the sacred place in familiar company, as effectively wrapped in a cocoon of identity with a particular community, language, and region as any modern mass tourist.

In the public accommodations available to pilgrims, moreover, considerable segregation by caste and region has been observed. Bhardwaj concludes that it is the nature of Hindu society itself which hinders the full realization of potential pilgrim interaction at the sacred places (Bhardwaj 1973, 217, 222). The regional exclusiveness of the hostels and *dharmasalas* (pilgrims' lodging) "minimizes pilgrim interaction," replicating the patterns of limited regional intercommunication within India as a whole.

Turner's description of medieval Europe (Turner 1973, 201-202) as "the continent of the great regional and protonational pilgrimage centers," in which a few important ones, such as Compostela, attracted huge crowds of pilgrims from every country in Europe, but where "any region possessing a certain cultural, linguistic, or ethnic unity, often corresponding also to an area of economic independence, tended to become at once a political unit and a pilgrimage catchment area," can stand, mutatis mutandis, for India, past and present. But while there are notable similarities in the pattern and structure of pilgrim flows, the integrative circulation in the reverse direction was not at all the same. In Europe there was an ecclesiastical structure that mediated that outward flow from the center, ideologically universalistic but tending to generate or exacerbate interethnic as well as center-periphery discordance. In India the reverse flow has been largely unstructured, a trickling through towns and villages of thousands of tiny rivulets, the circulation of religious teachers, ascetics, poets — the "great integrators" at both the level of the entire civilization and of individual regions.

Such persons have often had a base in one of the great pilgrimage centers, where they would be part of a polyglot population sustaining a religious and philosophic discourse across language, regional, and even caste boundaries. In contrast to the normally restricted interaction among parties of pilgrims from different regions, there is an openness and receptivity to religious conversation, both in such sacred centers and in the population at large, with "foreigners" from other parts of India. An illustration is provided by the Tamil institution of the Karikatha, in which a discourse in Tamil on the life of a saint — Telugu, Marathi, Hindi, or Bengali — will include songs of the saints in any of these languages (Raghavan 1966, 48).

To comprehend the social implications of the entire phenomenon of Indian pilgrimage with its many different levels, we may see it as having been given shape from below and above. What Eck calls the basic "locative" religious impulse (Eck 1979) is indeed local and probably has been since prehistoric times, never extending far beyond the horizons of familiar, everyday experience. The association of a particular collective with a particular place is thereby consolidated. The special virtue attached to some of these religious foci and the manipulation of religious symbols by local rulers in order to validate their control would produce an uneven scatter of holy places with varying intensity and range of attachment, but still expressing a powerful connection with place and region. The mythopoeic work of the epics and later sacred texts was, I suggest, to tie existing centers of sanctity together into a loosely bound aggregate. A complex, psychologically profound body of myth was superimposed on the surface of place-rooted sanctity. It thereby provided a mythic geographic structure on a grand scale, limning a subcontinent and holding fast in time a blurred protohistoric human geography. This mythic structure could be extended subsequently and at the same time be given over to an enormously involved elaboration. The mythologized places that are a part of the structure are seen from above, as it were. The place-bound meanings of the chthonic religion which lives on in folk belief and custom are abstracted and refashioned in a corpus of mythic geography that is about place but detached from it. Place is replaced by sacred notes and geography itself becomes a cosmic geometry.

It is a geometry that is given life by the institution of pilgrimages. A question remains as to the pristine purpose of setting in motion this massive circulation. In contrast to what was the case in ancient Israel, there is no sign in its inception of an integrative strategy, for which the mode of solitary pilgrimage envisaged could not have been effective. An integrative purpose, moreover, would have been frustrated by the lack of compulsion attached to pilgrimage and also by the recognition that "those whose hearts are aglow with righteousness had the Ganga in their own homes." That position, transcending the urge to pilgrimage, has been voiced in epic and Purana, by philosopher and mystic, in folk tales and essays, side by side with extravagant praises for the blessings to be obtained by pilgrimage to the tirthas. Here is Lalla, the Kashmiri woman mystic writing in the fourteenth century: "I, Lalla, went out far in search of Shiva, the omnipresent lord; having wandered, I found him in my own body, sitting in his house (Raghavan 1966, 144)." There is in this mystical intuition a detachment from place that nevertheless has an effect convergent with expressions of the opposite sentiment. One informant among a group of villagers in Saurashtra told me with a shrug of the shoulders that he had never gone on pilgrimage to a tirtha. His *dharma* (duty; obligation) was farming and the only pilgrimage he made was to his fields.

Paradoxical as it may seem, the commitment to place expressed in this remark is the very motivation of the impulse to pilgrimage of the kind generated "from below," with pilgrim journeys ramifying outward within one's own region. It is a way of extending the scope of propitiations, bargains, alliances that secure one's place and one's well-being in a world beyond the limited sway of one's own village deity, a proceeding that may be enhanced by the support and company of one's fellows. The same consciousness of place may remain as a theme in the formation of larger pilgrim networks spread over whole regions, and it is a consciousness that grows with repetition. But the saint mystics who turn away from pilgrimage have at the same time detached themselves from place. That also is the purpose of the pilgrimage constructed "from above," which is always intended to bring release in preparation for the final one. The pilgrim's goal, not the journey, is truly the end of the pilgrimage. It is release from both structure and communitas.

At two different scales, then, pilgrimage in India involves two different sets of relationships between people and places that have been saturated with sacred meaning for tens of centuries, that are alive in the minds of tens of millions; the message says that place is an illusion which being there is meant to dispel.

Notes

1. Turner (1978, 250) states that communitas, or social antistructure, is a relational quality of full unmediated communication which arises spontaneously in all kinds of situations. "The bonds of communitas are undifferentiated, egalitarian, direct, extant, nonrational, existential...." Communitas "does not merge identities; it liberates them from conformity to general norms, though this is necessarily a transient condition if society is to continue to operate in an orderly fashion." (Ed.)

2. For a fuller explanation of this term (which is sometimes translated roughly as "pilgrimage," see the discussion by Bhardwaj in his Introduction to Chapter 1. (Ed.)

3. More information on the role of the panda is given by Caplan in Chapter 11. (Ed.)

References

Bhardwaj, S. M. 1973. *Hindu places of pilgrimage in India: A study in cultural geography.* Berkeley: University of California Press.

Bharati, A. 1963. Pilgrimage in the Indian tradition. *History of Religions* 3:135-67.

Binford, M. R. 1976. Mixing in the color or Ram of Ranuja: A folk pilgrimage to the grave of a Rajput hero-saint. In *Hinduism: New essays in the history of religions,* ed. B. L. Smith, 120-42. Leiden: Brill.

Chandola, S. 1977. Some goddess rituals in non-narrative folk songs of India. *Asian Folklore Studies* 36:57-68.

Eck, D. 1981. India's tirthas: "Crossings" in sacred geography. *History of Religions* 20:323-44.

Ensink, J. 1974. Problems of the study of pilgrimage in India. *Indologica Taurinesia* 2:57-79.

Pfaffenberger, B. 1979. The Kataragama pilgrimage: Hindu-Buddhist interaction and its significance in Sri Lanka's polyethnic social system. *Journal of Asian Studies* 38:353-70.

Raghavan, V. 1966. *The great integrators: The saint-singers of India.* New Delhi: Publications Division, Ministry of Information and Broadcasting.

Sopher, D. E. 1967. *Geography of religions.* Englewood Cliffs, NJ: Prentice-Hall.

Stoddard, R. H. 1966. Hindu holy sites in India. Ph.D. diss., University of Iowa, Iowa City.

Turner, V. 1973. The center out there: Pilgrim's goal. *History of Religions* 12:191-230.

Turner, V., and E. Turner. 1978. *Image and pilgrimage in Christian culture: Anthropological perspectives.* New York: Columbia University Press.

Sacred Space and Pilgrimage in Hindu Society: The Case of Varanasi

Rana P. B. Singh
Banaras Hindu University

Abstract

Pilgrimage has been one of the strongest traditions in Hindu religion since the Vedic time. In the course of time, Varanasi has been eulogized and accepted as the most sacred city in Hinduism. By the turn of the 13th century, many pilgrimage circuits and spatially manifested holy sites and shrines developed in Varanasi. The re-establishment of important pan-Indian holy sites in Varanasi makes this city a microcosm of India. Many cosmological symbols also occur, such as the 56 Vinayaka shrines representing a multiple frame of eight directions and seven layers of the atmosphere. Similarly the five most popular pilgrimage circuits represent the five gross elements making life, according to the Hindu cosmogony. All these pilgrimage circuits are associated with the shrines referring to numerical symbolism. The pilgrimage journeys are described according to months and seasons for which specific shrines or holy spots are prescribed.

To engage in the special ritual honoring the patron deity, Vishveshvara or Vishvanatha, is the purpose for about sixty percent of the pilgrims to Varanasi; and the sacred journey around his temple is known as the "inner sanctum" route of the city. In geographic symbolism, the three forms of Shiva (with the respective segmented circuits Omkareshvara, Vishveshvara, and Kedareshvara) make the shape of a trident, which is why the city is perceived as lying on Shiva's trident. The sacred topography of the city shows one of the best known examples of mesocosm (earthly) representation interlinking macrocosm (heavenly bodies) and microcosm (individual being, or deity, or inner sanctum of a temple).
Key words: cosmology, circumambulatory circuits, pilgrimage, Varanasi, Shiva.

The spatial components of pilgrimage involve more than just traveling from one's residence to a *tīrtha* (sacred site); they may also incorporate elements of religious space at the pilgrimage site. In the case of Varanasi, such spatial manifestations of the sacred are expressed by pilgrim movements which reflect the patterns of urban features, the areal analogies

Sacred Places, Sacred Spaces: The Geography of Pilgrimages, edited by Robert H. Stoddard and Alan Morinis, 1997. Geoscience and Man, vol. 34, pp. 191-207. Dept. of Geography and Anthropology, Louisiana State University, Baton Rouge, LA 70893-6010.

191

based on spatial transposition, and cosmological configurations (Singh 1994a). Furthermore, not only are ritualistic movements prescribed spatially but they are also related temporally to a sacred calendar (Singh 1994b).

After an introductory section on the role of pilgrimages in Hinduism, this paper focuses on the expression of worship through spatial and temporal frameworks in Varanasi, the pilgrimage center with two thousand sanctuaries and a half million images (Pavitrananda 1956, 498-99).

The Role of Pilgrimages

The Vedic literature (ca. 2000 - 500 B.C.) does not refer directly to pilgrimages, but traveling was considered an essential part of fulfillment (e.g., *Aitareya Brahmana*, VII.15). In Vedic literature, the Sanskrit word *yātra* referred to "travel" rather than "pilgrimage", but the Puranic literature (ca. 500 B.C. - A.D. 700) did accept yātra as meaning "pilgrimage". Yātra, as a symbol of union and joining, has somehow or other become an essential part of all Hindu religious activities. At the local level, movement is expressed by *parikrama* (circumambulation), which through time has become an invariable central ritual during pilgrimage.

Detailed information about sacred sites and pilgrimages is found in Puranic literature. The *Mahābhārata* (ca. 300 B.C.) may be considered the first Hindu book providing glorious descriptions of sacred places. It clearly indicates that going on pilgrimages (*tīrtha-yātras*) is superior to sacrifice (Bhardwaj 1973, 29). The *Matsya Purana* (ca. A.D. 400) enumerates a large number of sacred places with descriptions of associated schedules, gestures, dreams, and auspicious signs and symbols. Similarly other Puranas describe sacred places and pilgrimages.

Motives for pilgrimages, as stipulated in the Puranas, may be categorized in four broad groups: *putreshana* (desire for a son), *vitteshana* (desire for wealth), *mukteshana* (desire for liberation or atonement from sin), and *lokeshana* (desire for worldly gain). But all centers of pilgrimage have the merits of general purification and bliss. In most cases, the act of pilgrimage is performed as an expression of devotion to a deity and ultimately to gain blissful satisfaction through the fulfillment of a particular desire.

It is a very common tradition in Hinduism to endow more sacredness to some places than to others, even though no single system defines which place is the most sacred for all times, for all sects, and for all regions. Certainly Varanasi (ancient Kashi and the place the British called Banaras or Benares) ranks among the major Hindu pilgrimage places.

Varanasi is not universally regarded as the most sacred. For example, it is not held in especially high regard by pilgrims from Gujarat. And, from the perspective of Tamils, the Gaṅgā itself "is forced to worship in a south

Indian shrine in order to become free of the sins deposited by evil-doers who bathe in the river at Kashi" (Shulman 1980, 18).

In spite of some regional differences, numerous texts cite Varanasi as a primary place for pilgrimage. The *Bhavisya Purana* (as referred to in *Tristhalisetu* 141-142) mentions that a person taking a bath anywhere in the Gangā can achieve merit, but that merit increases ten times where the river touches the Vindhyachal range, one hundred times where it takes a westerly flow, and one thousand times where it has a northerly flow, which is the case at Varanasi.

The *Kashi Khanda* (6.68) states that there are seven sacred cities (*puris*) which bestow salvation: Ayodhya (the capital of Lord Rama), Mathura (the birthplace of Lord Krishna), Kanchi (sacred to Lord Vishnu), Dwarka (the capital of Lord Krishna), and Kashi/Varanasi (the city of Lord Shiva) (fig. 1). According to popular belief, those who die in Kashi will receive direct liberation, while in any of the other six cities they will receive liberation only indirectly because they will be reborn in Kashi. In fact, the whole area of Varanasi is so sacred that a person dying anywhere in this territory receives *moksha* (liberation from transmigration) and pilgrims can obtain sufficient merit for salvation by visiting only a few places.

A Sanskrit stanza (translated by Chaudhuri 1979, 172) declares: "Kashi is for them whose salvation is not to be had anywhere. For those who die ignorant of the revealed scriptures and sacred traditions, for those who have abandoned purity and proper conduct, or for those who have nowhere else to go, for them Varanasi is refuge."

Arrangements and Movements within Varanasi

At the national or pan-Hindu scale, Varanasi is considered a sacred site to which many pilgrims travel long distances. At the local scale, however, Varanasi is an area of sanctity in which spatial patterns and behavior are important. For example, on the 84 ghats along the banks of the Gangā are located 96 distinct tīrthas. Of these 96, five are known as the *Panchatīrtha*. The eighth-century text, *Matsya Purana* (185.69) refers to the meritorious glories of these five ghats. In an early fourteenth-century text, the *Kashi Khanda* of *Skanda Purana* (84.107-10), their importance is extoled in the following manner: "There, O Prince, is the very excellent Five Tīrthas, the Panchatīrtha; having bathed in which a person shall never again be born ... rather he becomes the five-faced Shiva in Kashi."

Pilgrims perform rituals by proceeding in order from Assi Ghat to Dashasvamedha to Adi Keshava, to Panchaganga, and finally to Manikarnika Ghat. At each of these ghats, pilgrims take baths and worship prominent deities (Singh 1994c). After taking the final ritual bath at Manikarnika Ghat, they pay homage to the patron deity of the city, Lord Shiva in the form of Vishvanatha, and to other deities nearby (Eck 1982, 220).

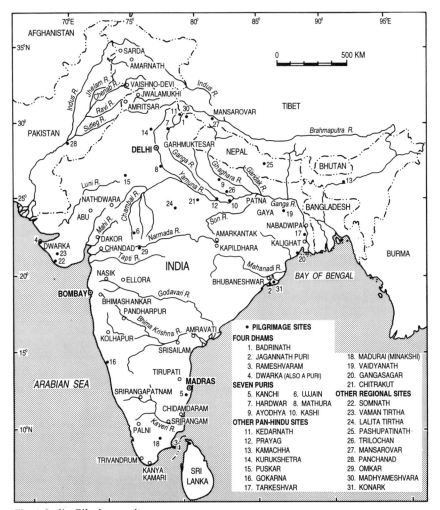

Fig. 1. India: Pilgrimage sites.

Spatial Transposition

One of the factors affecting the arrangement of holy places within Varanasi involves spatial transposition, which is the re-establishment of religious patterns at a different place and different scale from the original. It has been said that "all the sacred places of pilgrimages are in Varanasi, and if one stays in Varanasi there is no need to go anywhere else on pilgrimages" (Eck 1982, 283).

Because of the notion of spatial transposition, Varanasi reflects the very depth of India's spiritual geography. Through spatial transposition, the six other puris are re-created in the sacred geography of Varanasi (compare figs. 1 and 2). Thus, while moving around within this holy city, pilgrims can, in effect, worship at the seven puris (Singh 1995a).

Likewise, all twelve light-reflecting (*Jyotir*) *lingas* (phallic symbols representing Shiva), which are distributed throughout India, are transposed to Varanasi. Specifically, Someshvara (originally Somnath, Gujarat) appears at Man Mandir Ghat in Varanasi; Mallikarjuna (Hyderabad) at Tripurantakeshvara; Mahakaleshvara (Ujjain) at Briddhakala; Omkareshvara (Mandhata) at Omkareshvara; Vaidyanatha (Deoghar) at Kamachha; Bhimashankara (Pune) at Bhimeshvara; (Rameshvaram) at Ramkund; Nageshvara (near Dwarka) at Bhonsala Ghat; Tryambakeshvara (Nasik) at Baradeo; Kedareshvara (Chamoli) at Kedara Ghat; Ghushmeshvara (Ellora) near Batuka Bhaivara; and Vishveshvara, already in Varanasi at Jnanavapi.

Another example of spatial transposition is the representation of the four *dhams* (abodes of gods) lying at the four cardinal directions of India (fig. 1). The northern dham of Badrinath has its counterpart near Trilochana Ghat in Varanasi (fig. 2). The southernmost sacred site of Rameshvaram is reproduced at the Man Mandir Ghat, and the western dham of Dwarka is replicated at Shankhudhara. The fourth is Jagannath Puri in the east. Near Assi Ghat, Puri has been transposed to a compound where a large sandalwood Jagannath statue has been installed.

Other illustrations of spatial transposition of various gods and goddesses in Varanasi are the eight Bhairavas for the eight directions, the nine Durgas and nine Gauris for the nine planets, and the 42 Shivas. Just as there are three important layers of Shiva-lingas, each having 14 lingas, distributed over the subcontinent, the same are represented within the confines of the sacred precincts of Varanasi.

Although it has little impact on the topic of pilgrimages within Varanasi, it should be noted that spatial transposition also moves away from Varanasi to other sacred sites. Eck notes: "Varanasi is present in a thousand places in India, each with its own temple of Kashi Vishvanatha, some even boasting a Panchakroshi road. Kashi is the paradigm of the sacred place, to which other places subscribe in their claims to sanctify" (Eck 1982, 283-284).

Cosmology

As implied by the location of sacred sites within Varanasi having directional importance, cosmological concepts influence arrangements. The cosmology of Varanasi, which is described in Puranic literature as the first city after the great cosmic dissolution (*mahapralaya*), can be represented as a series of concentric circles. In total there are seven circles, each of which is intersected by eight radials located at the prime directions. The 56 inter-

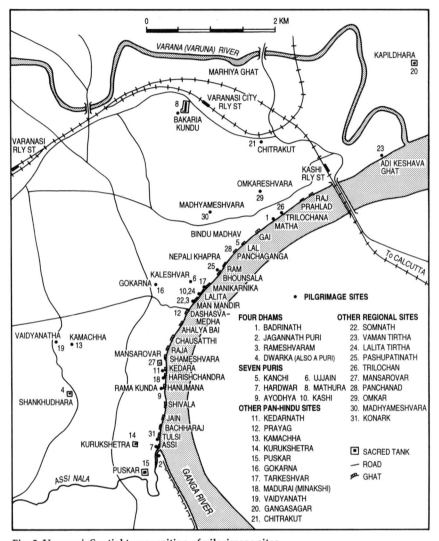

Fig. 2. Varanasi: Spatial transposition of pilgrimage sites.

sections are manifested by 56 shrines dedicated to Lord Ganesha in the form of Vinayaka (fig. 3). Thus, pilgrims who visit the 56 Vinayakas observe the differential sanctity of space by following a prescribed route that takes them through the seven protective rings to reach the holy of holies, the Vishvanatha (Vishveshvara) Temple (Singh 1995b).

Sanctity within the concentric rings varies, with the intensity of sanctity increasing as the center is approached. Or, stated in common geographic terminology, variations in sanctity can be expressed by a distance

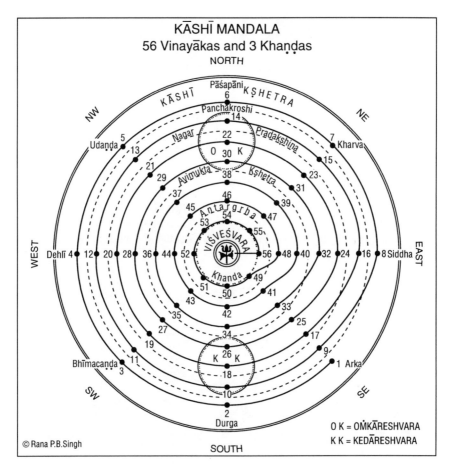

Fig. 3. Mandala of the city of Kashi, now Varanasi, showing location of 56 Vinayakas (Ganesh) and three segments. *Source:* The *Kashi Khanda* 57:59-116.

decay function. Consequently, the complexity of rituals and the overall importance of a pilgrimage site is related to its position within this zone of sacred space. The differentiation of sanctity, in turn, greatly affects the movement of worshipers within the precincts of the pilgrimage place.

The seven concentric rings are identified with the seven routes of pilgrimage. From outer to inner, these are the following: Chaurashikroshi, marking the cosmic circuit; Panchakroshi, which delimts the sacred territory; Nagar Pradakshina, corresponding with the circumambulatory route of the main city; Avimukta Kshetra, delimiting the inner sacred territory; Omkareshvara Khanda Yātra, the northern segmentary pilgrimage route; Vishveshvara Khanda Yātra, known as Vishveshvara Antargriha, the bounds of the most sacred inner sanctum of the holy territory; and Kedar-eshvara Khanda Yātra, the southern segmentary pilgrimage route sur-rounding the Kesareshvara temple.

The first known map of Kashi showing its yātras and main pilgrimage stations, as based on Puranic literature, was prepared by Kailashnath Sukal in 1875 (fig. 4). The map clearly shows the holy realm of Kashi with an outer limit in a circular form around its center at the Madhyameshvara Temple and a square at the most holy place of the patron deity, Vish-vanatha (Vishveshvara). Thus, the map depicts the concept of a universe within the universe (Singh 1982) (figs. 5 and 6).

Circumambulation

Circumambulation (parikrama) can be thought of as a pilgrimage at a local scale that involves moving along a prescribed route which commences and terminates at the same place. In fact, because the circumference of the

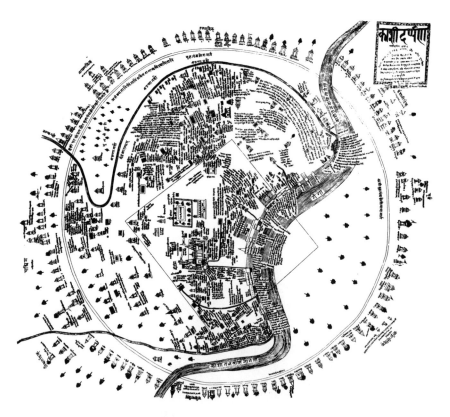

Fig. 4. Map of Kashi, based on Puranic literature, prepared by Kailashnath Sukal, 1875.

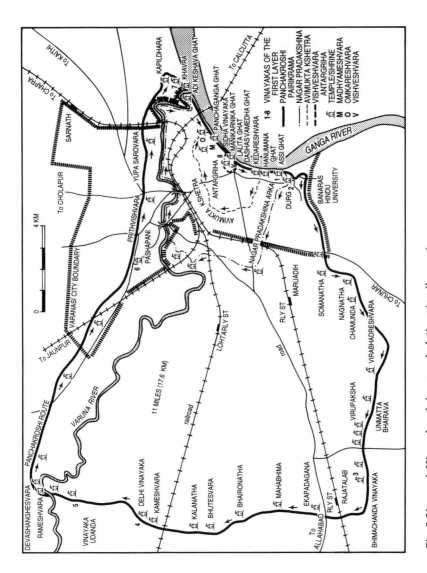

Fig. 5. Varanasi: Hierarchy of circumambulations (parikramas)

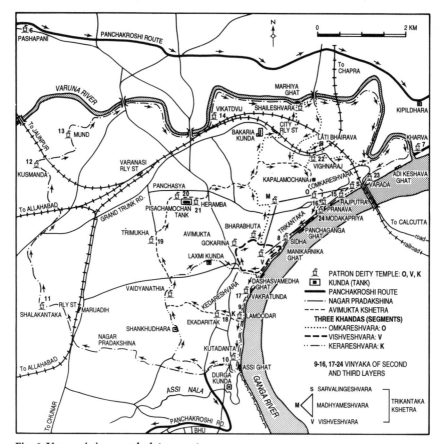

Fig. 6. Varanasi circumambulatory routes.

route may vary from a few meters to many kilometers, a long circumambulation is transitional to a short pilgrimage. For example, the now abandoned *Chaurashikroshi Parikrama*, which involved a length of 270 kilometers around Varanasi, could be considered either a long circumambulation or a short pilgrimage (Singh 1993, 38-43).

Religious movements are associated not only with differentiation of sacred space but also by sacred time. Although all days that are auspicious for traveling are considered good for pilgrimages, a particular day is preferred for worship of a specific deity and for a distinct goal. For instance, pilgrims, who observe differences in space when visiting the 56 Vinayakas, also recognize variations in the sanctity of time because the most auspicious times for such are the fourth days during the waning fortnights of Bhadrapada (August-September) and Magha (January-February).

Yātras (pilgrimages and circumambulations) can be classified according to timing as annual, seasonal, monthly, weekly, and daily. Among the annual circumambulations in Varanasi, Panchakroshi is the most common (fig. 5). Each of the five parts (*panch* or five; *krosha* or 3.2 kilometers) is approximately 16.1 kilometers; thus the entire route totals about 80.5 kilometers. The concept of five denotes wholeness through Shiva as the lord of four directions and the center of a circle. Thus, this yātra represents the whole world. The number of temples on this Panchakroshi route is 108, which corresponds to the product of 12 months and 9 planets. By performing this circumambulation, a pilgrim can receive the meritorious benefits of the whole cosmos (Singh 1991).

The most popular months for the Panchakroshi are Agahana/Margashirsha (November-December) and Phalguna (February-March). Although pilgrims may undertake this yātra during either season, the latter time is more popular because it is believed that Lord Shiva and other gods performed this pilgrimage at this time. During this season, the plays of Rama and Krishna are presented at the five sacred resting sites: Kandawa, Bhimachandi, Rameshwar, Shiopur, and Kapildhara (Vidyarthi, et al. 1979, 83-85). On the morning of the sixth day, after taking baths at the Manikarnika Kunda (sacred well or pond), pilgrims return to their starting point. At the conclusion of their ritual journey, they worship Lord Shiva.

The Panchakroshi parikrama is continued for a month during the leap-year month (Malamasa), which is considered especially auspicious. Pilgrims, who come from all over the country, are guided by professional priests (*paṇḍās*), a custom that was initiated by a Brahmin priest of Varanasi for this particular ritual about a century ago (although paṇḍās have served elsewhere since the eleventh century). Associated with this pilgrimage is a grand feast called *bhandara*, for which subscriptions and alms are collected in both cash and kind from various groups of pilgrims. The bhandara was first organized during a parikrama in 1973 during which about 500 persons — including Brahmins, Shudras, Sannyasis, and beggars — were fed (Vidyarthi, et al. 1979, 87).

Since the Panchakroshi parikrama is not possible for everyone, the main territory of Kashi (i.e., Varanasi Nagar) has been accepted as an alternative circumambulatory route. This route, which is only about 25 kilometers long, passes through the area between the Assi Nala and Varana River that is known as Nagar Pradakshina (fig. 6). As usual, the actual pilgrimage is preceded by preparatory rituals that include taking a bath in the Gaṅgā at Manikarnika Ghat, making a sacred vow (*sankalpa*) at Jnanavapi and worshipping Vishvanatha (Vishveshvara) in the adjacent temple, and proceeding southward to Assi Ghat. From there, pilgrims go westward as they move clockwise by visiting Shalakantaka Vinayaka and then Kusmanda Vinayaka shrines, following the Varana (Varuna) River to its mouth, worshipping at the Adi Keshava, and finally returning to Vish-vanatha.

This shortened circumambulation is to be performed at least twice each year according to the movement of the sun: once during the six months from summer to winter when the sun progresses northward (Uttarayana) and once when the sun moves southward (Dakshinayana). Considering the difficulties of performing both pilgrimages, the scriptures suggest that performance of either in a year provides considerable spiritual merit.

The parikrama of Avimukta (never forsaken) is a second abbreviated version of the great Panchakroshi. According to *Kashi Khanda* (39.77), pilgrims are to take a bath at Manikarnika Ghat, make a sacred vow at Jnanavapi and worship Avimukteshvara, both in the compound of Vishvanatha, and then return to Manikarnika Ghat. Afterwards, they are to follow a clockwise circular route to visit Kedara, Vaidyanatha, Pisha-chamochana, Omkareshvara, and Trichona Ghat before returning to Vishvanatha.

The circumambulation that is seasonal is associated with the seven sacred cities (table 1). In Varanasi, it occurs at Lalita Ghat where Shiva, in the form of Karuneshvara (lord of sympathy), is worshiped every season. The patron deity is also worshiped in the Hemanta (winter) season as Ma-hakaleshvara (lord of time and death).

The monthly pilgrimage is associated with a holy bath in a *kunda* (sacred pond) for a particular purpose. The practice of combining a sacred

Table 1. Seasonal pilgrimages to seven *puris* (sacred cities) in Varanasi.

Puri	Place in Varanasi	God	Hindu Season	Roman Season	Roman months
Dwarka	Shankhudhara	Lord Krishna	Varsha	Rains	July-Sept
Kanchi	Bindumadhav	Vishnu	Sharada	Autumn	Sept-Nov
Ujjain	Kaleshvara	Mahakalesh-vara	Hemanta	Winter	Nov-Jan
Hardwar	Assi Ghat	Vishnu	Shishira	Cold	Jan-Mar
Mathura	Bakaria Kunda	Child Krishna	Vasanta	Spring	Mar-May
Ayodhya	Ramakunda	Rama	Grishma	Summer	May-July
Kashi	Lalita Ghat	Karunesh-vara	- - - - - - - - all seasons - - - - - - - -		

bath with circumambulation is regarded as having been introduced by supernatural beings and great sages. The circumambulations are around the kundas and their associated Shiva temples at a variety of places. Monthly pilgrimages, therefore, are a form of worshipping Lord Shiva in his different forms (table 2).

Among the daily pilgrimages, Antargriha (inner sanctum), with 75 shrines and temples along its path, is one of the most important. According to Puranic sources, the Antargriha of Vishvanatha/ Vishveshvara is very meritorious. The *Kashi Khanda* (74.45) describes the boundary of Vishvesh-

Table 2. Monthy pilgrimage sites in Varanasi

Bathing pond	Location of pond	Hindu month	Roman month	Motive	Initiator
Kamakunda	Mahatir-lochan	Chaitra	Mar-Apr	To fulfill desire	Gods
Bimala-kunda	Jangam-bari	Vaishakha	Apr-May	To get peace	Demons
Rudrabasa Tirtha	Manikar-nika	Jyeshtha	May-June	Relieving difficulty	Gods
Lakshmi-kunda	Lakshmi-kund	Ashadha	June-July	To get wealth	Celestial musicians
Kamachha-kunda	Kamachha	Shravana	July-Aug	To get energy	Inspired sages
Kapala-mochan	Lata Bhairava	Bhadra-pada	Aug-Sept	Relieving fear	Celestial beings
Markandeya Tirtha	Jnanavapi	Ashvina	Sept-Oct	To satisfy manes	Manes
Pancha-ganga	Bindu-madhav	Karttika	Oct-Nov	To purify	Sages
Pishacah-mochan	Pishacha-mochan	Marga-shirsha	Nov-Dec	Relief from spirits	Inspired sages
Dhanada Kunda	Annapurna temple	Pausha	Dec-Jan	To get rich	Guhayak(?)
Koti-tirtha	Sakhi Vinayaka	Magha	Jan-Feb	To purify	Vegetal godling
Gokarna Kunda	Kodaike Chauki	Phalguna	Feb-Mar	Atone from sins	Flesh-eating demons

vara Antargriha as: "On the east, Manikarnoka; in the south, Brahmesh-vara stands; in the west, Gokarna; and in the north, Bharatbhuteshvara." Most pilgrims who come to Varanasi, as well as many pious residents of the city, traverse this circumambulation route daily.

In the course of time, the Antargriha of the other two of the three *khan-das* (segments) also became popular. The importance of all three segments probably resulted from the Puranic literature that describes Varanasi as being raised above the earth on the three points of Shiva's trident. This no-tion has been distinctly presented in a lithograph of Varanasi pilgrimages, which is popularly sold in shops of religious materials (fig. 7). The circu-mambulatory route linking the Omkareshvara khanda in the north and the Kedareshvara khanda in the south completely encircles the zone of the patron deity and delimits the sacred territory of the deity. Nowadays, however, pilgrims rarely perform parikrama along the Omkareshvara segment, which surrounds the oldest occupied settlement in Varanasi (Singh 1980, 41).

The parikrama of the Kedareshvara khanda includes worship at many temples and shrines. According to *Kashi-Kedar Mahatmya* (29.38), "It is known as the Kedara (field) where the crop of liberation grows. There-fore, that place became famous as the Kedara, both in Kashi and in the mountains." In fact, Kedareshvara in Kashi is the spatial transposition of the well-known Kedara in the Himalaya. The Puranic literature declares that the Himalayan Kedara liberates anyone who sees it. Of course it is very difficult for most pilgrims to accomplish the rigorous journey into the high Himalaya, so it was transposed to Kashi. Lord Shiva agreed that Ke-dareshvara would bestow liberation directly and unconditionally.

Concluding Remarks

More than half of the 500 pilgrims interviewed by Vidyarthi et al. in 1972-73 stated that they had come to Varanasi for special performances (table 3). It would seem that these respondents exemplify the typical pil-grim who travels to a distant place because the object of devotion is locat-ed there. Although the journey itself may be meaningful, the primary reason for movement is merely to get from one place to another (i.e., from home to the tirtha). However, another 13 percent of the interviewed pil-grims reported that they came to Varanasi to undertake a circumambula-tion associated with funeral ceremonies. Furthermore, because pilgrims often have multiple reasons for their yātras, numerous respondents who came to Varanasi "for special performances" undoubtedly engaged also in at least one parikrama.

The geography of pilgrimages is frequently studied at the scale that reduces the sacred sites to points and focuses attention on movements across long distances. It is important to remember that the movement

Fig. 7. Map of Kashi, based on early lithograph.

Table 3. Main purpose for pilgrims' visits to Varanasi, 1972-73

Purpose		Percent
Special performances		59.0
Vishvanatha worship	57.2	
Worship of other deities	1.8	
Funeral ceremonies		13.0
Pindadana	7.8	
Throw ashes into the Gaṅgā	2.8	
Cremation	2.4	
Tīrtha yātra (as part of religious duty)		12.8
Special tīrtha yātra (on auspicious occasion)		4.2
Mundana (ritual hair cut)		2.0
No answer and miscellaneous		9.0

Source: After Vidyarthi et al. (1979, 136)

within a sacred area is also a part of the spatial component of pilgrimages. Consequently, to gain a full understanding of the geography of religious behavior, it is essential that the routes and timing of movements be studied at several scales. Varanasi with its annual, seasonal, monthly, weekly, and daily parikramas well illustrates this characteristic of pilgrimages (Singh 1993, 215-24).

References

Bhardwaj, S. M. 1973. *Hindu places of pilgrimage in India: A study in cultural geography.* Berkeley: University of California Press.
Chaudhuri, N. C. 1979. *Hinduism: A religion to live by.* London: Chatto & Windus.
Eck, D. 1982. *Banaras: City of light.* New York: Alfred A. Knopf.
Pavitrananda, S. 1956. Pilgrimage and fairs: Their bearing on Indian life. In *The cultural heritage of India*, ed. H. Bhattacharya, 495-502. Calcutta: Ramkrishna Mission.
Shulman, D. D. 1980. *Tamil temple myths: Sacrifice and divine marriage in the South Indian Saiva tradition.* Princeton: Princeton University Press.
Singh, Rana P. B. 1980. The socio-cultural space of Varanasi. *Art and Archaeology Research Papers* 17:41-46.
———. 1982. Image of Varanasi City: Reflections on geography of tourism. *Frankfurter Wirtschafts und Sozialgeographische Schriften* 41:161-74.
———. 1991. *Pancakrosi yātra, Varanasi: Sacred journey, ecology of place, and faithscape.* Varanasi, India: Tara Book Agency.
———, ed. 1993 *Banaras (Varanasi): Cosmic order, sacred city, Hindu traditions.* Varanasi, India: Tara Book Agency.
———. 1994a. The sacred geometry of India's holy city, Varanasi: Kashi as cosmogram. *National Geographical Journal of India* 40:1-31.

——. 1994b. Time and Hindu rituals in Varanasi: A study of sacrality and cycles. *Geographia Religionum* 8:123-38.

——. 1994c Water symbolism and sacred landscape in Hinduism: A case of Benares (Varanasi). *Erdkunde* 48:210-27.

——. 1995a. Varanasi: Cosmic order and cityscape. III: Shiva's universe and pilgrimage journeys. *Architecture and Design* 12:83-85.

——. 1995b. Varanasi: Ganesha images and shrines in the cityscape. In *Pilgrimage Studies*, Pub. 3, ed. D. P. Dubey, 209-20. Allahabad: Society of Pilgrimage Studies.

Vidyarthi, L. P., M. Jha, and B. N. Saraswati. 1979. *The sacred complex of Kashi*. Delhi: Concept Publishing Co.

The Role of Pilgrimage Priests in Perpetuating Spatial Organization within Hinduism

Anita Caplan
Council for International Exchange of Scholars

Abstract

This study examines the role of pilgrimage and pilgrimage priests at Prayag (Allahabad), India, in perpetuating the spatial organization of Hinduism. The physical landscape of Prayag as a major all-India pilgrimage center is a manifestation of Hindu myths and gods from some of Hinduism's Great Traditions. Pilgrimage priests (paṇḍās) occupy this landscape and keep pilgrims aware of the sanctity of the sacred center.

Data show that the profession of paṇḍā is a long-established institution recognized by the government as well as by the devout pilgrims. Analysis of paṇḍā activities demonstrates in several ways how the paṇḍās' work is integral to the pilgrimage tradition at Prayag: (a) paṇḍās maintain a geographical division of India into areas (symbolized by flags) wherein the pilgrims from each area are "owned" by particular paṇḍās; (b) paṇḍās provide facilities for the pilgrimage including a place to stay, make travel arrangements, loan money, obtain medical help, and arrange for food; (c) paṇḍās assist in the performance of religious rituals — especially ash immersion and ancestor worship; and (d) paṇḍās strengthen the tie to their pilgrim-clients in a number of ways including their acceptance of donations (dāna), the use of admonitions, recruitment, and the information they keep for pilgrim families in their pilgrimage records (bahīs).

The paṇḍā is a professional whose entrepreneurial and managerial role works to maintain geographic channels of communication between the sacred center and client families from all over India. Paṇḍā activities publicize the pilgrimage and maintain its tradition. By managing the annual religious fairs, or melās, and by officiating in ritual observances at Prayag, the pilgrimage priests become caretakers of Prayag's sacred geography as well as perpetuators of Hindu tradition. Their work significantly contributes to pilgrimage to Prayag and in this way ensures that pilgrimage remains an important feature of Hinduism.

Key words: pilgrimage, pilgrimage priests (paṇḍās), Hinduism, India, pilgrimage services

The survival of Hinduism as a major religion for over four thousand years has occurred without relying on a formal organization of an official

Sacred Places, Sacred Spaces: The Geography of Pilgrimages, edited by Robert H. Stoddard and Alan Morinis, 1997. Geoscience and Man, vol. 34, pp. 209-233. Dept. of Geography and Anthropology, Louisiana State University, Baton Rouge, LA 70893-6010 governing body (such as a hierarchical church authority). It has survived even though its specific characteristics vary from region to region. If Hinduism lacks uniformity of belief and lacks formal organization, what is there that reinforces Hindu tradition? What informal means of organization have caused this religion to persist for so long?

One potential mechanism is the pilgrimage — the focus of this paper. Hindu pilgrimage, it will be shown, displays a spatial organization that is maintained partly by pilgrimage priests. These priests, Brahmans who are called *tīrtha purohits* (literally "pilgrimage priests"), act as entrepreneurs and organizers catering to the physical and spiritual needs of pilgrims at most of India's major religious centers. It is suggested here that the tīrtha purohits are in the critical position of translating, interpreting, and teaching Hinduism's Great Traditions to pilgrim clients. Each priest is in the position of encouraging and maintaining the geographic organization of India's major pilgrimages by taking responsibility for potential and actual pilgrims from a specific region.

While such spatial distinctions are maintained, the pilgrimage site becomes a point for reinforcement of a common Hindu identity and for the dissemination outward of this identity. When participants share religious activities with fellow pilgrims from all over India, they may sense that they belong to the large cultural tradition that is Hinduism. A homogenizing effect may occur because pilgrims, coming from diverse linguistic areas and representing different castes and occupations, participate together in a standardized set of religious activities. When they meet priests and revered saints gathered at sacred places, the pilgrims become the recipients of religious knowledge. They take this knowledge with them back to their homes and share it with fellow villagers and relatives. In sum, the pilgrimage can be characterized as a spatially-organized network which joins the various outlying points to sacred pilgrimage centers (nodes), thereby defining the region of Hinduism.

To explore the plausibility of these points, this study examines the spatial organization and operation of a major Hindu pilgrimage, Prayag's Magh Melā.[1] About one million people attend the annual Magh Melās at Prayag, which takes place during the winter months of Magh (Hindu calendar). This should not be confused with the Kumbh Mēla, which occurs every twelve years and attracts even more pilgrims; for example, about five million attended the Kumbh Melā in Prayag in 1977.

Sources of Data

Data were collected in Allahabad during 1978-1979 and 1983-1984. The main sources of data examined here include (1) printed materials, the *Prayāg Māhātmya* of the ancient *Purāṇas* and the contemporary guide books which evolved from it, (2) interviews with 95 pilgrimage priests, and (3) a survey of approximately 1,696 pilgrims at Prayag. Other data include hundreds of pilgrimage records kept by the priests and interviews with officials.

Texts

The *Prayāg Māhātmya,* literally "the glorious praise of Prayag," is both an ancient and a popular publication. It is said to be the authority regarding the greatness, the ceremonies, and the rules regarding a pilgrimage to Prayag. The *Prayāg Māhātmya* was originally a part of several of the *Purāṇas* and finds its most complete form in chapters 103-112 of the *Matsya Purāṇa.* Hazra (1940, 177) dates these chapters as having been written between A.D. 850 and 1250. The contemporary *Prayāg Māhātmya* is a continuously evolving treatise which, while it bears considerable resemblance to the Puranic version, appears also to reflect current behavior and beliefs of today's pilgrims at Prayag. That is, several parts of the contemporary *Prayāg Māhātmya* do not appear in the older *Purāṇas,* but do incorporate current beliefs and practices.

The edition of the *Prayāg Māhātmya* examined here is written in very simple modern Hindi, rather than the original Sanskrit, and was sold very cheaply. It is designed for pilgrim-tourists as a sort of religious guidebook. The text is one of the literally hundreds of pamphlets on religious matters that are available at shrines and temples throughout India. It is not known when the *Prayāg Māhātmya* was first translated for popular use from Sanskrit into Hindi nor how much credit should be given to Nirbhai Tripati (1978), the author of the version examined, for the translation and interpretation. As a guidebook, the *Prayāg Māhātmya* describes the contemporary perception and organization of Prayag's sacred space and thus was used as an authoritative source in the mapping of the sacred geography of Prayag.

Interviews with Pilgrimage Priests

Ninety-five interviews with pilgrimage priests (the tīrtha purohits) provide data on the role of these religious guides. These priests were selected from a 1975 census of the tīrtha purohit community in Prayag (the Prayagwal Sabha). Of the 1,484 tirtha purohit families in Prayag, only 322 were registered by the Prayagwal Sabha to work as priests. Some of these families reported as many as 26 members, but generally with the male members —fathers, brothers, sons, and nephews — working together. An attempt was made to interview one male member of as many separate member families as possible during a four-month period (December 1978 - March 1979). The tīrtha purohits who were not located, and therefore not represented in the sample, were not as active in the work of priest as those that were interviewed. Some that are missing from the sample had other jobs, such as in law, government, education, and medicine. Thus, although the 95 interviewed represented only 30 percent of the tirtha purohit families registered by the Prayagwal Sabha, they were the most active in their profession.

Survey of Pilgrims

Eight interviewers conducted a survey (the pilgrim-stream survey) of 1,696 pilgrims from streams of worshipers on their way to the bathing site at Prayag. In an attempt to make comparisons between places of origin, another sixteen interviewers conducted lengthy interviews (the state-selected survey) in pilgrim camps with at least 20 pilgrims from each state in India, collecting 697 interviews in all.

The remainder of this paper is divided into two parts. The first part describes the importance of Prayag as a sacred center; the second part examines the role of pilgrimage priests in the spatial organization of pilgrimage to this holy place.

Prayag's Sacred and Secular Geography

During special holidays, when it is especially auspicious, a city of tents is erected in Prayag (Allahabad) on the banks of the Rivers Gaṅgā (Ganges) and Yamunā (Jumna) and their confluence, the saṅgam. The site then becomes a center of activities, complete with areas of camping and a variety of services provided (fig. 1).

This tent city largely disappears at the end of the fairs, or melās, although smaller numbers of visitors come throughout the year. When the monsoon is in spate, the rivers actually cover the physical location of the former tent city. In the aftermath of the flooding, the physical reappearance of the saṅgam indicates a new physical geography that has been altered by the water currents and deposition of sand on the floodplain.

What factors contribute to the periodic establishment of this religious center located at the saṅgam? What are some of the activities, especially those that encourage pilgrimages, that occur at this site?

Mythical and Astrological Explanations for Pilgrimages at Prayag

According to the Puranic mythology, gods and demons churned the ocean to obtain a precious nectar which gave immortality. In a popular and contemporary ending of the myth, when the coveted kumbha (or pitcher) of nectar was obtained, one of the gods whisked the pitcher away from the demons. The god evaded the demons, spilling a few drops of the nectar at four places — Prayag, Hardwar, Nasik, and Ujjain — before reaching the safety of heaven. Tradition has it that since then sages, saints, and pil-

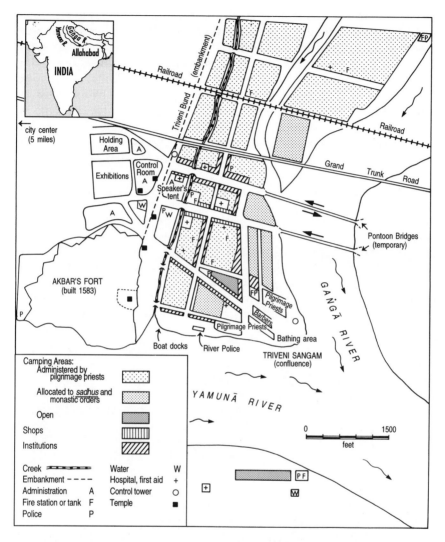

Fig. 1. Pilgrimage grounds of Prayag's Magh Melā, Allahabad, India, January 14 to February 12, 1979 (Hindu date: Magh, Samwat 2035). *Source:* Adapted from the official plan provided by J. N. Visvakarma, Head, Magh Melā Commission.

grims have periodically flocked to each of these four places to celebrate the divine event. The god's journey took twelve days, which corresponds to twelve years in the lives of humans. Consequently, the event is celebrated with greater intensity every twelve years as the Kumbh Melā.

The legend of the churning of the ocean is inadequate, however, to account for the periodic nature of Prayag's other melās. This is because long before Prayag and Hardwar were mentioned in the now popular myth, a regular cycle of melās was already established at those places during the month of Magh (Bonazzoli 1977, 106-119).

A second theory that accounts for the timing of the melās is related to astrology. The Kumbh Melās is held when the sun is in Aries and the planet Jupiter is in Aquarius (or Kumbh), which occurs every twelfth year, although the interval may, very rarely, be eleven or thirteen years. However, scholars (Bonazzoli 1977; Bedekar 1967) find both the mythical and the astrological explanations insufficient and continue to search for evidence documenting the origin of Prayag's melās.

Geographic Explanations for Prayag's Location

In general, population distribution does not entirely explain the locations of sacred places in India (Stoddard 1966). Physical landscape factors, however, do seem to play a significant role in the location of these places (Bhardwaj 1973). For example, Hindu sacred places are located at the four corners of the sub-continent, at natural rock and cave formations, on the coasts, and on mountain tops. Many of India's sacred places are located on rivers, not for economic reasons, but because rivers are manifestations of goddesses. Site characteristics — river, ocean, hilltop — are invariably tied into the myths of the sacred places and this relationship between the site characteristic and myth is often acted out in religious ritual. For example, water deified in the person of river gods cleanses the human spirit as well as the body. In fact, one of the few religious beliefs that Hindus unanimously agree on is that rivers are sacred. It is not surprising, therefore, that a holy site is located at the confluence of two important rivers, both believed to be goddesses.

In part, the mythical must be considered along with the physical when explaining Prayag's location. This is illustrated at Prayag by the Triveṇī Saṅgam, literally the meeting of three braids or streams. Thousands of years ago, as the Gaṅgā Valley became the heartland of Aryan-Hindu culture and the seat of empires, the Gaṅgā became established as the holiest of rivers, as a mother goddess. It continues to be venerated to this day, and Hindus sing hymns and recite prayers praising the river. Hindus obtain several benefits from bathing in the Gaṅgā, from drinking of the river, and from tasting a few drops of the stream's water brought from afar.

The Yamunā is the second sacred river at Prayag and flows from a source not far from the Gaṅgā in the Himalayas. Yamunā, the daughter of Sūrya (the sun god) and the sister of Yama (the lord of death), is best known for her association with the early life of Lord Kṛṣṇa (Krishna).

Devout Hindus believe that a third river, the invisible Sarasvatī, joins the Gaṅgā and the Yamunā at Prayag to form the Triveṇī Saṅgam. Sarasvatī, the goddess of learning, has no geographic reality at Prayag (other than being marked by the line where the silted, milky-appearing Gaṅgā merges with the blue-green Yamunā). It is possible that at one time there was a river named Sarasvatī somewhere to the west of Prayag (Godbole 1963; Spate, Learmouth, and Farmer 1967).

Historical Factors in Prayag's Religious Importance

Evidence for Prayag's antiquity comes from the R̥g Veda which, by the early half of the first millennium B.C., mentioned that the confluence of the rivers Gaṅgā, Yamunā, and Sarasvatī is a holy place capable of bestowing immortality upon the faithful (Müller 1892, 9:533). By the seventh century, Prayag was certainly well established both as a center of pilgrimage and as an urban place. At that time, the Chinese pilgrim, Hsüan-tsang, observed that Hindus sought salvation in the belief that dying at Prayag meant the attainment of heaven. Hsüan-tsang saw pilgrims throw themselves from the Patalpuri temple, located right at the saṅgam, down into the paved court below (Beal 1884). Near the court at the temple was a sacred tree, the Akṣayavaṭa ("Everlasting Fig Tree"), from which Hsüan-tsang observed pilgrims throwing themselves into a deep reservoir.

These suicides give Prayag its name. This is because the name "Prayag" has the literal meaning in Sanskrit of excellent *yajña*, or excellent sacrifice. The sacrificial ceremony of yajña, which has been practiced by Hindus from time immemorial, has meant making offerings to the deities by putting the offerings in a fire which is the personification of the god Agni. The supreme sacrifice is the giving of the physical body in fire. While the Vedic religion condemned it, suicide, or at least death, at the saṅgam promised immortality. This is demonstrated by a verse of a R̥g Veda Khila:

Those who take a bath at the place where the two
rivers, white and dark, meet together, rise
up (fly up) to heaven;

those determined men who abandon their body there
(i.e., commit suicide by drowning themselves)
secure immortality (or *mokṣa*). (Kane 1973, 596-597)

Some of the same benefits of yajña may be gained today at Prayag by sacrificing wealth in lieu of sacrificing one's life. The giving of even the smallest donation at Prayag is believed to be far better than a donation made at any other place in India. Today pilgrims give donations to the pilgrimage priests, saints, and sādhus, as well as to the thousands of beggars who congregate during the annual melās.

The Akṣayavaṭa tree, which Hsüan-tsang wrote about in the seventh century, was called the "Tree of Prayag" by the time of al-Biruni (about A.D. 1030), and religious suicide was still being practiced (Sachau 1910). The twelfth-century historian Kalhana (Stein 1961, 1:94) recounted that a king of Kashmir visited Prayag at the end of the eighth century. The king made a very large donation to the Brahmans at Prayag. Whether or not these Brahmans were the ancestors of today's hereditary caste of pilgrimage priests is unknown.

By the sixteenth century, shifting rivers and flooding probably led to the ruin of whatever large urban settlements were previously at Prayag (Singh 1966, 32); and by the time the great Mughal emperor Akbar visited in 1567, the city was reduced to little more than a village. Nevertheless, Prayag continued to be an important religious center.

Akbar was the first Mughal ruler to lay claim to Prayag. He appreciated the strategic importance of the location between two important rivers, so in 1583 he commanded that a fort and a city, which he made his capital, be built at the confluence (Smith 1958, 351). He had the massive fort erected over the Pātālpuri temple and the soon-to-die Akṣayavaṭa tree (Irwin 1983), and changed the name of the city to Ilahabas (later, Allahabad). To protect the fort from flooding and damage by the ever-shifting River Gaṅgā, Akbar had two massive embankments or bunds built (fig. 2). The temple, now a set of dimly-lit subterranean corridors, and a relic of the tree, can still be visited by going inside and under the fort.

Recent Economic and Political Importance of Allahabad as a Factor in Maintaining the Pilgrimage

Allahabad, still called Prayag by devout Hindus, has been an important settlement for at least two thousand years. It became a notable economic and administrative center during the Muslim period (roughly the 1560s to 1760s). In 1801, political power in Allahabad was ceded to the British East India Company. The British brought to the city the railroad and various institutions. The University of Allahabad was the fourth university to be built during the British period (Schwartzberg 1978, 104). In 1860, the British made the city the provincial capital of the Northwest Provinces (Schwartzberg 1978, 65), and the provincial high court was transferred there in 1868.

Allahabad was probably the most important city in the independence struggle as a place for the exchange of ideas and strategies among the political elite. For example, the Indian National Congress with Moti Lal Nehru as its president had its early significant meetings in Allahabad.

The internal variations of the city can be displayed simply by noting the locations of the three main areas of the city: the commercial, administrative, and sacred sectors (fig. 2). The commercial sector (called the Chowk) is centered in the older section of the city, just south of the railroad lines. Administrative activities were shifted by the British from the fort to the newer Civil Lines, located just north of the railroad tracks. The sacred sector of Allahabad, with most of the well-known temples, is located pri-

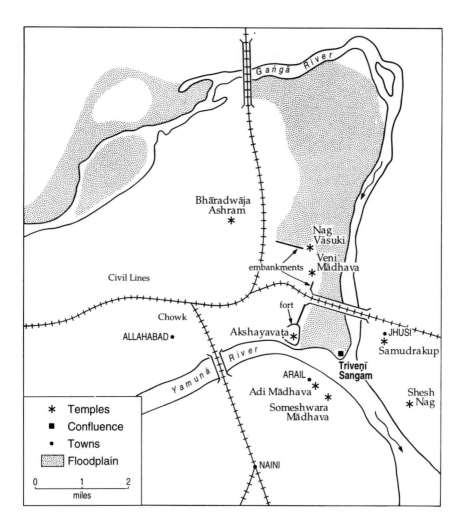

Fig. 2. Sacred and secular features of the contemporary city of Allahabad, situated between the Gaṅgā and Yamunā Rivers.

marily along the banks of the Rivers Gaṅgā and Yamunā. The homes of the priests are on both sides of the two rivers.

Allahabad's contemporary landscape (the Chowk, the Civil Lines, High Court, University, Mughal tombs, fort, and so on) reflects the evolution of the city as an important economic, administrative, and educational center. In addition, these secular attractions are linked to the center's sacred attractions because a substantial number of visitors to the secular city also visit the saṅgam. For example, Hindus who come to Allahabad for business at the High Court, banks, or the University are likely to take the opportunity to have a bath at the saṅgam during their visit. The railroad is another relevant secular feature because it provides direct links to all corners of the country and facilitates travel to this sacred center.

Satsang: *In the Company of the Holy*

The attraction to this pilgrimage site is maintained partly by presence of saints and sādhus at the melās. For many participants at Prayag, to have the *satsang* (good company) of saints is a compelling attraction. This desire may go back more than a thousand years.

It is possible that melās may have originally been regular assemblages of sādhus, *rishis*, holy men, and teachers. The great theologian and famous sādhu Sankara (c.788-820), who was also known as an *acārya*, or fighter (defender of the faith), traveled all over India to preach his doctrines. He is popularly believed to have organized the Kumbh Melās to serve as a regular meeting place as well as a seat of learning, although no evidence has been found to support this theory (Bonazzoli 1977, 110).

Today the assemblage of sādhus from all parts of India, which has been described vividly by Bharati (1961), Mehta (1972), and Ghurye (1964), is one of the most important features of the melās. Ghurye (1964, 95), in describing the various groups of Hindu ascetics and their monastic organizations, notes that their attendance at the Kumbh Melās at Prayag is the "cherished desire of most Sannyāsis, if these renouncing persons may be said to cherish any desire." Associated with such an assemblage is an attraction that draws laypersons to this religious environment.

The Sacred Geography of Prayag Today and How It is Used by Pilgrims

Allahabad's contemporary landscape also includes sacred features such as temples and ashrams and the facilities associated with the annual Magh Melā. These provide a sacred geography, which is a manifestation of Hindu myth. The geographic pattern in which gods and mythical events have become fixed in Prayag's physical space are best illustrated in the sacred precinct of the saṅgam, melā grounds, and major temples (fig. 2).

Since the annual melās take place on the floodplain between the rivers Gaṅgā and Yamunā, the courses of the streams determine how much land is available at any particular time. In any case, the entire melā grounds are sacred and one must refrain from desecrating the land by improper behavior such as eating meat or eggs there. Some people avoid wearing leather shoes.

Most pilgrims spend a few days camping at the sacred confluence in the melā grounds, the huge sandy area filled with tents erected especially for the melā (see fig. 1 for a typical arrangement). Those pilgrims who spend a month residing on this holy ground are called *kalpavāsī*, "a person who spends a period of time." In 1979, the melā officer-in-charge, K. K. Visvakarma, estimated there were 400,000 pilgrims who participated as kalpavāsī, but this was probably an exaggeration. In that year, the temporary tent city occupied 93 hectares (230 acres).

After the melā is over in mid-February, the tent city is dismantled. About four months later, the yearly monsoon floods return, inundating the plain and changing, forever, the precise outlines of the melā and the location of the sangam.

The overall orderliness with which such a large event takes place is due in part to the support of the government. Past governments — Hindu, Muslim, and British — as well as the present government, have all protected the rights of pilgrims to visit Prayag. The British began a policy which continues to this day of appointing commissions to oversee the operation of the melās. The commissions take responsibility for the installation of water pumps, the stringing of electric lines, the erection of police observation towers, the digging of latrines, and the building of a pontoon bridge across the Gangā. The melā commission works to safeguard the lives of pilgrims, provides medical facilities, and aids pilgrims in many other ways. Government expenditure is substantial. According to Visvakarma, the government yearly spends over Rs. 16,00,000 ($200,000) and takes in only 30 percent of that in revenue.

One of the goals for today's pilgrims to Prayag is to visit a number of temples. There is no consensus on exactly which places must be visited, but most priests agree that the places listed in the various versions of the *Prayāg Māhātmya* are important. For example, the 1910 *Prayāg Māhātmya* enumerates some of the places pilgrims should visit:

> I salute Triveṇī, Mādhava, Soma, Bharadwaja,
> Vāsuki, Akshayavata, and Shesha, in Prayag,
> which is the chief among tīrthas. (Bhattacharya 1910, 66)

The name Triveṇī refers to Triveṇī Sangam, the site of the three-braided stream (fig. 1). All other names listed refer to temples. Mādhava and Soma are manifestations of Visnu, the tutelary deity of Prayag. Bharadwaja is the name of an ashram, which is near the site mentioned in the epic *Ramayana* as the place at which Lord Rama stopped to rest while in exile on his way to Chitrakut (Valmiki 1976, Canto 54 & 55:435-442). The names of the other temples represent Vāsuki, a snake god, Akṣayavaṭa, the undying tree, and Shesha, another snake god.

Although several gods and goddesses are said to reside in temples at Prayag, the city, unlike many other places of pilgrimage in India, is not regarded as a temple city. Hindus do not come specifically to this center to worship the images of particular gods. Rather the primary focus of their devotion is a ritual bath at the confluence of the rivers — an entirely natural site unadorned with human artifacts. At the sangam one feels and sees the mingling of the white, silt-laden waters of the Gangā with the blue-green waters of the Yamunā; and the believer experiences the presence of the cleansing water of the invisible Sarasvatī. At no other place of worship in India do Hindus experience as many gods in such a direct tangible manner as at the sangam. Worship of god-images at temples at Prayag is an extra accoutrement to the pilgrimage to the sangam and a bath at this holy place.

It is clear, therefore, that numerous site features, and religious associations with that site, contribute to the importance of Prayag as a major pilgrimage center. In addition, though, there is an organization of space that facilitates pilgrimage to this place.

Pilgrimage Priests: Agents of a Spatial Organization of Hinduism

When Hindu pilgrims travel away from home to visit sacred places, they usually are confronted with changes in culture and language. Often pilgrims feel uncomfortable with local languages or dialects and need help in making arrangements for lodging and travel. Many also feel the need for structure and direction in performing religious activities.

To address these needs and problems, the institution of pilgrimage priest has developed through the centuries. Several researchers (Goswamy 1966; Vidyarthi 1961, 1979; Bhardwaj 1973; Mehrotra 1977; Bharati 1963; and Saraswati 1975) describe how these men, working as religious guides, interpret Hinduism to their mostly-rural pilgrim-clients. At Kashi (Varanasi), for example, temple priests, *ghātiyās* (men who work on the bathing steps), paṇḍās (pilgrimage priests), and others work in roles that transmit Hindu religious tradition (Saraswati 1975; Sopher, this volume). Saraswati (1975, 28) suggests that these men, whether or not they are versed in the shastraic knowledge, contribute to the perpetuation of the tradition largely because they interact directly with the pilgrims.

The Role of Paṇḍās

Prayag's pilgrims call their tīrtha purohits by the colloquial name, paṇḍā. Paṇḍās have life-long relationships with client families and guide them through religious activities at Prayag.

Essential to the proper performance of all the rituals under a paṇḍā's direction is *godān* (literally donation of a cow). Godān is a symbolic gift of money to the officiating priest. The practice of godān at Prayag goes back to antiquity. For example, the *Mahābhārata*, composed in the latter half of the first millennium B.C., documents the giving of wealth to Brahmans at Prayag (Buitenen 1975, (3)93:408). Likewise, the *Matsya Purāṇa* describes the merit and virtue one might get by making gifts of cows at the confluence of the Gangā and Yamunā.

A gift of a cow is the highest traditional donation, even though one of the interviewed pilgrims gave a baby elephant, costing more than Rs. 10,400 ($1300), to his paṇḍā. Large gifts such as cows and elephants are not generally given; most donations are only a few rupees, with the minimum gift being 1.25 rupees (worth about 12 U.S. cents at the time of this research). Meant to symbolize the gift of a cow, most donations are still called godān, although the term *dāna* is also used to refer to payment.

Although dāna implies an honorific gift, there are differences of opinion, albeit rare, regarding whether or not it should have a sacred or secular meaning. The elected leader of the community of pilgrimage priests at Hardwar (Avinash Vashisht) had a very secular attitude about taking donations from pilgrims; he suggested that pilgrimage priests are no more and no less than travel agents. They provide needed services: lodging mainly, but also food, travel arrangements, and protection of travelers' belongings. They keep written records and tell pilgrims how to conduct rituals. For those real services, Vashisht said, and not because they are holy and deserve honor, tirtha purohits should receive fees and thereby earn their living. A look from the outside suggests that Vashisht's characterization has some validity.

Only a few of the pilgrimage priests in Prayag, however, offered this same viewpoint. In fact, at least one family of priests in 1979 performed a ritual to repent for their acceptance of donations. This reflects an attitude about the taking of dāna that relates to the origin of Prayag's paṇḍās.

Prayag's Paṇḍās: Their Origins

Prayag's paṇḍās believe that they are not the original Brahmans who lived in Prayag in Vedic times. This is because there are injunctions in the *Śastras* and the *Purāṇas* that prohibited the native Brahmans of Prayag from accepting and living off donations given to them at the holy confluence. For example, the *Matsya Purāṇa* says: "A Brahmana should, however, avoid, as far as possible, the accepting of any gift at sacred places. He should be on his guard, that is, should not yield to temptation" (a Taluqdar of Oudh 1916, Ch.105, 15:286). Contemporary paṇḍās believe, therefore, that Brahmans came from outside Prayag to assist pilgrims and accept their donations.

The taking of dāna by the paṇḍās of Prayag may have led to their becoming a distinct subcaste (Prayagwal) of Brahmans, at least by Mughal times, and probably for many centuries before then. Several early documents from the Mughal period legitimize the rights of Prayagwals to perform services for their clients. Some of these documents are edicts, or *firmāns*, from Indian maharajas and Muslim rulers giving Prayagwal families the right to conduct rituals and collect donations from Hindus coming from the ruler's area of jurisdiction.[2] For example, one document (fig. 3) dated 1874 by the King of Sohagpur (located in what is now Shahdol District, Madhya Pradesh) states:

> that any from my state who goes to Prayag, should recognize Purohit Rameshwar and if he goes to some other Purohit, he should pay damages to Purohit Rameshwar. If I find out that anyone did not follow this order, I will punish him. Rameshwar is the Purohit of Sohagpur, therefore no one should go to others. This order issued by the court of Anupper on Miti Vaishakh Sudi 3 Samwat 1930 [A.D. 1874].

The Organization of Prayag's Paṇḍās

The paṇḍās at Prayag belong to the Prayagwal Sabha, "Organization of Prayagwals." The organization, which was registered with the government in 1860, has elected officers and neighborhood councils. It has four main functions. One function is the protection of members' rights to provide services to pilgrim families from each paṇḍā's regional jurisdiction. Another is the maintenance of quality and integrity of members so the reputation of the group as a whole is protected. A third function is the annual allocation of space on the melā grounds to the members of the organization. And, lastly, the group occasionally resolves disputes among members.

When the Prayagwal Sabha serves as protector and preserver of the rights of its members to conduct rituals and accept donations at the sangam, it may link with the legal system. In 1979, for example, the group had a petition in the court to reaffirm that only the Prayagwals have the right to accept dāna at the sangam or on the banks of the Gangā and Yamunā. They collected documents, including quotations from sacred texts and other historical items, to support their position.

The Geographic Division of Hindu Lands by the Paṇḍās

How does the pilgrim know which paṇḍā to go to? Whether the pilgrim knows it or not, every Hindu has a paṇḍā at Prayag (fig. 4). Each paṇḍā has the designated right to perform services for pilgrims from a particular area of India, Nepal, or other country. In essence, India is divided into geographical areas, in each of which pilgrims are "owned" by the particular paṇḍā who has jurisdiction over it. Each area's paṇḍā speaks Allahabad's local Hindi as well as the regional language of his clients.

To facilitate the separation of pilgrims according to client territories, each paṇḍā uses an identifying flag. These flags provide a simple way for illiterate pilgrims to remember and find their paṇḍās in Prayag. The pilgrim has only to remember the name of the flag (such as "green flag," "basket," or "bear") rather than the name of the particular man he met on his last visit, a name that might change depending on which family member

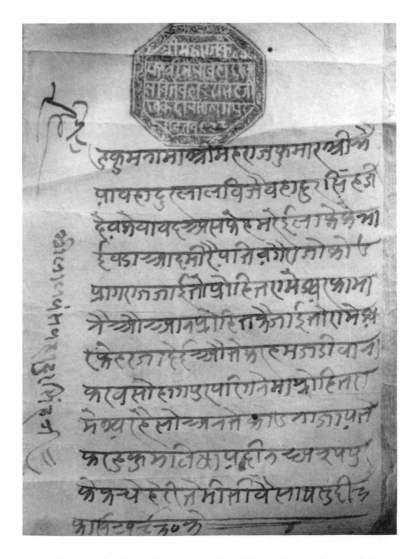

Fig. 3. An order from the King of Sohagpur to his subjects . See text for translation.

Fig. 4. Pilgrim (right) has traveled from the state of Tamil Nadu in the south of India to Prayag to consult with his pilgrimage priest (left).

provided services. In some cases, the flags provide meaningful associations with their regions, such as a *pān* (betel) leaf representing a region known for its pān production or the *kukṛī* sword symbolizing the Gurkha region of Nepal (fig. 5).

Some indication of the magnit ude of paṇḍā activity can be gained from a count of flags. On December 19, 1978, an ordinary weekday with no particular religious significance, this researcher counted 79 flags erected near the daises of the paṇḍās working at the saṅgam. Some of the paṇḍās displayed more than one flag and some flags were displayed by more than one paṇḍā (due to consolidation or splitting of families) so the number of paṇḍā families working that day was probably about 60. Several hundred flags fly during the days of the melās. The flags do not appear to have any religious significance beyond providing help for pilgrims in locating their paṇḍās. The author did, however, tape-record a religious ceremony in which a pilgrim was instructed by his paṇḍā to promise to never forget the name of the paṇḍā's flag.

Pilgrims who seek out their paṇḍā's flag are likely to be reinforced for this behavior by the paṇḍā's use of their regional language and by the presence of other clients from the same region. Other activities that bond pilgrims to paṇḍās are considered below.

Secular Functions of the Paṇḍās

The most important facility provided by paṇḍās is a place to stay. During the 1979 melā, 38 percent of the 1,696 pilgrims interviewed in a pilgrim-stream survey were staying with paṇḍās. About two-thirds of the pilgrims who remained at the melā at least one night and thus needed accommodations stayed with paṇḍās. Some pilgrims stay in the paṇḍā's guest houses, but most sleep in tents in the melā area. These tent enclaves, which cover over forty hectares (one hundred acres), are set aside for administration by the paṇḍās. The area is divided by the paṇḍās, so each enclave represents a different geographic region.

Pilgrims usually bring their own blankets and cooking utensils and prepare their own meals; but paṇḍās may also loan them bedding and utensils and help them buy food and wood. (As noted above, other necessities such as water, latrines, and medical facilities are provided by the melā commission or volunteer groups.)

One important function of the paṇḍā is to provide security. Pilgrims can leave their money and their belongings with the paṇḍā while they go to take their holy bath and visit nearby temples. Pilgrims often fear for their personal safety when they leave the familiar confines of their home villages, so they are relieved to put themselves into the hands of paṇḍās whom they usually respect.

Sometimes paṇḍās loan money to pilgrims who run short of cash during the melā. The paṇḍā extracts a pledge and during the next few months he visits client villages to collect donations and repayment of loans. Such visits by paṇḍās during the ensuing year are very common. Of the paṇḍās interviewed, 83 percent had visited client villages in the previous year; and 98 percent reported that they normally go. They spend from one to five months traveling to clients, with 46 percent of them spending two months. The state-selected survey of pilgrims found that 52 percent of the pilgrims staying with paṇḍās had been visited in their villages by their paṇḍās in the previous year. Twenty-six percent of those visits were primarily to collect donations. Often the donations were in kind, such as agricultural produce, which the paṇḍā will usually sell locally before returning to Prayag.

Religious Functions of the Paṇḍās

Paṇḍās have lifelong relationships with client-families, guiding them through religious activities at Prayag. Some of the typical rituals in which paṇḍās assist their clients include *veṇīdān* (a gift of hair in which a hus-

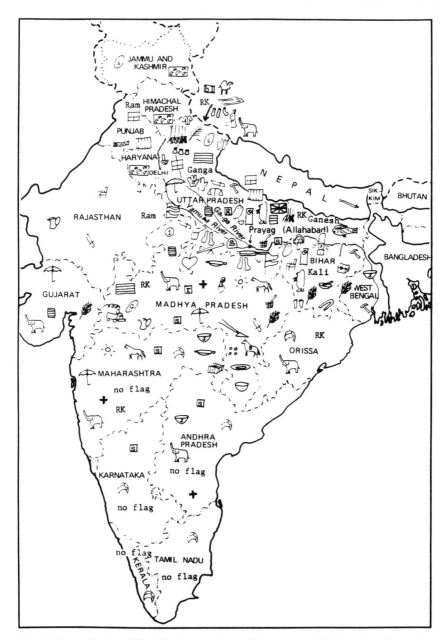

Fig. 5. The territories of the pilgrimage priests of Prayag as marked by their flags. Symbols representing the flags of pilgrimage priests are located on the map of India according to the states from which the priests' client-pilgrims come. The key to the flag symbols is on the facing page.

Fig. 5 (*continued*). Key to the flag symbols on facing page.

band and wife participate), *asthi visarjan* (ash immersion), and *śrāddha* (ancestor worship). By far the greatest number of pilgrims come to the saṅgam for the *snān*, the simple ritual bath. Although only a small percentage of pilgrims really need a paṇḍā's assistance for the bath itself, most do visit their respective paṇḍās.

Prayag is one of the most important places in India for ash immersion (asthi visarjan). Typically Hindu villagers come to Prayag several months or even years after the death of a family member (usually a father or mother) carrying the ashes of the deceased tied in a small piece of cloth. A typical villager may travel, along with his family or other men from his home village, to Prayag to perform the special *pūjā* (worship), with assistance from his paṇḍā, and to immerse the ashes in the saṅgam.

Another frequent ceremony performed at Prayag is ancestor worship (śrāddha), which is almost always done under the guidance of a paṇḍā.

Active Recruitment of Pilgrims

From the pilgrim's viewpoints, the paṇḍās' first role in the yearly religious festivals is to publicize the event. By sending postcards to their clients and by annually visiting client villages, paṇḍās encourage Hindus to go on pilgrimages. Such efforts seem to pay off. Of 697 pilgrims who were interviewed in the state-selected survey, 288 reported that paṇḍās usually visited them in their home villages. In 279 cases, pilgrims reported that the paṇḍā had suggested they visit Prayag. Obviously a few hundred paṇḍās and their agents cannot publicize the merits of the saṅgam in all the villages in India; nevertheless, a large percentage of those villagers contacted by the paṇḍās do come to Prayag.

Quite often the paṇḍā will admonish pilgrims to let family members know that when they come to Prayag in the future, they should accept this paṇḍā as their pilgrimage priest and not go to another. The admonition is well-taken by pilgrims because it assures them that they are being served by a paṇḍā family that is trusted by their own family.

Pilgrimage Records

Pilgrimage priests keep permanent records in large ledgers, called *bahīs*, at many of the important pilgrimage places in India, such as Hardwar, Puri, Gaya, Varanasi, and Prayag. Besides being pilgrimage records, the bahīs serve as permanent genealogical records that can be consulted by future generations. The registers are usually organized first by place and then by family. Information recorded in these registers includes pilgrims' names, the dates of their visits, family genealogies including the names of male members of the extended family, and the names of women in the pilgrimage party. Often the Prayag paṇḍās record the purpose of the pilgrimage, especially if it is to immerse the ashes of a dead relative. Almost all paṇḍās record the addresses of their clients in a bahī. The paṇḍās use these addresses to write to clients, reminding them to come to Prayag next year, and to find the client-villagers during their spring and summer visits.

No interviewed paṇḍā could specifically tell the oldest date recorded in his bahīs. The majority said they went back one to two hundred years, with one claiming his went back a thousand years. The relatively recent part of old bahīs are generally recopied into new volumes in the same way that Mayer (1966, 197-98) described how bards recopy genealogies. Recopying provides a readily available contemporary version of the list of client families. This availability is important because when a pilgrim visits his paṇḍā, it takes the paṇḍā only about five minutes to locate a written record of the most recent visit by a member of the client family — even if the visit had been several years earlier. Such quick retrieval impresses clients, particularly new ones, with the conclusion that they have located their family's paṇḍā. On this matter, paṇḍās have been accused of faking records, but the author is convinced of their knowledge and ability to organize records systematically for quick retrieval. This study found no evidence of faking.[3]

The system of keeping bahīs has a primary effect of proving to each pilgrim that a particular paṇḍā is his. Most pilgrims would never knowingly seek and receive services from any other paṇḍās. Such loyalty may be partly because the bahīs prove previous religious behavior of family members. These continuities are particularly important because devout Hindus believe it is an obligation and duty for the living to remember and conduct rituals for the spirits of dead parents, grandparents, and great-grandparents. One gains merit in the performance of such acts, and it is believed that the spirit of the dead relative also receives some satisfaction. The bahīs document these religious performances. For example, a man might read in a bahī that his father conducted rituals for his grandfather some years back. This would provide some satisfaction and also enhance a feeling of family solidarity. Furthermore, members of the present generation are motivated to have their names taken down because that insures that after death a future generation will honor them with the appropriate rituals.

Some Modifications of the Paṇḍā System

Many pilgrims from the four southern states of India are served by priests at Prayag who insist on the more formal title of "tīrtha purohit." These pilgrimage priests differ from others at Prayag in other ways: they do not use flags and they do not sit on thatch-roofed daises by the holy confluence. Instead they receive clients at their homes, which contain temples and rooms in which pilgrims can stay. In fact, 58 percent of the 45 pilgrims in the pilgrim-stream survey who were from the four southern states stayed in the homes of their tīrtha purohits; only 29 percent stayed in camps.

In general, the "southern" tīrtha purohits serve an educated, urban, and sophisticated clientele that is capable of writing and making reservations for visits. The pilgrims tend to know the names of and are able to locate their tīrtha purohits without needing flags. It is generally claimed that the "southern" pilgrims, because of their high level of education and religious sophistication, demand that their tīrtha purohits at Prayag be masters of Sanskrit and perform no shortcuts in the rituals.

My observations of rituals conducted by both groups of pilgrimage priests confirmed that there are differences in the patron-client (*jajmānī*) relationships between the "southern" versus "northern" pilgrims and priests. The "southern" tīrtha purohits and their educated, assertive pilgrims appeared equal in social status. In contrast, there appeared to be a social gulf between the "northern" paṇḍās and their mostly illiterate, rural, and relatively submissive pilgrim-clients. These generalizations, however, require further research to document their validity.

The tīrtha purohits whose clients come from the four southern states do not keep exactly the same form of bahī as the paṇḍās. Rather, their bahīs resemble visitors' registers in that information is arranged chronologically by date of visit, with columns for names, addresses, and comments.

In spite of these differences, the tīrtha purohits do provide the same services to their clients as other paṇḍās and live in the same neighborhoods of Allahabad as other paṇḍās.

Criticisms of Paṇḍās

In general, I found the paṇḍās to be relaxed, easy-going, and sociable. Nevertheless, because they are considered to be saints by their devout clients, they easily switch roles, playing the priest without embarrassment when they are given gifts and worshipped. Paṇḍās appear confident in their role as they guide their clients through each step of various religious rituals.

Many educated Hindus, however, characterize paṇḍās as cheats and confidence men. Mehrotra (1977), for example, points to the paṇḍās' use of argot, that is, a secret dialect known only to the paṇḍās, which he says is designed to trick, cheat, and dupe clients. Several Indians residing in the United States have said that paṇḍās have tried to deceive them, claiming to be their family priests, when in fact it was unlikely that their family had ever contacted priests at those pilgrimage places. Avinash Vashisht (the secretary of the organization of pilgrimage priests at Hardwar) suggested that non-religious and Western-educated Indians whose families do not have previous ties with paṇḍās may well be in the most danger of being taken advantage of.

Vashisht also remarked that, on the other hand, those pilgrims, educated or not, whose families have maintained relationships with paṇḍā
families for several generations are protected from being duped by people
posing as paṇḍās. It is likely that the majority of Indian pilgrims who are
illiterate peasants feel great satisfaction and receive security and confidence when they meet their family paṇḍās. Pilgrim families who have
maintained close relationships with paṇḍā families over generations have
trust that their spiritual and physical needs will be cared for when they
visit Prayag. Such patron-client relationships have self-policing effects:
paṇḍās do not jeopardize their future relationships with client families,
and possibly with other pilgrims from the same villages, by cheating or
otherwise antagonizing clients.

Some of this criticism must be legitimate, however, because the paṇḍā
community does admit that a small segment of their society has been
guilty of cheating pilgrims. For several years, the paṇḍās in Prayag have
been working to self-police their community through the Prayagwal Sabha. In a pamphlet published by this organization in 1977, Pandit Shesh
Narayan Shokaha (1977) describes both opportunists who pose as paṇḍās
and a few actual paṇḍās who cheat pilgrims. He notes that such persons
hurt the reputation of all paṇḍās because most people cannot tell which
paṇḍās are honest.

Other criticism of Prayag's paṇḍās are that they do not know Sanskrit
texts well and that they employ many shortcuts in the rituals. As a result
of complaints that have been made to the central government about the
paṇḍās' lack of training and knowledge, the paṇḍā community has established Sanskrit schools. Other changes that are occurring include further-
ing the education of paṇḍā children, girls included, so the paṇḍās will
project a better image.

In addition to education, self-policing, and defending its legal rights,
the paṇḍā community is also reacting to pilgrim interest in secular services
of a touristic nature. Paṇḍās are providing improved food and lodging as
well as complete travel arrangements as part of their professional services.
As a result, their income has other bases besides donations for conducting
religious services. It is not known whether or not these additional activities will affect the image of the paṇḍās.

Summary

Analysis of several paṇḍā activities demonstrates how they aid in further-
ing the pilgrimage tradition at Prayag. First, paṇḍās perpetuate a division
of India into regions over which specific areas are "owned" by particular
pilgrimage priests. The paṇḍās reinforce the ties between potential pilgrims within their regional jurisdiction and Prayag by visiting and corresponding with client villagers. Second, paṇḍās assist pilgrims by

providing a place to stay in Prayag, making travel arrangements, and helping them obtain food, loans, and medical aid. Third, paṇḍās assist in the performance of important religious rituals, especially ash immersion and ancestor worship. Fourth, paṇḍās strengthen the tie to their pilgrim-clients by accepting donations, recruiting, and keeping records of pilgrim visits to Prayag.

The paṇḍā is a professional; he has an entrepreneurial and manageri-al role in providing both religious and secular facilities and services. By maintaining geographic channels of communication between the sacred center and client families from all over India, he publicizes the pilgrimage and its tradition. By managing the annual melās and officiating in ritual observances at Prayag, the pilgrimage priests transmit the traditions to the people. They are caretakers of Prayag's sacred geography and perpetua-tors of Hindu tradition. Their work significantly contributes to pilgrimage to Prayag and in this way ensures that pilgrimage remains an important feature of Hinduism.

Notes

1. For more details, see Caplan 1982. Additional observations for this paper were gath-ered in 1983-84.

Other studies documenting regional centers throughout India as places for the perpet-uation of Hindu tradition include Eschmann, Kulke, and Tripathi (1978), Patnaik (1977), Vid-yarthi (1961) (Vidyarthi, Jha and Saraswati 1979), Saraswati (1975), and Eck (1982).

2. Most paṇḍās said that many such documents establish their legitimacy, but when pressed to display them, most paṇḍās alleged that the documents may have been lost to floods. A difficulty with locating and preserving more of these documents is that many paṇ-ḍās are unaware that their old legal records might be of historical value. It would be invalu-able if the paṇḍā community would conduct a systematic search of old legal documents, catalog them, and provide for better preservation.

3. Some of the older bahī entries are in Indian Persian and are difficult to translate. Moreover, even volumes that are written in the Devanāgarī script are difficult to read. Vow-el diacritics are often missing and words are run together.

References

Beal, S. 1884. *SI-YU-KI, Buddhist records of the Western World*. Translated from the Chinese of Hsüan-tsang (A.D. 629). London: Trübner and Co.
Bedekar, V. M. 1967. The legend of the churning of the ocean in the Epics and the Purāṇas: A comparative study. *Purāṇa* 9:7-61.
Bharati, A. 1961. *The ochre robe: An autobiography*. London: George Allen & Unwin.
——— . 1963. Pilgrimage in the Indian tradition. *History of Religions* 3:135-67.
Bhardwaj, S. M. 1973. *Hindu places of pilgrimage in India: A study in cultural geography*. Berke-ley: University of California Press.
Bhattacharya, A. 1910. *Prayag or Allahabad*. Calcutta: The Modern Review Office.
Bonazzoli, G. 1977. Prayāga and its Kumbha Melā. *Purāṇa* 19:81-179.
Buitenen, J. A. B. van, trans. and ed. 1975. *Mahābhārata*. Book 3 in v. 2. Chicago: The Uni-versity of Chicago Press.

Caplan, A. L. H. 1982. Pilgrims and priests as links between a sacred center and the Hindu culture region: Prayag's Magh Melā pilgrimage (Allahabad, India). Ph.D. diss., University of Michigan.

Eck, D. 1982. *Banaras: City of light.* New York: Alfred A. Knopf.

Eschmann, A., H. Kulke, and G. C. Tripathi. 1978. *The cult of Jagannath and the regional tradition of Orissa.* New Delhi: Manchar.

Ghurye, G. 1964. *Indian sadhus.* Bombay: Popular Parkashan.

Godbole, N. N. 1963. *Rig-Vedic Saraswati.* Government of Rajasthan: Cabinet Secretariat.

Goswamy, B. N. 1966. The records kept by priests at centres of pilgrimage as a source of social and economic history. *The Indian Economic and Social History Review* 3:174-83.

Hazra, R. C. 1940. *Studies in the Purānic records on Hindu rites and customs,* Bulletin No. XX. Dacca: University of Dacca.

Irwin, J. 1983. The ancient pillar-cult at Prayāga (Allahabad): Its pre-Aśokan origins. *Journal of the Royal Asiatic Society* 2:253-80.

Kane, P. V. 1973. *History of Dharmasastra,* v.4. Poona, India: Bhandarkar Oriental Research Institute.

Mayer, A. C. 1966. *Caste and kinship in Central India: A village and its region.* Berkeley: University of California Press.

Mehrotra, R. R. 1977. *Sociology of secret languages.* Simla, India: Indian Institute of Advanced Study.

Mehta, V. 1972. *Portrait of India.* Baltimore, MD: Penguin Books.

Müller, F. M., ed. 1892. *Ṛg Veda.* London: Oxford University Press.

Patnaik, N. 1977. *Cultural tradition in Puri: Structure and organization of a pilgrimage centre.* Simla, India: Indian Institute of Advanced Study.

Sachau, E. C., trans. 1910. *Alberuni's India.* London: Trubner.

Saraswati, B. 1975. *Kashi: Myth and reality of a classical cultural tradition.* Simla, India: Indian Institute of Advanced Study.

Schwartzberg, J. E., ed. 1978. *A historical atlas of South Asia.* Chicago: The University of Chicago Press.

Shokaha, S. N. 1977. Tīrthrāj Prayāg kā mahākumbha: Tīrth purohit aur tīrthyātri. In *Maha Kumbh Smarika 1977,* ed. R. Sharma, 16-19. Allahabad, India: Prayagwal Sabha.

Singh, U. 1966. *Allahabad: A study in urban geography.* Varanasi, India: Banaras Hindu University.

Smith, V. A. 1958. *The Oxford history of India.* London: Oxford University Press.

Spate, O. H. K., A. T. A. Learmonth, and B. H. Farmer. 1967. *India, Pakistan and Ceylon: The regions.* London: Methuen.

Stein, M. A., trans. 1961. *Kalhana's Rajatarangini: A chronicle of the kings of Kasmir,* v. 1. Delhi, India: Motilal Banarsidass.

Stoddard, R. H. 1966. Hindu holy sites in India. Ph.D. diss., University of Iowa, Iowa City.

a Taluqdar of Oudh, trans. 1916. *Matsya Purāṇa: The sacred books of the Hindus,* v. 17. Allahabad, India: Apurva Krishna Bose.

Tripati, N. 1978. *Prayag Mahatmya.* Varanasi, India: Thakur Prasad and Sons Booksellers.

Valmiki. 1976. *Śrīmad Vālmīki-Rāmāyana,* v. 1. Gorakpur, India: Gita Press.

Vidyarthi, L. P. 1961. *The sacred complex in Hindu Gaya.* New York: Asia Publishing House.

Vidyarthi, L. P., M. Jha, and B. N. Saraswati. 1979. *The sacred complex of Kashi.* Delhi: Concept Publishing Co.

Section V:
PILGRIMAGES IN OTHER RELIGIONS OF ASIA

The Jaina Ascetic as Manifestation of the Sacred

Thomas McCormick
Independent Scholar

Abstract

In addition to making pilgrimages to holy sites, which are called *tīrtha*s, devotees of the Jaina religion often visit "walking tīrthas," the Jaina ascetics. Since homelessness is a basic holy concept for Jainas, their ascetics have no established place of residence or congregation, except during the monsoon season, when every ascetic ceases wandering and remains for four months as a guest of a local group of Jaina laity. There he or she acts as spiritual leader and may also attract "pilgrims" from other places. No group is visited every year by the same ascetic. Thus, locational impermanence is an invariable characteristic of one type of Jaina "pilgrimage."
Key words: Jaina, pilgrimages, wandering ascetics.

The Jaina religion is prominent in the cultural landscape[1] of northwestern India, particularly in the state of Gujarat.[2] This is true not only in the sense that Jaina temples and shrines appear frequently or that the prosperous Jaina community maintains homes and businesses in all the cities and most villages and towns. No visitor can fail to notice these things or fail to guess that the Jainas have an influence all out of proportion to their small portion of the population. But the visitor will be especially intrigued by another frequent sign of Jaina presence, namely the white-robed monks and nuns as they walk from village to village or from house to house in town or in the city.

The Jaina community[3] is a very ancient one, having originated at least two and a half millennia ago as one of the numerous ascetically oriented sects of the Gangetic valley.[4] It is the only one of those sects to survive into the present as a distinct social and religious entity. The fundamental social fact of the Jaina community has always been the presence of two "classes" of believers: the ascetics, who act as religious teachers and exemplars, and the laity that reverently supports them. Between the two, as P. S. Jaini

---

Sacred Places, Sacred Spaces: The Geography of Pilgrimages, edited by Robert H. Stoddard and Alan Morinis, 1997. Geoscience and Man, vol. 34, pp. 235-256. Dept. of Geography and Anthropology, Louisiana State University, Baton Rouge, LA 70893-6010.

(1979, 120) puts it, "a very real feeling of mutual affection and respect has prevailed."

One example of the mutuality between lay and ascetic Jainas should be of special interest to geographers, and it can be expressed thus: while the layperson cherishes family, friends, and home, the ascetic is, above all, homeless. With no more attachment to place than to possessions, ascetics must usually live a wandering life as "guests" of successive local *sanghas* or congregations of laity. Save during the monsoon season, they should follow the practice of *māsakalpa*; that is, they should sojourn no longer than a month with any particular sangha and should then change residence. The veneration shown to the monastics by the laity, and the latter's duty of attending on the former, mean that every locale that "hosts" an eminent monk or nun is capable of becoming a holy place. This is particularly true during the *caturmāsa*, or four months of the monsoon season. For during that season, every ascetic must cease wandering and reside for the four months with one sangha, where he (or she) acts as a leader and focus of local religious activities. It is this custom of the monsoon retreat, or *paryūsanakalpa*, and its potential for generating a unique sort of pilgrimage, that I want to explore in this paper.

Ascetics and Householders

The homelessness of the ascetic, and much else in Jaina religious geography, may be explained by two notions which Jainas share with their Hindu and Buddhist neighbors, but which they interpret in distinctive ways. The first is that there exist two sorts of human beings. There are, in the first place, those men and women who follow ordinary desires and occupations, whose broad aim it is to prosper in this life and in the next. These are the laity, who must perforce go about their business regardless of the fact that their mundane thoughts and activities inevitably attract something called *karma*. This is a kind of fine substance, according to Jainas, that clings to the *jīva* (that is, to the soul or sentient essence), "defiling" it and compelling it to undergo various pleasant and unpleasant destinies. Association with karma is regarded by Jainas as the reason why all jīvas are subject to reincarnation. This fate is shared not only by human beings but by animals and plants, by the inhabitants of the many heavens and hells recognized by Jainas, and, as we shall see, by many entities that other traditions do not regard as animate.

But there also exists a superior sort of men and women, namely, the Jaina ascetics. These have renounced wealth and progeny in order to work toward *moksa*, that is, toward bliss, beatitude, and freedom from the karma-induced inadequacies and disappointments of this life. The way to moksa consists of avoiding those actions and thoughts, such as anger, greed, and lust, which make the jīva receptive to karma. Since such acts are inevitable in the course of a householder's life, any serious attempt to avoid them presupposes monastic renunciation. The attempt cannot succeed without many lifetimes of ascetic discipline.

The Jaina ascetic, then, hopes to overcome all attachment to the world. From the moment of entrance into the monastic life, the ascetic is "oriented" not, like the laity, toward home and workplace but toward the *siddhaloka*, the abode of those souls (called *siddhas*) who have attained mokṣa. The ascetic's life is a perpetual pilgrimage toward that world. The *upāśraya*, the temporary "monastery" where the ascetic rests briefly from his or her journey, is the property not of the monastic order but of the local lay saṅgha, and the monk or nun is strictly that saṅgha's guest. By this hospitality, the layperson is partially redeemed from the evils committed in the course of the worldly vocation. The ascetic, for his or her part, preaches the sacred doctrine to the lay hosts, and by word and example encourages them to assume temporary monastic vows, to perform acts of charity, to meditate, and to do other good works that will give them worldly success and otherworldly merit (figs. 1 and 2).

Of course, Jainas are well aware that the style of life followed by the renunciate is extreme and frankly unnatural. They know that what their

Figure 1. A Jaina monk giving a spiritual lecture in the *upāśraya*.

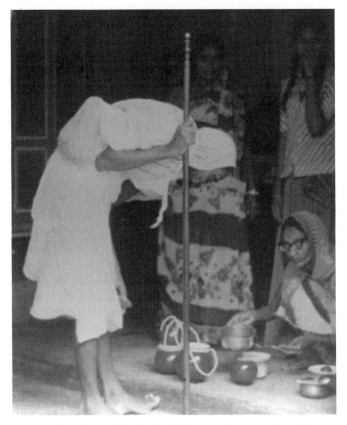

Figure 2. A monk receiving food offerings and homage from laity.

sacred canon calls "going forth from home into homelessness" contradicts their own natural desires and legitimate needs. Indeed, they know that the purpose of the monastic discipline is to negate precisely the basic values and emotions without which no family member, businessman, or citizen could function. These values and emotions include especially what Yi-Fu Tuan (1974) calls topophilia, "the human being's affective ties with the environment." As the traditional Indian symbolism of renunciation puts it, the Jaina ascetic opts for "the forest" over "the village"; or, as Tuan (1974, 116) would say, for wilderness over kosmos. In terms of non-ascetic values, whether Western or Indian, such a decision is extraordinary and perhaps perverse.

But the ascetic's negation of the world is not as radical as would seem to be indicated by the symbolism that expresses it. In theory as well as in practice, the ascetic lives in association with the lay community as spiritual leader and teacher.

The Fourfold *Tīrtha*

It is the company of monks and nuns, with their male and female devotees, that Jainas call the fourfold *tīrtha*. The tīrtha is founded anew in every age by the preaching and example of a succession of perfected ascetics who thereby become *Tīrthaṅkaras* ("makers of the tīrtha") before passing out of embodied existence and into the siddhaloka, and whose images the Jainas reverently worship in the temples. This concept of tīrtha is the second notion I want to discuss.

As all students of South Asian religion are aware, a tīrtha is literally a ford, a way of crossing the river of life, so to speak, to the far shore of mokṣa. Almost all religious traditions indigenous to India use the word to mean something like "manifestation of the sacred," "person, place, or thing that imparts holiness or communicates divine power," or "hierophany." To Hindu devotees, tīrtha most often connotes an object of pilgrimage, a holy place, although it can also mean a holy person, a ritual, or even a piece of religious paraphernalia with special power or significance.[5] In Jaina theory, such an object is a *dravya-tīrtha* (a "specific tīrtha"); the *bhava-tīrtha* ("true tīrtha" or "tīrtha par excellence") is the Jaina community, or rather the doctrine which that community perpetuates and embodies.

Jainas, like other Indians, make pilgrimages to holy places; and, like other Indians, they call such places tīrthas. Most of these sites (which, as we know, are properly dravya-tīrthas) are associated with the lives of Tīrthaṅkaras, their great disciples, or various other siddhas. At these places there are great shrines, where Jainas make *tīrtayātrās*, "journeys to tīrthas," in fulfillment of vows or simply for the spiritual benefit of *darśana*, "sight," of holy things. Wealthy and devout Jainas acquire further merit by organizing mass tīrthayātrās for those who find the expense of such a journey prohibitive and by providing meals and lodgings to the pilgrims.[6]

However, tīrthayātrās are not the only sort of pilgrimages undertaken by Jainas. Monks and nuns are sometimes called *jaṅgamatīrthas*, "walking tīrthas," and one of the most important religious duties of a Jaina householder is to approach a monastic and to salute him or her reverently. (Monastics, of course, have the same duty toward their preceptors and toward elder monastics.) To make an extended effort in doing this duty is especially meritorious, for as one Jaina layman told me, "If I have to travel far to see holy monks or holy nuns, I am more likely to come into their presences with proper humility."

To approach a holy being, symbolically or physically but in any case humbly, is indeed the basic Jaina act of worship. The object of such worship may as easily be a living monastic as the Tīrthaṅkara. After all, even though the latter is often called "God" in English and by equivalent terms in Indian languages, he is not properly a supernatural being but an ascetic who has succeeded fully in the practice of austerities. This fact explains why one of the Tīrthaṅkara's most popular epithets is Jina ("conqueror," "victor"), whence the word Jaina is derived. It is also why the most widely used Jaina litany invokes not only the Tīrthaṅkaras but all Jaina monastics, past and present.[7] These great men and women differ among themselves in rank but not in nature; in degree but not in kind. Tīrthaṅkara and living ascetic are incomparably superior to the celestrial beings, called *devas*, who are properly "the gods," and whose main function in Jaina legend is that of titanically powerful equivalents of human beings who miraculously help or hinder the fourfold tīrtha.

So it is that the homely image of the neighborhood monastery, with its monk or nun bestowing benediction by means of holy words and darśana, is in Jaina minds not far removed from that of the *samavasarana*, the great preaching hall which the devas routinely build as a place of enthronement for every Tīrthaṅkara after his enlightenment. Indeed, the feelings of the Jaina laity toward their monastics are not easily explicable without an understanding of the samavasarana and its symbolism.[8]

Jainas believe that every Tīrthaṅkara sat for a time in his samavasarana, "immobile, bathed in omniscient glory, 'preaching' by means of the miraculous sound emanating from his body." He and three holographs of himself faced in the four cardinal directions, benefitting the human beings, gods, and animals who gathered around him in concentric circles. Jaina piety sees the temple that houses the Tīrthaṅkara's image "as a representation of the samavasarana....The layman comes near as though he were actually approaching" it (Jaini 1979, 196; see also Dundas 1992, 30-3).

The magnificence of this vision of a human *axis mundi* should not make us forget that it is essentially a picture of a preaching monastic. It will not then be surprising that sacred journeys to both static and "walking" tīrthas should be undertaken by Jainas. Especially pious laypeople visit monks and nuns many times in the course of a year. But it is during the monsoon season, when every monastic's whereabouts are established for four months, that a "pilgrimage" to one's favorite monk or nun becomes a very popular form of devotion.

The Monsoon Retreat

The Jaina monk (or nun) is quite literally a walker. The vow of nonattachment reduces his (or her) possessions to a staff, two bowls for food and water, and religious objects. The larger branch of Jainas, the Śvetāmbaras (the object of this study), permit their monastics only a few cotton and wool cloths as raiment; the male ascetic of the other major Jaina persuasion, the Diagambaras, goes without clothing. The ascetic may not maintain a home or ride in a vehicle. Thus, whatever the merits of the general social theory for which he offered the Jainas as evidence, Max Weber was certainly correct in pointing out that "homelessness is the basic holy concept" in Jainism. "It signifies the break of all worldly relations, and thus, above all, indifference to sense pleasures and avoidance of all actions based on worldly motives" (Weber 1958, 189, 190).[9] As we have seen, it is in accordance with this concept that the monks and nuns must wander for eight months of the year and may compromise this regime during only the monsoon season, when they practice paryūṣaṇakalpa.

The idea of paryūṣaṇakalpa may seem to contradict the general rationale for the monastic life. But Jainas justify this apparent inconsistency by invoking the doctrine of *ahiṃsa* or "non-injury," a virtue which they esteem above all others. To observe perfect ahiṃsa is impossible for the laity, and is difficult even for the most advanced ascetic. Jainas believe that air, water, fire, and many other substances which few traditions regard as capable of suffering harm, in fact possess jīvas. Accordingly, the requisites of an ascetic include a cloth to hold before the mouth while speaking, in order to avoid injury to the jīvas of the air, and a broom or *rajoharaṇa* for carefully sweeping dust and small animals away from every object he or she touches. Ascetics may not drink non-sterile water, which houses water-jīvas, nor light a fire, thus killing fire-jīvas when the light is extinguished.[10] And if the killing even of such elementary bodies is forbidden to ascetics, it is all the less permissible for them to make long journeys through the lush growth of the monsoon season, where they would surely trample small plants and animals in their progress. Hence during this season they must compromise their ascetic "topophobia" and remain in one place.[11]

This rationale for the monsoon retreat seems reasonable enough in view of the heavy rains that prevail in the eastern Gangetic region, where Jainism first emerged into history during the eighth to sixth centuries B.C. But in Gujarat, Karnataka, and Rajasthan, the regions of northern and western India where the majority of Jainas live nowadays, one often sees neither very lush growth nor heavy rains, and we must explain the survival of the custom of paryūṣaṇakalpa in some other way. This is not difficult, for, by favoring a particular place for four months, monks and nuns are investing that place with their sacredness and benefitting the laity who look to them for blessing and spiritual guidance. Further, this practice helps to integrate a small and widely distributed community.

Not surprisingly, caturmāsa is regarded by Jainas as an especially sacred time of the year, when many who do not ordinarily perform their religious duties become observant, and those normally observant will find their piety increasing.[12] As one monk remarked to me, "Where there is no monk, there will be less devotion to religion. But if a monk is here for a long time, a kind of religious atmosphere will build up."

The Jaina canonical works, none dating from more recently than the sixth century of the Christian era,[13] tell us that the leader of each group of monastics, who is generally the guru or spiritual preceptor of the others, is to choose their monsoon retreat, for monks and nuns are forbidden by custom to travel or stay alone. As for their places of residence, they are to stay in caves, in abandoned houses, or under trees. No special house is to be prepared for them, since this would attract to them the karma resulting from acts of "violence" committed in the course of building the house. In modern practice this rule is ignored, for all acknowledge the need for shelter if the monastic is to study and to preach. We have already seen that special buildings, called upāsrayas or monasteries, are provided as residences for the monks and nuns by the respective saṅghas. The latter must decide whom to invite, and the invitation must be accepted or rejected by the leader of the monastic group in question.[14]

The saṅgha leaders' decision on whom to invite for caturmāsa is often the most important one they will make during the year, and it is made carefully. Their first choice may refuse the invitation, for there is much competition among saṅghas for the honor of hosting monastics who are famous for their preaching abilities, their miraculous healing powers, the holiness of their lives, or their knowledge of the scriptures. Nonetheless, the saṅgha will try its best to attract such guests. The saṅgha may also seek out a guest who has wealthy lay devotees, since the latter's generosity will benefit the local charitable works, and also aid in feeding and housing those who come for the guest's darśana.

Very importantly, the best monastic guest is able to inspire large numbers of lay Jainas to become tapasvins, that is, to undertake the long fasts and other mortifications that are customary during caturmāsa, and which are regarded as particularly effective removers of karma.[15] Every saṅgha is proud of its tapasvins and vies with other saṅghas to produce the longest list.

More worldly motives are sometimes at work. I heard it said of one saṅgha trustee, "He wants a famous monk here only in order to make sure the shops will be open!" In this case, an eminent monk accepted the invitation, and a steady stream of visitors kept the shops quite open.

More frequently, the saṅgha must be content with receiving a monk of lesser stature, or perhaps with hosting only nuns. The latter, while they greatly outnumber the monks, are not thought to possess the same power to inspire religious conduct.

A Contemporary Caturmāsa

The group of monks whose caturmāsa I observed is headed by a monastic scholar long known to Sanskritists for his work in editing Jaina religious texts. His host was the saṅgha of a town of 11,000 inhabitants, about 600 of whom are Jainas. The town is located on the highway from Ahmedabad, chief city of Gujarat, and the major Jaina pilgrimage site of Śaṅkheśvara. Given the presence of an eminent monk, the location was certain to attract many "pilgrims" throughout the season.

The saṅgha was expecting this to be a memorable caturmāsa for one reason in particular. It seems that three years previously, the monks in question had stayed for caturmāsa in a certain small and most obscure village, one which had allegedly never hosted a monk before, but the sort of town preferred by this monastic scholar for the peace and quiet that enable him to do his work efficiently. But at that time the number of tapasvins taking major fasts was surprisingly large, and this was attributed by all to his unusual spiritual power. In this manner of a self-fulfilling prophecy, his subsequent caturmāsas have been marked by the same phenomenon, much to the credit of the saṅghas where these events took place.

This monk has, in fact, tended to avoid towns in favor of villages precisely because his reputation might attract large numbers of visitors, disturbing his editorial work. But in this year, other factors influenced him to make an exception. His late father, who had become also his guru when father and son together became monks, was born in this town, making it already a holy place in his eyes. Further, the town is associated with an institution of which all Jainas approve, namely, the largest *pañjrapoḷ* (a shelter where injured, sick, and unwanted animals are cared for by the compassion of the Jaina community) in Gujarat.[16] After making certain that provisions would be made for the large number of expected visitors, he accepted the invitation. The saṅgha, meanwhile, busied itself in preparing the community kitchen which was to serve visitors throughout the season.

To begin caturmāsa in an auspicious manner is always important to the monastics. In this case, it was doubly so: after all, this town was a sacred place as far as their leader was concerned. He consulted astrology to determine the direction from which the town was to be approached as well as the day on which the walk was to be made. A number of Jainas from his previous town of residence accompanied him all or part of the way, and received his blessing for this act of devotion (fig. 3). Festooned streets and a brass band greeted his arrival. A large audience was present at the upāśraya to hear his first sermon of the season, in which he urged the assembled Jainas to take vows as tapasvins.

There was a steady stream of visitors. Many, who were returning to Ahmedabad from pilgrimages to Śaṅkheśvara, made a stop here in order to receive the blessing of the monks and of the group of nuns who had likewise accepted an invitation from the saṅgha. The nuns were there only because of this eminent monk; they wished to study under him and to enjoy the spiritual benefit of his company. Caturmāsa is a time for monastics to devote themselves to study, since they will not be interrupted by the necessity of frequent movement.

The number of those taking extended fasts was, as predicted by everybody, very high. Two hundred and fifty tapasvins fasted for at least eight days, seventy-two for thirty, and one for forty-five days. These figures are not as mind-boggling to Indians as to Westerners, who commonly disbelieve in the possibility of such long fasts. Nevertheless, they were considered quite impressive in a saṅgha of less than 700. (Actually, some tapasvins were not local residents but had come especially to take their vows in the presence of a great monk and to be inspired by his daily presence) (fig. 4).

Figure 3. Monks, accompanied by laý followers, journeying to *caturmāsa* quarters.

Food and lodging were no problem for the visitors; the custom of town exogamy, and the Jaina involvement in commerce, meant that any tapasvin from any town had relatives here to receive him or her as an honored guest. Many other Jainas came to visit their tapasvin relatives, to give them gifts, and to receive their darśana; indeed, a tapasvin's friend or relative who failed to do so would have been guilty of discourtesy. These visits often assumed a secular tone as the visitors took the opportunity to discuss family matters or business with their hosts.

The tapasvins ascribed the success of their austerities to the spiritual power of their monastic guest, although he denied himself any credit. Reverence for the monk began, indeed, to surpass all reasonable bounds. One resident, who had been worried by the long drought in this supposed monsoon season, said earnestly, "We must ask Mahārāj ["great king," a title of respect applied to monks] to do something quickly! God may not listen to the prayers of us ordinary people, but if a great monk prays for rain, He is sure to hear. Why, didn't you notice that a few drops of rain fell when he entered the town, although the sky was clear?" Another citizen alleged that the monk had performed a miraculous cure.

Figure 4. Laypeople taking vows of *tapas* before a monk.

To my knowledge, no one had ever before told such stories about this quiet scholar, and I asked him for his reaction. "I have no such power," he replied with some exasperation. "I tell this to the people and they think I'm only being humble. I too am in the temple daily, praying for rain."

To the townsfolk, his arrival had begun the sacralization of this town and had set in motion two other factors which were now working independent of his intentions: the tapas, which he had encouraged, and a series of superstitious tales, which he was trying unsuccessfully to discredit. Apparently, the popular mind had focused different and unrelated characteristics of tirthas, including the power of working miracles and of inspiring religious conduct, upon him. But in his own view, this town possessed a sacred character only because his father-guru had been born here. As for the miraculous power that sustained the tapasvins in their austerities, he credited it to the same source and to the grace of Pārśvanātha, the Tīrthaṅkara to whom both father and son had always been especially devoted.[17]

That this town had become a religious center was especially evident as the holiest period of the Jaina year, and the climax of caturmāsa, approached. This is the *paryūsana*, a nine-day celebration which includes a joyous remembrance of the birth of Mahāvīra, last of the Tīrthaṅkaras of our age and a contemporary and rival of the Buddha. It culminates in the annual rite of confession of sins and is followed by the breaking of the tapasvins' fasts and by ceremonies and parades in their honor.

Paryūsana and Its Aftermath

The holiest period of the Jaina year is approached and experienced with an intensity of emotion familiar to observers of sacred times and places. Every Jaina practices at least some small fast or other austerity and makes some donation to the saṅgha. And at no time does the monastic guest seem more a part of his host community than during paryūsana.

During paryūsana, great importance is given to the practice of *dāna*, or charity and generosity toward the Jaina religion. Paryūsana is marked by large donations to the saṅgha and its good works, earnestly solicited from the many visitors and often quite conspicuously given. One sees much of the *bolī*, the characteristic Jaina form of fund-raising, in which the right to perform a particular religious function, such as presiding at a ritual, is given to the highest bidder after the manner of an auction.[18] There were bolīs to benefit the saṅgha's religious school, for the pañjrapol, and for the local dispensary. These appeals were usually conducted in the upāśraya, and always in the presence of the monks, who were quite literally the "sacred center" of the saṅgha's religious activity (fig. 5).

If the boḷīs give the Jaina laity a chance to practice dāna, the comple-mentary virtue of *tapas* (austerity) is especially evident on the ninth day, the most sacred event in the Jaina calendar. This is the day of *saṃvat-sarīpratikramaṇa*, the great annual rite of confession and penitence, in which monastics and laity alike ask and grant forgiveness for all transgres-sions committed during the past year. All good Jainas fast on this day, and for the three-hour duration of the rite, everyone dresses as a monastic and observes monastic vows. If a monk is present in the locality, he presides over the rite, which in any case takes place in the upāśraya. Similar and shorter *pratikramaṇa*s are conducted daily, fortnightly, and seasonally; all of these are obligatory for monastics and tapasvins.

It is the day following saṃvatsarīpratikramaṇa that marks the true climax of caturmāsa. Certainly it drew the most visitors, many in char-tered buses furnished by the generosity of rich and devout Jainas. The tapasvins were taken in a procession of great pomp to a public celebration in which they broke their fasts. A program of music and theater was pre-sented in their honor while the monks presided from a dais. Each tapasvin came forward to receive a garland of flowers and a blessing from the monk

Figure 5. *Saṅgha* leaders conducting *boḷī*.

who had inspired the heroic austerity. Professional photographers were on hand to record what was declared to be "the greatest tapas in all of Jaina history" (fig. 6). In the next day's edition of the largest newspaper in Gujarat, there appeared an account that praised the tapasvins and that attributed all manner of miraculous powers to the scholar-monk.

In the days before and after saṃvatsarīpratikramaṇa, when laypeople were observing monastic vows, the monk for his part became very actively involved in the affairs of the local laity. Certain boḷīs had had encouraging or disappointing results, and he had to discuss the reasons with saṅgha leaders. The pañjrapoḷ was seriously overcrowded with animals during this drought year, and he had himself to compose a leaflet appealing for funds for fodder. There was a special problem facing the ambiḷśālā, a special kitchen for those undergoing partial fasts, whose budget had been in deficit for many years, and whose trustees asked the monk if he might say a few words on its behalf to the assembled faithful. This he did, choosing the tapasvins' celebration as the time and place to make his appeal for one lakh rupees ($10,500 U.S.). The goal was exceeded within an hour after the appeal was made.

This apparent reversal of the roles of monk and layperson — the former working and appealing for funds for the saṅgha, the latter approx-

Figure 6. Formal group portrait of *tapasvins*.

imating the monastic estate through austerity — is paradoxical only if one fails to consider that the two halves of the fourfold tīrtha exist as a conjoined polarity. As this well-worn analogy with electricity implies, the opposite poles interact and transform one another when a high current, so to speak, is flowing. This interpenetration of the sacred and the profane, or at least, of the functions of the estates corresponding to those categories, was neither ritualized nor theorized, but simply accomplished.

After the great rite of confession was completed and the tapasvins had "returned to the world," the line between monastic and lay functions was reestablished. The last festivity of caturmāsa has in fact the effect of emphasizing the difference between these two modes of living. This festivity is dīvālī, the festival of lights, so-called from the custom of lighting lamps, candles, and fireworks in celebration of it. To most lay Jainas, dīvālī is the Hindu New Year, a time for dedicating the next year's account books and worshipping them as manifestations of Lakṣmī, goddess of wealth (fig. 7); to the monastic, and the very observant layperson, it is most importantly the day of Mahāvīra's passing, a time for fasting and meditation. Shops, Jaina and non-Jaina, are closed for five days and are reopened on the day of dhanapañcami ("the fifth of money"). But in the upāśraya, that same day is called jñānapañcami ("the fifth of knowledge"), when sacred books are dusted, arranged, and worshipped as tīrthas, often with an effigy of Sarasvatī, goddess of wisdom, in a place of honor.

Since it is a saying in India that Lakṣmī and Sarasvatī cannot live in the same house (a saying whose truth scholars may readily appreciate!), it is perhaps appropriate that at this time lay-monastic interactions are at a minimum, save in the case of those observant laity who wish to follow the monastics in their austerities. In most cases, one wishes to celebrate dīvālī in one's own house or to exchange home-baked sweets with neighbors. The sacredness of caturmāsa is not, of course, forgotten as dīvālī approaches. Visitors still come for the monks' blessing; a teacher of meditation comes to learn more of Jaina yoga, and gives a series of lectures in the temple courtyard; students from Ahmedabad and from abroad come to study sacred texts, taking advantage of the relative quiet; and the community kitchen remains open, though less busy than before. But monastic and lay Jainas are going about their separate businesses, contributing to the Jaina way of life in their respective ways.

The end of this caturmāsa was anticlimactic. The monks did not leave the town immediately, due to the illness of one of their number, but they noted the date by ceremonially changing their residence, for one day, to the house of a layman. When the chief monk did decide that it was time for him to depart with his disciples, it was to the tīrtha of Śaṅkheśvara, to whose miraculous image of Pārśvanātha he and his father-guru had always been particularly devoted. I visited him there and found him occu-

Figure. 7. Merchants dedicating new account books on *dīvali*.

pying a small, dark, and uncomfortable-looking room. My surprise at his choice of quarters amused him. "My father," he explained, "spent his last earthly moments on this very spot." Did I not know what made one place more comfortable than another?

Some Conclusions

Readers are perhaps entitled to feelings of annoyance when a contributor to a scholarly volume says his paper is intended primarily as a stimulus to further research. This remark, after all, seems something of a truism to anyone who views scholarly endeavor as a continuous process, and who looks forward, as all good scholars do, to the day on which his own research will be made obsolete. Nonetheless, it seems to me that some such remark must be made in order to emphasize properly the very tentative nature of my observations. There are two reasons why this emphasis is important.

One is that the living Jaina tradition, or "popular Jainism" if one prefers the jargon, has until recently attracted very little interest from Western students.[19] For example, although excellent geographic studies of Hindu pilgrimage have been made (Bhardwaj 1973; Caplan 1982; Sopher 1968;

Stoddard 1966), no geographer has studied the Jaina tīrtha-complex, despite its spiritual importance to Jainas, the historic and artistic significance of many of their shrines, and the great amount of theorizing that Jainas have done on the subject of pilgrimage. The whys and wherefores of this scholarly indifference are outside the scope of this paper.

Much more importantly, my conclusions are tentative because the problem I am posing — the role of the holy man or woman as manifestation of the sacred — has been oddly overlooked by scholars. Indeed, one may carefully study Mircea Eliade's classic study of hierophanies (that is, of tīrthas) without finding any discussion of the holy man or woman (Eliade 1974). This fault holds true for almost every treatment of the subjects of hierophany and holiness, with a few happy exceptions such as Peter Brown's (1982) learned and thoughtful study.

Perhaps this neglect follows from the fact that a hierophany is easier to study if it stays put; or, which is the same thing, perhaps an established hierophany is easier to study than one whose "myth" is still in the process of formation. Indeed, some geographers may argue that this formative stage is simply beyond their disciplinary scope.[20] But the rewards of studying this process are great indeed, and certainly the materials are close at hand: in India, and particularly among the Jainas, the holy man or woman is by far the most accessible of hierophanies.

Like every Jaina ascetic, the monk we have been following in this paper gives different locales a chance to share in his sacredness. In this way, he defines a geographic entity (namely the region within which he chooses to wander) no less definitely, in spite of all the changes in its configuration. At his next caturmāsa, many Jainas from the town we have described will go to him in order to renew a sacred relationship. It will be the turn of another town to receive them as honored guests, tapasvins, and worshippers. Those several Jaina communities bound together by ties of blood, marriage, and business will use the occasion, as they used similar past occasions, for gatherings to exchange gossip, to discuss business, and to reaffirm old ties and Jaina identity. The presence of the legatees of Mahāvīra and exemplars of his doctrine will dignify and spiritualize these gatherings and will give the participants worldly success and otherworldly merit. The next caturmāsa site will not be entirely similar to the town we have described. It will be smaller, carefully chosen for its obscurity and its distance from the main thoroughfare. But in Jaina minds, it will be transformed into an abode of the holy.

We are certainly dealing here with an object of pilgrimage, but one which we may at first find difficult to recognize as such. It may seem strange to us that in the Jaina religion, just as any human being may attain perfection through austerity and nonviolence, so in the same way any humble village may become a holy place by manifesting those qualities.

But in truth, the insight that great pilgrimages are not always directed to established religious centers should be quite acceptable to us Westerners. Our own traditions tell of kings who came to offer gold to a child born in a stable. "The wind blows where it chooses, and you hear the sound of it, but you do not know where it comes from or where it goes. So it is with everyone who is born of the Spirit."[21]

Acknowledgment

This paper is dedicated to the memory of Kendall Folkert and Thomas Zwicker.

Notes

1. This phrase, cultural landscape, has been defined by Wagner and Mikesell as "the typical complexes of environmental features, including the manmade ones, that coincide with each cultural community" (Wagner and Mikesell 1962, 10). This formulation may be applied to much more than static geographic features or the movement and distributions of large numbers of people. My example, the wandering ascetic, is a most significant "environmental feature" of India, for many reasons. One reason, which is my concern here, is the ascetic's refusal to share the laity's attachment to home and to village. Because of that radical denial, the ascetic's very presence in the landscape is a critique of the inadequacy and parochiality of our "normal" attitudes toward place and space. More specifically, it criticizes the failure of those attitudes to take eternity into account. It would be surprising if such a presence were not capable of becoming an object of interest to geographers of religion.

2. Gujarat, where the research resulting in this paper was conducted, is one of the twenty-two states of the Indian Union and has a population of about forty-one million. Slightly under one million of these are Jainas. Gujarat has been a Jaina center at least since the second century A.D. and has especially been a stronghold of the Śvetāmbara sect. Gujarat is distinctive for its prosperous merchant community, of which the Śvetāmbara Jainas are very much a part.

Gujarat is not the only area of India where Jainas are concentrated. The strongholds of the other large persuasion of Jainas, the Digambara sect, are in southern Maharastra, northern Karnataka, and several northern states. Sthānakavāsīs and Terapanthis, influential offshoots of the Śvetāmbaras, are concentrated in Rajasthan. Śvetāmbaras, most of them of Gujarati culture, may also be found in most of these areas and in all the larger cities of India, especially Bombay (see Schwartzberg 1978, 232). For the Śvetāmbara-Digambara division, and other sectarian groupings, see Dundas 1992, 119-23.

3. "Community" is the term commonly preferred in contemporary India, over the more traditional "caste," to translate *jāti*. The latter denotes the social group into which an Indian is born and which traditionally governs his position in society, his choice of spouse, and his means of livelihood. In its colloquial use, the term is notoriously imprecise. While many Jainas will answer "Jaina" to the question, "What is your caste?", Jainas belong to many different jātis. The jātis to which the Jainas of northern India belong are of the group usually called *vāniyā*, whose traditional occupation is that of merchant and financier. Most of the Digambaras of Karnataka and Maharastra are not vāniyās but agriculturalists (Sangave 1959, 73ff).

4. The most widely known introduction to the Jainas in English is still that of Stevenson (1970), despite, as P. S. Jaini rightly remarks, "the clearly biased conclusions arrived at by its Christian missionary author" (Jaini 1979, xi). Much more balanced and objective are Jaini's own introductory volume (Jaini 1979) and the more recent work by Dundas (1992). The best

short account is Folkert's (1984). To place Jaina origins in historical context, see Jaini 1970 and Basham 1981.

5. For a lucid description of this most basic of all Indian religious concepts, see Eck 1981.

6. Ratnasekhara, a Jaina monastic writer of the fourteenth century, described the proper way of making pilgrimages to sacred places and the duties of those who sponsor mass pilgrimages (Williams 1963, 234, 235). An excellent study of contemporary Jaina pilgrimage is Cort 1988.

7. This is the Pañcamaskaramantra or "salutation to the five." It runs:
"Homage to the *arhats* [the Jinas]!
"Homage to the *siddhas*!
"Homage to the *ācāryas* [a class of advanced monks]!
"Homage to the *upādhyāyas* [monastic teachers]!
"Homage to all the *sādhus* [ascetics] of the world!
"This fivefold salutation is of all auspicious things the most auspicious."

8. The samavasaraṇa is a frequent subject of Jaina sacred art and legend, and it plays a large role in the design of Jaina temples. See Shah 1955, 85-95. For an extended analysis of the samavasaraṇa and some speculations on its psychological significance, see Norton 1981.

9. Of course, the Jainas are far from being the only Indian religion whose monastics are homeless, or which regards homelessness as a prerequisite for sanctity. Compare, for example, the practice of the Rāmānandī sect as described by Burghart, where homelessness "represents the form of the ascetic liberated from the world" (Burghart 1983, 380). Compare also Bharati's account of his initiation as an ascetic of the Daśanāmi order and of his monastic pilgrimage (Bharati 1970, 144-73); and note Bharati's exegesis of his own monastic name, Agehananda: "Bliss through homelessness, bliss that is homelessness, bliss when there is no home..." (Bharati 1970, 154). The attitudes cited by Burghart and by Bharati are similar to that of the Jainas, to whom the homeless state of the monk is an anticipation of his final goal of bodiless existence in the siddhaloka.

10. It is interesting that the many ascetic traditions of India, all of which regard their monastics as homeless at least in theory, forbid them in any case to light fires and to cook. As Kim Dovey has pointed out in a paper which has many implications for this study, the creation of a home is powerfully symbolized by "the fire and the hearth that shelters it" (Dovey 1978). One might add two observations: first, that the preparation and serving of food in one's home is the most elementary duty of the host toward a guest; and secondly, that fires played an essential part in the hospitality rites, directed toward the Vedic gods conceived as guests of the worshipper, which are among the earliest attested forms of Indian religious behavior.

11. As described by Deo (1956, 246): "With a view of not inflicting injury to living beings in the overgrowth of vegetation in the rainy season, the monk spent the four months of the rainy season (*vassā*) in one place."

12. Sangave (1959, 343, 344) remarks: "The four months of the rainy season, known as caturmāsa, are selected for the special observances of religious practices and that is why those who cannot perform religious practices for the whole year are advised to at least perform them during caturmāsa."

13. "Canonical literature," among Śvetāmbara Jainas, refers to forty-four texts and their commentaries, written in various Prakrits (early Indian vernacular languages). See Dundas (1992, 53-73) for an account of the canon. The Sanskrit writings of later Jaina masters have a quasi-canonical character.

14. Deo (1956, 247-49) has summarized the practices set forth in the Prakrit canon for searching out a monastic residence. The system he describes bears no similarity to what I observed in Gujarat in 1982.

15. The Jaina tradition is distinguished by the attention it has paid to the subject of lay discipline in general and for the severity of the penances undertaken by the laity. It has been

suggested that the quasi-monastic character of the penances has been partially responsible for the cameraderie and affection that often characterizes monastic-lay relationships among Jainas, and it may help to explain the continued vitality of the tradition. See Williams (1963) for an account of the vast literature on the subject of lay discipline produced by Jaina spiritual masters, and Norman (1991) for the treatment of this subject within the Jaina canon.

16. The pañjrapol is a characteristic Jaina institution, although homes for unwanted cows and other animals are a Hindu and a Buddhist custom as well. See Lodrick (1980) for an account of animal homes in India.

17. "Grace" is the English expression used by Hindus and Jainas to render the Sanskrit terms *prāsāda* and *krpā*. Both connote favor or blessing. One would not theoretically expect Jainas to employ such a concept, for the Jaina "God," being a soul in moksa, immersed in timeless beatitude, should neither be pleased by prayers nor answer them; hence a Jaina should approach "God," whether in the form of a physical or a mental image, only to create a feeling in himself that will turn his own mind toward moksa. The fact, however, seems to be that many and perhaps most Jainas do ask Tīrthaṅkaras for favors, mundane and otherwise, and this fact has led to considerable casuistry. For example, it is sometimes alleged that the Tīrthaṅkaras' attendant demigods and goddesses, sometimes called *śāsanadevas*, give blessings and answer prayers on their behalf, "God" himself remaining unmoved.

This insoluble philosophical problem is perhaps one reason among many why Jainas show such reverence to monastics. The latter are "available" in a sense in which the siddhas, depending on one's views, may not be. Jainas also dedicate temples to "future Tīrthaṅkaras" whom they know by name, and to Tīrthaṅkaras who are presently living in other universes. None of these, of course, is yet in moksa, and no Jaina doubts that they answer prayers and give blessing. For Jaina theory regarding the "purpose" of prayer and worship, see Dundas 1992, 179-81 and Humphrey 1985.

18. For example, on Mahāvīra's birthday celebration, Jainas remember that his mother had fourteen beautiful dreams during her pregnancy: dreams of a smokeless fire, of a ship with banners, and of other auspicious sights. The saṅgha celebrates this event by lowering silver images of the dreams from the ceiling of the upāśraya in order to symbolize the descent to earth of divinity. The right to catch the silver image as it falls belongs to the one who makes the most generous offer.

19. I say "until recently" because the situation has changed radically for the better in the past decade. Arcane studies of the minutiae of monastic praxis and logical theory, which were virtually the sole interest of generations of Western Jainologists, have been supplemented by the fine historical and field studies of Cort (1988, 1989, 1991), Reynell (1985), Banks (1986), and others. Anyone who needs to be convinced of the new vitality of Jaina studies need only peruse the volume edited by Carrithers and Humphrey (1991).

20. Support is perhaps lent to such a position by David Sopher's remark, "Geography cannot deal with the personal religious experience, which is to some the core of religion" (Sopher 1967, 1). The great usefulness of Sopher's survey of religious-geographical themes, the only survey of its kind, is yet lessened by this self-imposed restriction. The individual's self-image in relation to space, place, and the natural world in general is, in fact, a vital theme in any human geography and of the geography of religions in particular. As Yi-Fu Tuan puts it, "A human geography requires that we be aware of the differences in the human desire for coherence, and note how these differences are manifest in the organization of space and time, and in attitudes toward nature" (Tuan 1976).

A viable geography of religions should deal with the following themes: (1) the worshipper's self-image in relation to nature, to cosmos, and to the transcendent (this theme should include the study of religiously-based cosmologies); (2) the influence of these cosmological and other images on the organization of space and sense of place; (3) the influence of religious ideas on the use of resources and on the landscape; and (4) the effect of geographical constraints and opportunities on the spread and interaction of religions. (This scheme is, of course, not original but is an adaptation of Sopher's.)

21. John 3:8 in the New Revised Standard Version (NRSV).

References

Banks, M. J. 1986. Defining division: An historical overview of Jaina social organization. *Modern Asian Language Studies* 20:447-60.

Basham, A. L. 1981. *History and doctrines of the Ājīvikas, a vanished Indian religion*. Delhi, Motilal Banarsidas.

Bharati, A. 1970. *The ochre robe: An autobiography*. London: George Allen and Unwin.

Bhardwaj, S. M. 1973. *Hindu places of pilgrimage in India: A study in cultural geography*. Berkeley: University of California Press.

Brown, P. 1982. The rise and function of the holy man in Late Antiquity. In *Society and the holy in Late Antiquity*, 103-52. Berkeley: University of California Press.

Burghart, R. 1983. Wandering ascetics of the Rāmānandī sect. *History of Religions* 22:361-80.

Caplan, A. L. H. 1982. Pilgrims and priests as links between a sacred center and the Hindu culture region: Prayag's Magh Mela pilgrimage (Allahabad, India). Ph.D. diss., University of Michigan.

Carrithers, M. and C. Humphrey. 1991. *The assembly of listeners: Jains in society*. Cambridge: Cambridge University Press.

Cort, J. E. 1988. Pilgrimage to Shankesavar Parshvanatha. *Bulletin of the Center for the Study of World Religions, Harvard University* 14: 163-72.

———. 1989. Liberation and well being: A study of the Svetambar Murtipujak Jains of Northern Gujarat. Ph.D. diss., Harvard University.

———. 1991. The Svetambar Murtipujak Jain Mendicant. *Man* 26: 651-71.

Deo, S. B. 1956. *History of Jaina monachism from inscriptions and literature*. Poona, India: Deccan College Postgraduate and Research Institute.

Dovey, K. 1978. Home: An ordering principle in space. *Landscape* 22:27-30.

Dundas, P. 1992. *The Jains*. London, New York: Routledge.

Eck, D. 1981. India's tīrthas: 'Crossings' in sacred geography. *History of Religions* 20:323-44.

Eliade. M. 1974. *Patterns in comparative religion*. New York: New American Library.

Folkert, K. W. 1984. Jainism. In *A handbook of living religions*, ed., J. R. Hinnels, 256-77. New York: Viking.

Humphrey, C. 1985. Some aspects of the Jain puja: The idea of "God" and the symbolism of offerings. *Cambridge Anthropologist* 9:31-39.

Jaini, P. S. 1970. Śramaṇas: Their conflict with Brahmaṇical society. In *Chapters in Indian civilization*, v. 1, ed. J. W. Elder, 39-81. Dubuque, Iowa: Kendall/Hunt.

———. 1979. *The Jaina path of purification*. Berkeley: University of California Press.

Lodrick, D. 1980. *Sacred cows, sacred places: Origins and survivals of animal homes in India*. Berkeley: University of California Press.

Norman, K. R. 1991. The role of laymen according to the Jain canon. In *The assembly of listeners: Jains in Society*, ed. M. Carrithers and C. Humphrey, 31-39.Cambridge: Cambridge University Press.

Norton, A. W. 1981. The Jaina Samavasaraṇa Ph.D. diss., New York University, School of Fine Arts.

Reynell, J. 1985. Honour, nurture and festival: Aspects of female religiousity amongst Jain women in Jaipur. Ph.D. diss., Cambridge University.

Sangave, V. A. 1959. *Jaina community: A social history*. Bombay, India: Popular Book Depot.

Schwartzberg, J. E., ed. 1978. *A historical atlas of South Asia*. Chicago: The University of Chicago Press.

Shah, U. P. 1955. *Studies in Jaina art*. Varnasi, India: Jaina Cultural Research Society.

Sopher, D. E. 1967. *Geography of religions.* Englewood Cliffs, NJ: Prentice-Hall.
——. 1968. Pilgrim circulation in Gujarat. *Geographical Review* 58:392-425.
Stevenson, M. 1970. *The heart of Jainism.* Bombay, India: Munshiram Manoharilal.
Stoddard, R. H. 1966. Hindu holy sites in India. Ph.D. diss., Department of Geography, University of Iowa, Iowa City.
Tuan, Y-F. 1974. *Topophilia: A study of environmental perception, attitudes and values.* Englewood Cliffs, NJ: Prentice-Hall.
——. 1975. Place: An experiential perspective. *Geographical Review* 65:151-65.
——. 1976. Humanistic geography. *Annals of the Association of American Geographers* 66:266-76.
Wagner, P. L., and M. W. Mikesell. 1962. The themes of cultural geography. In *Readings in cultural geography,* eds. P. L. Wagner and M. W. Mikesell, 1-24. Chicago: University of Chicago Press.
Weber, M. 1958. *The religion of India: The sociology of Hinduism and Buddhism.* Trans. H. H. Garth and D. Martindale. Glencoe, IL: Free Press.
Williams, R. 1963. *Jaina yoga: A study of the medieval Śrāvakācāras.* London: Oxford University Press.

Patterns of Pilgrimage to the Sikh Shrine of Guru Gobind Singh at Patna

P. P. Karan
University of Kentucky

Abstract

The four major sacred places for Sikh pilgrimages are the Akal Takht in Amritsar, the Takht Sri Kesgarh in Anandpur, the Takht Hazur Sahib in Nanded, and the Takht Sri Harmandirji Patna Sahib (or Takht Janamstan) in Patna. A survey of 437 pilgrims at the Takht Sri Harmandirji Patna Sahib provided information about the patterns of movement and the socio-economic characteristics of pilgrims to this shrine. Although pilgrim flows are affected by numerous factors (such as religious promotional lectures at local *gurdwaras*, or temples, participation in theological discourses, desires to enhance the Sikh brotherhood, and opportunities for promoting trade and commerce), three variables were examined statistically: annual per capita income, percentage of Sikh population, and distance to Patna from the largest city. When related to the percentage of pilgrims interviewed at Patna originating from each district, the income variable produced the highest level of correlation. The importance of this wealth factor was substantiated by comparing socioeconomic characteristics of the interviewed pilgrims with the general population of India. The Sikh pilgrims were richer, more urban, and had more schooling. Furthermore, those pilgrims who had come to this shrine more than once were even more likely to be rich, urban, and well educated.
Key words: pilgrimage, Sikh shrines, pilgrimage flows, pilgrimage characteristics, Patna.

Pilgrimage to sacred places is an important institution in nearly all major religions. Followers of every religion perceive certain places as sacred, and it is their ambition to visit holy places at least once in their life time. What places are considered sacred, and why, often depends on the recorded, or sometimes unrecorded, religious events associated with specific geographic sites.

Cultural geographers have long been concerned with the study of religious phenomena, including the journeys or pilgrimages to sacred places. Particularly noteworthy are geographic studies on pilgrimage to

Sacred Places, Sacred Spaces: The Geography of Pilgrimages, edited by Robert H. Stoddard and Alan Morinis, 1997. Geoscience and Man, vol. 34, pp. 257-268. Dept. of Geography and Anthropology, Louisiana State University, Baton Rouge, LA 70893-6010.

257

Hindu, Moslem, Buddhist, and Christian sacred places (Stoddard 1966; Bhardwaj 1973; Sopher 1968; Shair and Karan 1979; Tanaka Shimazaki 1977; Gurgel 1976). As a companion study, the geographic aspects of the Sikh pilgrimage to the sacred shrine of Guru Gobind Singh (also known as Takht Janamsthan and Takht Sri Harmandirji Patna Sahib) at Patna, Bihar, are considered in this paper.

Three questions are examined here. (1) What is the spatial pattern of pilgrimage to the Sikh shrine of Guru Gobind Singh? (2) What are the socioeconomic attributes of those pilgrims? (3) What is the relationship between the socioeconomic characteristics of the pilgrims and their frequency of pilgrimage to this shrine?

Data for this study were collected through a quasi-random sample survey of pilgrims during the months of October-December 1980. During that period, 437 pilgrims (231 men and 206 women) were interviewed. During the interviews, information was collected on each pilgrim's home district, occupation, age, literacy, annual income, mode of travel, and the number of times pilgrimage was undertaken to Patna.

Before analyzing the results of the collected data, it may be useful to discuss briefly the development of the Sikh religion as it relates to the sacred places of Sikh pilgrimage in India.

Religion of the Sikhs

Sikhism developed out of Hinduism into a distinct religion with belief in ten Gurus, and reverence for the Holy Book, Guru Granth Sahib, and certain symbols, ceremonies, shrines, and places of pilgrimage. Of the ten Gurus, the personalities of Nanak, Angad, Amar Das, Arjan, and Gobind Singh left a deep impression on Sikhism (Cunningham 1966). The teachings of Guru Nanak (1469-1539), founder of the religion, formed the nucleus of the Granth Sahib. The second Guru, Angad (1539-1552), invented the Gurmukhi alphabet, the sacred script of the Sikhs. Amar Das (1552-1574), the third Guru, started the institution of *langar* (common kitchen) to abolish caste distinctions. Ram Das (1574-1581), the fourth Guru, founded the city of Ramdaspur, which later came to be known as Amritsar, and started the construction of the Golden Temple, which then became a major center of Sikh pilgrimage.

Arjan (1581-1606), the fifth Guru, infused vigor into Sikhism. He enhanced the religious importance of Amritsar by making it his headquarters, and he completed the construction of the Golden Temple (Harmandir) and the surrounding tank. His religious activities incurred the enmity of Mogul Emperor Jahangir, and he was tortured to death in 1606. This created a rift between the Sikhs and Moguls and started the process by which Sikhism became militant. Guru Har Gobind (1606-1645) sanctioned the use of steel in the defence of religion and for the protection of the oppressed. The intolerance of Emperor Aurangzeb to the proselytizing activities of Sikhs led to the seizure and execution of the ninth Guru, Teg Bahadur (1664-1675). Religious persecution inevitably led the Sikhs to take up arms against the Moguls and paved the way for the transformation of Sikhism into a militant theocracy under Guru Gobind Singh (1675-1708), the tenth and last Guru.

Guru Gobind Singh was the most famous of all the Gurus after Nanak. Born at Patna on 22 December 1666, he became Guru at the age of nine. He founded the Khalsa, the militant Sikh theocracy, and infused new life and vigor by introducing baptism and adding the suffix "Singh" (lion) to names. He organized Sikhs into a well-knit religious and social body; he abolished the succession of Gurus by replacing them with the Granth Sahib. On Baisakhi Day (30 March 1699), he baptized five of his followers with *amrit* (water of immortality). As the outward and visible signs of this discipline, they were enjoined at the time of baptism to wear five K's: *kes* (unshorn hair) associated with saintliness, a *kangha* (comb) for keeping the hair clean and tidy, *kacha* (shorts) which ensured briskness of movement during action and served as comfortable underwear at times of rest, a *kara* (bangle or bracelet) as sign of sternness and constraint, and a *kirpan* (sword) as an instrument of offence and defence, and as an emblem of power and dignity. The disciples were also asked to follow rules of conduct such as abstaining from smoking tobacco and drinking alcohol.

Thus was born in 1699 the Khalsa Brotherhood which rejuvenated Sikhism with disciplinary forms and vows secured by religious ceremonies (Rataul 1974). With a new script, a new scripture, new centers of worship, and new symbols and ceremonies, the Sikhs acquired a distinct religious individuality. During the following decades, the blood of martyrs nurtured the Sikh community with tremendous communal pride. Two sons of Guru Gobind Singh became martyrs, and he himself was assassinated on 7 October 1708 at Nanded.

Sikhism, as a religion, is a way of life based upon the belief that the Sikh disciple (*sisya*) incorporates or embraces the Guru, which is linked with an inexhaustible source of power. Meditation on God, utterance of the Name (*nam*), the guidance of the Guru, the company of saints, righteous living, and the service of humanity (*seva*) are the means of salvation (Singh, T. 1968).

Although Sikhism is a religion with a distinct way of life, it shares some Hindu beliefs such as the doctrine of the immortality and transmigration of the soul. In common with many religions, Sikhs maintain temples (*gurdwaras*), celebrate religious festivals (such as the birthdays of Guru Nanak and Guru Gobind Singh, the installation of Sri Guru Granth Sahib and the Khalsa, and the anniversaries of the martyrdom of Guru Arjan and Guru Teg Bahadur), and participate in pilgrimages.

Distribution of Sikhs

The number of Sikhs in India is about 18.3 million (13.1 million according to the 1981 census), constituting almost 2 percent of the national population. The highest proportion of Sikhs is in the state of Punjab (78.62%), followed by Haryana (6.08%), Uttar Pradesh (3.56%), Rajasthan (3.30%), and Delhi (2.81%). A large number of small Sikh communities are scattered throughout the various urban centers of the country (Dutt and Devgun 1977).

Before India's independence, the Sikhs numbered 5.7 million and were mostly concentrated in the Punjab. The partition of the Punjab (1947) led to considerable redistribution of the Sikh population from their original homelands. In 1961, Sikh totals (in millions) by states were as follows: Punjab 6.7; Uttar Pradesh 0.3; Rajasthan 0.3; and Delhi 0.2. The total for India that year was 7.8 million, up from 6.2 million in 1951 (but less than the 1971 figure of 10.3 million).

The great bulk of the Sikh population in the Punjab is rural, with only 12 percent living in urban areas. Outside of Punjab state, nearly 80 percent of the Sikhs live in urban areas and engage in commerce, crafts, and military service. Many of these urban families migrated to Indian cities as refugees from Pakistan in 1947.

Four Sacred Places of Sikh Pilgrimages

There are four famous holy places of Sikh pilgrimage in India: (1) the Akal Takht at Amritsar, Punjab; (2) Takht Sri Kesgarh at Anandpur, Ropar District, Punjab; (3) Takht Janamsthan (also known as Takht Sri Harmandirji Patna Sahib) in Patna, Bihar; and (4) Takht Hazur Sahib in Nanded, Maharashtra.

The Takht, the place of exaltation, is the seat of religious authority. The first Takht, the Akal Talkt in the front of the Golden Temple at Amritsar, was the seat from which the Guru exercised authority until the death of Guru Gobind Singh. In 1708, when the Order of the Khalsa was invested with spiritual and secular authority in conjunction with the Guru Granth, four sacred places — Amritsar, Anandpur, Patna, and Nanded — were recognized as Takhts. These four kept in view the geography of India as well as doctrinal and practical considerations in establishing a national religious fraternity (Singh, K. 1958). Each of these four sites is historically associated with Sikh Gurus. As mentioned above, the fourth and fifth Gurus constructed the Golden Temple and surrounding tank in Amritsar. Patna, which is described in greater detail below, is the birthplace of the Guru Gobind Singh.

Anandpur was founded in the year 1664 by Guru Teg Bahadur, the ninth Guru. It is also the ancestral home of Guru Gobind Singh, who spent twenty-five years of his life there. Anandpur Sahib grew into prominence as the birthplace of the Khalsa in 1699, when Guru Gobind Singh baptized his five followers and gave them the name Panj Pyare (the five loved ones). The spot where Guru Gobind Singh formed the first Khalsa is now the actual location of the Gurdwara Kesgarh of Anandpur.

Situated on the banks of the Godavari River, Nanded is a small town visited by thousands of Sikh pilgrims. They come to pay homage to Guru Gobind Singh at the site where he was assassinated in 1708. Because the rituals at Nanded vary slightly from those in the Punjab, they have been the source of some controversy between the Akalis of the Punjab and the Dakkhanis (Southern Sikhs).

Like the four *dhams* of the Hindus (Badrinath, Rameswaram, Dwarka, and Puri), the four Takhts are places of primary sanctity and pilgrimage. Each has a large gurdwara which receives wide attention as a sacred spot with inspiring traditions and legends. Sikh pilgrims are attracted to these places from various parts of India and abroad, and many contribute to the costs of gurdwara expansion.

The growth of Sikh pilgrimage to these four places speaks highly of the spiritual significance of the sacred spaces which continue to attract huge numbers of pilgrims. The number of pilgrims who visit Patna is estimated at about 90,000 per year; the number at Nanded at approximately 50,000; at Anandpur about 500,000; and the number who visit Amritsar is many times as great (fig. 1).

Sikhs attach special value to pilgrimage and consider it an important part of one's religious life, mental discipline, and internal purification. The institution of pilgrimage among the Sikhs can be traced back to Guru Nanak, who undertook a series of journeys and pilgrimages to various sacred places in India and Southwest Asia. Like Nanak, Sikhs go to sacred places for spiritual practices. In all sacred places, it is not what is seen with the naked eye that matters, but the venerable association and religious experience that counts. Where skeptics see only stone and marble of the shrine, the pilgrims and devotees feel the touch of divine life.

Sikh Pilgrimage to Takht Patna Sahib

Takht Sri Harmandirji Patna Sahib

Takht Sri Harmandirji Patna Sahib (figs. 2, 3 and 4) is situated in the eastern part of Patna, an area which has been renamed Patna Sahib because of its sanctity as the place where Guru Gobind Singh was born. The shrine, located in the city's old quarter at a site known as Harmandir Gali, was completed in the eighteenth century (Singh, S. 1983). The original building of Harmandir has undergone several changes. At the beginning of the nineteenth century, a devastating fire damaged the old edifice, and in 1934

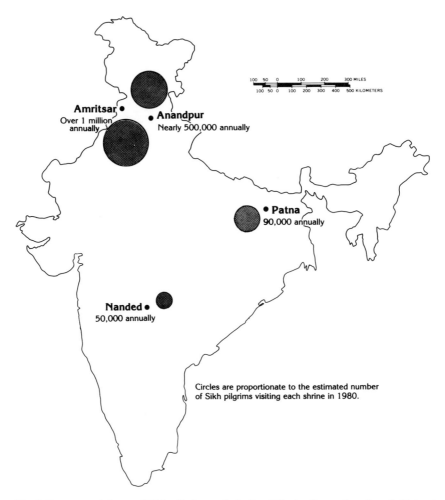

Fig. 1. Four sacred places of Sikh pilgrimage in India. (Pilgrim figures based on field data.)

an earthquake destroyed a portion of it. Construction of the present building was started in 1954 and completed by 1957 with the help of contributions by devotees from all parts of the world. The Harmandir is managed
by 15 trustees representing various Sikh organizations (Sikhs of Patna District, Sikh Societies of North and South Bihar, Sikhs of Calcutta, Uttar
Pradesh Sikh Pratinidhi Board, Sikhs of Delhi State, Sikh Gurdwara of
Amritsar, and Chief Khalsa Diwan of Amritsar).

A spacious congregation hall adjoins the sacred spot where Guru
Gobind Singh was born. Near the main entrance of the shrine is a marble-

Fig. 2. Sacred shrine of Guru Gobind Singh at Patna. The shrine, called Sri Harmandirji, located in the older eastern section of Patna City, where the Guru was born in 1666.

lined well, near which the Guru played during his childhood. Attached to the Harmandir is the Guru Ka Langar (community kitchen) where every one is served. Relics preserved in Harmandir include a copy of Sri Guru Granth Sahib, called Bare-Sahib and signed by Guru Gobind Singh, and several items relating directly to Guru Gobind Singh: Chhaabi Sahib, the only painting of him; Pangura Sahib, a small cradle (with four stands covered with golden plates) in which he slept as a child; a sword; a pair of ivory sandals; and a gown.

The Pilgrims

Our knowledge of the number and volume of Sikh pilgrims to the shrine of Guru Gobind Singh at Patna during the past 275 years since it was rec-

Fig. 3. **View of the altar at Sri Harmandirji Shrine, where the** *Granth Sahib* **(sacred scriptures) decorated with flowers is kept. Pilgrims and other worshipers gather in the courtyard below for prayer, singing of hymns, and religious discourses.**

ognized as a Takht is very limited. No accurate record or account of the volume of pilgrims exists. Presumably the number of pilgrims has increased from the mid-nineteenth century onwards as a result of improvements in the transportation system that allow Sikhs from the Punjab to perform the pilgrimage within two weeks. Since the end of the nineteenth century when the Punjab was directly connected with Patna by railway, the volume has increased. In recent years, pilgrim traffic has been increasing as a result of faster trains to the Patna Sahib Railway Station, improved bus routes, more cars, and better air service. A significant increase has occurred within the last decade, with, according to local officials, the estimated number of 90,000 pilgrims in 1980 being twice that of 1970.

Fig. 4. Buildings surrounding the sacred shrine of Sri Harmandirji. These buildings house pilgrims visiting the shrine from various parts of India and abroad. One also contains *Guru Ka Langar* (the free community kitchen) where pilgrims are served meals.

Currently, most Sikh pilgrims from parts of Bihar and eastern Uttar Pradesh come by road. According to pilgrims interviewed, train was the mode of travel for the majority of pilgrims from other places: Punjab (92%), Haryana and Delhi (89%), western districts of Uttar Pradesh (87%), Rajasthan (85%), and Calcutta (91%).

According to the data collected, 89 percent of the pilgrims to Patna come from the area consisting of the Punjab, Haryana, Delhi, Uttar Pradesh, and Rajasthan. That is, the majority of pilgrims come from the states having the major concentrations of Sikh population. At the district level of areal generalization, the largest number of pilgrims come from Amritsar, Ludhiana, Jullundur, Sangrur, Patiala, and Kapurthala districts of Punjab. Secondary pilgrim-supplying areas include Bhatinda, Firozepur, Ropar, Hosiarpur, Gurdaspur, and Delhi. Only small percentages come from urban centers in Bihar, Orissa, West Bengal, and Rajasthan, and from large cities such Bombay, Madras, Kanpur, Nagpur, and Hyderabad.

The economic prosperity of Sikhs communities in general, and the Punjab in particular, accounts for a steady growth during the 1970s (Karan and Bladen 1975). In addition to the economic conditions, the pilgrim flow is influenced by other factors such as religious promotional lectures at local gurdwaras, participation in theological discourses, the social goal of enhancing the Sikh brotherhood, and opportunities for promoting trade and commerce.

A multiple regression model was employed to discover the most significant factor influencing the number of pilgrims from a given district in India. The dependent variable was "percentage of pilgrims interviewed at Patna originating from each district" and the three independent variables for each district were: "annual per capita income," "percentage of Sikh population," and "distance to Patna from the largest city." The results reveal that income is the most important factor determining the volume of pilgrims, with a R^2 value of 0.82. Adding the variable termed "percentage of Sikh population" increased the coefficient to 0.88, and combining all three variables yielded 0.89.

During the 1980 interviews with pilgrims, data were collected to determine the effect pilgrims' visits had on the economy of the city. Questions were asked about the length of stay and the amount of money spent by pilgrims in the local area. The survey revealed that for pilgrims coming from outside Bihar the length of stay was between three to five days. The general pattern was for pilgrims from the Punjab, Haryana, and Delhi to stay longer than pilgrims from Uttar Pradesh and West Bengal. Pilgrims from within Bihar reported the shortest stay.

Data obtained from pilgrims indicate that on an average each pilgrim family spent approximately 200 Indian rupees on various goods and services during their stay in Patna. The estimate for the total direct spending by visitors is approximately 3.6 million rupees annually. Information and data collected from owners and operators of businesses in Patna Sahib indicate that they receive nearly 61 percent of this total trade, with the remainder being spent in other parts of Patna.

According to the sample of pilgrims, 68 percent of the pilgrims to the shrine of Guru Gobind Singh come from urban areas while only 32 percent are from rural parts of the country. This urban dominance is also reflected by the occupational distribution of pilgrims: 29 percent are engaged in service activities; 27 percent are in manufacturing and small business enterprises; and 18 percent are in the armed forces — all being occupational categories that are normally associated with urban residences. Only 21 percent of the pilgrims are engaged in farming and related services. (The remaining 5 percent are in miscellaneous other categories.) In a country where approximately three-fourths of the population lives in rural areas, this low participation of rural pilgrims may seem surprising; however, it must be remembered that, except for the Punjab, most Sikhs are urban dwellers with urban-based occupations.

This same urban/occupational pattern is displayed by the educational levels of the pilgrims. Almost half (49%) of the sampled pilgrims have completed high school; in contrast, only 8 percent have no formal schooling. According to the 1981 census, less than 8 percent of the Indian population has a high school degree or higher and 64 percent is illiterate. Therefore, these statistics about pilgrims certainly do not support the popular image of pilgrimages being composed primarily of illiterate peasants.

Income data are also consistent with the characterization of pilgrims' not being poor peasants. Although there is an element of uncertainty in drawing conclusions from information about income provided voluntarily by informants themselves, the sample data indicates the following: 19 percent have high incomes (Rupees 20,000 or more annually), 63 percent are in the middle income category (Rupees 12,000-18,000 per year), and 18 percent are defined as having low income (less than Rupees 12,000 per year, the category that includes the national GNP per capita value).

Data about the age of pilgrims indicate that pilgrims generally matched the national age structure. The percentage of pilgrims for the age categories of 16 - 30, 31 - 50, 51 - 70, and 71 and above were respectively: 32, 43, 22, and 3. National census data for 1981 for the age categories of 15 - 24, 25 - 44, and 45 and above were respectively: 30, 41, and 28. In any case, the Sikh pilgrims to Patna cannot be characterized as being mainly the elderly.

An attempt was made to learn about the importance of pilgrimage in the lives of Sikhs by asking the sample of visitors at the shrine about their priorities. According to their declared motivations, more than half (58%) of them give a higher priority to making a pilgrimage than to other activities such as doing business, visiting with relatives, or traveling.

Data obtained about the characteristics of pilgrims and the frequency of their pilgrimage to this shrine did not reveal a distinct relationship between these two variables. Most pilgrims at the shrine of Guru Gobind Singh are first-time visitors: of the pilgrims interviewed, fewer than 10 percent were on their second or third pilgrimage to Patna. This small percentage did not allow for much generalizing about variations in frequency of pilgrimages. Nevertheless, it was observed that those pilgrims who had returned for a second or third pilgrimage had characteristics similar to those of the entire group. Nearly all who had made multiple pilgrimages were of urban origin, occupied in services, and in the highest income category. In fact, if any distinction can be made, it is that those who might be regarded as more devout because of their multiple pilgrimages to this holy place were even farther than the total set of interviewed pilgrims from the popular image of pilgrims as being poor, rural, and uneducated.

In many respects, pilgrimages in the Sikh tradition are similar to those of other religions, with this type of religious movement manifesting a universal urge to visit those special places endowed with sanctity. However, as evidenced by data collected at the Takht Sri Harmandirji Patna Sahib,

Sikh pilgrims do not fit the popular image of pilgrims' being primarily from rural areas and being poorer and less educated than the general population. Whether the richer, better educated, urban pilgrims observed at this shrine typify other pilgrim populations of recent times will remain unknown until researchers examine this aspect of pilgrimage in greater detail.

Acknowledgment

I wish to thank Professor Shamsher Singh, Research Scholar at Takht Patna Sahib for assistance and support.

References

Bhardwaj, S. M. 1973. *Hindu places of pilgrimage in India: A study in cultural geography.* Berkeley: University of California Press.

Cunningham, J. D. 1966. *A history of Sikhs.* New Delhi, India: S. Chand and Company.

Dutt, A. K., and S. Devgun. 1977. Diffusion of Sikhism and recent migration patterns of Sikhs in India. *GeoJournal* 1:81-89.

Gurgel, K. K. 1976. Travel patterns of Canadian visitors to the Mormon culture hearth. *Canadian Geographer* 20:405-17.

Karan, P. P., and W. A. Bladen. 1975 Interregional disparities of income in India. *Geographical Review of India* 37:210-20.

Rataul, S. S. 1974. *The Khalsa.* Amritsar, India: Shiromani Gurdwara Parbandhak Committee.

Shair, I. M., and P. P. Karan. 1979. Geography of the Islamic pilgrimage. *GeoJournal* 3:599-608.

Singh, K. 1958. A New Takht - Seat of authority. *The Sikh Review* July:30-35.

Singh, S. 1983. *Takht Patna Saheb in its historical and spiritual perspective.* Patna Saheb: Takht Sri Harmandirji.

Singh, T. 1968. *The Sikh prayer.* Amritsar, India: Shiromani Gurdwara Parbhandhak Committee.

Sopher, D. E. 1968. Pilgrim circulation in Gujarat. *Geographical Review* 58:392-425.

Stoddard, R. H. 1966. Hindu holy sites in India. Ph.D. diss., University of Iowa, Iowa City.

Tanaka Shimazaki, H. 1977. Geographic expression of Buddhist pilgrim places on Shikoku Island, Japan. *Canadian Geographer* 21:116-24.

The Shikoku Pilgrimage:
Essential Characteristics of a Japanese Buddhist Pilgrimage Complex

Hiroshi Tanaka Shimazaki
University of Lethbridge

Abstract

The pilgrimage to multiple sacred places on Shikoku Island, Japan, is representative of Buddhist pilgrimage popular since the seventeenth century. Associated with Kōbō-Daishi, founder of the Japanese Shingon Mikkyō sect, it incorporates 88 temples located along a 1,545-kilometer circular route. Towards an understanding of pilgrimage places, four essential aspects of the sacred sites are considered: the association of the sites with various sacred beings; the temple landscapes in terms of their assemblages of physical features; the relationship between geographic setting and ritual behavior; and the spatial interactions among the 88 places. The geographic setting of the sacred places is characterized by the assemblage of landscape markers invested with special meaning and the expression of this cultural preference, both in frequency of occurrence and in spatial organizations, within the temple precincts. The association of each of the temples with Kōbō-Daishi and Buddhist deities is central to its acknowledged sanctity. This recognized association is expressed in the landscape and in the ritual behavior occurring at each of the temples. While there is some variation in the physical setting of each of the sacred places, particular pilgrim activities are repeatedly linked to specific physical features. When the pilgrimage places are considered collectively, a distinctive spatial-temporal order in pilgrimage ritual emerges. The 88 places are united into distinct, though often overlapping, groups by pilgrim movement. These temple groupings, bound by underlying meaning, provide guidelines for the institution of pilgrimage as a spatial-symbolic system.
Key words: pilgrimage, Buddhist pilgrimage, Japan, sacred landscape, spatial symbolism.

Introduction

The diversity of pilgrimage forms and traditions makes it difficult to find a single method adequate for the study of pilgrimage in general. As well,

Sacred Places, Sacred Spaces: The Geography of Pilgrimages, edited by Robert H. Stoddard and Alan Morinis, 1997. Geoscience and Man, vol. 34, pp. 269-297. Dept. of Geography and Anthropology, Louisiana State University, Baton Rouge, LA 70893-6010.

the complex nature of pilgrimage invites a variety of research perspectives and results in difficulties in relevant comparison of the essential nature of pilgrimage the world over. While each differs in character, all pilgrimages rest on the existence of pilgrimage places. Compared with the considerable attention given to pilgrimage as a human movement over a given space, less emphasis has been placed on the understanding of the pilgrimage places themselves.

In this study, the significance of the institution of pilgrimage is conceptualized under the rubric of "places" as a formal integration of particular physical features, recognized association, corresponding behavior, and interaction with other places. In order to capture the character of places of religious significance, a representative pilgrimage within one particular cultural context is investigated through the identification, description, and synthesis of the non-mentalistic "external" dimensions of the 88 sacred places of the Shikoku pilgrimage in Japan. (The location and names of the 88 pilgrimage places are indicated in figure 1 and table 1 respectively. The data for this paper was collected during my 78-day walking pilgrimage in 1972 and numerous return visits to Shikoku.)

In Japan, a religious journey to multiple pilgrimage places is usually referred to as *junrei*, meaning pilgrimage, while a visit to a single site is often referred to as *sankei* or *sanpai*, meaning temple prayer visit, thus indicating that a journey to multiple sites is a characteristic aspect of the idea of pilgrimage in Japan.[1] Among the various types of pilgrimages to multiple sites, pilgrimages to 88 and 33 places are two major types. Of these, the pilgrimage to the 88 sacred places on Shikoku Island is perhaps the best known and is the original model from which all other pilgrimages to 88 places emerged.[2]

Association of the Pilgrimage Places with Sacred Beings

Central to the acknowledged sanctity of the Shikoku sacred places is their recognized association with deities and/or saintly beings. The particular significance of each of the 88 places rests on its twofold association with Kōbō Daishi (A.D. 774-835) and with a particular *honzon* or chief deity. Such association is the foundation of both the history and the legends of each of the 88 places and a variety of points along the pilgrimage route and is the basis of contemporary pilgrimage customs and beliefs.

Kōbō Daishi

Today, pilgrims believe that the Buddhist priest Kukai, posthumously known as Kōbō Daishi, established the 88 sacred places. He visited China early in the ninth century to study Shingon Mikkyō Buddhism, the sect he later established in Japan, and probably was aware of the idea of pilgrim-

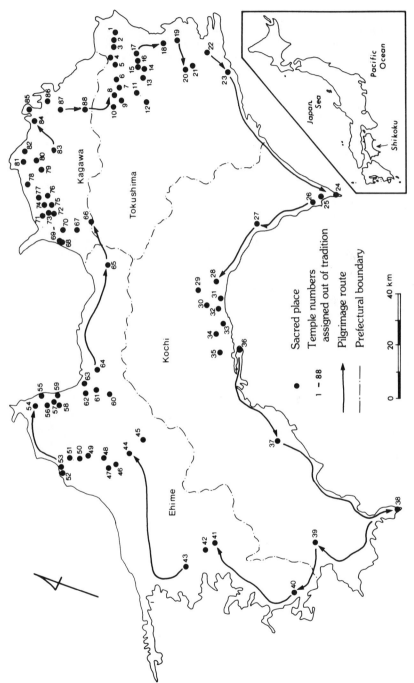

Fig. 1. Eighty-eight Buddhist pilgrimage places on Shikoku Island, Japan.

Table 1. Temple names of the 88 Buddhist places, Shikoku, Japan

Assigned number*	Temple name	Assigned number	Temple name	Assigned number	Temple name
1	Ryōzen-ji	31	Chikurin-ji	61	Kōon-ji
2	Gokuraku-ji	32	Zenjibu-ji	62	Hōju-ji
3	Konsen-ji	33	Sekkei-ji	63	Kisshō-ji
4	Dainichi-ji	34	Tanema-ji	64	Maegami-ji
5	Jizō-ji	35	Kiyotaki-ji	65	Sankaku-ji
6	Anraku-ji	36	Seiryū-ji	66	Unpen-ji
7	Jūraku-ji	37	Iwamoto-ji	67	Daikō-ji
8	Kumadani-ji	38	Kongofuku-ji	68	Jinne-in
9	Hōrin-ji	39	Enkō-ji	69	Kannon-ji
10	Kirihata-ji	40	Kanjizai-ji	70	Motoyama-ji
11	Fujii-dera	41	Ryūkō-ji	71	Iyadani-ji
12	Shōsan-ji	42	Butsumoku-ji	72	Mandara-ji
13	Dainichi-ji	43	Meiseki-ji	73	Shusshaka-ji
14	Jōraku-ji	44	Taihō-ji	74	Kōyama-ji
15	Kokubun-ji	45	Iwaya-ji	75	Zentsū-ji
16	Kannon-ji	46	Jōruri-ji	76	Konzō-ji
17	Ido-ji	47	Yasaka-ji	77	Dōryū-ji
18	Onzan-ji	48	Sairin-ji	78	Gōshō-ji
19	Tatsue-ji	49	Jōdo-ji	79	Kosho-in
20	Kakurin-ji	50	Hanta-ji	80	Kokubun-ji
21	Tairyū-ji	51	Ishide-ji	81	Shiramine-ji
22	Byōdō-ji	52	Taisan-ji	82	Negoro-ji
23	Yakuō-ji	53	Enmyō-ji	83	Ichinomiya-ji
24	Hotsumisaki-ji	54	Enmei-ji	84	Yashima-ji
25	Shinshō-ji	55	Nankō-bō	85	Yakuri-ji
26	Kongōchō-ji	56	Taisan-ji	86	Shido-ji
27	Kōnomine-ji	57	Eifuku-ji	87	Nagao-ji
28	Dainichi-ji	58	Senyū-ji	88	Ōkubo-ji
29	Kokubun-ji	59	Kokubun-ji		
30	Zenraku-ji	60	Yokomine-ji		

* Over the centuries these numbers have come to be assigned to the temples to indicate the preferred order of visits.

age, but there is no reference to the Shikoku pilgrimage in his writing. It is known, however, that Kōbō Daishi was born on Shikoku and traveled to several places on the island.[3] The 88 temples of the Shikoku pilgrimage are not the only ones that existed on Shikoku during Kōbō Daishi's lifetime. There were at least 165 temples of which 130 claim Kōbō Daishi as either their founder, consecrator, or sculptor of their honzon, or claim association with his life activities.

When and how, then, did the pilgrimage come to encompass the present 88 places? These questions were raised as early as the late seventeenth century when they appeared in one of the earliest pilgrim guide books written by the Buddhist priest Jakuhon (1689). The answers were not known then, nor are they now, although there has been considerable speculation (Kondō 1971). Jakuhon himself introduced 92 temples. But by the early eighteenth century, the total had become fixed at 88 and each temple had been assigned a number in a clockwise order beginning with Ryōzen-ji (Tanaka Shimazaki 1981). The historical records indicate that the pilgrimage was well established by the beginning of the eighteenth century.

Whether Kōbō Daishi was the originator of the pilgrimage or not, the strong association of Kōbō Daishi with the pilgrimage is clearly evident in the landscape. Pilgrims, whether they walk or use some vehicular mode of transportation, carry staves that symbolize Kōbō Daishi. Written on them are the words "*Dōgyō ninin*," meaning "together with Kōbō Daishi." The belief of the pilgrims in the presence of Kōbō Daishi is acknowledged through their behavior at each of the 88 temples (see below).

Honzon

While the association of Kōbō Daishi is shared by all 88 sacred places and varies only in its extent, the association with the honzon or principal deity varies according to the particular type of honzon with which each sacred place is associated. While it is common for each place to be associated with several Buddhist deities and to enshrine representations of these deities, one among them has been designated as the honzon. There are twelve types of honzon found within the 88 sacred places (table 2). The frequency with which each type of honzon occurs is indicative of its relative popularity. Because the twelve types of honzon are representative of various facets derived from the greatness of the Buddha and are thus parts of a complex, unified whole, there is an inherent relationship among them.

The nature of the twelve types of honzon may be defined according to "hierarchy," "temporal position," and "functional significance." First, the honzon are hierarchically conceptualized as *nyorai*, the Buddha in his enlightened state; *bosatsu*, the Buddha in his candidacy, that is, in his training for enlightenment; and *myōō* and *ten* protectors. Second, with regard to temporal position, the honzon may be conceived as occupying positions either in the "present world," that world in which the soul presently resides, or in the "future worlds," the successive worlds in which the soul will reside when it departs from the human body it now inhabits. Third, in terms of functional significance, all the honzon contribute to the salvation of humanity either "practically" or "theoretically."

Table 2. Frequency of occurrence of the type of honzon
(principal deity) within the 88 sacred places

Type of honzon	Frequency	Percent
Kanzenon-bosatsu	30	32.5
Jūichimen K-b	14	
Senju K-b	10	
Shō K-b	5	
Batō K-b	1	
Yakushi-nyorai	24	26.1
Amida-nyorai	10	10.9
Dainichi-nyorai	6	6.5
Jizō-bosatsu	6	6.5
Shaka-nyorai	5	5.4
Fudō-myōō	4	4.4
Kokūzō-bosatsu	3	3.3
Miroku-bosatsu	1	1.1
Monju-bosatsu	1	1.1
Daitsuchishō-bosatsu	1	1.1
Bishamon-ten	1	1.1
Total	92*	100.0

* Total exceeds the number of sacred places, 88, as Iwamoto-ji
(#37) is associated with five honzon.

Practical salvation refers to the concrete assistance with the affairs of the secular world offered by certain honzon and theoretical salvation to the soul's salvation afforded by others. The essential character of the twelve honzon is defined within this framework (schematically shown in fig. 2). For example, Shaka is more theoretical and current, and holds a higher position, than Miroku, which tends to be more practical and futuristic.

When the association of the 88 sacred places with honzon is viewed in terms of the frequency of occurrence of the types and their essential characteristics, it becomes evident that the majority of honzon are nyorai, residing in the present world and serving the practical needs of humanity. The syncretic nature of the association of the temples with Kōbō Daishi and the Buddhist deities serves to accommodate a variety of pilgrim needs and draws pilgrims to the 88 sacred places located along the periphery of Shikoku Island.

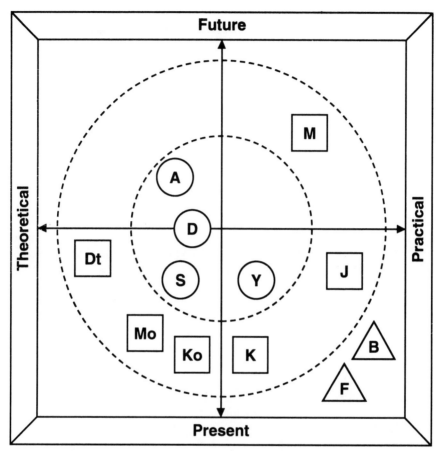

Hierarchy shown by centrality
Temporal occurrence shown by position of horizontal axes
Functional significance shown by position of vertical axes

Y   Yakushi - nyorai
A   Amida - nyorai
D   Dainichi - nyorai
S   Shaka - nyorai

K   Kanzenon - bosatsu
J   Jizō - bosatsu
Ko Kokūzō - bosatsu
M   Miroku - bosatsu
Mo Monju - bosatsu
Dt Daitsūchishō - bosatsu

F   Fudō - myōō
B   Bishamon - ten

Fig. 2. Conceptualization of the 12 types of honzon found within the Shikoku 88 pilgrimage places in terms of hierarchy, temporal position, and functional significance.

Spatial Expression of the Pilgrimage Places
Peripherality and Centrality of Pilgrimage Places

The nature of the location of pilgrimage places has been given consider-able attention.[4] With regard to the Shikoku pilgrimage, the locational char-acteristics of the sacred places differ depending on the scale of observation.

When the set of 88 places is viewed within Japan as a whole, the sa-cred places may be said to be peripherally located on the island of Shikoku and separated by the Inland Sea from Honshu, the economic and political heart of Japan. Historically Shikoku was considered to be *hedo* or *heji*, "land on the edge." The image held by the majority of those who lived on the "mainland" was that the Shikoku sacred places existed in a separate world outside of everyday space.

When the distribution of the 88 places is viewed at a scale that in-cludes only Shikoku Island, however, the conclusion is different (fig. 1). The distribution of temples and population roughly correspond, with the greatest number of temples located in the areas of concentrated popula-tion, the centers of which are the four prefectural capitals.

The centrality of distribution observed for Shikoku Island once again gives way to peripherality when the pilgrimage sites are viewed at yet an-other scale. That is, when the locations of temples are examined within ur-banized areas, it is seen that the majority of the pilgrimage sites lie on the fringe of the cities.

Historically, temples near urban centers attracted local residents and as a result they became the foci of local pilgrimages to small groups of tem-ples. On the other hand, a small number of temples located in remote areas and lacking ready accessibility were the training sites and references points for priests and devotees undertaking serious and lengthy pilgrim-ages. It is possible that these two historical practices of pilgrimage merged to form the Shikoku pilgrimage system as we know it today and provided the foundation for the concept of Shikoku as a Buddhist *dōjō*, or holy place.

Shikoku as a Buddhist Dōjō

The fact that the 88 sacred places are distributed over Shikoku's four pre-fectures has contributed to the concept of Shikoku as a Buddhist dōjō, or holy place of learning and practicing The Way. Within this larger dōjō, there are four smaller dōjō, each serving a specific purpose reflected in its name (table 3). These four dōjō correspond to Shikoku's four "countries," as they were traditionally called, or present day prefectures.

Within each dōjō, one sacred place functions symbolically as a *sekisho* or, in this context, the spiritual checkpoint which sinners cannot pass.

Table 3. Shikoku as a dōjō complex

Prefectural name			
Contemporary	Traditional	Name of dōjō	Purpose of dōjō
Tokushima	Awa	Hosshin	To determine that supreme enlightment will be attained
Kochi	Tosa	Shugyō	To practice that which has been determined
Ehime	Iyo	Bodai	To attain wisdom and under-standing of life
Kagawa	Sanuki	Nehan	To satisfactorily complete everything

Their locations do not follow any particular rule with respect to their spatial relationship to other sacred places within the dōjō, but, with the exception of the sekisho in the first dōjō, the sekisho is one of the most difficult sacred places to reach within each dōjō.

In addition to the four prefectural sekisho, there is the *ura-sekisho*, a fifth sekisho for the four dōjō together. Located approximately halfway along the circular route from Ryōzen-ji (temple 1), it is the first sacred place pilgrims visit after crossing into the third dōjō.

The traditional integrated spatial and symbolic organization of the 88 sacred places is summarized schematically in figure 3. Each temple occupies a prescribed position along the established circular pilgrim path. The spatial organization of the 88 places is shown in the outer ring, and their symbolic organization into four dōjō is shown in the inner circle. Shown in the center of the figure are Kōbō Daishi and the 12 honzon with which the 88 places are associated.

Pilgrimage Circulation and Spatial Structure of the Pilgrimage Places

The spatial structure of the 88 places of the pilgrimage is the outcome of the various ways in which the sacred places have been visited over the centuries. Three spatial types of pilgrimage may be observed.

The first is the pilgrimage to all 88 sacred places at once covering the 1,385 kilometer route. Although the pilgrimage normally commences at Ryōzen-ji, pilgrims may enter the circuit at any point.[5] They usually travel in a clockwise direction and return to their starting point to complete the circuit.[6] The majority of pilgrims leave the circuit at this point and return

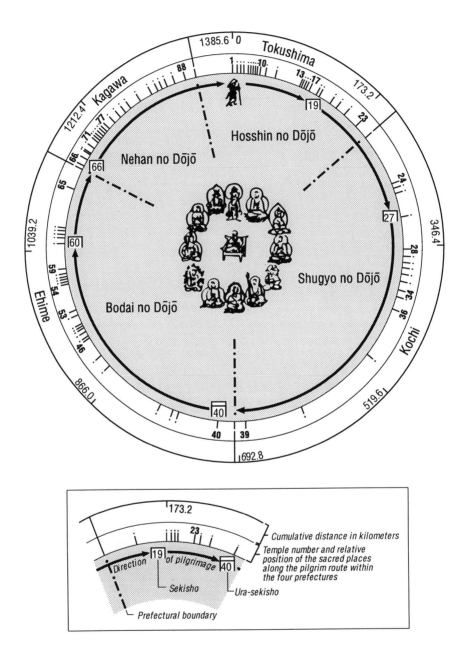

Fig. 3. Shikoku as a Buddhist Dōjō, consisting of 4 integrated dōjō, showing spatial and symbolic organization of the 88 sacred places. Central illustration represents Kōbō-Daishi and the 12 Buddhist deities associated with the 88 sacred places.

home, but some, especially in earlier times, would repeat the pilgrimage again and again without ever leaving the closed circuit.[7] To make the pilgrimage to all the places in the traditional manner, on foot, requires 40 to 60 days. In the past, for the sick and crippled who visited the sacred places hoping to be cured of their afflictions, it took even longer.

Among those who cannot afford the time to visit all of the sacred places at once, making a pilgrimage to all of the temples in only one prefecture is popular. This second type of pilgrimage, called "one-country visit," may be repeated on successive occasions until all 88 places have been visited, one prefecture at a time.

The third spatial type — the local pilgrimage — is practiced primarily by Shikoku residents. Through the division of the 88 sacred places into smaller groups, pilgrims have been permitted to make the pilgrimage in convenient segments. With the completion of each segment, certain religious merit is believed to have been attained; and when all segments of the pilgrimage have been completed, the religious merit is almost equal to that gained when the pilgrimage is made all at once.[8]

These types are expressed by the relationships between the Shikoku pilgrimage and its twelve sub-pilgrimages (fig. 4). Eight of these, encompassing anywhere from five to 17 temples each, are local pilgrimages, while the remaining four are "one-country" (i.e., one prefecture) visits.

Diffusion of the Shikoku Pilgrimage System

In addition to the Shikoku pilgrimage system, elsewhere in Japan there are numerous miniature pilgrimages to 88 sacred places patterned after the Shikoku model. At least 41 of them are considered major ones (fig. 5).[9] Like the original pilgrimage sites, the miniature routes are circular in arrangement, although, in some cases, the assigned temple numbers do not conform to the sequential spatial order of the sites. Compared with the Shikoku pilgrimage, however, miniature ones are much shorter, although there is considerable variation in circuit length. Some, if made on foot, take two weeks to complete, while others can be made in one day.

These replica pilgrimagtes have emerged over the centuries as another means of facilitating pilgrimage participation, and their existence has contributed to the spread of the idea of pilgrimage. Although each of the imitative pilgrimages had an enthusiastic local initiator who traveled to Shikoku, each region is believed to have been visited by Kōbō Daishi. All of the pilgrimage sites have an association with Kōbō Daishi and one or more Buddhist deities, but the association with Buddhist deities differs from the Shikoku model with regard to the range and frequency of occurrence of images enshrined.

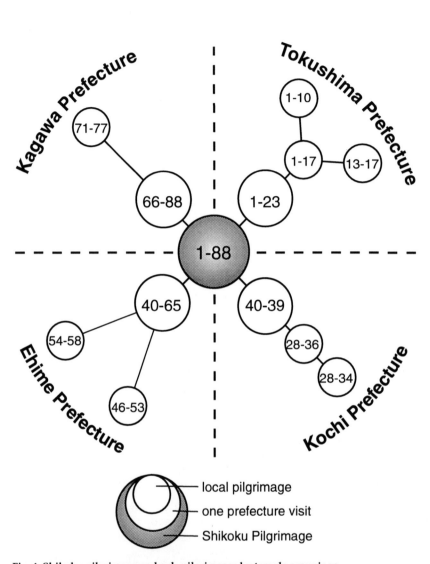

Fig. 4. Shikoku pilgrimage and sub-pilgrimages by temple groupings.

Fig. 5. Distribution of 41 sites throughout Japan, each having an 88-place sacred pilgrimage in miniature.

These miniaure pilgrimages afford individuals greater accessibility to this type of religious activity. The traditional walking pilgrimage of two months' duration after traveling to Shikoku from other parts of Japan was difficult for many. Personal considerations of finances and time were barriers to participation in the pilgrimage, as were political constraints during the Edo Period (1603-1868), when free movement from one prefecture to another was hindered.

While the Shikoku 88 places are each marked by a temple complex which consists of a variety of structures, the miniature pilgrimage sites have smaller structures with limited variety. In some cases, the sites are marked by natural features such as caves or waterfalls. The transfer of soil from the Shikoku sites to their counterparts in the miniature pilgrimages has played an important role in the designation and sanctification of the new sites.

Stability of Sacred Sites

Not only has there been a shift of sanctity among the Shikoku sites (as well as the transfer of the sanctity to other areas of Japan through the establishment of miniature pilgrimages), but changes in location have also occurred from time to time.

As far as can be determined, 14 of the 88 sacred places have changed locations since the middle of the sixteenth century, the earliest period for which records exist. Six were closely associated with Shinto shrines, and the changes in location occurred when Buddhism and Shinto were forced to separate in the early 1870s under the Haibutsu Kishaku movement (when the Meiji Government declared Shinto to be the state religion and attempted to abolish Buddhism). Another seven were moved after the original sites were destroyed by fire. One temple, Hōju-ji, moved twice: the first time after being destroyed by fire and the second time to make way for railway construction.

Today, almost no pilgrims visit the original sites from which sacred places have been moved. It may be argued, therefore, that the geographic setting of the sacred place is characterized not solely by the site as its exists unaltered by man, but rather primarily by the assemblage of landscape markers that have been invested with special meaning. What then are the constituent parts of the pilgrimage place as a physical complex?

Landscape of the Pilgrimage Places
Variation of Landscape Features and Frequency of Occurrence

The landscape, "the typical association of concrete geographic features" (Wagner 1972, 59), of the 88 sacred places is at the same time an essential aspect of the character of the pilgrimage and an expression of this character. Each sacred place encompasses a variety of features, both artificial and natural, each with its own distinctiveness. When the 88 places are viewed as a whole, however, shared characteristics permit categorization of the features into representative types. The provision of a morphology of temple landscape is accommodated through the selection of 36 representative types of landscape units found within the precincts of the 88 places.[10] A model of a temple complex is shown in figure 6.

The frequency of occurrence of the features within the temple precincts were classified into three groups: those occurring at more than 75 percent of the 88 sacred places (called "dominant"), those occurring at between 50 and 75 percent of the temples ("common"), and those occurring at less that 50 percent of the sacred sites (termed "less common"). According to this classification, 44 percent of the 36 landscape units are dominant (table 4).

Comparison of Temple Landscape: Old and New

A capacity for change is inherent in the character of the temple landscape and is expressed through temporal variation in the emergence and decline of landscape components. Comparison of temple landscape units at two time periods — the latter part of the seventeenth century and the present century — illuminates the changing character of the pilgrimage places (table 5).[11]

Based on the difference in the frequency of occurrence of the landscape units for the two time periods, the units may be defined as new, progressive, less progressive, or regressive. New units are those which did not occur at all in the latter part of the seventeenth century, while regressive ones are those which occur with less frequency now than they did earlier. The remaining features occur with greater frequency today than earlier are considered "progressive" or "less progressive," depending on whether the quantitative difference in occurrence between the two time periods is equal to or greater than the average difference, which was 33 percent, or less than that 33 percent.

The 12 new landscape units and the 22 "progressive" and "less progressive" features are directly or indirectly related to the pilgrimage ritual and reflect the increasing importance of the 88 places as active pilgrimage centers.

The decline of *yashiro*, the building which houses the Shinto gods, is perhaps indicative of the decreased association of Buddhism with Shinto. The decreasing occurrence of *mizu* ("sacred" water) is indicative of a decrease in the importance of natural bodies of water, which are still important within Shinto. This stands in marked contrast to the dramatic increase

1. Daishidō	7. Tōrō	13. Ishidan	19. Hōkyōintō	25. Settaisho	31. Tsuyadō
2. Kuri	8. Mon	14. Dō	20. Ishidatami	26. Hyakudoishi	32. Jishikoku
3. Chōzubachi	9. Meihyō	15. Hōnōsekihyō	21. Haka	27. Torii	33. Komainu
4. Kōro	10. Shōrō	16. Kuyōtō	22. Gorintō	28. Mizu	34. Dōkutsu
5. Rōsokutate	11. Jizō	17. Dōhyō	23. Zō	29. Tō	35. Shintokaikan
6. Hondō	12. Hei	18. Yashiro	24. Shokubutsu	30. Ishi	36. Soseki

Fig. 6. A model of the physical setting of the pilgrimage places, showing the relative positions of the 36 landscape units. (Artwork by the author.)

in the occurrence of *chōzubachi*, or ablution basins, which is perhaps expressive of an increasing ritualization within the Shikoku pilgrimage.

Spatial Arrangement of Landscape Features

While the frequency of occurrence of specific landscape features has changed over time, the spatial relationships among the features within the compounds remain relatively fixed.

Although the compounds of more than 90 percent of the sacred places have a southern or eastern orientation, no fixed geometrical arrangement of the 36 landscape units is apparent. There are two reasons for this. First, the majority of the sacred places are situated on "mountain" sides,[12] each one having distinct topographic characteristics. Second, there is considerable variation in the size of the compounds. When the arrangement is viewed within the broader context of relative position, however, the positions of the units appear to show some organizational patterns. The position of each unit may best be grasped if the compound is conceived as having two parts: fringe (which is frequently at a lower elevation) and interior (which is often, but not necessarily, higher). There is generally little variation in the spatial arrangement of the landscape units for the 88 sacred places.

Although all 36 types of physical features function symbolically, some may be said to fulfill a "practical" purpose in that they are directly associated with observable pilgrim activities. There are 17 types of physical features, the relative positions of which are stable. Of these, nine are dominant features with which pilgrim ritual is associated. Four of these nine are located in the interior of the compound. Two of these structures, the *daishidō* (daishi hall) and *hondō* (main hall), are associated with Kōbō Daishi and the honzon and are located in the most interior part of the compound.

Pilgrimage Places as Ritual Centers

A sacred place declares its underlying intent and its ideal meaning when pilgrims activate it and actualize it. One of the significant aspects of the place of pilgrimage is that they are the focal points of various ritual activities performed by countless numbers of pilgrims. Such pilgrim ritual is rooted in Buddhist teaching and has been tempered by Japanese cultural tradition.[13] The activities performed at the sacred places are the "accounts" of the pilgrimage process, which occurs not only at the sacred centers but also along the route linking them. The character of the 88 places of pilgrimage is expressed through the correspondence between specific structures and pilgrim activities.

The relationship between pilgrim activities and physical setting and variations in pilgrims' ritual behavior is examined here in an attempt to understand the nature of the pilgrim sites as the stage of pilgrim ritual. Through empirical observation it is possible to determine which of the 16 dominant physical features found in the sacred places most frequently elicit visible responses from pilgrims. Of the 16 dominant features, nine are most commonly associated with 13 discrete sets of pilgrim activities. These are considered to be the ritual units.

Structure of the Pilgrimage Ritual

The ritual units are listed in the order in which they ideally occur and an alphabetical label is assigned to each unit (table 6). Ideal order, as it is understood here, functions as a conceptual tool.[14] In reality, there are many variations within the sequential order of the ritual units. Nevertheless, on the basis of empirical observations, the relative sequence can be generalized (fig. 7). Variations that do occur in the sequence of ritual units occur only within demarcated fields: entrance, preparation for worship, worship, proof of worship, and departure. There is no interchange between the fields. The ritual units that constitute the worship field occupy the spatial interior. Those units that constitute the other ritual fields — entrance, preparation for worship, proof of worship, and departure — occupy the spatial fringe.

The relationships between the particular physical features and specific pilgrim behavior are supported both by the occurrence of the physical features and the pilgrims' recognition of and response to the meaning embodied in the features. When the pilgrimage ritual is considered as a whole, the temporal position of ritual units may be said to be "physically" determined according to the geographic location of physical features within the compound (as in the cases of A, B, L, and M) or "behaviorally" determined according to the point within the ritual at which pilgrims choose to perform specific activities (as with C through K). This dimension is termed "determinant of temporal position." Thus, the relative position of particular physical features together with pilgrim behavior in the ordered use of the features give rise to the relatively fixed structure of the pilgrimage ritual.

Range of Ritual Variation

The occurrence of the selected ritual units with regard to the sequential order presented in figure 7 must be understood in relation to the total framework. Whenever a specific physical feature does not exist within a particular temple compound, the corresponding behavior is usually omitted. Particular ritual behavior may also be omitted at the discretion of

Table 4. Physical featurers of the 88 Buddhist temple compounds in order of frequency of occurrence, Shikoku, 1973

Occurrence grouping	Rank order	Frequency of occurrence	Landscape unit Name	Approximate translation	Artifical or natural	Dominant material*
	(1)	88	Daishidō	Daishi hall	A	W
	(2)	88	Kuri	Priest's residence	A	W
	(3)	88	Chōzubachi	Ablution basin	A	S
	(4)	88	Kōro	Incense burner	A	S (M)
	(5)	88	Rōsokutate	Candle receptacle	A	M
	(6)	87	Hondō	Main hall	A	W (C)
	(7)	86	Tōrō	Lantern	A	S
	(8)	84	Mon	Gate	A	W
Dominant 75%	(9)	82	Meihyō	Temple name marker	A	S
	(10)	81	Shōrō	Belfry	A	W
	(11)	78	Jizō	Jizō statue	A	S
	(12)	75	Hei	Wall	A	C (clay)
	(13)	72	Ishidan	Stone steps	A	S (C)
	(14)	70	Dō	"Small" building	A	W
	(15)	70	Hōnōsekihyō	Donation stone	A	S
	(16)	69	Kuyōtō	Memorial "stupa"	A	S

(continued)

Table 4. *(concluded)*

| Occurrence grouping | Rank order | Frequency of occurrence | Landscape unit | | Artifical or natural | Dominant material* |
			Name	Approximate translation		
	(17)	60	Dōhyō	Pilgrim road sign	A	S
	(18)	55	Yashiro	Kami building	A	W
	(19)	54	Hōkyōintō	Hōkyōin "stupa"	A	S
Common	(20)	54	Ishidatami	Stone walk	A	S
50%	(21)	54	Haka	Grave(s)	A	S
	(22)	45	Gorintō	Five-ring "stupa"	A	S
	(23)	44	Zō	Statue	A	S (M)
	(24)	31	Shokubutsu	"Sacred" tree	N	W
	(25)	28	Settaisho	Settai building	A	S
	(26)	27	Hyakudoishi	Hundred-times stone	A	S
	(27)	26	Torii	Shinto gate	A	S
	(28)	22	Mizu	"Sacred" water	N	W (C)
	(29)	21	Tō	Pagoda/stupa	A	W (C)
	(30)	19	Ishi	"Sacred" rock	N	W
Less	(31)	18	Tsuyadō	Overnight building	A	W
common	(32)	14	Jishikoku	Own Shikoku	A	S
	(33)	9	Komainu	Wolf dog	A	S (M)
	(34)	9	Dōkutsu	Sacred" cave	N	
	(35)	7	Shintokaikan	Congregation's bldg.	A	C
	(36)	4	Soseki	Foundation stone	A	S

Source: Personal observations, 1972-73.

* W = wood, S = stone, C = concrete, M = metal

Table 5. Comparison of the frequency of occurrence of the
landscape units at the present time with their frequency
of occurrence at the end of the 17th Century.

Landscape Unit		Frequency of occurrence		
#	Name	20th C	17th C	Difference
1	Daishidō	88	35	+53
2	Kuri	88	76	+12
3	Chōzubachi	88	2	+86
4	Kōro	88	0	+
5	Rosokutate	88	0	+
6	Hondō	87	85	+ 2
7	Tōrō	86	3	+83
8	Mon	84	51	+33
9	Meihyō	82	0	+
10	Shōrō	81	44	+37
11	Jizō	78	4	+74
12	Hei	75	44	+31
13	Ishidan	72	39	+33
14	Dō	70	39	+31
15	Hōnōsekihyō	70	0	+
16	Kuyōtō	69	4	+65
17	Dōhyō	60	0	+
18	Yashiro	55	77	-22
19	Hōkyōintō	54	0	+
20	Ishidatami	54	0	+
21	Haka	54	6	+48
22	Gorintō	45	11	+34
23	Zō	44	6	+38
24	Shokubutsu	31	11	+20
25	Settaisho	28	0	+
26	Hyakudoishi	27	0	+
27	Torii	26	12	+14
28	Mizu	22	25	- 3
29	Tō	21	13	+ 8
30	Ishi	19	5	+14
31	Tsuyadō	18	1	+17
32	Jishikoku	14	0	+
33	Komainu	9	0	+
34	Dōkutsu	9	8	+ 1
35	Shintokaikan	7	0	+
36	Soseki	4	3	+ 1

Table 6. Ritual units: Relationship between the physical features and the "behavioral units."

Ritual units	Physical features	↔	Activity	Associated behaviour — Meaning
A	Mon	↔	Entering the gate	— Passing from the secular world into the sacred enclosure
			Throwing money/rice	— Offering to niō
			Spitting paper	— Requesting a healthy body
			Leaving straw sandals	— Asking for a safe journey
B	Ishidan		Climbing the steps	— Proceeding to the sacred higher interior — Elimination of bonnō or wordly desires
		↔	Leaving money on the steps	— Asking for yakuyoke or calamity-free years
C	Chōzubachi	↔	Washing hands and gargling	— Spiritual purification
D	Shōrō	↔	Hitting the bell	— Announcing arrival to deities and Kōbō-Daishi
E	Kōro(1)	↔	Burning incense	— Veneration of and communication with the deities
F	Rōsokutate (1)	↔	Lighting candles	— Veneration of and giving light to deities, Kōbō-Daishi and the dead
G	Hondo		Leaving ofuda	— Identification and "eternification"
			Leaving money	— Offering to Buddha
			Leaving objects	— Praying for individual desires, gratification
		↔	Chanting okyō: Hannya-shingyō Honzon no Shingon Daishi no Hōgō	— Invocation — Praising the greatness of Buddha — Praising the greatness of Kobo-Daishi — Communication with Buddha
			Praying	

(continued)

Table 6 (concluded)

Ritual units	Physical features		Activity	Associated behaviour
				Meaning
H	Kōro (2)	↔	Burning incense	— Veneration of and communication with the deities
I	Rōsokutate (2)	↔	Lighting candles	— Veneration of and giving light to deities

J	Daishido	↔	Leaving ofuda
			Leaving money
			Leaving objects
			Chanting okyō:
			  Hannya-shingyō
			  Honzon no Shingon
			  Daishi no Hōgō
			Praying
				— Identification and "eternification"
				— Offering to Kobo-Daishi
				— Praying for individual desires, gratification
				
				— Invocation
				— Praising the greatness of Buddha
				— Praising the greatness of Kobo-Daishi
				— Communication with Buddha

K	Nōkyōsho	↔	Receiving hōin and honzon's image	— Reciept for offering okyo and proof of having visited the temple
L	Ishidan	↔	Descending steps	— Proceeding back to secular word
M	Mon	↔	Leaving through the mon	— Passing from the sacred enclosure back into the secular world

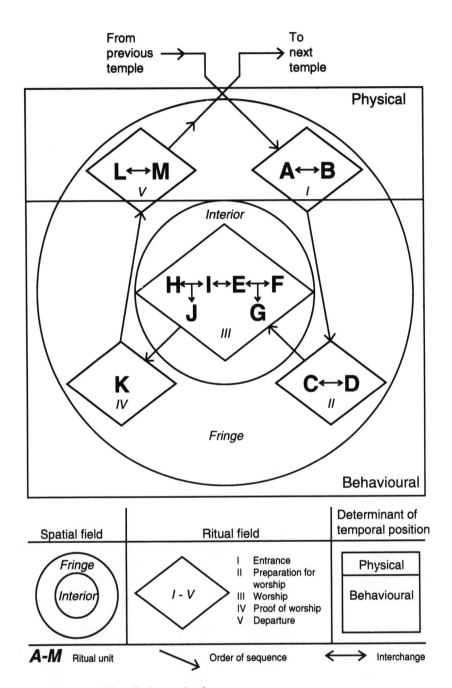

Fig. 7 Structure of the pilgrimage ritual.

individuals or groups. For example, although all pilgrims have to enter and depart via the temple gate and stone steps, there is considerable difference in the performance of entrance and departure activities. Some pilgrims perform all of the identified rituals while others may omit the preparation rituals, daishidō rituals, hondō rituals, or, in extreme cases, omit all the rituals except those necessary for proof of temple visit. When they are traveling in groups by chartered bus and the allotted time at each temple is limited, it is customary for the majority of pilgrims to perform all the rituals except the proof of visitation because certain people (often drivers or travel guides) are delegated to obtain the temple stamp (proof) for all the pilgrims.

One might be tempted to view such variations in pilgrim behavior as an indication of devoutness. Without analyzing the intensity of the behavior, however, such a generalization would be misleading. For example, a pilgrim might perform only those rituals directly focused on Kōbō Daishi but with great intensity, yet he might be viewed by observers incorrectly as a casual temple visitor because his ritual behavior was limited in range.

Among the many factors contributing to the variations in pilgrim behavior, motivation may play a significant role. Differences in pilgrim motivation are partially reflected in the forms, duration, and intensity of ritual behavior. Even so, similar externally observable behavior may derive from widely divergent pilgrim motivation, an indication of the complex nature of the relationships among physical features, forms, sequence of rituals, and pilgrim motivation.[15]

Summary

I have attempted to identify, describe, and synthesize what I consider the essential elements of the 88 sacred places of the Shikoku pilgrimage. The sanctity of each place derives from its association with Kōbō Daishi and one of twelve honzon or chief deities. Such association constitutes the essence and the ultimate source of the distinctive character of the places of pilgrimage. The pilgrimage is characterized by its ability to accommodate the practical needs of pilgrims through the association of the places with honzon which are believed to serve the practical needs of humanity.

The locational characteristics of the Shikoku sacred places can be said to be either peripheral or central depending on the geographical scale of observation. Over the ages, particular temples, ranging in number from all 88 places to only five places, have been linked into culturally recognized groups. The existence of these groups, supported by underlying symbolic concepts, provides guidelines for the practice of pilgrimage. The Shikoku 88 places provided the original model for the emergence of the miniature pilgrimages to other 88 sacred places throughout Japan.

The positions of the sacred places are not necessarily absolutely fixed. Thus, the geographic setting of the sacred place is characterized not solely by the site as it exists unaltered by man, but rather primarily by the assemblage of landscape markers that have been invested with special meaning and the expression of this cultural preference and organization in the landscape. The dynamic character of the places is reflected in the landscape.

There is some variation in the physical setting of each of the 88 sacred places, yet particular pilgrim activities are repeatedly linked to specific physical features. The spatial temporal order within the set of relationships between the physical features and pilgrim activities may be considered as a characteristic expression of the earth-bound institution of pilgrimage. Through ritual activity, humans activate and interact with pilgrimage places and at the same time these places accommodate humans' needs and intentions.

While this study focused on one specific pilgrimage, the aspects of the pilgrimage places examined are not unique to the Shikoku sacred places. These aspects are shared by pilgrimage places throughout Japan and are a commonly shared dimension of pilgrimage places within other religious contexts.

Notes

1. T. Nakao and A. Saitō (1973 and 1975) suggest that there are at least 150 multiple pilgrimages encompassing a minimum of 6,876 sites in Japan.

2. The Shikoku pilgrimage attracts pilgrims from all over Japan, male and female, representing all walks of life and a variety of religious sects besides Shingon Mikkyō, the sect to which the vast majority of the 88 sacred places belong. Estimates of the volume of pilgrim traffic annually range from 50,000 to 80,000.

3. Places which Kōbō Daishi visited for training and documented in his writings include Tairyū-san (temple 21), Muroto Cape (temple 24), and Ishizuchi-san (temple 60). For a good biography of Kōbō Daishi, see Hasuo (1931).

4. One of the earliest geographic analyses of the locational characteristics of pilgrimage places is by Robert H. Stoddard (1966). Victor Turner (1973) suggests a spatially peripheral location for the pilgrim's destination. Further analysis of this proposition is found in Sopher (this volume).

5. Jakuhon (1689) suggests that in the seventeenth century the Shikoku pilgrimage may have begun with Zentsū-ji, the birthplace of Kōbō Daishi and presently designated as temple 75. The shift in initiation point of the pilgrimage probably came about as the pilgrimage gained popularity. Ryōzen-ji was the first temple to be reached by pilgrims coming from central Japan, the major catchment area of the pilgrimage, via Awaji Island. As well, historical records suggest that pilgrims (primarily priests) may have started the pilgrimage by visiting Kōyasan, the "headquarters" of the Shingon Mikkyō sect established by Kōbō Daishi and the place where he died. The direct route from Kōyasan to Shikoku brings the pilgrims to a point close to Ryōzen-ji.

So it seems that the convenience of beginning the pilgrimage at Ryōzen-ji, supported by the proximity of this temple to Kōyasan and thus to Kōbō Daishi, gradually overruled the desirability of beginning at Kōbō Daishi's birthplace. Over the years, repeated practice of the pilgrimage starting at Ryōzen-ji and continuing in a clockwise direction, supported by constant reference to this order in the pilgrim guides books and maps, may have consecrated the sequence.

6. Many pilgrims believe that Kōbō Daishi is making the pilgrimage in a clockwise direction and they are following his footsteps, from which it is further believed that by following the prescribed order, a deep religious experience can be realized.

As more and more pilgrims use some form of motorized transportation, fewer and fewer follow the prescribed order exactly. The recent opening of a bridge linking Honshu with Shikoku at Marugame has also influenced the flow of pilgrimage traffic. Because it was designed for travel on foot, it is not always well suited to the use of vehicles. These changes are relatively minor, though, and only occur within small groups of temples within each prefecture — the altered order of places visited never crosses prefectural boundaries.

Visiting the 88 places in a counter-clockwise direction is not prohibited and is done occasionally by pilgrims. Nevertheless, the overall sequential relationship remains.

7. Such perpetual pilgrims are often societal outcastes. For a discussion of this fact, see Hoshino (1981).

8. Traditionally made on foot, the Shikoku pilgrimage is being affected by modern modes of transportation. Today the most common form of transportation is by chartered bus, but pilgrims also travel by taxi, private car, bicycle, and motorcycle. Using modern transportation, the time required to complete the pilgrimage is reduced from the original two months to about two weeks. With the reduction of time comes also a reduction in cost of accommodation, so today the most expensive way to make the pilgrimage is likely on foot.

These reductions in time and expense required to complete the pilgrimage have increased the frequency with which the pilgrimage, or portions of it, may be made by any one individual. This, in turn, has increased the opportunity to accumulate religious merit. Yet the traditional practice of journeying on foot to the sacred places still appears to be considered by most pilgrims to yield the greatest religious merit. For those with a limited amount of time, it seems a conflict exists between the desire to gain the greatest possible merit from making the entire pilgrimage circuit and the merit gained by making the journey on foot. For a discussion of various ways the conflict between religious merit and convenience has been met, see Tanaka Shimazaki (1976).

9. In addition to the 41 miniature pilgrimages identified here, there are numerous others of a much smaller scale. In these, the 88 sacred places are represented by a set of stone markers, each of which has carved on it the name of one temple and the figure of the chief deity of that temple. Very often these stone markers stand side by side in a row, though sometimes they are spread over a more extensive area. Often they stand within a temple compound and can be visited in a matter of minutes. They particularly attract the residents of the local area (Tanaka Shimazaki 1983).

10. The data on which the landscape inventory is based was collected during 1972-73 field research and were confirmed by Omoto, the head priest at Taisan-ji (temple 56) early in 1974 (Tanaka Shimazaki 1977).

11. Data for the latter part of the 17th century was derived from the description and sketches provided by Priest Jakuhon (1689). The landscape units encompass all the features cited by Jakuhon.

12. Mikkyō means "hidden doctrine" and the school exhibits a strong preference for mountain or "mountain-like" sites on which to locate its temples. When the sacred places are observed, most are seen to occupy mountain-like sites. Although the absolute elevation may not necessarily be great, the approach to the temple is often via a steep hill, or the temple may be situated on a low hill in a forested area that gives the atmosphere of a mountain setting. From empirical observation, it would appear that of the 88 sacred places, 61 are situated within the mountains. Of these, 25 are located on or near the top of a mountain (with the highest elevation being that of Unpen-ji [temple 66] at 911 meters) and 36 are surrounded by

mountains or have mountains behind them. The remaining 27 temples are clearly situated on a plain, although often surrounded by forest.

13. Pilgrims apparently learn the prescribed rituals from their leaders, from guide books, and from observation of other pilgrims. It should be noted that in actuality the behavior within the units is as diverse as the pilgrims themselves. There is, for example, wide variation in behavior in front of the hondō and daishidō with regard to length of time spent in worship and the intensity of worship as evidenced through facial expressions, body movements, and tone of voice.

The meanings of chanted and spoken utterances, rhythmical sounds, body movements, and objects commonly associated with ritual activity may be standardized to the point where their employment in ritual behavior not only expresses but also stimulates feelings which are supposed to be experienced on given ritual occasions. Without examining the inner feelings of pilgrims, however, their actual intensity cannot be evaluated. The concern of this discussion is on the observable forms of behavior; the degree to which pilgrims understand the underlying meaning of the ritual is not a part of this paper.

14. From repeated observation of pilgrim ritual, discussions with pilgrim leaders and priests, and examination of published pilgrim diaries and guide books, various aspects of pilgrim behavior were selected, fused, and simplified to facilitate the construction of this ideal order.

15. In the Shikoku pilgrimage, at each temple pilgrims deposit *ofuda* or calling cards on which they indicate those things for which they are praying while making the pilgrimage. I had an opportunity to examine 1,552 ofuda left at two temples (Ryōzen-ji and Jizō-ji on March 30th and April 1st, 1973). From these it became apparent that pilgrims pray for such things as safety for the family, prosperous business, improved financial situation, freedom from traffic accidents, good health, pregnancy, safe delivery of baby, world peace, and the ability to pass university examinations. Many give thanks for desires which have been fulfilled. Some pilgrims with whom I walked part of the route indicated that they were making the pilgrimage in order to test physical endurance, to contemplate life after retirement, and, in some cases, as a substitute for someone who could not make the pilgrimage. Still others indicated that the primary motivation was to get away from routine life and enjoy the countryside.

References

Hasuo, K. 1931. *Kōbō Daishi-den* (Biography of Kōbō Daishi). Kōyasan: Kongōbu-ji.

Hoshino, E. 1981. *Junrei* (Pilgrimage). Tokyo: Kodansha.

Jakuhon. 1689. *Shikoku Henrei Reijō-ki* (Description of the sacred places of the Shikoku pilgrimage), 7 vols. Reprinted in *Shikoku Reijō-ki-shū* (Collection of descriptions of Shikoku sacred places), ed. Y. Kondo, 1973. Tokyo: Benseisha.

Kondō, Y. 1971. *Shikoku Henro*. Tokyo: Ōfūsha.

Nakao, T., and A. Saitō, eds. 1973. *Koji Junrei-jiten* (Dictionary of pilgrimage). Tokyo: Toyo-do.

Nakao, T., and A. Saitō. 1975. *Bukkyō Junrei-shū* (Buddhist pilgrimage). Tokyo: Bukkyō Minzoku Gakkai.

Stoddard, R. H. 1966. Hindu holy sites in India. Ph.D. diss., University of Iowa, Iowa City.

Tanaka Shimazaki, H. 1976. Religious merit and convenience, the resolution of a conflict with a pilgrimage through spatial-temporal adjustments. In *New themes in Western Canadian geography*, ed. B. M. Barr, B. C. Geographical Series No. 22, 109-18. Vancouver: Tantalus Research Ltd.

———. 1977. Geographic expression of Buddhist pilgrim places on Shikoku Island, Japan. *Canadian Geographer* 21:116-24.

——. 1981. The evolution of a pilgrimage as a spatial-symbolic system. *Canadian Geographer* 24:240-51.

——. 1983. *Junreichi no Sekai* (The world of pilgrimage places). Tokyo: Kokon Shoin.

Turner, V. 1973. The center out there: Pilgrim's goal. *History of Religions* 12:191-230.

Wagner, P. L. 1972. Cultural landscapes and regions: Aspects of communication. In *Man, space and environment*, eds. W. English and R. C. Mayfield, 55-68. New York: Oxford University Press.

Section VI: POSTLUDE

Pilgrimage: Culture and Geography

Philip L. Wagner
Simon Fraser University, Emeritus

Abstract

Geographical principles illuminate the nature of pilgrimage, and pilgrimage in turn illustrates important principles of geography. Thus, a pilgrim site in Shiraz, Iran, exemplifies the privileged and bounded character of particular places. The great Izumo Taisha, reputedly Japan's oldest shrine, evokes the ceremonious entry and exit behavior appropriate to transgressions of the boundaries of privileged places. The arduous journey of simple Mexican pilgrims to the national shrine of the Virgin of Guadalupe reveals the preparatory sacrifice and enterprise required for worthiness to transgress such boundaries.

The converse of place-exclusivity, too, is manifested in the concourse assembling from all quarters and corners of the world at St. Peter's Basilica in Rome. But particularism associated with national or regional identity constitutes another prevalent pilgrim theme, as found for example in Esquipulas, the major Central American shrine.

The human construction of places through action alone, applying to sites of pilgrimage as well as to all other recognized places, explains the distinctiveness of Tenri, the holy center of a Japanese "new religion." And the communicative function of that defining action is well shown, paradoxically, in the astonishing silence that attends the Holy Week processions in Popayán, Colombia.

In a geographical sense, all pilgrimage sites are "resources," available for actions propitious to spiritual welfare. The Bavarian monastery at Altötting, with its striking assemblage of votive objects, displays the signs of such spiritual resource exploitation. Pilgrimage shows that geography deals with more than one world.

Key words: pilgrimage, privileged places, spiritual resources, communicative functions.

A pilgrimage cannot convene just anywhere. In fact, it may be fair to say not merely that pilgrimages always presuppose some pre-existing sacred site, but even that many more such valid sites may well exist than have developed pilgrim traffic. Finding the place of a pilgrimage is an act of geographical discovery.

Some attendant geographic aspects thus deserve consideration in any comprehensive discussion of pilgrimage phenomena. But diverse religious traditions select or discover their pilgrimage sites. Does this very

Sacred Places, Sacred Spaces: The Geography of Pilgrimages, edited by Robert H. Stoddard and Alan Morinis, 1997. Geoscience and Man, vol. 34, pp. 299-323. Dept. of Geography and Anthropology, Louisiana State University, Baton Rouge, LA 70893-6010.

fact not preclude any general geographic characterization of all such sites? In a sense, it does so; indeed, we have no single material criterion except behavior by which we might infallibly identify a pilgrim place, wherever found, as one token of a single type. However, we likewise probably possess no assured touchstone for distinguishing "pilgrimage" absolutely from all other kinds of behavior.

On the other hand, known pilgrim sites do resemble each other in many respects. The difficulty is that they sometimes likewise resemble some kinds of non-pilgrimage places. Accordingly, an attentive study of the sites (and routes) of pilgrimage may contribute more to understanding of geography than of pilgrimage.

One virtue of research upon this eminently virtuous kind of human activity lies in its immunity to utilitarian or purely economic explanations. Pilgrimage, like only a few other human activities, expressly defies that brand of rationality. Hence it invites an interpretation of geography invoking other sorts of motivations, and thereby focuses awareness differently. Let us try to develop that awareness on the concrete basis of some personal experiences, and to sketch out such an interpretation.

Shiraz

The tomb of Sayyed Ala'ud din Hussein (d. A.D. 835) (fig. 1), brother of the last Imam, in the Shrine of the Mirrors in Shiraz, is the target of a celebrated Shi'a pilgrimage and one of the holiest places in Iran.[1] It is justly famous for its fine tiled dome and its doors of precious woods, delicately

Fig. 1. The tomb of Sayyad Ala'ud din Hussein in the Shrine of the Mirror in Shiraz is one of the holiest places in Iran. (Artwork by the author.)

worked and richly encrusted with silver. Above all, its glittering interior, resplendent with reflections from uncounted particles of shiny glass embedded in the walls, might have lured the tourist when Iran had tourists, were the place not sacrosanct to faithful Muslims. The inner chamber, in particular, with the elaborate tomb of the saint at its center, is holy space and not a place to be defiled by infidel incursions.[2]

But my dusty field boots having been exchanged in the vestibule for soft, silent slippers, there I was, the incautious geographer, moving slowly along counterclockwise in the midst of a reverent crowd of rather ragged men, women, and children around the ornate stone form of the tomb. Some among the faces glowered at me. Shortly I found myself next in line behind an elderly veiled lady who was lifting the *chador* from her face to kiss a well-worn spot on the pillar, as all the other pious visitors had evidently been doing. I became even more aware that I was transgressing forbidden boundaries. It was like suddenly noticing that one was in a stranger's occupied bedroom. Just then a young girl directly behind me noticed my discomfiture and indicated emphatically by her gestures that I should follow the ritual. I leaned forward, gingerly bestowed a kiss on the pillar, and thereupon as quickly as I could, I retreated to reclaim my boots and depart from the place I had desecrated.

Having visited at most just over a dozen pilgrimage sites of any consequence, I consider myself almost as much an intruder among the learned authors of this volume as I was in the Shrine of the Mirrors. In this situation as in that, I have only my geographer's inveterate curiosity to offer as an excuse. But in expiation of my imprudence (or impudence!) I should like in this essay, insofar as I can, to put curiosity to work in order to interpret the phenomenon of pilgrimage in general, as well as to comprehend geography a little better. Let me ask first what the incident at the Sayyed's tomb might teach about either pilgrimage or geography.

Pilgrim sanctuaries count among the most distinctive kinds of geographic places. They comprise not simply uniquely located points or areas (in itself a trivial attribute), but also sites of highly particular human activities, usually performed by people of some special background and at only given times; and the behavior proper to them tends to confer both external boundaries and internal spatial structure on them, often evidenced in artifactual components. The foregoing properties, I should contend, define what we mean by a "place."[3]

The features here recounted do not, of course, exhaust the attributes of pilgrim places; and furthermore, the same attributes characterize all other places of whatever kind, including simple brief encounters among people anywhere. These are thus not what makes a site of pilgrimage special.

In addition, even if the boundaries surrounding holy pilgrimage places do sometimes, as in the case of the Shrine of the Mirrors, tend to discourage intrusion by the uninitiated (always excepting geographers!), in this respect they do not differ at all from barriers enclosing altogether ordinary places, to pass across which may require the presentation of credentials or some minor ritual observance. Although strangers just must stay out of Brahmin kitchens, Muslim women's quarters, and Chicago bedrooms, access even to less intimate places, in most if not all societies, demands at least a perfunctory ritual exchange with the established occupants. We tend to overlook the frequency of the greetings and goodbyes we utter, the number of doors we knock at, and the readiness with which we say "excuse me." We are always asking permission to come in, pass by, or go away, for we are constantly crossing invisible but always intensely sensed place boundaries, throughout every day and lifelong. We could not get along without passwords and pretexts.

Thus the everyday spaces of humanity consist not primarily of the endless perspectives of uniform planes, but of infinite little compartments.[4] In order to traverse the limits of even the least of them, both strangers and their occupants themselves must perform small acts of deference. Any displacement within such configured space — even, indeed, among the rooms of a family's own house — calls for its rituals. At each entry or exit, joining or parting, there takes place a minute rite of passage, initiating the newcomer into, or discharging someone from, the company present within the respective bounded space.[5]

Probably what most sets pilgrimage apart is that for pilgrims this company is supernatural. Its rites of passage sanction entry into contact with another world and its powers, but only for those people qualified in some special fashion to perform them — which I was not when I intruded into the Shrine of the Mirrors.

Let us reflect further on such rites of passage.

Izumo

Reputedly the oldest of the ancient Shinto pilgrim places of Japan, and among the holiest of all, the Izumo Taisha, or great Izumo shrine, nestles at the foot of heavily forested hills adjacent to the Sea of Japan.[6] I had the good luck on a winter day to be there when the customary rites through which the pilgrim enters into close communion with the gods — the purification; the clapping of hands before the vacant tabernacle; the tolling of a great bell; the lighting of candles or incense; the waving of *sakaki* twigs; the tying of votive strips of white paper to the branches of surrounding trees — acquired additional significance as elements within another ritual complex (fig.2).

A thousand variegated bright kimonos blossomed in the dusty-muddy open area before the major wooden buildings of the shrine, displayed against the somber background of the consorts' invariably dark Western suits. These prospective brides and grooms had traveled to Izumo for a special festival propitious for their coming union, just as thousands of other young lovers would that same day visit other Shinto shrines throughout the country.[7]

The visit to a shrine ensues upon a series of preliminary steps, and is followed by yet other steps, prescribed in order, that will culminate in the couples' entry into the new state of marriage, and, with it, entry into different residences, and new relationships with domestic space.[8] Thus the visit at the shrine, and the whole progression through an established sequence of delineated places and defined assemblies of persons, entailing the successive solemn crossing of recognized thresholds and boundaries, enacts in a ritualized, spatially manifested fashion the transition from one stage or phase of life into another. Furthermore, the performance of the exquisitely spatial ritual then entitles the newlyweds to new spatial prerogatives: they may henceforth dwell — insofar as Japan's acute housing shortage may permit — together, either in the house of the father-in-law

Fig. 2. Buildings and votive papers on branches at the ancient Shinto shrine, the Izumo Taisha, reputedly the oldest of the Shinto shrines in Japan.

or, today, in their own separate quarters. The marriage bed itself, though, is the place most expressive of their new prerogatives.

Similar small spatial passages and prescribed positionings characterize all the other major ceremonies marking life transitions in any society whatsoever. These striking rites of passage include those that, in virtually any human society, welcome the newborn, by means of christening or varied other ceremonies, into the world of the group; those which, often with a period of ritual banishment or other uncomfortable ordeals, initiate the adolescents into new sorts of association and perhaps admit them to a new residence such as the long-house, or permit them to take part in martial or hunting expeditions; those that induct certain individuals into priesthoods, judicial authority, military command, or similar dignities, each possessing its particular spatial preserves or places of office; and the rites of the dead, involving reverent processions and physical removal from the vicinity of the living. In each such practice, a spatially programmed ceremonial is crucial, involving the traversing of boundaries of a series of significant places, each with its appropriate officiants and witnesses. And in each case the transition signals a new position within the entire society, relative not only to other individuals, but also to the spatial order of that society. Any of the major types of rites of passage, then, manifests a doubly spatial character.

Pilgrim rituals, involving a progression through minutely configured places containing seried stations for performances of their several successive observances, of course epitomize the spatial principle. Therein, as remarked, they differ little from itineraries followed in the course of daily living everywhere by everyone, which likewise call for frequent deference to boundaries, and sequences of minor ceremonial positions and progressions. But in addition, pilgrimage implies not just traversing nearby boundaries, but traveling a distance, too.

Thus a distant journey, often dangerous and difficult, is typical of pilgrimage wherever and whenever undertaken. Indeed, some pilgrims may adopt ascetic or penitential practices of their own volition, rendering their progress still more arduous but also yet more meritorious from a spiritual standpoint.

The great Izumo shrine is reached by railway, but circuitously and somewhat awkwardly, because its situation on the western coast, across the central mountain ranges, makes it rather remote from the main centers of population and arteries of circulation. In former times it must have been considerably more difficult of access, and constituted a more demanding target of pilgrimage. The difficulty of a journey to it, though, is far less than that elected by some pilgrims elsewhere in the world. Consider now a case from Mexico.

Guadalupe

The major national highway connecting Mexico City, D.F., with Veracruz by way of Puebla and Córdoba skirts the loftiest volcanoes, then tumbles steeply several thousand meters down the staircases of lava toward the Gulf of Mexico. This road is spectacular. It affords abrupt views of the great snowy cones, and, sometimes, vistas out toward the coast. In spring, sudden wild gardens that clothe the ground beneath the pines brighten the route. But it was around the first of December one year that I saw the most arresting and most moving sight I can remember in the region.

As I drove downhill, I encountered a seemingly endless file of people of all ages, dark-skinned mostly and poorly clad on the whole, bearing all manner of bedding, cooking vessels, and other equipment — even live birds in cages and family dogs frisking alongside — as they trudged up the slope. The column extended for many miles, and in fact I came across stragglers all the way out to Campeche, on the Yucatan Peninsula.

The feast of the Virgin of Guadalupe, celebrated on December twelfth at the national shrine in the northern part of the capital district, is, along with the festivals at Chalma, the greatest Indian religious event in the country.[10] Although pilgrims and penitents visit the basilica of Guadalupe throughout the year, the feast in December attracts by far the largest concurrence. People set out on foot or by bus from towns, poor villages, and remote hamlets all over the country in order to celebrate and supplicate the miraculous Virgin, often honoring her with performances of their own special dances, songs, and oratory. The ant-like column I had met was making this pilgrimage in its own devout and humble style.

Corresponding streams of pedestrian pilgrims converge on the Valley of Mexico from all over the Republic, as no doubt they used to on Compostela and Cambridge, too. These people belong largely to the poorest class, yet the journey on foot with so many possessions is not just a matter of expense, for the working time lost would impose greater costs than the price of an easier trip on the bus.[10] Rather, the preliminary journey afoot is an ascetic performance guaranteeing the efficacy of the later visit to the shrine.

If we look on pilgrimage as an epitome of the devout life, the laborious procession up to Guadalupe can be seen to exemplify the virtuous regime of humility and simplicity, unswerving faith, and patient effort held essential to salvation. It certifies the devotees as worthy of the spiritual benefits (and practical assistance) that they expect the entry into holy places to confer, and may even atone for derelictions in the past. In manifesting their sincerity and purity of heart, it qualifies them to cross the boundaries that separate the supernatural from everyday. Transgression of the ritual perimeters in any other state not only bestows no blessings, but may count as sacrilegious.

In this respect as well, this pilgrimage, or any other that evokes analogous preliminaries, illustrates a universal feature of human spatial behavior. Within the universe of tiny bounded spaces — places that we live in — crossing any boundary requires not merely little deferential rituals such as passwords and polite requests. As well, it calls for evidence of appropriate identity and of worthiness. Doors do not open to whoever knocks. Recognized position and affiliation in society, along with attributes of competence, authority, or merit, differentiate the individuals permitted entry to a place from those excluded. Admission to any place is almost invariably selective. Places sort out a society.

This principle could be applied in the actual mapping of the places to which given individuals within communities enjoy a ready, welcome access. No single human being has unlimited prerogatives of entry everywhere.[11] Hence the map of anyone's itineraries in itself reflects innumerable exclusions, and the distinctive set of places where that person might be willingly received would nicely index a particular compound position in society, corresponding faithfully to a determinate array of concrete and specific incidents of social interaction. Place in society, or what we call social position, describes its own figure in space.

Herein the grander rites of passage — the minute positionings and crossings marking out spatially enacted observances analogous to christening, initiation into adulthood, acceptance into sects or clubs, nuptial ceremonies, investiture into priesthood or other dignities, promotion to new levels of authority, even academic honors and degrees — play a crucial part. The altered social standing and attendant spatial rights these all signify, the recognition and respect they confer, determine to a large extent the spatial circulation patterns of their beneficiaries. In order to deserve admission to the Shrine of Mirrors, I should have undergone the Muslim circumcision and made public profession of the articles of Islamic faith; to participate in Shinto rites at Izumo, I ought at least (less heroically!) to have purified myself by dipping water from the trough provided in the outer temple compound, and rinsing hands and mouth, as well as letting a priest wave over me the cleansing *haraigushi* wand. These small rites of passage would in effect have created me anew, as a person then qualified to enter the respective holy places — altering thereby my spatial personality.

Pilgrimage, then, may involve antecedent, more or less ritualistic, spatial behavior marking passage into a condition of preparedness for the actual encounter with the supernatural. Ordinarily, however, the social and even ethnic differences among the pilgrims have otherwise no significant bearing on their visit to the holy place, for such rites of passage as are deemed to legitimize their pious pilgrimage are spiritual, not temporal, as the next experience I can recount will demonstrate.

Rome

One day in Rome I walked across the city, pausing to regard the Colosseum and the Forum of the Caesars and, following the Tiber, found myself within the Vatican. Strolling through the colonnade that partially encircles the great piazza, I arrived before the massive doors of the Basilica of Saint Peter, the largest church in Christendom (except, it is said, for the princely abbey church of St. Blasien in Baden-Württemberg). My intention was to see the ceiling frescoes by Michelangelo in the Sistine Chapel, but a vast congregation of people obstructed my passage. Saint Peter's was packed, and so I stood among the crowd and waited for whatever might be taking place.

Soon, in the distance deep within the basilica, I could discern the pope's palanquin in its gradual advance. The pontiff and his retinue of priests and nuns and deacons paused at each few steps to give a blessing to the multitude that pressed around them. When the august procession reached my own position, I could watch His Holiness, in close proximity, high on his exalted throne, gazing benignly down on the faithful and addressing them. I heard him speak in Latin, as expected, and likewise in Polish, Italian, German, Vietnamese, English, and French, and at least a dozen other languages, lovingly encouraging the members of his worldwide flock and pronouncing benedictions over them. Filipino pilgrims, Mexicans, and Africans stood entranced alongside me hearing the papal message of love and faith. I could well appreciate the unity transcending, but respecting, all the great diversity of humankind that shares in the pilgrimage to Rome.

The gathering of pilgrims at Rome, as well as at Varanasi or Mecca, pays little heed to difference of language or of origin. All peoples and social levels are equally received and sanctified. Not only ethnic circumstances but also social stations are irrelevant, poor and rich alike stand side by side. And this conveys another geographic lesson.

A pilgrimage affirms the oneness of humanity. Despite the boundaries that segregate the families, localities, and social sectors of communities no matter where, all individuals regardless of position and identity are both entitled and enjoined to partake in the common blessings of the sacred journey.

Perhaps, apart from tourist travel, which remains dependent on prosperity and privilege, the pilgrimage phenomenon most clearly manifests that most remarkable reality — that humanity indeed is one great family, and even much more remarkably, a worldwide family. Geographers, unless they be very perceptive biogeographers, tend not to accord sufficient importance to the singular fact of human ubiquity, yet the worldwide distribution of this one aberrant species, *Homo sapiens sapiens*, constitutes a gross exception to conditions otherwise prevailing in the realm of nature.

Humanity, indeed and uniquely, forms a single great gene pool and spectrum of localized minor phenotypic diversity all over the globe, and this fact has come about, historically, in consequence of certain peculiarly human capabilities exemplified in pilgrimage.

Pilgrimage, of course, is possible only because people can travel comparatively freely and securely for considerable distances. Their circulation is by no means analogous, however, to the seasonal migrations of so many animal species, from butterflies to bison and from hummingbirds to humpback whales, for such animal migrant aggregations are great massed collectivities, and non-territorially subdivided (at least during the long distance displacement). But human beings may carry out a pilgrimage either individually or in organized groups, and furthermore must reckon with the partitioning of the spaces they traverse into an infinity of bounded places, to enter or to leave which ceremonials are potentially required. Although in the human case no ineluctably confining territoriality of the sort affecting countless animals is present,[12] crossing boundaries and borders constantly demands both potent ritual performances and, often, some enabling evidence of worthy status.

This exacting requirement attaching to pilgrimage finds counterparts in any major spatial displacement of people or social groups. Migrants or wanderers must possess means of legitimizing their repeated transgressions of place limits. Yet unlike so many other creatures, people possessing such means can and do travel long distances, circulating frequently and widely. They have been able to meet and exchange and mix and move, in such a way as not only to maintain the genetic unity of the species for millennia, but also to extend its geographic range worldwide and incorporate it eventually into a single interconnected communication network and cultural and economic exchange system — on which pilgrimages themselves depend.

The flexible spatial order constructed of a place mosaic through which human individuals can circulate when they possess the proper passwords and performances helps to explain the terrestrial ubiquity of humankind, and, in addition,the development of "culture" as a human trait. For relatively free meeting and merging are essential to the imitative diffusion of behavioral routines, as also to the spread of their products in trade.[13] Even pilgrimage itself, as spatial blending, must evidently favor cultural diffusion, whether the congregation be worldwide, as at Rome, or much more regionally limited.

In addition, however, some important pilgrimages, as in the next example, although still democratic, often display, so to speak, the other side of the coin from such universality.

Esquipulas

The late afternoon had turned chilly, as always at this season in the mountains. In the gathering mist I could see the dim glow around the side of the
church. As I passed through, I entered a fragile, cavernous half-darkness.
Feeble candlelight, the murmur of muted prayer, and a faint fragrance of
copal incense confronted my senses, but only gradually could I make out
the forms of the pilgrims filling the church and the monks moving almost
stealthily among them. This somehow almost secret, quiet, crepuscular
place appeared uncannily removed from everyday reality, a world apart.
And in fact it was and is so: Esquipulas is the very core of the isolated and
devout Indian and poor Ladino world of Central America.[14]

Just at the Honduran frontier and adjacent to the continental divide,
the little Guatemalan settlement of Esquipulas lies in a montane basin at
nearly the exact midpoint of Central America, approximately halfway in
the distance from Tehuantepec to Panama. It is certainly no city. A small
huddle of old adobe structures and their newer board companions constitutes whatever "central business district" it can boast. The mountains, clad
in pine and oak, rise all around, and at a little distance toward them from
the modest town itself, there stands the stark white pilgrim church, surrounded by a tidy garden neatly fenced. Approaching over the pass from
the south, one may notice first the dramatically isolated church, if it is not
concealed within the mists that often heavily invest the valley. It is said
that on initially discerning the towers from the rocky hillocks in the pass,
pilgrim Indians used to break out in a special dance of celebration, as indeed they still may do.

The months from December through April, in the dry season, are the
special ones of pilgrimage to Esquipulas, and only in that period do am-
bulant street vendors install themselves directly in the area before the
church to offer trinkets and sweets and beverages to the throngs of devotees. Then the swarthy lifesized image of Christ crucified, the "Cristo de
los Indios," yet another of the those dark-visaged figures venerated at so
many pilgrim places, receives the homage of devout people who assemble
here from all over Central America. The great majority of them are either
Indians or poor Ladinos (as are the majority of Central Americans in general), and they practice Indian or other rustic devotions.

The Christ of Esquipulas shares some special attributes with several
other famous figures venerated in great pilgrimages. Like the Virgin of
Guadalupe herself, the Matka Boska in Caęstochowa, and the Virgin of
Montserrat, as well as a number of other well-known images of Christ, the
Esquipulas statue has a nearly black visage. Miraculous dark-faced statues, however, as a couple of the foregoing examples show, do not correlate
particularly well with populations of African or Indian descent. Postpon-
ing for the moment speculation on the reasons for their frequency, let us

take note instead of another attribute of the Christ of Esquipulas and the three Virgins mentioned: they are expressly and emphatically national, as well as simply religious, shrines. Even agnostic or backsliding Mexicans, Poles, and Catalans accord some deference to their respective national patronesses, and a great many Central Americans generally tend to acknowledge their Indian Christ at Esquipulas as perhaps the only surviving expression of their common identity and natural unity.[15]

A distinctive great national pilgrim cult focused on such a shrine, or even a multiplicity of them, often ranks with a flag and an anthem, and with patriotic histories and legends, as expression of a people's separateness and solidarity. To be sure, somewhat more circumscribed local pilgrimages do attract their own traffic in many countries, but the expressly national center of pilgrim devotion ordinarily draws far larger numbers, and usually not more than a few of those attending may be foreign. Truly international pilgrimages do occur, indeed, in addition, and generate a worldwide circulation, sometimes responding to an obligation incumbent on all believers, as in Islam.

Pilgrimages thus are conducted at several distinct geographic scales, which in this case may represent substantial diversity among the corresponding practices as regards their intended functions, meanings, and benefits. Local, national, and international pilgrimages may prove distinct in kind as well as in spatial scope. They do not necessarily constitute an actual hierarchy, either spatially or in regard to pious practice, for persons undertaking one type, say a journey to a national shrine, may often not participate at all in others. Accordingly, pilgrimages that do occur at graded spatial scales but misleadingly appear to form a "nested hierarchy," in fact, do nothing of the sort. Although when plotted on an appropriate map the totality of pilgrimages over a large area may look like a "central place system," it isn't one. This demonstrates the principle, important for geographic understanding, that form does not always faithfully reflect function or functional interconnection.

The particular dark faces of the images mentioned (and various others elsewhere) justify the question of whether or not some sort of consistent material characteristics imply sanctity in a site. An association of important shrines with streams or springs, impressive boulders, mountains, caves, groves, or even certain animals has often been noted. Likewise, a profusion of artifacts and structures expressive of the religious tradition concerned tends to mark a sacred location. These coincidences, however, are perhaps of less interest for geography than the companion question of why closely similar natural features nearby, or even other assemblies of artifacts and constructions, are frequently not perceived as betokening a like degree of holiness to that of the given shrine. In this case again, form and function need not always correspond.

Something more of cosmological significance must render the features of a site particular in order for it to acquire a sacred character and attract a pilgrimage. Tenri City affords a striking example.

Tenri

The Kii Peninsula, extending southward from a base that runs from Osaka to Nagoya, contains the heart of early civilized Japan, and Kyoto and Nara, old capitals, and is as well perfused with religious significance. Its pilgrimage centers are numerous, beginning with the ancient shrine of the Imperial family at Ise, and including the many temples and Shinto shrines in and around the city of Kyoto, as well as the vast wooded compound at Nara where tame deer wander about and many important Buddhist sects and some Shinto schools have their headquarters. Nara's geographical features — the great pine trees and ginkgos there, the bamboo grass (burnt in an annual ceremony on the steep hillslopes just to the east), the limpid little murmuring stream, and the sacred deer — contrast with the urban hubbub nearby, and go with the variegated holiness of the place. And so do the awesome Buddha-hall, the *todaiji*, largest wooden structure in the world; the exquisite many-roofed pagodas and giant bronze bells; the ancient, austere log storehouse, *shosoin*, where imperial treasures from the earliest periods repose; and the brilliantly vermilion, greened-bronze lantern-bedecked Kasuga shrine, home to one branch of Shinto.[16]

But not very distant, south of Nara, an offshoot of Shinto possesses an especially remarkable pilgrimage site. One of the more prominent among the dozens of so-called New Religions in Japan, the Tenrikyo has its central seat in a city that grew up on account of it and adopted its name. An immense complex of enormous temples, administrative buildings, educational facilities, dormitories, and dining halls dominates the area (fig. 3).

There I saw the center of the world. It is a spot called the *jiba* enclosed in a great hall, in a sort of pit set off by polished wooden railings with ornaments of bronze. Nakayama Miki (1798-1897), the founder of Tenri, the "heavenly doctrine," enjoined her followers to make the pilgrimage to the world-center as frequently as possible, and many do so annually.[17] They come not simply to pause in prayer beside the holy spot, but likewise to attend religious study sessions and practice collective spiritual exercises. Undoubtedly the opportunity to approach the jiba and commune with the potent forces it represents fortifies the pilgrim in faith and reinforces the beneficial effects of the doctrines themselves.

The sacred landscape of Tenri lacks ostentation in spite of its generous scale. The demeanor of the pilgrims is calm, concentrated, and purposeful. They cluster to pray, discuss, or even (as it appeared) probably to dance; and as everywhere in Japan, they come and go in flocks and formations.

Fig. 3. Hall of the Jiba, or center of the world, in the Tenrikyo, seat of one of the New Religions in Japan. (Artwork by the author.)

The spirituality pervading Tenri's precincts stems not from opulent appointments or elaborate ceremonial, but also not from strenuous or sacrificial exercises. It simply arises out of confidence in cosmological conceptions, and the confrontation with their material embodiment in the holy world center. Herein another geographic principle is manifested.

Tenri is a sacred place essentially because a visionary peasant woman there discerned the Center of the World. Like any other place less sanctified, it needed to be recognized in order to become a place of any consequence. Hence it illustrates the fact that places are perceptions.

It constitutes a place for the reason also that it has been made — transformed — by human action. The construction of the courts and buildings of the sect endows it with an even more definitive concreteness. These features have been located there in conformity with Tenri's sacred character, and their individual forms and collective spatial disposition reflect, in turn in their detail, the tenets of the faith. As a group, they express the principle that, likewise, "places are expressions."

Nonetheless, perceptions may be lost, and human expression can become inscrutable or undetectable. Think, for instance, of the holy places once revered by Indians in many parts of North America. A place retains identity and significance only so long as human behavior continues to affirm and indicate them. Thus, certain constantly repeated actions on the part of people preserve the special reality of Tenri. Beginning with the rituals of entry and concluding with those of departure, they include detailed routines finely attuned to the internal configuration of the place as a whole. Were they not duly heeded and performed, after all, Tenri would count as no pilgrimage center and impress the visitor as nothing but one more cluster of tile-roofed buildings in a big courtyard, like countless others in Japan. A holy place, then, can only exist through living behavior.[18]

Conversely — and here is the great rationale for pilgrimage — certain sorts of behavior are conceived of as possible exclusively at specific places. Pilgrim places accommodate the particular rituals considered to establish contact with supernatural powers that are not so directly accessible elsewhere. This conforms to the general rule that places are potentialities of action.

If such a place as Tenri constitutes, among other things, an expression, so indeed do all other known places whatsoever, distinguished as they must be by some human action, realized or yet potential. And this implies that places and their contents comprise communicative elements. Assimilated into the spatial circulation patterns and the collective routines of activity, as well as the shared perceptual domains of given human populations, recognized places and the usages associated with them both arise originally out of, and continue to enter into, human communication. Only it, in fact, maintains and vouches for their reality.

But a pilgrimage place plays a very special role in human communicative behavior, for it provides, as it were, privileged channels over which the devotee can communicate not merely with human fellows but with sacred beings and forces. Depending on the settings and occasions, the pilgrim dialogue with the divine takes many forms and avails itself of varied means of expression. One of the most moving moments of pilgrim communication that I ever witnessed used nothing but absolute silence.

Popayán

In Holy Week, just before Easter, a multitude of pilgrims and local folk assembles in certain old cities either to walk in, or to watch, spectacular processions that recapitulate the story of the Passion, Crucifixion, and Resurrection of Jesus. On these great occasions, revered statues of Christ and of saints in various churches and chapels are adorned with elaborate costumes, mounted on litters, and hoisted onto the honored shoulders of chosen members of various pious societies, in order to be borne through the streets in solemn progression to visit several sister churches. The processions of Sevilla, most famous of all, have counterparts in a few other cities, one of which is Popayán in Colombia.[19]

Popayán nestles in a cool, verdant valley among the northern outliers of the Andes. It has preserved much of its Colonial character, as it was in the time of Alexander von Humboldt's residence here, despite recurrent and destructive earthquakes. Off the main routes of travel and axes of modern development, it remains the seat of a major — and exceedingly colorful — market for the produce of a large surviving Indian population in the countryside. But Popayán is surely best known for the Holy Week procession of its city folk (fig. 4).

On Palm Sunday, a week before Easter, much tolling of bells, a solemn high mass, and the draping of the cathedral facade with fronds inaugurate the Holy Week observances. Sacristans and sodality members in the various parishes busy themselves with dressing the images and cleaning and decorating their centuries-old, tile-roofed, massive-doored homes. On the Wednesday and each succeeding night, one selected company of bearers, consisting of a score or so of men of both humble and eminent families admitted to this much envied office, collects at their respective church or chapel. Just as dark begins to fall, they lift their ponderous, towering litter high and, pacing sedately and painfully, set forth into the town.

Along the cobbled streets that lead down to and around the tree-crammed central plaza, meanwhile, pilgrim visitors and townsfolk have gathered. The city is darkened, but the lighted tapers grasped by most of the long rank of people provide just a faint illumination. The procession is still far up the street. The crowd waits; there are mufffled voices; somewhere a dog barks. Then, of a sudden, an utter hush descends on the whole city, with not a stir, not so much as a whisper. As the litter comes forth with replacement bearers darting in, now and then, to spell exhausted comrades, everyone along the way — children and all — stands perfectly still and barely breathes. The candlelit silence swells up like a prayer.

The quiet continues to reign for a while after the procession has completed its ceremonial itinerary and vanished from view. Then Poyayán returns to profane reality, and the people bustle away toward their beds.

Nothing could be more eloquent, more communicative, than that city of absolute silence. The fine old Colonial buildings, the richly decorated images, the almost penitential toil of the litter bearers, the candlelight — all the elements of ceremony — merge with that sublime stillness into an intense experience of the sacred.

All such immensely diverse forms of human utterance, just as effectively as speech, can communicate. They intermingle and augment one another. Not only do such dissimilar means of expression blend together,

Fig. 4. Holy week procession in Popayán, Colombia. (Artwork by the author.)

however. They often may alternate. Thus spoken words, silence, and gestures may enter into discourse by turns as two individuals communicate. Artifacts likewise often become enlisted in dialogue, perhaps interchanging with vocal or gestural utterance. Their display, like that of bodily gestures or sounds, becomes part of the flow of "meanings" exchanged. Human beings characteristically communicate over several such channels — by several such means — either simultaneously or in succession, as part of the give-and-take of shared, continuous discourse.

But not only do artifacts, gestures, and vocalizations serve in human communication. The very production of artifacts, too, the act of creating or manufacturing or building (or destroying) something, is enmeshed in communicative action. Work occurs as part of an interactive process among human beings that employs not only speech but both gesture and artifacts, and as it goes along produces other artifacts or artificial substances that carry a significance for human beings — and hence have communicative potentiality. The influence that human societies exert on their environments is not only entirely dependent on descriptions, explanations, instructions, requests, promises, and so on, but even more crucially upon material responses to such verbal (or sometimes gestural) promptings: together, the triggering words or motions and the labor that follows mostly occur within an ongoing communicative process, and remain rare in its total absence.

The type of communication most important to pilgrims, however, is one in which the response to a reverent gesture, an artifact given as offering, a prayer, or production of something, cannot be manifested so concretely as it might be in more mundane interactions. Similarly, the building of a chapel, shrine, or mosque as an act of devotion may attract worldly responses, but whatever supernatural rejoinder it might evoke has to be inferred on faith alone. The creation of a pilgrim place may doubly communicate, but the dialogue for which it matters most is eternally mysterious and private.

The lonely, secret, personal experience of dialogue with hidden powers is seldom sought most fruitfully through striving and struggle of the sorts that count for most in human interaction, those which communicate by commanding notice and conferring renown through material production and possession, and transform the earth in doing so. The former kind of dialogue is often fragile and furtive, not meant for human attention. The perceptions and practices that establish and maintain a pilgrim place, along with whatever special habitat features they may produce, provide a locus for communication of a special kind. The pious voyager can there transcend the everyday earthly boundaries and reach out toward the supernatural. For the believer at least, a pilgrimage site affords a distinctive and highly desirable medium of communication. It cannot fail to encourage, sustain, and strengthen those who make use of it. Dare we call a pilgrimage place a "supernatural resource"?

As resource sites, pilgrimage places must resemble in some fashion other localities at which resources are developed and exploited. It appears, besides, that many of the former harbor more than one activity, and afford a range of possibilities of exploitation. An example of such a pilgrimage center with multiple functions will facilitate reflection on these matters.

Altötting

A short distance southeast of Munich high enough up on a hill to afford a sweeping view of the tailored Bavarian countryside, the ancient Carolingian monastery of Altötting attracts a sizeable annual stream of pilgrims, largely from Southern Germany and neighboring Austria. In this respect it represents a typical regional pilgrimage.

Altötting is widely known for three things: the splendid view that appeals to weekend excursionists; its miraculous cures of physical ailments and accidental injuries; and the beer brewed right at the monastery. Unlike big centers such as Guadalupe, for example, it lacks a vast gathering of souvenir shops and hucksters' stalls. Probably its modest reputation would not support much such business, so that it fails to show one kind of exploitation commonly associated with the sites of larger pilgrimages. The beer for which it is renowned, however, can be enjoyed on the premises or bought to take out, and definitely counts as one of the local resources exploited.

The resource of primary interest and importance, though, is, to put it plainly, miracles. The monastery's image of the Virgin has been credited with numerous improbable cures, or rather needed intercessions. The walls of the shrine bear ample witness to this fact. Written testimonial plaques hang here and there, among a profusion of votive figurines of arms and legs and other assorted organs that attest to their possessors' cure in the corresponding part. These miniscule bits of anatomy, many finely crafted of silver, adorn the place densely, and, hanging among them or propped somewhere, abandoned crutches, braces, and canes proclaim yet other exceptional recoveries. This display permits of no doubt regarding the miraculous potentialities of Altötting. It indicates a preferential place for productive interaction with the supernatural, a veritable gold mine of grace.

This miraculous property, attributed also to the several other Christian pilgrimage sites herein described, raises the question of whether or not the same potentiality inheres as well in non-Christian pilgrim places — or, more generally, of whether or not the miraculous constitutes an essential and inherent aspect of all pilgrimage. Is pilgrimage in every case a trusted means of seeking benefits that natural, profane reality could never offer?

However the pilgrims account for their blessings, the sites of their devotions are distinctive for a special resource attribute and the behavior it evokes. Relative scarcity, comparative accessibility, costs of exploitation, and probably other, similar considerations that apply to resources in general will prove, no doubt, germane in this case too. One might even expect prospective visitors to engage in rational calculation of costs and benefits, like proper economic men and women, before resolving to set forth. However, the product or service acquired is not, in fact, a commodity: it cannot be sold or traded or used in making anything for sale.

On the other hand, a notorious benefit to be gained from making pilgrimage — made manifest, for example, in the Muslim title of Haji, the little stamped papers certifying Buddhist temple visits, or the scallop-shell badges of Compostela pilgrims — is a change in the social identity of the returned pilgrim. Insofar as a pilgrim journey does thus alter to some degree the permanent social position of an individual, it indeed partakes of the character of a genuine rite of passage. Furthermore, whatever transformation may have occurred is accompanied by an enhanced reputation. In this respect, the exploitation of this kind of resource does not really differ entirely from the ostensibly practical, utilitarian employment of resources to create commodities which, becoming possessions of someone, can be accumulated and displayed in order to claim attention and respect.

The pilgrim enterprise may then be considered as, among other things, an investment in social power and prestige, and perhaps one yielding just as large a return as would investment in material goods of this world intended to impress. Like property, the pilgrim's merit can be employed as a communicative device in order to convey an image or impression of the person, and hence corresponds to goods and services thus employed in any sort of consumption. For as this notion suggests, what the economist calls "consumption" is itself a kind of production from the standpoint of communication. Like acquired merit, the possession, display, and even destruction of objects condition the social position and accordingly also the spatial mobility and viability of human beings. They enter into, and are indispensable for, the ritual performances that constitute boundary behavior, aiding in negotiating circulation through socially fragmented space and gaining access to places. Just as pilgrim journeys have a bearing on a person's future possible itineraries and investitures, so do almost every other public act an individual performs and nearly all the earthly things an individual possesses. Hence, this one particular motive for pilgrimage is an integral part of the necessary psychological makeup of a peculiarly space-transcending species that both establishes and circumscribes, but also ceremoniously circulates among, the myriad places making up the spatial universe of human societies.

However, even insistent psychological needs for display could not alone inspire pilgrimage. Its motivations, as some foregoing examples indicate, not only transcend utilitarian considerations, but reach even deeper than those of communicative sociality and public expression. They reflect as well a longing for an intimate aloneness with the beings of another world.

Motivation of this latter sort is neither recondite nor rare. Indeed, although no doubt essential to the pilgrimage phenomenon, it manifests itself in forms more commonplace by far. The geographic evidence for it extends much beyond recognized pilgrimage sites and crops up far closer to home, as the following example shows.

Fraserview

Overlooking the river, a great grassy expanse with scattered groves of trees and rows of graves interrupts the grid of Vancouver's city streets. Within this quiet domain of the dead, I discovered a section reserved to deceased Chinese and another for the Japanese; then out in the northwest corner an orchard of double Eastern Orthodox crosses; then Catholic ground, distinct from the neighboring Protestant zone; and a Hebrew burial ground surrounded by an iron fence; and somewhere else the Veteran's quarter, with its uniform crosses drawn up at attention in a final military formation. (The Hindu, Sikh, and Muslim cemeteries are elsewhere, and there is even a native Squamish Indian one on the hill near my house.)

Undiscouraged by the persistent gray drizzle, people of all the respective faiths arrived in goodly numbers on Remembrance Day to distribute themselves among the various sectors of the cemetery, in order to pause at relatives' graves and leave behind a few fresh or plastic flowers. The concourse, rather silent and solemn, hardly resembled the polyglot crowds encountered in the shopping malls or the underground downtown retail passages: they looked better dressed and behaved with self-conscious dignity.

The decorous visitors to Fraserview Cemetery had come from not very far, to be sure, but apart from that qualification, the scene that I witnessed resembled a pilgrimage. The various denominational tracts themselves appear to conform to the characterization proposed herein for pilgrimage sites. Sharply set off by material markers or barriers from their urban surroundings and from one another, they consist each of a distinct domain not only perceived as such but expressly so constructed. Their integrity is indicated, furthermore, by correspondingly distinctive behavioral routines — revealed in the finer details of their visitors' conduct — for which their sites likewise afforded the requisite potentialities of place.

Perhaps, then, it will not be amiss to suggest a deep and close relationship between the circumscribed places that most human settlements set aside for their dead to repose in and the sacrosanct sites of actual pilgrimage. Not only do both sorts of places attract ceremonial visits, but in fact a great many important pilgrimage centers are associated with the graves of holy persons. It may be justified to look on cemetery visits as more closely akin to pilgrimage than gatherings for worship are, and also to see in cemeteries something more like pilgrim places than an ordinary mosque or church or temple is. Whatever kind of communication may belong to ordinary worship or attendance at religious rituals, that which motivates both pilgrimage and cemetery visitations has an intensely personalized character and addresses an explicitly otherworldly interlocutor.

Furthermore, it may be permissible to regard pilgrimage traditions, equally with mortuary ones, as rather more conservative and long enduring than are the current creeds and ceremonials of religion more generally. The practice of recognizing certain localities as points of direct contact with another world constitutes part of a people's construction of a proper geography. Both graveyard ghosts and holy grottoes go along with geomantic lines of power and sacred cardinal directions to configure the lived space of awareness and action. This sort of areal differentiation attests to the fact that geography deals with more than one world.

Conclusion

A duality or plurality of worlds imagined or experienced defines a different geography and generates, within it and responsive to it, pilgrimage. In this particular geography, abstract spatial relationships count for infinitely less than do the properties of given places. Yet those properties themselves consist far less of physical peculiarities than of activities and inferred attitudes distinguishing respective places and, conversely, those who frequent them — the pilgrims.

The geography of pilgrimage detects a special rituality, not unseldom tinged with rigorous asceticism, associated with the sites it studies. In order to account for the pilgrim's ritual behavior, geography looks at the places themselves, yet, as just mentioned, at other than simply physical features. It has to visualize a pilgrimage site as a place discovered, or perceived in a certain fashion; as a bounded sector of space; as an expression, probably of both some supernatural and some human intervention; as a partial transformation of the physical environment; as a potent communicative element; as the embodied potentiality of certain efficacious behaviors; thus, as a sort of supernatural resource; and of course as the orienting and justifying goal of a meaningful journey.

The rituality of pilgrimage reveals itself, among other ways, in the internal spatial differentiation of its target places into more minute, particular locations proper to component phases of the overall performance, as described in several papers in this volume. And architectural features may mark out the corresponding divisions. So too may pilgrim places sometimes be associated with distinctive kinds of physical surroundings, although as some of the accompanying papers show, this is not invariably the case.

Although discussion in this final article has concentrated on the sites, not routes, of pilgrimage — the targets of the pilgrim journey — the very term "pilgrimage" connotes travel, as well illustrated in some of the preceding papers. The broader spatial aspect is, of course, important too. But pilgrim paths permit of less confident generalization than do pilgrim places. To be sure, as some papers demonstrate, the contribution of pilgrim traffic to total circulation in an area can be assessed or even quantified. And the ethnic composition, local origins, and other social attributes of participants can be traced, and even reconstructed sometimes for past periods. Clearly, however, in many pilgrimages the manner or even the distance or direction of travel to the final site is not nearly so crucial as the arrival there and the subsequent circuit of sacred stations. Furthermore, qualifications other than ethnic affiliation or social status count the most for the legitimacy of pilgrim visits; equally as vital as presence and performance at the pilgrim place, for example, is motivation — which may elude any accurate measurement.

Most geographers who study pilgrimages, including those represented in this volume, have tended to avoid both its theological and its psychological aspects. Nonetheless, these very aspects are surely the most crucial in inspiring and sustaining any pilgrimage. This circumstance encourages geographers to get as close as they can to pilgrimage by other means. Accordingly, as this volume richly illustrates, they do their best to capture the immediacy of pilgrim gatherings and their specific settings and events. Particularities of place provide their clues to generalities, and the yield contributes to theories of place, not of pilgrimage alone.

Such a program of research conforms to a general trend in the study of human activity, which lately has begun to pay much greater heed to temporal and locational factors. In a way, the geographers' oft-bemoaned lack of expertise in psychological, sociological, and abstract cultural explanation almost compels them to march in the forefront of a new movement toward more circumstantial modes of explanation. Through deepened empirical appreciation of concrete detail within this firm framework, traditional assumptions concerning psychological and cultural and even theological irregularities become subject to testing and questioning, and may well undergo fruitful modification as a result.

The pilgrimage phenomenon, as noted above, largely confounds utilitarian economic reasoning. Few other forms of human activity lend themselves so poorly to that sort of analysis, or so insistently demand other kinds of interpretation.

Inevitably, research on pilgrimage must first concern much more than religion, or circulation, or given places as such. It belongs to the project of comprehending human activity much more concretely, as a reliable means toward attaining an ever more general and fundamental understanding of the principles that govern it. This is the burden of modern geography, as it has been of science for centuries. And the geography of pilgrimage affords a singularly favorable vantage point for new and telling insights.

Notes

1. The shrine is commonly referred to as Shah-e-Cheragh — meaning something like "lord of lights. " The name of the crypt's incumbent has also been given as Ahmed ibn Mosua and Amir Ahmed. No matter; he was the martyred brother, in any case, of the great Imam Reza, whose enormous and incomparably sacred shrine dominates Mashad.

2. As *Les Guides Bleu: Iran-Afghanistan* (Anon. 1974) puts it, "Ce monument est l'une des plus vénérables sanctuaires du chiisme, aussi vous abstiendrez-vous d'y pénétrer."

3. To the voluminous literature on the concept of place, well known to geographers, I should like to nominate for addition the profoundly scholarly book of Jonathan Z. Smith, *To Take Place: Toward Theory in Ritual* (1987), which not only reviews existing ideas in masterly fashion, but offers some important new insights.

4. Geographers, understandably intrigued with the fruitful concept of time-distance decay and its extensions and applications, have sometimes tried to make a science out of that conceptual system alone (cf. Peter Gould's eloquent and entertaining book, *The Geographer at Work* [1989]). But everybody knows that distance alone is not the only thing that limits movement and confines us; much of the world around a person is just "off limits" for the stranger. Our geographies have strangely overlooked this crucial fact (although the "coupling constraints" postulated by the Swedish School of Time Geography at least acknowledge it by implication).

5. The idea of rites of passage goes back to Arnold Van Gennep (1908), whose book of corresponding title gave rise to a multitude of later studies.

6. Lafcadio Hearn (1905) wrote an interesting description of Izumo in his chapter, "Kitzuki: The Most Ancient Shrine of Japan. " See also Watanabe (1974).

7. As I recall, this would have been on January 15, the national holiday on which men and women at the age of 20 are recognized as adults, and free to marry without parental sanction.

8. For a detailed account of the markedly spatial behavior incident to marriage, see especially Edwards (1989).

9. Descriptions of the Guadalupe Shrine and interpretations of its meaning abound. Compare, for example, Antonio Pompa y Pompa (1967) and Rafael Aguayo Spencer (1971).

10. Many or most people who come to Guadalupe do indeed ride the bus or a truck — or an airplane, train, or private car.

11. Symbolically, American partisans of "free choice" (or abortion) decline to allow the State — or the Pope — into their bedrooms, whereas they may themselves not be allowed access to the communion rail by the Church.

12. Cf. "Territory" in the *Oxford Companion to Animal Behaviour* (Anon. 1981).

13. See my article "Why diffusion?" (1988), and *Showing Off* (1996).

14. Cf. Castañeda 1955.
15. This is, of course, the major theme of Castañeda (1955).
16. See Ooka 1973.
17. Cf. *Japanese Religion: A Survey by the Agency for Cultural Affairs* (Anon. 1972) and *Religions of Japan: Many Traditions Within One Sacred Way* by Earhart (1984).
18. Some form of behavior is, of course, required even to indicate internal mental events that may concern place, and only when somehow thus manifested do they become subject to public discussion.
19. See Varona (1983) and Negret (1937).

References

Aguayo Spencer, R. 1971. *La Virgen de Guadalupe en la historia de México*. Mexico.

Anon. 1974. *Les Guides Bleu: Iran-Afghanistan*. Paris: Hachette.

Anon. 1972. *Japanese religion: A survey by the agency for cultural affairs*. Tokyo and Palo Alto: Kodansha International.

Anon. 1981. Territory. *Oxford companion to animal behavior* Oxford: Oxford University Press.

Castañeda, G. A. 1955. *Esquipulas. Descripción geográfica, histórica, legendaria y etimológica del municipio y de la villa de Esquipulas, donde se alza el santuario a la imagen de Cristo crucificado, con que se pudo y se puede aún aglutinar los varios y dispersos elementos centroamericana*. Mexico: Biblioteca de Cultura Popular.

Earhart, H. B. 1984. *Religions of Japan: Many traditions within one sacred way*. San Francisco: Harper & Row.

Edwards, W. 1989. *Modern Japan through its weddings: Gender, person, and society in ritual portrayal*. Stanford: Stanford University Press.

Gennep, A. van. 1908. *Rites of passage*. Paris: Nourry. Trans. M. D. Vizedom and G. L. Caffee, 1960. Chicago: University of Chicago Press.

Gould, P. 1989. *The Geographer at work*. Oxford: Oxford University Press.

Hearn, L. 1905. Kitzuki: The most ancient shrine of Japan. In *Glimpses of unfamiliar Japan*, 72-210. London: Kegan Paul, Trench, Trübner & Co.

Negret, R. 1937. *Guía histórico-artística de Popayán*. Popayán: N. Castillo.

Ooka, M. 1973. *Temples of Nara and their art*. New York and Tokyo: Tuttle.

Pompa y Pompa, A. 1967. *El gran acontecimiento guadalupano*. Mexico,D.F.: Editorial Jus.

Smith, J. Z. 1987. *To take place: Toward theory in ritual*. Chicago: University of Chicago Press.

Varona, J. V. 1983. *Popayán: ciudad única; pasado, presente, futuro*. Cali, Colombia: Feriva.

Wagner, P. L. 1988. Why diffiusion? In *The transfer and transformation of ideas and material culture*, eds. B. Dickison and P. Hugill, 179-93. College Station, TX: Texas A & M Press.

——. 1996. *Showing off: The Geltung hypothesis*. Austin: University of Texas Press.

Watanabe, Y. 1974. *Shinto art: Ise and Izumo shrines*. New York: Tuttle.